Foodi Multi-Cooker Cookbook For Beginners

Top 500 Quick, Easy and Delicious Foodi Multi-Cooker Recipes to Pressure Cook, Air Fry, Dehydrate, and More

Emma Rollins

Copyright © 2019 by Emma Rollins All Right Reserved.

No part of this publication may be reproduced, distributed, or transmitted in any form or by any means, including photocopying, recording, or other electronic or mechanical methods, or by any information storage and retrieval system without the prior written permission of the copyright holder.

Effort has been made to ensure that the information in this book is accurate and complete, however, the author and the publisher do not warrant the accuracy of the information, text and graphics contained within the book due to the rapidly changing nature of science, research, known and unknown facts and internet. The Author and the publisher do not hold any responsibility for errors, omissions or contrary interpretation of the subject matter herein. This book is presented solely for motivational and informational purposes only.

TABLE OF CONTENTS

Introduction 1
- Benefits of Using Foodi Multi-Cooker 2
- Foodi Multi-Cooker Functions & Buttons 3
- Pressure Releasing Methods 4
- Steps to Use Your Foodi Multi-Cooker 5
- Useful Tips 6
- Foodi Multi-Cooker Trouble Shooting 7
- Foodi Multi-Cooker FAQs 8

Breakfasts 10
- Broccoli, Ham, and Pepper Frittata 10
- Strawberries Breakfast Risotto 10
- Cheesy Egg Breakfast 11
- Poached Eggs & Tomatoes 11
- Chicken and Arugula Casserole 12
- Honey Cinnamon Apple sauce 12
- Tasty Mini Frittatas 12
- Breakfast Casserole 13
- Cilantro Bacon Breakfast Mix 13
- Tomato Frittata 13
- Cinnamon and Apples Oatmeal 14
- Tomato, bacon, and Spinach Omelet 14
- Egg Cups 15
- Bacon and Onions Quiche 15
- Soft, Medium, And Hard-Boiled Eggs 16
- Apple, Bacon and Grits Casserole 16
- Bulgur, Oat, And Walnut Porridge 17
- Cherries Oats 17
- Chicken Crunchadilla breakfast 18
- Apples and Cinnamon Oatmeal 18
- Spring Onions Frittata 18
- Egg, Sausage Chorizo and Cheese Cake 19
- Grits with Cheese & Bacon 19
- Blueberries Breakfast Mix 20
- Vanilla Banana Bread 20
- Delicious Giant Pancake 21
- French Toast Bread Pudding 21
- Breakfast Quinoa Bowl 22
- Red Onion and Potatoes Casserole 22
- Tasty Salmon Veggie Cakes 22
- Grits with Cranberries Breakfast 23
- Tomatoes and Ham Bake 23
- Turkey Burrito 24
- Simple Banana Oatmeal 24
- Apple and Bacon Casserole 24
- Cheesy Hash Browns Mix 25

Pork 26
- Pork Shoulder Chops with Carrots 26
- Pressure Cooker Cassoulet 26
- Pork with Barbecue Sauce 27
- Cranberry BBQ Pulled Pork 27
- Pork Tenderloin and Coconut Rice 28
- Pulled Pork Taco Dinner 28
- BBQ Pork with Ginger Coconut and Sweet Potatoes 29
- Honey Pork Chops 29
- Delicious Braised Pork Neck Bones 30
- Pulled Pork Chipotle Salad Bowl 30
- Pork Belly 31
- Classic Red Cooked Pork 31
- Simple Spare Ribs with Wine 32
- Pork Roast with Spicy Peanut Sauce 32
- Pork Loin Chops with Pears 33
- Pulled Pork with Crispy Biscuits 33
- Cilantro Pork Tacos 34
- Tandoori BBQ Pork Ribs 34
- Tasty Ranch Pork Chops 35

Honey Mustard Pork Tenderloin Recipe 35

Amazing Pork Chops with Applesauce 36

Pork with Apple Juice 36

Pork and Egg Fried Rice 37

Pork Chops with Mushroom Gravy 37

Pulled Pork Tacos 38

Pulled Pork Burgers 38

Asian Pork 39

Delicious Pork Carnitas in Lettuce Cups 39

Pulled Pork Lettuce Wraps 40

Pork Loin and Apples 40

Shoulder Ribs with Barbecue Rub and Sauce 41

Sausage and Cheesy Mashed Potatoes 41

Pork Chops 42

Pork with Hominy 43

Peppers and Pork Stew 43

Pork Loin with Vegetable Sauce 44

Pulled Pork 44

Tasty Crispy Pork Carnitas 45

Pork Tenderloin Braised Apples 46

Beef & Lamb 47

Round Roast and Veggies 47

Seasoned Italian Beef 47

Lamb Steaks with Feta and Potatoes 47

Cheesy Beef Pasta 48

Balsamic Maple Beef 48

Awesime Beef Roast 49

Stuffed Rigatoni 49

Pressure Cooker Chili 50

Lamb Shanks 50

Corned Beef and Cabbage 51

Korean Style Braised Short Ribs 51

Texas Beef Chili 52

Beef Chili 52

Beef Tacos with Chili Sauce 53

Braised Beef Shank in Soybean Paste 53

Beef and Pasta Casserole 54

Lamb Shanks with Pancetta 54

Marinated Steak 55

Easy Osso Bucco 55

Lamb Stew with Brussels Sprouts 56

Goulash 56

Tender Pot Roast 57

Classic Brisket with Veggies 57

Beef Bourguignon 58

Easy Sausage and Peppers 59

Pasta with Meat Sauce 59

Steaks with Garlic Cream Sauce 60

Lamb Skewers with Pita Bread and Eggplant Dip
.... 60

Beef Chili & Cornbread Casserole 61

Mongolian Beef 61

BBQ Pulled Beef Sandwiches 62

Cold Beef Noodle Salad 62

Shredded Barbecue Skirt Steak 63

Shredded Pepper Steak 63

Beef and Bean Pasta Casserole 64

Braised Short Ribs 64

Pot Roast 65

Red Beef Curry 66

Delightful Lamb Shanks with Pancetta 66

Chili Con Carne 67

BBQ Baby Back Ribs 67

Beef Barley Mushroom Stew with Sour Cream ... 68

Chinese Beef Stew 69

Lamb, Rice, And Chickpea Casserole 69

Beef Stuffed Peppers 70

Special Lamb Shanks Provençal 70

Mouthwatering Beef Stew 71

Beef Stew 72

Lamb with Enchilada Sauce 72

Lamb and Bulgur-Stuffed Acorn Squash 73

Beef Ribs 73

Moroccan Lamb and Couscous Stew 74

Tex-Mex Meatloaf Recipe 74

Sausage and Chard Pasta Sauce 75

Garlic Teriyaki Beef 76

Delicious Lamb Casserole 76

Easy Short Ribs and Root Vegetables 77

Teriyaki Beef 77

Mini Pork Roast 78

Meatballs with Artichokes 78

Mexican Beef 79

Poultry 80

Chicken Leg Quarters with Rosemary 80

Moroccan Chicken 80

Cacciatore Chicken 81

Lemon and Garlic Chicken 81

Sesame Ginger Chicken 81

Chinese Chicken and Rice 82

Lemongrass Chicken 82

Turkey Mix and Mashed Potatoes 83

Turkey Meatballs 83

Salsa Chicken 84

Chicken BBQ 84

Filipino Chicken Adobo 85

Chicken Sandwiches 85

Sweet and Tangy Chicken 86

Chicken in Tomatillo Sauce 86

Chicken Congee 86

Chicken And Rice 87

Chicken Romano 87

Chicken Korma 88

Chipotle Chicken, Rice, and Black Beans 88

Chicken Piccata 89

Turkey Chili 89

Chicken with Cherries & Pumpkin Seed Wild Rice
.... 90

Chicken Alfredo Pasta 90

Baked Chicken 91

Fall Off the Bone Chicken 91

Turkey Thighs 92

Filipino Chicken 92

Lemon Garlic Chicken 92

Delicious Chicken Dinner 93

Turkey Sausage and Macaroni Casserole 93

Turkey Gluten Free Gravy 94

Honey Barbecue Chicken Wings 94

Stuffed Chicken Breasts 95

Crack Chicken 95

Shredded Chicken Breast 95

Cilantro Chicken Meatballs 96

Braised Chicken with Capers and Parsley 96

Chicken Pina Colada 97

Chicken with Soy Sauce 97

Cordon Blue Chicken Casserole 98

Easy Turkey Drumsticks 98

Chicken and Potatoes 98

Duck and Vegetables 99

Asian Chicken 99

Chicken Rogan Josh Curry 100

Crispy Chicken Thighs with Carrots and Rice Pilaf
.... 100

Bone Broth 101

Chicken Salad 101

Ginger Garlic Drumsticks 101

Curried Lemon Coconut Chicken 102

Thai Lime Chicken 102

- Turkey Legs 103
- Chicken and Sausage Stew........................... 103
- Sweet Chipotle Chicken Wings 104
- Instant Penne with Chicken 104
- Chicken and Green Chile Stew 105
- Chicken with Mushrooms 105
- Honey Sriracha Chicken Wings 106
- Whole Chicken Recipe 106
- Turkey Chili 107
- Now and Later Butter Chicken 107
- Stuffed Chicken Recipe 108
- Mozzarella Marinara Chicken 108
- Chicken Breasts with White Wine 109
- Chicken Ragú 109
- Delicious Chicken and Coconut Curry 110
- Texas Trail Chili 110
- Turkey Meatballs in Tomato Sauce 111
- Green Chicken Curry 111
- Turkey Breast 112
- Awesome Turkey Sloppy Joes 112
- Chicken with Mushrooms and Artichoke Hearts 113
- Cranberry Braised Turkey Wings 114
- Yummy Spicy Turkey Chili 114
- Olive and Lemon Ligurian Chicken 115
- Delicious Frozen Chicken Dinner 115
- Enchilada Chicken Breasts 116
- Herbed Whole Roasted Chicken 117
- Delicious Chicken Pot Pie Recipe 117
- Aromatic Turkey Breast 118
- Sweet Soy Chicken Wings 119

Fish & Seafood 120
- Salmon with Bok Choy 120
- Tuna and Capers Tomato Pasts 120
- Tuna and Buttery Crackers Casserole 121
- Trout-Farro Salad 121
- Seafood Paella 122
- Pernod Mackerel and Vegetables Recipe ... 122
- Special Farro with Fennel and Smoked Trout .. 123
- Coconut Fish Curry 123
- Tomatillo and Shrimp Casserole 124
- Cod Fillets with Almonds and Peas 124
- Caramelized Haddock 125
- Lemon Dill Cod with Broccoli 125
- Special Fish Filets 125
- Alaskan Cod with Pinto Beans 126
- Southern Shrimp Chowder 126
- Delightful Tuna Noodle 127
- Mackerel Salad 127
- Lemon and Dill Fish 128
- Cod Chowder 128
- Pasta with Tuna 129
- Delicious Cuttlefish 129
- Monk Fish with Power Greens 130
- Creamy Garlicky Oyster Stew Recipe 130
- Potato Beer Fish 130
- Cheesy Tuna Helper 131
- Fish Curry 131
- Green Chili Mahi-Mahi Fillets 132
- Fish and Vegetable "Tagine" with Chermoula .. 132
- Red Curry Cod with Red Beans 133
- Lime Saucy Salmon Recipe 133
- Shrimp with Risotto Primavera 134
- Coconut Fish Curry 134
- Scallops with Butter Caper Sauce 135
- Shrimp and Tomatillo Casserole 135
- Steamed Fish 136
- Chili Garlic Black Mussels Recipe 136
- Salmon Steaks with Creamy Mustard Sauce 136

Lobster Bisque 137
Tasty Mahi Mahi Recipe 137
Clams in White Wine 138
Carolina Crab Soup Recipe 139
Steamed Salmon with Garlic Citrus 139

Soups 140

Creamy Potato Cheese Soup 140
Buffalo Chicken Soup 140
Colombian Chicken Soup 141
Chicken Noodle Soup 141
Potato Soup with Leek and Cheddar 142
Cream of Asparagus Soup 142
Hamburger Soup 143
Mushroom Barley Soup 143
Asian Beef Soup with Rice Noodles 144
Carrot Soup 144
Beef Stock 145
Bean Soup 145
French Onion Soup 146
Chicken Soup 147
Cheese Tortellini and Chicken Soup 147
Chicken and White Bean Chili with Tomatoes . 148
Corn Chowder 148
Beef and Rice Soup 149
Creole White Bean Soup 149
Butternut Squash Soup 150
Creamy Tomato Soup 150
Roasted Tomato Soup 151
Chops, Rice and Cheese Soup 151
Butternut Squash Sweet Potato Soup 152
Cream of Spinach with Chicken Bites 152
Split Pea and Ham Soup 153
Corn Soup 153
Chicken Stock 153

Beef, Barley, And Mushroom Soup 154
Poblano and Chicken Soup 154
Chicken Tortilla Soup 155
Butternut Squash Soup with Chicken Orzo 155
Split Pea Soup 156
Beef and Vegetable Soup 156
Barbecue Brisket Soup 157
Enchilada Soup 157
Chicken and Wild Rice Soup 158
Special Chicken Soup 158
Cream of Sweet Potato Soup 158
Beef Stew 159
Chicken and Tomato Soup 159
Chicken Stew 160
Chicken Cream Cheese 161

Snacks, Appetizers & Side Dishes 162

Lime Carrot Sticks 162
Parmesan Brussels Sprouts 162
Garlicky Cauliflower 162
Vegetarian Rigatoni Bolognese 162
Pepper Jack Mac and Cheese 163
Crispy Broccoli Side Salad 163
Artichokes with Ghee 164
Thyme Celeriac Fries 164
Couscous and Vegetable Medley 164
Italian Potatoes 165
Rainbow Fingerling Potatoes 165
Rigatoni with Meat Sauce 165
Simple Potato Salad 166
Spaghetti Squash with Garlic and Sage Brown . 166
Honey Glazed Carrots with Dill 167
Vegetables and Rice 167
Sushi Rice 167
Coriander Zucchinis 168

Honey Garlic Chicken Lettuce Wraps	168
Smoky Mushrooms + Onions	169
Spicy Peppers	169
Mix Bean Salad	169
Carbonara	170
Paprika Potatoes	170
Mixed Mushrooms	170
Oregano Chickpeas Spread	171
Spice Rubbed Cauliflower Steaks	171
Lime Potatoes	171
Cilantro Brussels Sprouts	171
Crispy Turkey Bites	172
Saffron Risotto	172
Peas and Walnuts Mix	172
Balsamic Parsnips Chips	173
Coconut Carrot Chips	173
Buttery Chicken Bites	173
Broccoli and Bacon Mix	173
Green Beans and Cherry Tomatoes	174
Zucchini and Dill Spread	174
Vegan Alfredo Sauce	174
Coconut Potatoes	174
Sweet Potato Wedges	175
Thyme Baby Carrots	175
Paprika Potato Chips	175
Ginger Mushroom Sauté	175
Simple Cilantro Parsnips	175
Celeriac Sticks	176
Celery Dip	176
Chickpeas Salad	176
Lime Cabbage	176
Black Olives Spread	177
Pork Bites	177
Peppers Salsa	177
Simple Green Beans	177
Lentils Salsa	178
Minty Turkey Bites	178
Caramel Sauce	178
Basil Beet Chips	178
Herbed Squash	179
Chives Chips	179
Cranberry Apple Sauce	179
Basil Shrimp	179
Chinese Beet Slices	180
Vegetable Stock	180
Carrot Sticks	180

Vegetables 181

Curried Cauliflower	181
Potato Salad	181
Braised Red Cabbage and Apples	182
Sugar Glazed Carrots	182
Smashed Sweet Potatoes with Pineapple and Ginger	183
Brussels Sprouts	183
Wrapped Carrot with Bacon	183
Rye Berry and Celery Root Salad	184
Quinoa and Potato Salad	184
Braised Celery and Tomatoes	185
Zucchini and Mushrooms	185
Buttered Brussels Sprouts	186
Polenta with Honey and Pine Nuts	186
Collard Greens in A Tomato Sauce	186
Pumpkin Puree	187
Vinegary Collard Greens	187
Crispy Ratatouille Recipe	187
Steamed Artichokes	188
Carrots Escabeche	188
Butter Spaghetti Squash	189
Cauliflower Mac and Cheese	189

- Breakfast Kale 190
- Mushroom Gravy 190
- Simple Potato Wedges 191
- Buffalo Cauliflower Bites 191
- One Pot Pasta Puttanesca 192
- Artichoke Hearts 192
- Carrot Puree 193
- Roasted Rainbow Fingerling Potatoes 193
- Spaghetti Squash and Spinach Walnut Pesto 193
- Spring Vegetable Ragù 194
- Polenta with Fresh Herbs 194
- Vegetable Stew Recipe 195
- Stewed Broccoli 195
- Maple Mustard Brussels Sprouts 196
- Zucchini Fries with Marinara Sauce 196
- Greens and Beets with Horseradish Sauce 197
- Smooth Carrots with Pancetta 197
- Chickpea Stew with Carrots 198

Rice & Pasta 199

- Lentil Sauce for Pasta 199
- Brown Rice Pilaf with Cashews 199
- Tasty Ninja Fagiole 200
- Turkey and Veggie Casserole 200
- Seafood Risotto 201
- Cannellini in Tomato-Sage Sauce 201
- Fried Rice 202
- Wild Rice Salad with Apples 202
- Rice Stuffed Acorn Squash 203
- Curried Chicken and Pasta 203
- Rice and Kale 204
- Pasta Puttanesca 204
- Italian Pasta Casserole 205
- Armenian Rice Pilaf 205
- Rice & Chickpea Stew 206
- Portuguese Tomato Rice with Shrimp 206
- Lentil and Wild Rice Pilaf 207
- Ninja Brown Rice 207
- Rice and Artichokes 208
- Quinoa Risotto with Bacon 208
- Chicken in Peanut Sauce 209
- Wild Rice with Sweet Potatoes 209
- Beetroot Rice 210
- Spanish Rice 210
- Barley Risotto with Fresh Spinach 211
- Wild and Brown Rice Pilaf 211
- Pineapple Fried Rice 212
- Long Grain White Rice 212
- Tiger Prawn Risotto 213
- Brown Rice Stuffed Cabbage Rolls with Pine Nuts and Currants 213
- Mexican Rice 214
- Brown Rice with Lentils 214
- Lamb Pasta Casserole 215
- Foodi Brown Rice 215
- Brown Rice Medley 215
- Risotto with Butternut Squash and Porcini 216
- Risotto with Peas and Shrimp 216
- Asian Veggie Pullow 217
- Rice and Mushrooms 217
- Rice and Lentils 218
- Fresh Tomato and Basil Sauce 218

Beans & Grains 219

- Stewed Tomatoes and Green Beans 219
- White Bean Dip with Tomatoes 219
- Pinto beans with bacon 220
- Refried Bean Nachos 220
- Cuban black beans with ham 221
- Perfect Refried Beans 221
- Spice Black Bean and Brown Rice Salad 222

Spicy Black Eyed Peas	222
Basic Boiled Beans	223
White Bean, Sausage, And Escarole Stew	223
Green Bean Casserole	224
Cracked Wheat Surprise	224
Barley with Vegetables	224
Italian Cannellini Beans and Mint Salad	225
Hummus	225
Black bean and corn salad	226
Barley and Mushroom Risotto	226
Quick Soaking Dry Beans	227
Wheat Berry Salad	227
Rich and creamy lentils	227
Cracked Wheat and Vegetables	228
Franks and Beans	228
Black Bean and Sweet Potato Hash	229
Refried Beans	229

Dessert Recipes **230**

Chocolate Cheesecake	230
Vanilla Pudding with Berries	230
Delicious Chocolate Fondue	231
White chocolate lemon pudding	231
Rich Chocolate Pudding	232
Poached peach cups with ricotta and honey	232
Molten gingerbread cake	232
Chocolate Fondue with Coconut Cream	233
Vanilla Pots de Crème	233
Pumpkin Pie Pudding	234
Blackberry swirl cheesecake	234
Pumpkin Chocolate Cake	235
Mango Cake	235
Pineapple upside-down cake	236
Awesome Honey Flans	236
Strawberry Shortcake Mug Cake	237
Vanilla Ginger Custard	237
Chocolate pudding	238
Cookies and Cream Cheesecake	238
Lemon Ricotta Cheesecake with Strawberries	239
Chocolate Zucchini Muffins	239
Chocolate Brownie	240
Apple Bread	240
Blueberry clafouti	241
Chocolate Custard	241
Apple Ricotta Cake	242
Apricot jam	243
Chocolate Lava Cake	243

Introduction

The Foodi Multicooker is revolutionary! You can cook virtually anything - It is an all-in-one multi-functional kitchen appliance, which can be used as pressure cooker, slow cooker, rice cooker, air fryer, etc. That means you can almost make all your dishes from meats and main courses to rice, potatoes, vegetables of every description, dessert to even yogurt. Better yet, pressure cooking and air frying cooking allows you to prepare foods up to 70% faster, and 75% less fat, on average, than conventional cooking methods do, which means you save energy in addition to your precious time.

Foodi is really very convenient and can save users too much time and money! Meantime, the recipes it provides are nutritious and delicious, even tender inside and crispy outside. It really can give people all kinds of flavors! It is very easy to use, usually all you need to do is just dump all ingredients into the pot, then close the cover and wait for few minutes, and finally you will get your favorite tasty dish!

The recipes are simple and easy to understand. By using this cookbook Anyone can make the delicious recipes with the Foodi. You just need to know the right measurements, and you will have a great recipe ready for you. You do not have to deal with fire or flames on the stoves, Foodi has made life easier for the people now.

This cookbook presents a carefully hank-picked easy and delicious recipes that you can cook in your Foodi. Just Pick the best recipes you like and start cooking with your ninja Foodi now. You will be amazed at how simple it is to use. The machine plays with you, but you need to make sure to handle it with care. It gives you healthy food with all the nutrients your body requires. Thus, you can feed your family with healthy meals without stressing yourself too much or spending long hours inside the kitchen.

The Foodi Multicooker is a real kitchen partner. And this amazing cookbook is the ultimate companion to your Foodi Multi-Cooker.

Benefits of Using Foodi Multi-Cooker

Pressure cooking is a very healthy way to cook food to preserve more nutrients and shorten the cooking time for beans, grains, and other foods. And so has the invention of the pressure cooker. Foodi is the best kitchen appliance that I know of, it always tops my list of kitchen appliances, whenever, and this is because of some of the fantastic functionalities of the Foodi. So here are some of the benefits of ninja foodi

Fast cooking: It greatly decreases typically long cooking times for all dishes. Cooking time can be reduced 60% to 80% (depending on the ingredient). Faster cooking times mean you can cook real foods from scratch in the time it takes for pizza delivery or to prepare a frozen dinner. Vegetable stock can be ready in 5 minutes; you can cook wholesome soups from scratch in 20 minutes, roasts in 30, braise meat in 40, and desserts in just 20 minutes.

Preserving Nutritional Value: Most of our existing cooking methods destroy or drain nutrition of the food, and we are actually eating foods which are not able to fulfill the nutrition requirement of our body. Pressure cooking method prevents the ingredients from exposing to extreme heat. Pressure cooking also requires less time to cook, and so ingredients remain safe from nutrient destruction.

Safe and Easy to Operate: This revolutionary product is pre-programmed, and therefore, you do not have to worry about cooking time or dangerous incidents like exploding of the cooker. The features are extremely easy as the programs are pre-set, and all you need to do with the foodi cooker is to select the right cooking button

Extraordinary Energy Saver: With a shorter cooking time, plus more efficient electrical modes than most appliances you'll be saving not only time but valuable electricity too. To top it off, this will be the only kitchen appliance you'll be using -- which makes it even more economical. You can see why you will soon make your money-back on your purchase in no time. Simply by conserving energy

Boosting the Digestibility.: The important thing to maximizing the potential nutritional value is increasing the digestibility of your foods. Pressure cooking method helps in boosting the digestibility of the nutrients present in the food. The combination of pressure and steam makes the ingredients tender as well as, succulent

Minimum Exposure to Health Harming Compounds: our existing cooking methods not only destroy nutrients but also produce certain compounds, which can be harmful to health such as cancer-causing elements. But when meals are prepared using pressure cooking method, these harmful compounds. aren't produced. The foods are actually bathed in steam while cooking, also it can make them tastier as well as, juicier

One-Pot Cooking; The Convenient Solution: No longer do you have to bother about the size of your kitchen or where you will store the multitude of kitchen appliances needed to concoct one single home cooked meals. Simply place all of your ingredients in your foodi and then allow the ninja foodi work do its thing automatically.

Foodi Multi-Cooker Functions & Buttons

Function Buttons

PRESSURE - The pressure cooker button is used to tenderize food quickly while locking in all the moisture and flavor.

AIR CRISP - The air-frying function is great for making crisp foods like French fries, zucchini wedges, and onion rings without having to deep-fry them. This function is ideal for making golden-skinned roast chicken or roast pork belly with crackling

SLOW COOK - The slow cooker function cooks food at a lower temperature for longer lengths of time. This is great for dishes like pulled pork and fall-off-the-bone pork/beef ribs

STEAM - The steam function uses heated water vapor to cook delicate foods gently at a high temperature. This is ideal for perfectly cooking fish and vegetables

SEAR/SAUTE - The searing/sautéing function transforms the Foodi into a stovetop for sautéing vegetables like garlic and onions, simmering sauces, browning meats prior to stewing/braising for more flavor, as well as a host of other uses

BROIL - The broiling function allows you to caramelize or brown food. You can do this at the start of the cooking process to caramelize the sugar in meats and vegetables for a more flavorful stew or broth

BAKE/ROAST - The baking/roasting function transforms the Foodi into an oven so you can make baked treats, tender meats, and even pizza with crisp cheesy top

DEHYDRATE (Only available in certain models) - The dehydrating function lets you make dehydrated fruits, vegetables, and meats for healthy snacking as well as to increase the shelf life of these food items

Operating Buttons

POWER - This button shuts off the unit and stops all modes of cooking.

TEMP arrows - The TEMP arrows allow you to adjust the cooking temperature and/or pressure level by pressing the up and down buttons accordingly

TIME arrows - The TIME arrows allow you to adjust the cooking time using the up and down buttons

KEEP WARM - This button automatically switches on after steaming, slow cooking, pressure cooking, or another cooking function is finished. The KEEP WARM mode will stay on for 12 hours. To turn off the mode, just press the KEEP WARM button. The KEEP WARM button keeps food warm at a food safe temperature. In other words, it is not meant to be used to warm food from a cold/frozen state

START/STOP - To start cooking, press the START/STOP button after selecting the temperature/pressure and time. To stop the machine's cooking function, press the START/STOP button again

STANDBY MODE: The unit will enter STANDY MODE when there is no interaction with the control panel for 10 minutes.

Pressure Releasing Methods

Natural Release:

There's really nothing you have to depressurize your pressure cooker. Once the cooking is finished, the pressure will automatically slowly drop inside the electric pressure cooker. Because of this slow drop in pressure and heat, when using natural release, food continues cooking even though active cooking is complete. Your stocks and soups come out cleaner and food are more likely to stay intact.

After the cooking cycle ends, wait until the Floating Valve completely drops before opening the lid

*(*For Example, in our recipes, you may see "**Release the pressure naturally for 10 minutes**," – this means after the cooking cycle ends, wait for 10 minutes and then release remaining pressure by turning the valve to 'Venting')*

Use this method when cooking meat, foods that increase in volume or foam (like dried beans and legumes), soups, or any other foods that are primarily liquid.

Quick Release:

Quick release works by turning the valve once active cooking is complete. This process takes an extra degree of care, as a loud burst of steam is released from the valve. Rapid release takes no more than a minute or two, and works best with foods, like eggs, vegetables, or delicate ingredients that don't benefit from any extra cook time.

Use Quick release when adding additional ingredients to the pot (like with a stew), or cooking eggs, vegetables, delicate foods, or ingredients that don't benefit from additional cook time.

*(*It's best to avoid using Quick release when cooking foods that increase in volume, froth, or foam, like legumes, or those that are mostly **liquid**, like **soup**, as the liquid can boil up and vent through the release valve.)*

Steps to Use Your Foodi Multi-Cooker

Step 1: Preparing your ingredients

Prepare ingredients according to the directions in the pressure-cooking recipe you have selected. For extra flavor, use the brown or sauté functions first, just like you would when cooking with conventional cookware. For instance, brown the meat and vegetables for a stew, before adding other liquids and cooking under pressure.

Be sure to deglaze the pot, scraping up any browned bits clinging to the bottom with a small amount of wine, broth or even water, so they loosened, adding flavor to your food, as well as discouraging scorching

Step 2: Add Liquid

After the aromatics softened, add the remaining ingredients and pour liquid, into the cooker body, as specified in the recipe or timetable. This fluid is usually water. However, some recipes will call for other liquids, such as wine

Step 3: Lock the lid

Assemble the pressure lid by aligning the arrow on the front of the lid with the arrow on the front of the cooker base. Then turn the lid clockwise until it locks into place. Make sure the pressure release valve on the lid is in the SEAL position.

Step 4: Select the function

Select the function, according to the recipe. Press the START/STOP button to begin. Your Foodi will begin to build pressure, indicated by the rotating lights. The unit will begin counting down when it is fully pressurized.

Step 5: Turn off the cooker and release the pressure.

When the countdown is finished, the Foodi will beep, automatically switch to the Keep Warm mode, and begin counting up. After the pressure-cooking time has finished, turn off the cooker by selecting "Start/Stop" button. You can release the pressure two ways: quick release or natural release, according to the recipe or timetable instructions.

Step 6: Air Frying and Finish the dish

In some cases, after releasing pressure and carefully removing the lid, some dishes need Air fry, bake, roast, or broil to evenly crisp and caramelize meals to golden-brown perfection, finish with a crisp to create Crisp meals or simmer to help thicken, reduce, or concentrate the liquid; others require to add more ingredients to finish the recipe.

Useful Tips

1. Watch out about overfilling. Your foodi should not be completely filled. Ever! You need space for pressure and/or steam to build up. Whether you are filling it with food or fluid, always make sure there is plenty of space from the top

2. For consistent browning, make sure ingredients are arranged in an even layer on the bottom of the cooking pot with no overlapping. If ingredients are overlapping, make sure to shake half way through the set cook time.

3. Use the Keep Warm mode to keep food at a warm, food-safe temperature after cooking. To prevent food from drying out, we recommend keeping the lid closed and using this function just before serving. To reheat food, use the Air Crisp function

4. Press and hold down the Time Up or Down arrows to move faster through the display to get to your desired time

5. For smaller ingredients that could fall through the reversible rack, we recommend first wrapping them in a parchment paper or foil pouch

6. To have your unit build pressure quicker, set it to **SEAR/SAUTÉ HIGH**. Once ready to pressure cook, press the PRESSURE button and continue as you normally would

7. When switching from pressure cooking to using the crisping lid it is recommended to empty the pot of any remaining liquid for best crisping results

8. **DO NOT** attempt to open the lid during or after pressure cooking until all internal pressure has been released through the pressure release valve and the unit has cooled slightly. If the lid will not turn to unlock, this indicates the appliance is still under pressure - **DO NOT** force lid open. Any pressure remaining can be hazardous. Let unit naturally release pressure or turn the Pressure Release Valve to the **VENT** position to release steam. Take care to avoid contact with the releasing steam to avoid burns or injury. When the steam is completely released, the red float valve will be in the lower position allowing the lid to be removed

9. **Unplug from outlet when not in use** and before cleaning. Allow to cool before putting on or taking off parts.

10. **DO NOT** use a damaged removable cooking pot, silicone ring or lid Replace before using

11. **DO NOT** touch hot surfaces. Appliance surfaces are hot during and after operation. To prevent burns or personal injury, **ALWAYS** use protective hot pads or insulated oven mitts and use available handles and knobs

12. **DO NOT** soak in water or use any liquid material while cleaning the cooker base of the Foodi

13. **DO NOT leave the house when it is on.** Unlike with a traditional slow cooker, the Foodi reaches high temperatures, can carry a high voltage, and involves literal pressure.

Foodi Multi-Cooker Trouble Shooting

1. How long does it take for the unit to depressurize?

Depending on how much food or liquid is inside the pot, quick release can take up to 2 minutes while natural release can last up to 20 minutes or longer

2. I can't take the pressure lid off.

As a safety feature, the pressure lid will not unlock until the unit is completely depressurized. To release pressure, turn the pressure release valve to the VENT position to quick release the pressurized steam. A quick burst of steam will spurt out of the pressure release valve. When the steam is completely released, the unit will be ready to open Turn the pressure lid counterclockwise then lift it up and away from you.

3. The unit is taking a long time to come to pressure.

Cooking time is affected by the temperature or quantity of the ingredients, the current temperature of the cooking pot, and the selected temperature. If the unit is taking time to build pressure, ensure that the pressure lid is fully locked and that the release valve is in the SEAL position. You should also make sure that the silicone ring is fully seated and that it is flush against the lid. If you live in a high-altitude area, building pressure may also take longer

4. The ingredients were not crispy enough.

The quality of the ingredients as well as the temperature affect the doneness of food. To make sure your food is cooked the way you want, check the food in the middle of cooking. If the food is not crispy enough, cook it longer.

5. There is a "VENT" error message on the screen.

If you are slow cooking or searing/sautéing, the VENT error message will appear when the pressure release valve is in the SEAL position. To correct this, turn the release valve to VENT and leave it in that position until you're finished cooking

6. The unit is hissing and not reaching pressure.

Check that the pressure release valve is in the SEAL position. If there are still some hissing sounds, the silicone ring may not be completely in place.

To stop the cooking, press the START/STOP button and VENT accordingly. Then, remove the pressure lid and ensure that the silicone ring is inserted fully and that it lies flat under the ring rack

7. There is a lot of steam coming from my unit when using the Steam function.

It's normal for steam to release through the pressure release valve during cooking. Leave the pressure release valve in the VENT position for Steam Slow Cook and Sear/Sauté

Foodi Multi-Cooker FAQs

1. How do I set the cooking temperature?

To set the cooking temperature, look for the TEMP arrows on the left side of the digital display. Press the up or down buttons until you get the desired temperature. If you want to adjust the temperature during cooking, you can but you won't be able to change the pressure setting when pressure cooking has already started

2. The unit has started pressure cooking. Can I still move it?

No, it is NOT recommended that you move the unit once pressure cooking has started.

3. Can I cook pasta in the Foodi?

Yes, you can cook pasta in the Foodi. Refer to one of the recipes in the Inspiration Guide that comes with the unit.

4. Is the outside of the Foodi safe to touch when cooking?

The outside unit of the Foodi will get hot so be careful when touching anything other than the control panel, the handle on the lid, and the exterior handles.

5. Why the two lids?

The Foodi has two lids that serve different purposes. The pressure lid allows you to make use of the pressure cooking, steaming, slow cooking, and searing/sautéing functions. The crisping lid, on the other hand, allows you to use the air-frying, baking/roasting, and broiling functions.

6. When using the Air Crisp function, do I need to pre-heat the unit?

Yes, but to pre-heat the unit before air-frying, just add 5 minutes to the total cooking time. Then, allow the unit to come to temperature first before putting in the ingredients

7. How do I set the cooking time?

To set the cooking time, look for the TIME arrows on the right side of the digital display. The clock will display HH:MM. You can change the cooking time at any point during cooking.

8. How do I remove the diffuser from the bottom of the Cook & Crisp Basket?

Grasping the diffuser by the edge and pulling it straight back will allow you to remove it from the Cook & Crisp Basket

9. The display shows "E." What does this mean?

An error message denoted by "E" means the unit is not working properly. If this happens, call Customer Service at 1-877-646-5288

10. How often should I clean the silicone ring and how?

It is recommended that you clean the silicone ring after every use. Wash the silicone ring in warm, soapy water. If cleaning the silicone ring in the dishwasher, place it on the top rack.

11. I want to cancel a cooking function. How do I do that?

Pressing either the START/STOP or POWER buttons will cancel the cooking

12. How do I clean my Foodi?

1. Clean the unit thoroughly after each use. Before cleaning, unplug the unit. Remove all the accessories and the pressure lid.
2. Use a clean, damp cloth to wipe down the cooker base and control panel. You can clean the crisping lid the same way but make sure you allow the heat shield to cool first.
3. You should never immerse the cooker base in water or any liquid
4. Also, you should never put the cooker base in the dishwasher.
5. The cooking pot, silicone ring, and steam rack are dishwasher-safe. However, the pressure lid needs to be handwashed in warm, soapy water
6. Remember to use a non-abrasive sponge or cloth when cleaning the unit.

Breakfasts

Broccoli, Ham, and Pepper Frittata

(Prep + Cook Time: 30 Minutes | **Servings:** 4)

Ingredients:
- 8 oz. ham; cubed
- 2 cups frozen broccoli florets
- 1 cup half-and-half
- 1 cup sliced bell peppers
- 1 cup grated Cheddar cheese
- 4 eggs
- Vegetable oil or unsalted butter; for greasing the pan
- 1 tsp. salt
- 2 tsp. freshly ground black pepper

Instructions:
1. Grease a 6-by-3-inch pan extremely well so the egg does not stick to it once cooked. I use a silicone brush to get oil or butter into every crevice of the pan
2. Arrange the sliced peppers in the bottom of the pan. Place the cubed ham on top. Cover with the frozen broccoli.
3. In a medium bowl, whisk together the eggs, half-and-half, salt, and pepper. Stir in the cheese.
4. Pour the egg mixture over the vegetables and ham. Cover the pan with aluminum foil or a silicone lid.
5. Pour 2 cups of water into the inner cooking pot of the Pressure Cooker, then place a trivet in the pot. Place the covered pan on the trivet
6. Lock the lid into place, Select Manual or Pressure Cook and adjust the pressure to High. Cook for 20 minutes. When the cooking is complete, let the pressure release naturally for 10 minutes, then Quick Pressure Release any remaining pressure. Unlock the lid
7. Carefully remove the pan from the pot and remove the foil. Let the frittata sit for 5 to 10 minutes. Using a knife, gently loosen the sides of the frittata. Place a plate on top of the pan and, holding it in place, invert the frittata onto the plate. If you want the pepper and ham side up, you're done. If you want the cheese side up, flip it on a plate once more.
8. Serve as is, or brown the top of the frittata under the broiler for 3 to 4 minutes

Strawberries Breakfast Risotto

(Prep + Cook Time: 16 Minutes | **Servings:** 6)

Ingredients:
- 1 pint fresh strawberries; hulled and sliced (about 2 cups)
- 1½ cups medium-grain white rice; such as Arborio
- 2 cups unsweetened apple juice
- 1/2 cup heavy or light cream
- 2 tbsp. unsalted butter
- 1/2 tsp. ground cinnamon
- 1/2 tsp. salt
- 2 tbsp. honey

Instructions:
1. Melt the butter in the Foodi turned to the *Sautéing/Browning* function. Stir in about 1 cup strawberries; cook for 2 minutes, stirring often, to soften
2. Pour in the rice; add the cinnamon and salt. Stir over the heat for 1 minute until the rice begins to turn translucent. Pour in the apple juice and 1¾ cups water; stir well
3. Lock the lid onto the pot. Set the Foodi to cook at High pressure for 12 minutes. To get 12 minutes' cook time, press *Pressure* button.
4. Pressure Releas. Use the Quick Pressure Release method
5. Unlock and open the cooker. Turn the Foodi to its *Sautéing/Browning* mode. Stir in the cream, honey, and the remaining cup (or so) of strawberries; bring to a simmer, stirring constantly. Simmer until thickened, about 3 minutes, stirring frequently but gently so as not to break down the strawberries.
6. Unplug the Foodi, cover loosely with its lid, and set aside for 5 minutes to blend the flavors in the rice. Serve

Cheesy Egg Breakfast

(Prep + Cook Time: 10 minutes | **Servings:** 2)

Ingredients:
- 2 English muffins
- 1 cup water, for steaming
- 1 tsp. unsalted butter, at room temperature, divided.
- 2 tbsp. grated aged Cheddar or Parmesan cheese, divided.
- 2 large eggs
- 1/4 tsp. kosher salt, divided.
- Freshly ground black pepper

Instructions:
1. Using 1/2 tsp. of butter each, coat the insides of 2 heatproof custard cups or small ramekins. Crack 1 egg into each cup and carefully pierce the yolks in several places to make sure the yolk cooks through evenly
2. Sprinkle each with 1/8 tsp. of kosher salt, some pepper and 1 tbsp. of Cheddar cheese, covering the eggs. Cover the cups with aluminum foil, crimping it around the sides.
3. Add water and insert the steamer basket or trivet. Place the cups on the insert
4. High pressure for 4 minutes. Lock the lid in place and bring the pot to high pressure for 4 minutes.
5. To get 4 minutes' cook time, press the *Pressure* button and adjust the time
6. Pressure Release. After the timer reaches 0 the cooker will automatically enter Keep warm mode.
7. Press the Start/Stop button and carefully release the pressure.
8. Finish the dish. Toast the English muffins while the eggs cook
9. Unlock but don't remove the lid for another 30 seconds; this helps ensure that the whites are fully cooked. Using tongs, remove the cups from the cooker and peel off the foil
10. Using a small offset spatula or knife, loosen the eggs, then tip each one out onto the bottom half of one of the English muffins. Top with the other half and enjoy.

Poached Eggs & Tomatoes

(Prep + Cook Time: 15 minutes | **Servings:** 4)

Ingredients:
- 2 large Heirloom Ripe Tomatoes, halved crosswise
- 1 tsp. chopped Fresh Herbs, of your choice
- 2 tbsp. grated Parmesan Cheese
- 4 large Eggs
- 1 cup Water
- Salt and Black Pepper to taste
- Cooking Spray

Instructions:
1. Pour the water into the Foodi and fit the reversible rack. Grease the ramekins with the cooking spray and crack each egg into them
2. Season with salt and pepper. Cover the ramekins with aluminum foil.
3. Place the cups on the trivet. Seal the lid. Select Steam mode for 3 minutes on High pressure. Press Start/Stop.
4. Once the timer goes off, do a quick pressure release. Use a napkin to remove the ramekins onto a flat surface.
5. In serving plates, share the halved tomatoes and toss the eggs in the ramekin over on each tomato half
6. Sprinkle with salt and pepper, parmesan, and garnish with chopped herbs.

Chicken and Arugula Casserole

(Prep + Cook Time: 40 Minutes **| Servings:** 4)

Ingredients:
- 1 lb. chicken meat, ground.
- 12 eggs, whisked
- 1 cup baby arugula
- 1 tbsp. canola oil
- ½ tsp. thyme, chopped.
- Salt and black pepper to the taste

Instructions:
1. Set the Foodi on Sauté mode, add the oil, heat it up, add the chicken meat, stir and brown for 5 minutes.
2. In a bowl, mix the eggs with salt, pepper, thyme and the arugula and whisk well
3. Pour this over the chicken meat, toss, set the machine on Bake mode, and cook the mix at 350°F for 25 minutes.
4. Divide the casserole between plates and serve for breakfast.

Honey Cinnamon Apple sauce

(Prep + Cook Time: 12 minutes **| Servings:** 6 to 8)

Ingredients:
- 3 lb. medium-tart baking apples, such as McIntosh, cored, peeled and roughly chopped
- 3/4 cup unsweetened apple juice
- 1 tbsp. fresh lemon juice
- 1/2 tsp. ground cinnamon
- 1/3 cup honey
- 1/2 tsp. salt

Instructions:
1. Mix everything in the Foodi Multi-cooker. High pressure for 6 minutes. Lock the lid onto the pot. Set the Foodi Multi-cooker to cook at high pressure for 6 minutes, using the "Pressure" Button and use the Time Adjustment button to adjust the cook time to 6 minutes. Turn off the Foodi Multi-cooker or unplug it, so it doesn't flip to its keep-warm setting.
2. Pressure Release. Reduce the pressure using the Natural Release Method. Unlock and open the Foodi Multi-cooker.
3. Finish the dish. Use an immersion blender or a potato masher right in the pot to puree the apples into a thick sauce
4. Close the crisping lid. Select "BROIL" and set the time to 5 minutes. Select START/STOP to begin. Cook until top is browned. Serve warm.

Tasty Mini Frittatas

(Prep + Cook Time: 15 minutes **| Servings:** 5)

Ingredients:
- 5 eggs
- Desired mix in's: cheese, veggies, meats the options are endless!
- Splash of milk (I use almond milk)
- Spices such as salt and pepper

Instructions:
1. Mix eggs, milk and mix-in's in a dish. Pour mixture into individual baking molds, I use silicone molds.
2. Place molds on rack in Foodi Multi-cooker with 1 cup of water.
3. High pressure for 5 minutes. Close the lid and the pressure valve and then cook for 5 minutes.
4. To get 5 minutes' cook time, press *Pressure* button and use the Time Adjustment button to adjust the cook time to 5 minutes
5. Pressure Release Use the quick release method when the timer goes off.
6. Close the crisping lid. Select "BROIL" and set the time to 5 minutes. Select START/STOP to begin. Cook until top is browned.

Breakfast Casserole

(Prep + Cook Time: 30 Minutes | **Servings:** 6)

Ingredients:
- 6 eggs
- 1 small onion; diced
- 1 yellow pepper; diced
- 1 small sweet potato; diced
- 1 cup water
- 1/2 tsp. garlic powder
- 1/2 tsp. onion powder
- 1/2 tsp. salt-free all-purpose seasoning
- 2 tbsp. cooking fat (ghee, olive oil, avocado oil)
- 1 tsp. sea salt
- Optional garnish: 1/4 cup green onions; diced

Instructions:
1. Combine all of the ingredients except for the green onions in a mixing bowl and stir well. Pour the mixture into a small casserole dish (mine was 7 × 5-inches (18 × 13-cm) and glass). Now pour the water into the stainless steel bowl of your Pressure Cooker and lower in the steam tray. Next, lower in your filled casserole dish and make a foil "tent" so the water will deflect off while cooking
2. High pressure for 30 minutes. Secure the lid and close off the pressure valve. Press the *Pressure* button and allow it to cook for the 30 minutes displayed. Quick-release the pressure valve when cooking is complete and carefully remove the lid when safe to do so
3. Remove the casserole dish when you are able to do so safely, and slice and serve with green onion garnish. Refrigerate individual slices and eat throughout the week as desired

Cilantro Bacon Breakfast Mix

(Prep + Cook Time: 30 Minutes | **Servings:** 4)

Ingredients:
- 1 lb. bacon, chopped.
- 2½ cups cheddar cheese, shredded.
- 4 eggs, whisked
- 2 tsp. canola oil
- 2 cups almond milk
- Salt and black pepper to the taste
- 3 tbsp. cilantro, chopped.

Instructions:
1. Set the Foodi on Sauté mode, add the oil, heat it up, add the bacon, stir and cook it for 10 minutes.
2. In a bowl, mix the eggs with the milk, salt, pepper and the cilantro and whisk well
3. Pour this over the bacon, sprinkle the cheese on top, set the machine on Bake mode and cook at 370°F for 15 minutes
4. Divide the mix between plates and serve for breakfast

Tomato Frittata

(Prep + Cook Time: 25 Minutes | **Servings:** 6)

Ingredients:
- 6 oz. canned tomatoes, chopped.
- 8 eggs, whisked
- 2 tbsp. chives, chopped.
- 6 tbsp. cream cheese, soft
- 1/2 cup cheddar cheese, shredded
- 2 tbsp. parsley, chopped.
- Cooking spray
- Salt and black pepper to the taste

Instructions:
1. In a bowl, mix all the ingredients except the oil and whisk well
2. Put the reversible rack in the Foodi, add the baking pan inside and grease it with cooking spray
3. Pour the eggs mix inside, spread, set the machine on Bake mode and cook the frittata at 350°F for 15 minutes.
4. Divide between plates and serve for breakfast

Cinnamon and Apples Oatmeal

(Prep + Cook Time: 18 minutes | **Servings:** 4)

Ingredients:
- 3/4 cup steel-cut oats
- 1 small apple, peeled, cored and diced
- 1 tsp. unsalted butter
- 1 tbsp. heavy (whipping) cream
- 2 tbsp. packed brown sugar
- 3 cups water
- 1/2 tsp. ground cinnamon
- 1/4 tsp. kosher salt

Instructions:
1. In the Foodi Multi-cooker, stir together the water, brown sugar, cinnamon and kosher salt, dissolving the salt and sugar. Pour in the oats, add the apple and stir again.
2. High pressure for 12 minutes. Lock the lid in place, cook for 12 minutes.
3. To get 12 minutes cook time, press the *Pressure* button and adjust the time to 12 minutes. When time up turns the Foodi Multi-Cooker off. (Keep warm* setting, turn off)
4. Pressure Release. Use the natural release method. Unlock and open the Foodi Multi Cooker.
5. Finish the dish. Stir the oats and taste; if you like them softer, place the lid on the cooker, but don't lock it. Let the oats sit for 5 to 10 minutes more. Close the crisping lid. Select "BROIL" and set the time to 5 minutes. Select START/STOP to begin. Cook until top is browned.
6. When are ready to serve, stir in the butter and heavy cream. Serve

Tomato, bacon, and Spinach Omelet

(Prep + Cook Time: 30 Minutes | **Servings:** 4)

Ingredients:
- 4 eggs
- 1/4 cup onion; diced
- 1/4 cup tomatoes; seeded and diced
- 1/4 cup fresh baby spinach; chopped
- 2 tbsp. dairy-free milk
- 2 tbsp. plus 1 tsp. (5 ml) ghee; olive oil, avocado oil or lard, divided
- 3 slices bacon; cooked and crumbled
- Optional: ham; mushrooms, dairy-free cheese, sliced jalapeños

Instructions:
1. In a bowl whisk together your 4 eggs and dairy-free milk and set it aside. Warm 1 tsp. (5 ml) of ghee or preferred cooking fat in the stainless steel bowl of your Foodi by pressing the Sauté button. Spoon in your diced onion and cook for about 5–8 minutes or until it softens, becomes translucent and begins to brown
2. Remove the cooked onions and set them aside. If you are including mushrooms in your omelet, you may sauté them at the same time as the onions and remove them accordingly. Cooking time may vary, as the mushrooms will release a lot of moisture while cooking
3. Melt the remaining 2 tbsp. (30 ml) of ghee in the Foodi, and then press the Keep Warm button once it's completely melted. Now pour in your egg mixture
4. Secure the lid, close the pressure valve and then cook for 5 minutes On High pressure. To get 5 minutes' cook time, press *Pressure* button and the *Time Adjustment* button to adjust the cook time to 5 minutes.
5. Quick-release the pressure and remove the lid once safe to do so
6. Carefully remove the cooked omelet from the bowl, using a thin flexible spatula. Transfer it to a plate and fill one half with the sautéed onion, diced tomato, bacon and spinach. Then fold the other half over and serve warm.

Egg Cups

(Prep + Cook Time: 10 Minutes | **Servings:** 4)

Ingredients:
- 2 large peppers (red or green bells work well)
- 1 cup water
- 8 pastured eggs
- 1 tsp. sea salt
- 1/2 tsp. onion powder
- 1/2 tsp. garlic powder
- 1/4 tsp. cumin
- 1/4 tsp. ground black pepper
- Optional garnishes: diced onion; tomato, avocado, salsa and cilantro sprigs

Instructions:
1. Start by slicing your peppers horizontally so that each one makes two "cups." Hollow out the interior of each to remove any seeds. Now crack two eggs into each of the pepper halves. Divide the seasonings among the 4 servings, so that each half gets a quarter of the seasonings
2. Now lower your Pressure Cooker steaming rack into the stainless steel POT bowl and pour a cup (240 ml) of water into the bottom of the bowl. Next, lower your egg-filled peppers onto the rack, placing them carefully so they do not topple over during cooking. Make a tin foil "tent" to place over the peppers so that extra water does not drip into the eggs while they are cooking
3. Now secure the lid and seal the pressure valve closed. Press the *Pressure* button and then the Pressure button so that the Low Pressure light is illuminated. Now press the "-" button until 4 minutes is displayed. Allow the cooking cycle to complete, and then Quick Pressure Release the pressure valve and remove the lid when safe to do so
4. Serve garnished with onions, tomato, avocado, fresh salsa or cilantro.

Bacon and Onions Quiche

(Prep + Cook Time: 13 Minutes | **Servings:** 2)

Ingredients:
- 2 bacon slices; diced
- 1/4 cup thinly sliced onion
- 2 large eggs
- Butter; at room temperature; for coating
- 1 cup water; for steaming
- 1/4 tsp. kosher salt; plus, additional for seasoning
- 2 tbsp. whole milk
- 2 tbsp. heavy (whipping) cream
- Freshly ground black or white pepper

Instructions:
1. Using a small amount of butter, coat the insides of 2 heatproof custard cups or small ramekins.
2. Set the Foodi to *Sautéing/Browning* add the bacon. Cook for 2 to 3 minutes, stirring occasionally, until the bacon renders most of its fat and is mostly crisp
3. Add the onion, and sprinkle with a pinch or two of kosher salt. Cook for about 3 minutes, stirring, until the onions just begin to brown. Transfer the bacon and onions to paper towels to drain briefly. Wipe out the inside of the Foodi. If you prefer, sauté the bacon and onions in a small skillet, and you won't have to clean out the Foodi.
4. Into a small bowl, crack the eggs. Add the milk, heavy cream, and 1/4 tsp. of kosher salt, and season with the pepper. Whisk until the mixture is homogeneous; no streaks of egg white should remain. Pour one-quarter of the egg mixture into each cup or ramekin. Sprinkle half of the bacon and onions over each, and evenly divide the remaining egg over the bacon and onions
5. Add the water and insert the steamer basket or trivet. Carefully transfer the custard cups to the steamer insert. Place a sheet of aluminum foil over the cups. You don't have to crimp it down; it's just to keep steam from condensing on top of the custard
6. Lock the lid in place, and bring the pot to High pressure, cook at High pressure for 7 minutes. To get 7 minutes' cook time, press the *Pressure* button and use the *Time Adjustment* button to adjust the cook time to 7minutes

7. Pressure Release Use the Quick Pressure Release method. Unlock and remove the lid. Using tongs, carefully remove the custard cups from the Foodi. Cool for 1 to 2 minutes before serving. If you want to unmold the quiches, run the tip of a thin knife around the inside edge of the cups. One at a time, place a small plate over the top of the cups, and invert the quiches onto the plate

Soft, Medium, And Hard-Boiled Eggs

(Prep + Cook Time: 8 Minutes | **Servings:** 1 to 12)

Ingredients:
- 1 to 12 cold; large eggs

Instructions:
- Set a large metal vegetable steamer in the Foodi multi cooker; Add about 2 inches of water to the cooker-not so much that it comes through the holes of the steamer. Set one or more eggs in the steamer

For soft-boiled eggs:
- Lock the lid onto the pot. Bring the cooker to High pressure by pressing the *Pressure* button. Allow to cook for 1 ½ minute and press Start/Stop
- Use the Quick Pressure Release method to bring the pressure in the pot back to normal.

For medium-boiled eggs:
- Lock the lid onto the pot. Close the lid and the pressure valve and then cook for 3 minutes On High pressure. To get 3 minutes' cook time, press *Pressure* button
- Use the quick Pressure Release method to bring the pot's pressure back to normal but do not open the pot. Set the cooker aside, covered, for 1 minute. Use the Quick Pressure Release method to bring the pot's pressure fully back to normal.

For hard-boiled eggs:
- Lock the lid onto the pot. Close the lid and the pressure valve and then cook for 3 minutes On High pressure. To get 3 minutes' cook time, press *Pressure* button and use the *Time Adjustment* button to adjust the cook time to 3 minutes
- Turn off the machine or unplug it; set aside for 8 minutes. Use the Quick Pressure Release method to bring the pot fully back to normal pressure
- For all eggs Unlock and remove the lid. Transfer the eggs to a large bowl. Cut the top off a soft-boiled egg and serve it in an eggcup; peel the other kinds of eggs while still warm

Apple, Bacon and Grits Casserole

(Prep + Cook Time: 35 Minutes | **Servings:** 4 to 6)

Ingredients:
- 2 large eggs; lightly beaten
- 3/4 cup quick cooking or instant grits
- 1/2 cup shredded Cheddar cheese (about 2 oz.)
- 2 tbsp. unsalted butter; plus, more for buttering the dish
- 8 oz. Canadian bacon; chopped
- 1 medium tart green apple; such as Granny Smith, peeled, cored, and chopped
- 4 medium scallions; green and white parts, trimmed and sliced into thin bits
- 1 tsp. dried thyme

Instructions:
1. Melt the butter in the Foodi turned to the Browning function. Add the Canadian bacon; cook, stirring often, for 1 minute. Add the apple, scallions, and thyme; cook for 1 minute, stirring constantly. Scrape the contents of the cooker into a large bowl. Wipe out the cooker with a damp paper towel
2. Turn the Foodi to its Browning mode. Add 3 cups water and bring to a boil. Whisk in the grits and cook, whisking all the while, until thickened, about 5 minutes. Scrape the grits into the bowl with the bacon mixture; cool for 10 minutes. Wash and dry the cooker.
3. Set the rack inside the cooker and pour in 2 cups water. Make a foil sling and set a 2-quart, high-sided, round baking or soufflé dish on top of it. Lightly butter the inside of the dish

4. Stir the eggs and cheese into the grits mixture until uniform and well combined. Spread the mixture in the prepared baking dish; cover and seal with foil. Lower the dish onto the rack in the cooker with the sling. Fold the ends of the sling so they'll fit inside the cooker
5. Lock the lid onto the pot and cook at High pressure for 22 minutes On High pressure. To get 22 minutes cook time, press the *Pressure* button and then use the "time adjustment" button to adjust to 22 minutes.
6. Use the Quick Pressure Release method
7. Unlock and open the cooker. Use the sling to transfer the baking dish to a wire cooling rack, steadying the dish as necessary. Uncover, cool a couple of minutes, and spoon the casserole onto individual plates to serve.

Bulgur, Oat, And Walnut Porridge

(Prep + Cook Time: 30 Minutes | **Servings:** 6)

Ingredients:
- 1/2 cup steel-cut oats
- 1/2 cup chopped walnuts
- 1/2 cup maple syrup
- 1/2 cup bulgur
- 1/2 tsp. ground cinnamon
- 1/2 tsp. salt

Instructions:
1. Mix everything with 4 cups water in the Foodi. Close the lid and the pressure valve and then cook on High pressure for 25 minutes. To get 25 minutes' cook time, press *Pressure* button and use the *Time Adjustment* button to adjust the cook time to 25 minutes
2. Use the Quick Pressure Release method to bring the pot's pressure back to normal.
3. Unlock and remove the lid. Turn the electric cooker to its browning function. Bring to a simmer, stirring often. Cook, stirring constantly, until slightly thickened, about 2 minutes. Serve

Cherries Oats

(Prep + Cook Time: 20 Minutes | **Servings:** 4)

Ingredients:
- 3 cups almond milk
- 1/4 tsp. cinnamon powder
- 1/4 cup cherries, pitted and chopped.
- 4 tbsp. cream cheese
- 1 tbsp. brown sugar
- 4 eggs, whisked
- 1½ cups rolled oats

Instructions:
1. In a bowl, mix all the ingredients and toss well
2. Pour this into the Foodi, put the pressure lid on and cook the mix on High for 15 minutes
3. Release the pressure naturally for 10 minutes, divide the oats into bowls and serve for breakfast.

Chicken Crunchadilla breakfast

(Prep + Cook Time: 25 minutes | **Servings:** 2)

Ingredients:
- 1 cup cooked chicken meat, shredded, divided.
- 1/2 package (4 oz.) prepared cheese product, cut in 1/2-inch cubes, divided.
- 1 flour tortilla (12 inches)
- 1/4 cup shredded Mexican cheese blend
- 1 Roma tomato, diced, divided.
- 2 scallions, thinly sliced, divided.
- 2 corn tostadas, divided.

Instructions:
1. Lay flour tortilla onto a clean surface. Place 1/2 cup shredded chicken onto center of tortilla. Sprinkle half of the cubed cheese evenly on top of shredded chicken, then sprinkle with half the tomatoes and half the scallions.
2. Place one tostada on top. Repeat step 1 with layers of remaining chicken, cubed cheese, tomatoes, and scallions. Top with second tostada and shredded cheese
3. Gently fold flour tortilla over the layers in a concentric pattern, about 4 folds, until the crunchadilla is securely wrapped
4. Using a broken piece of tostada or a torn piece of tortilla, cover the center opening of the crunchadilla so all contents remain secure during cooking
5. Gently flip crunchadilla over, seam-side down, and coat the top with cooking spray.
6. Place crunchadilla in Cook & Crisp Basket. Select AIR CRISP, set temperature to 360°F, and set time to 8 minutes. Select START/STOP to begin. When cooking is complete, crunchadilla is ready to serve

Apples and Cinnamon Oatmeal

(Prep + Cook Time: 17 Minutes | **Servings:** 4)

Ingredients:
- 3/4 cup steel-cut oats
- 1 small apple; peeled, cored, and diced
- 2 tbsp. packed brown sugar
- 1/2 tsp. ground cinnamon
- 3 cups water
- 1/4 tsp. kosher salt
- 1 tsp. unsalted butter
- 1 tbsp. heavy (whipping) cream

Instructions:
1. In the Foodi, stir together the water, brown sugar, cinnamon, and kosher salt, dissolving the salt and sugar. Pour in the oats, add the apple, and stir again
2. Lock the lid in place, cook for 12 minutes On High pressure. To get 12 minutes cook time, press the *Pressure* button. When the time is up turn the Foodi off. ("Keep warm" setting, turn off).
3. Use the natural release method. Unlock and open the Foodi
4. Stir the oats, and taste; if you like them softer, place the lid on the cooker, but don't lock it. Let the oats sit for 5 to 10 minutes more. When they are ready to serve, stir in the butter and heavy cream. Serve.

Spring Onions Frittata

(Prep + Cook Time: 20 Minutes | **Servings:** 4)

Ingredients:
- 4 eggs, whisked.
- 4 spring onions, chopped.
- 2 tsp. smoked paprika
- Cooking spray
- Salt and black pepper to the taste

Instructions:
1. In a bowl, mix all the ingredients except the cooking spray and whisk well
2. Put the reversible rack in the Foodi, add the baking pan inside and grease with the cooking spray
3. Pour the eggs mix inside, spread, set the machine on Bake mode and cook the frittata at 370°F for 15 minutes. Divide between plates and serve for breakfast

Egg, Sausage Chorizo and Cheese Cake

(Prep + Cook Time: 25 minutes | **Servings:** 6)

Ingredients:
- 8 Eggs, cracked into a bowl
- 8 oz. Breakfast Sausage, chopped.
- 1 large Green Bell Pepper, chopped.
- 3 Bacon Slices, chopped.
- 1/2 cup Milk
- 4 slices Bread, cut into 1/2 -inch cubes
- 1 tsp. Red Chili Flakes
- 1 large Red Bell Pepper, chopped.
- 1 cup chopped Green Onion
- 1 cup grated Cheddar Cheese
- Salt and Black Pepper to taste
- 2 cups Water

Instructions:
1. Add the eggs, sausage chorizo, bacon slices, green and red bell peppers, green onion, chili flakes, cheddar cheese, salt, pepper, and milk to a bowl and use a whisk to beat them together.
2. Grease a bundt pan with cooking spray and pour the egg mixture into it. After, drop the bread slices in the egg mixture all around while using a spoon to push them into the mixture
3. Open the Foodi, pour in water, and fit the rack at the center of the pot. Place bundt pan on the rack and seal the pressure lid.
4. Select Pressure mode on High pressure for 6 minutes, and press Start/Stop.
5. Once the timer goes off, press Start/Stop, do a quick pressure release
6. Run a knife around the egg in the bundt pan, close the crisping lid and cook for another 4 minutes on Bake/Roast on 380°F.
7. When ready, place a serving plate on the bundt pan, and then, turn the egg bundt over. Use a knife to cut the egg into slices.
8. Serve with sauce of your choice

Grits with Cheese & Bacon

(Prep + Cook Time: 25 minutes | **Servings:** 4)

Ingredients:
- 3 slices smoked Bacon, diced.
- 2 tsp. Butter
- 1/2 cup Water
- 1/2 cup Milk
- 1 ½ cups grated Cheddar Cheese
- 1 cup ground Grits
- Salt and Black Pepper

Instructions:
1. Preheat the Foodi by select Sear/Sauté mode and set to HIGH pressure. Then Cook bacon until crispy, about 5 minutes. Set aside.
2. Add the grits, butter, milk, water, salt, and pepper to the pot and stir using a spoon. Close the pressure lid and secure the pressure valve.
3. Choose the Pressure mode and cook for 3 minutes on High. Press Start/Stop
4. Once the timer has ended, turn the vent handle and do a quick pressure release. Add in cheddar cheese and give the pudding a good stir with the same spoon.
5. Close crisping lid, press BAKE/ROAST button and cook for 8 minutes on 370°F. Press Start key.
6. When ready, dish the cheesy grits into serving bowls and spoon over the crisped bacon. Serve right away with toasted bread

Blueberries Breakfast Mix

(Prep + Cook Time: 25 Minutes | **Servings:** 6)

Ingredients:
- 2 cups old fashioned oats
- 1 tsp. baking powder
- 2 cups blueberries
- 2 cups almond milk
- 2 eggs, whisked
- 1/3 cup brown sugar
- 1 tsp. cinnamon powder
- 2 tbsp. butter
- Cooking spray

Instructions:
1. In a bowl, mix all the ingredients except the cooking spray and whisk well
2. Put the reversible rack in the Foodi, add the baking pan inside, grease it with cooking spray and then add the blueberries and oats mix
3. Set the Foodi on Bake mode and cook the mix at 350°F for 20 minutes
4. Divide into bowls and serve for breakfast.

Vanilla Banana Bread

(Prep + Cook Time: 45 minutes | **Servings:** 4 to 6)

Ingredients:
- 1 large ripe banana, mashed
- 1/4 cup (1/2 stick) unsalted butter, melted, plus more for the pan
- 1/8 tsp. ground cinnamon, plus more for dusting
- 1/2 cup pecans, chopped.
- 1 cup all-purpose flour
- 1/2 tsp. baking powder
- 1/4 tsp. baking soda
- 1/2 tsp. kosher salt
- 2 large eggs
- 1/3 cup sugar
- 1/3 cup sour cream
- 1/2 tsp. pure vanilla extract

Instructions:
1. Close crisping lid. Preheat the unit by selecting BAKE/ROAST, setting the temperature to 325°F and setting the time to 5 minutes. Select START/STOP to begin.
2. Insert the steam rack into the Foodi Multi-cooker and add 1 ½ cups (350 ml) water. Butter a 6 × 3-inch (15 × 7.5 cm) round cake pan
3. In a medium bowl, whisk together the flour, baking powder, baking soda, salt and cinnamon.
4. In a second medium bowl, whisk together the eggs, sugar, sour cream, melted butter and vanilla. Mix in the banana. Add the dry ingredients and mix to combine; stir in the pecans
5. Scrape the batter into the prepared pan and cover with aluminum foil. Place the pan on the steam rack. Close the crisping lid.
6. Air Frying for 40 minutes. Select BAKE/ROAST, set temperature to 325°F and set time to 40 minutes. Select START/STOP to begin
7. Finish the Dish. When cooking is complete, remove pan from pot and place on a cooling rack. Allow bread to cool 30 minutes before serving. Serve.

Delicious Giant Pancake

(Prep + Cook Time: 30 minutes | **Servings:** 6)

Ingredients:
- 3 cups All-purpose Flour
- 3/4 cup Sugar
- 1 ½ tsp. Baking Soda
- 2 tbsp. Maple Syrup
- 5 Eggs
- 1/3 cup Olive Oil
- 1/3 cup Sparkling Water
- 1/3 tsp. Salt
- A dollop of Whipped Cream to serve

Instructions:
1. Start by pouring the flour, sugar, eggs, olive oil, sparkling water, salt, and baking soda into a food processor and blend until smooth.
2. Pour the batter into the Foodi and let it sit in there for 15 minutes. Close the lid and secure the pressure valve.
3. Select the Pressure mode on Low pressure for 10 minutes. Press Start/Stop.
4. Once the timer goes off, press Start/Stop, quick-release the pressure valve to let out any steam and open the lid.
5. Gently run a spatula around the pancake to let loose any sticking. Once ready, slide the pancake into a serving plate and drizzle with maple syrup. Top with the whipped cream to serve.

French Toast Bread Pudding

(Prep + Cook Time: 20 Minutes | **Servings:** 6)

Ingredients:
- 2 large eggs; at room temperature
- 5 cups of 1-inch bread cubes (about 7 oz.)
- 1/4 cup sugar
- 1/4 cup orange marmalade
- 1/4 cup raisins
- 1 cup whole or low-fat milk
- 1/2 tsp. ground cinnamon
- 2 tsp. vanilla extract

Instructions:
1. Lightly butter a 2-quart, high-sided, round baking or soufflé dish; set aside. Place the pressure cooker rack inside the Foodi; pour in 2 cups water
2. Whisk the eggs, milk, sugar, marmalade, vanilla, and cinnamon in a big bowl until smooth, with no bits of egg visible. Add the bread cubes and raisins; toss well to soak up the liquids. Pour the entire mixture into the prepared baking dish; cover and seal the dish with aluminum foil. Make a foil sling, set the filled baking dish on it, and lower the baking dish in the sling onto the rack. Fold the ends of the sling so they'll fit inside the cooker
3. Lock the lid onto the cooker, bring the cooker to High pressure by pressing the *Pressure* button and cook for 15 minutes.
4. Use the Quick Pressure Release method to bring the pot's pressure back to normal.
5. Unlock the lid and open the cooker. Use the foil sling to transfer the hot baking dish to a wire rack. Uncover and cool for 5 minutes before dishing it up by the big spoonful

Breakfast Quinoa Bowl

(Prep + Cook Time: 24 minutes | **Servings:** 4)

Ingredients:
- 1 cup quinoa
- 2 scallions (white and light green parts), thinly sliced
- 2 large eggs, hard-boiled, cooled and peeled
- 2 tbsp. chopped fresh flat-leaf parsley
- 1-pint cherry tomatoes (25 to 30 tomatoes)
- 1 tbsp. (15 ml) extra-virgin olive oil
- 1/4 tsp. freshly ground black pepper
- 1 ½ cups (350 ml) water
- 3/4 tsp. kosher salt, divided.
- 1 avocado

Instructions:
1. Preparing the Ingredients Using a fine-mesh strainer, rinse the quinoa, then place into the Foodi Multi-cooker. Add the water and 1/2 tsp. of the salt
2. High pressure for 7 minutes. Close the lid and Cook for 7 minutes.
3. To get 7 minutes' cook time, press the *Pressure* button and use the Time Adjustment button to adjust the cook time to 7 minutes.
4. Pressure Release. Use the *Natural Release* method for 5 minutes, then vent any remaining steam and open the lid.
5. Fluff with a fork. Press Start/stop, lock the lid and let sit for 5 minutes more.
6. Finish the dish. While the quinoa is cooking, preheat broiler. On a small rimmed baking sheet, toss the tomatoes with the olive oil, pepper and the remaining 1/4 tsp. salt. Broil until the tomatoes begin to burst, about 3 minutes. Toss with the scallions and parsley.
7. Pit, peel and dice the avocado. Divide the quinoa among bowls, top with the tomatoes and avocado and then coarsely grate the eggs on top. Serve

Red Onion and Potatoes Casserole

(Prep + Cook Time: 40 Minutes | **Servings:** 4)

Ingredients:
- 1 ½ pounds hash browns
- 1 sweet pepper, cut into strips
- 4 eggs, whisked.
- 1 red onion, sliced.
- Salt and black pepper to the taste
- 1 tsp. rosemary, chopped.
- 2 tsp. canola oil

Instructions:
1. Set the Ninja Foodi on sauté mode, add the oil, heat it up, add the hash browns, stir and sauté for 5 minutes.
2. Add the onions, sweet pepper, salt, pepper and the rosemary, stir and sauté for another 5 minutes
3. Add the eggs, toss, set the machine on Bake mode, heat it up at 350°F and cook the mix for 20 minutes
4. Divide the casserole between plates and serve for breakfast

Tasty Salmon Veggie Cakes

(Prep + Cook Time: 40 minutes | **Servings:** 4)

Ingredients:
- 2 (5 oz.) packs Steamed Salmon Flakes
- 1 Red Onion, chopped.
- 1 cup Breadcrumbs
- 1 Red Bell Pepper, seeded and chopped.
- 4 tbsp. Butter, divided.
- 4 tbsp. Mayonnaise
- 2 tsp. Worcestershire Sauce
- 1/4 cup chopped Parsley
- 1 tsp. Garlic Powder
- 2 tbsp. Olive Oil
- Salt and Black Pepper to taste
- 3 Eggs, cracked into a bowl
- 3 large potatoes, cut into chips

Instructions:
1. Turn on the Foodi and select Sear/Sauté mode on High pressure. Heat the oil and add half of the butter. Once it has melted, add the onions and the chopped red bell peppers.
2. Cook for 6 minutes while stirring occasionally. Press Start/Stop
3. In a mixing bowl, add salmon flakes, sautéed red bell pepper and onion, breadcrumbs, eggs, mayonnaise, Worcestershire sauce, garlic powder, salt, pepper, and parsley.
4. Use a spoon to mix well while breaking the salmon into the tiny pieces. Use your hands to mold 4 patties out of the mixture
5. Add the remaining butter to melt, and when melted, add the patties. Fry for 4 minutes, flipping once.
6. Then, close the crisping lid, select Bake/Roast mode and bake for 4 minutes on 320 °F. Remove them onto a wire rack to rest.
7. Serve the cakes with a side of lettuce and potato salad with a mild drizzle of herb vinaigrette

Grits with Cranberries Breakfast

(**Prep + Cook Time:** 15 Minutes | **Servings:** 4)

Ingredients:
- 3/4 cup grits or polenta (not quick cook or instant)
- 1/2 cup dried cranberries
- 1/2 cup slivered almonds; toasted
- 3 cups water
- 1/8 tsp. kosher salt
- 1 tbsp. unsalted butter
- 1 tbsp. heavy (whipping) cream
- 2 tbsp. honey

Instructions:
1. In the Foodi combine the grits, water, kosher salt, and dried cranberries
2. Lock the lid in place, and bring the cooker to High pressure by pressing *Pressure* button and cook for 10 minutes.
3. Use the Quick Pressure Release method
4. Unlock and remove the lid. Quickly add the butter, heavy cream, and honey, and stir vigorously with a wooden spoon or paddle until smooth and creamy. Spoon into bowls, top with the toasted almonds, and serve.

Tomatoes and Ham Bake

(**Prep + Cook Time:** 40 Minutes | **Servings:** 8)

Ingredients:
- 1lb. white bread, cubed
- 1 lb. ham, cooked and chopped.
- 30 oz. canned tomatoes, chopped.
- 1/2 lb. cheddar, shredded
- 2 tbsp. veggie stock
- 1/4 cup olive oil
- 1 spring onion, chopped.
- 2 tbsp. cilantro, chopped.
- Salt and black pepper to the taste
- 8 eggs, whisked

Instructions:
1. Set the Foodi on Sauté mode, add the oil, heat it up, add the ham and all the other ingredients, toss a bit, set the machine on Bake mode and cook at 360°F for 35 minutes
2. Divide the mix between plates and serve for breakfast

Turkey Burrito

(Prep + Cook Time: 12 Minutes | **Servings:** 2)

Ingredients:
- 1 big turkey breast, cooked and shredded.
- 3 eggs, whisked
- 1 avocado, peeled, pitted and sliced
- 1 red bell pepper, sliced
- Cooking spray
- Salt and black pepper to the taste
- 2 tbsp. mozzarella, shredded
- 2 corn tortillas

Instructions:
1. Put the reversible rack in the Foodi, place the baking pan inside and grease it with cooking spray
2. Add the whisked eggs mixed with salt and pepper, set the machine on Bake mode and cook at 400°F for 6 minutes
3. Arrange the tortillas on a working surface, divide the eggs mix on each, also divide the rest of the ingredients, roll into 2 burritos and serve for breakfast

Simple Banana Oatmeal

(Prep + Cook Time: 30 minutes | **Servings:** 4)

Ingredients:
- 2 ripe bananas, chopped
- 1/2 cup steel-cut oats
- 1/2 cup packed light brown sugar
- 1/4 cup heavy cream
- 2 tsp. vanilla extract
- 1/2 tsp. ground cinnamon
- 1/4 tsp. salt

Instructions:
1. Mix the oats, brown sugar, bananas, vanilla, cinnamon and salt with 2 ¼ cups water in the Foodi Multi-cooker until the brown sugar dissolves.
2. High pressure for 18 minutes. Lock the lid onto the pot and cook at high pressure for 18 minutes.
3. To get 18 minutes cook time, press the *Pressure* button and use the Time Adjustment button to adjust the cook time to 18 minutes.
4. Pressure Release. Turn off the Foodi Multi-cooker or unplug it, so it doesn't flip to its keep-warm setting. Allow the pot's pressure to come to regular naturally, 10 to 12 minutes
5. If the pot's pressure hasn't returned to normal within 12 minutes, use the quick release method to bring it back to normal.
6. Finish the dish. Unlock and open the cooker. Stir in the cream. Close the crisping lid. Select "BROIL" and set the time to 5 minutes
7. Select START/STOP to begin. Cook until top is browned. Set aside for 1 minute to warm before serving.

Apple and Bacon Casserole

(Prep + Cook Time: 43 minutes | **Servings:** 4 to 6)

Ingredients:
- 8 oz. Canadian bacon, chopped.
- 1 medium tart green apple, such as Granny Smith, peeled, cored and chopped.
- 4 medium scallions, green and white parts, trimmed and sliced into thin bits
- 2 tbsp. unsalted butter, plus more for buttering the dish
- 3/4 cup quick cooking or instant grits
- 2 large eggs, lightly beaten
- 1/2 cup shredded Cheddar cheese (about 2 oz.)
- 1 tsp. dried thyme

Instructions:
1. Melt the butter in the Foodi Multi-cooker, turn to the Sauté function. Add the Canadian bacon; cook, stirring often, for 1 minute.

2. Add the apple, scallions and thyme; cook for 1 minute, stirring constantly. Scrape the contents of the cooker into a large bowl. Wipe out the cooker with a damp paper towel.
3. Turn the Foodi Multi-cooker to its Sauté mode. Add 3 cups water and bring to a boil. Whisk in the grits and cook, whisking all the while, until thickened, about 5 minutes. Scrape the grits into the bowl with the bacon mixture; cool for 10 minutes. Wash and dry the cooker
4. Set the rack inside the cooker and pour in 2 cups water. Make a foil sling and set a 2-quart, high-sided, round baking or soufflé dish on top of it. Lightly butter the inside of the dish.
5. Stir the eggs and cheese into the grits mixture until uniform and well combined. Spread the mixture in the prepared baking dish; cover and seal with foil
6. Lower the dish onto the rack in the cooker with the sling. Fold the ends of the sling so they'll fit inside the cooker
7. High pressure for 22 minutes. Lock the lid onto the pot and cook at high pressure for 22 minutes.
8. To get 22 minutes cook time, press the *Pressure* button and then use the time adjustment button to adjust to 22 minutes.
9. Pressure Release. Use the quick release method.
10. Finish the dish. Unlock and open the cooker. Close the crisping lid. Select "BROIL" and set the time to 5 minutes. Select START/STOP to begin. Cook until top is browned.
11. Use the sling to transfer the baking dish to a wire cooling rack, steadying the dish as necessary. Uncover, cool a couple of minutes and spoon the casserole onto individual plates to serve

Cheesy Hash Browns Mix

(**Prep + Cook Time:** 30 Minutes | **Servings:** 4)

Ingredients:
- 1 ½ pounds hash browns
- 1 cup coconut milk
- 1 cup cheddar cheese, shredded.
- 2 tbsp. chives, chopped.
- 2 tsp. canola oil
- 8 oz. cream cheese
- 1 yellow onion, chopped.
- Salt and black pepper to the taste
- 4 eggs

Instructions:
1. In a bowl, mix all the ingredients except the oil and the yellow onion and whisk them well
2. Set the Foodi on Sauté mode, add the oil heat it up, add the onion, stir and sauté for 5 minutes
3. Add the eggs mix, toss, set the Foodi on Air Crisp and cook everything for 15 minutes more.
4. Divide between plates and serve for breakfast

Pork

Pork Shoulder Chops with Carrots

(Prep + Cook Time: 52 minutes | **Servings:** 4 to 6)

Ingredients:
- 3 lb. bone in pork shoulder chops, each 1/2 to 3/4 inch thick
- 6 medium carrots
- 1/3 cup maple syrup
- 1/3 cup chicken broth
- 3 medium garlic cloves
- 1 tbsp. bacon fat
- 1/3 cup soy sauce
- 1/2 tsp. ground black pepper

Instructions:
1. Melt the bacon fat in a Foodi Multi-cooker, turned to the browning function. Add about half the chops and brown well, turning once, about 5 minutes. Transfer these to a large bowl and brown the remaining chops.
2. Stir the carrots and garlic into the pot; cook for 1 minute, constantly stirring. Pour in the soy sauce, maple syrup and broth, stirring to dissolve the maple syrup and to get up any browned bits on the bottom of the pot. Stir in the pepper. Return the shoulder chops and their juices to the pot. Stir to coat them in the sauce
3. High pressure for 40 minutes. Lock the lid on the Foodi Multi-cooker and then cook for 40 minutes
4. To get 40 minutes' cook time, press *Pressure* button and use the Time Adjustment button to adjust the cook time to 40 minutes
5. Pressure Release. Let the pressure to come down naturally for at least 14 to 16 minutes, then quick release any pressure left in the pot.
6. Finish the dish. Close crisping lid and select Broil, set time to 7 minutes
7. Transfer the chops, carrots and garlic cloves to a large serving bowl. Skim the fat off the sauce and ladle it over the servings

Pressure Cooker Cassoulet

(Prep + Cook Time: 50 Minutes | **Servings:** 4 to 6)

Ingredients:
- 2 lb. boneless pork ribs, cut into 1-inch chunks Salt and pepper to taste
- 2 cups great northern beans (or similar)
- 4 cloves garlic; minced
- 2 cups herbed croutons
- 1 cup goat cheese; crumbled (optional)
- 1 cup beef broth
- 1 carrot, diced
- 1 celery stalk; diced
- 1/2 white onion, diced
- 2 tbsp. olive oil
- 2 tbsp. dried rosemary

Instructions:
1. Set the Foodi to *Sauté* mode, Add the olive oil Heat olive oil. Sprinkle pork ribs with salt and pepper, then brown in the Pressure Cooker on all sides
2. Then add the beans, broth, carrot, celery, onion, rosemary and garlic.
3. Close the lid and cook on High Pressure for 35 minutes. To get 35 minutes cook time, press *Pressure* button.
4. When cooking is complete, select cancel and use Natural Release
5. Dish cassoulet into 4 to 6 large soup bowls, then top with equal amounts of croutons and goat cheese. Serve.

Pork with Barbecue Sauce

(Prep + Cook Time: 30 Minutes | **Servings:** 2)

Ingredients:
- 3/4 lb. boneless pork shoulder, trimmed of as much visible fat as possible, cut into 2-inch chunks
- Buns or lettuce leaves, for serving
- 1 tbsp. yellow mustard
- 1 tbsp. Dijon mustard
- 1½ tsp. cider vinegar
- 1/2 tsp. Worcestershire sauce
- 1 tbsp. honey
- 3 tbsp. ketchup
- 1/4 tsp. kosher salt
- 1/2 tsp. ground cayenne pepper

Instructions:
1. In the Foodi, stir together the yellow mustard, Dijon mustard, honey, ketchup, cider vinegar, Worcestershire sauce, kosher salt, and cayenne pepper until thoroughly mixed. Add the pork, and toss to coat.
2. Lock the lid in place, and bring the pot to High pressure. Cook at High pressure for 25 minutes. To get 25 minutes' cook time, press *Pressure* button and use the *Time Adjustment* button to adjust the cook time to 25 minutes
3. Use the Natural Pressure Release method
4. Unlock and remove the lid. Pour the pork and sauce through a coarse sieve; set the pork aside to cool. Return the sauce to the cooker, and let it sit for 1 to 2 minutes so any fat rises to the surface. Skim or blot off as much fat as possible and discard.
5. Turn the Foodi to *Sautéing/Browning* Simmer the sauce for about 5 minutes, or until it's the consistency of a thick tomato sauce
6. While the sauce thickens, shred the pork, discarding any fat or gristle. Add the shredded pork to the sauce, and heat through. Serve on buns, or use as a filling for lettuce wraps.

Cranberry BBQ Pulled Pork

(Prep + Cook Time: 55 Minutes | **Servings:** 10)

Ingredients:
- 3 - 4 lb. pork shoulder or roast, boneless, fat trimmed off

For the sauce:
- 1 cup tomato puree
- 1 chipotle pepper in adobo sauce; diced
- 1/2 cup apple cider vinegar
- 3 tbsp. liquid smoke
- 2 tbsp. tomato paste
- 2 cups fresh cranberries
- 1/4 cup buffalo hot sauce
- 1/3 cup blackstrap molasses
- 1/2 cup water
- 1 tbsp. adobo sauce
- 1 tsp. salt, or more to taste

Instructions:
1. Cut the pork against the grain in halves or thirds and set aside
2. Press the *Sauté* key of the Foodi.
3. When the pot is hot, add the cranberries and the water
4. Let simmer for about 4 to 5 minutes or until the cranberries start to pop. Add the remaining sauce ingredients in the pot and continue simmering for 5 minutes more.
5. Add the pork in the pot. Press the *Cancel* key to stop the *Sauté* function. Cover and lock the lid.
6. Select *Pressure* and cook at HIGH pressure for 40 minutes
7. When the Foodi timer beeps, turn the steam valve to Venting to quick release the pressure. Unlock and carefully open the lid
8. With a fork, pull the pork apart into shreds. Serve the pork with plenty of sauce on rolls or bread or over your favorite greens.

Pork Tenderloin and Coconut Rice

(Prep + Cook Time: 20 Minutes | **Servings:** 4)

Ingredients:
- 1 lb. pork tenderloin, cut into 4 pieces
- 1 small leek; white and pale green parts only, halved lengthwise, washed and thinly sliced
- 1 (4½ oz.) can chopped mild green chiles (about ½ cup)
- 1 (15 oz.) can black beans; drained and rinsed (about 1¾ cups)
- 1 cup chicken broth
- 1 cup regular or low-fat canned coconut milk
- 1 cup white long-grain rice; such as white basmati rice
- 2 tbsp. packed light brown sugar
- 1 tsp. dried thyme
- 2 tbsp. peanut oil
- 1 tsp. ground cumin
- 1/2 tsp. ground coriander
- 1/4 tsp. salt
- 1/4 tsp. ground black pepper

Instructions:
1. Heat the oil in the Foodi turned to the *Sautéing/Browning* function. Add the pork tenderloin pieces; brown on all sides, turning occasionally, about 6 minutes. Transfer to a plate
2. Add the leek and chiles; cook, stirring often, until the leek softens, about 2 minutes. Stir in the thyme, cumin, coriander, salt, and pepper; cook until aromatic, less than half a minute. Stir in the beans, broth, coconut milk, rice, and brown sugar until the brown sugar dissolves.
3. Nestle the pieces of pork in the sauce, submerging the meat and rice as much as possible in the liquid; pour any juices from the meat's plate into the cooker
4. Lock the lid on the Foodi and then cook On High pressure for 15 minutes. To get 15 minutes' cook time, press *Pressure* button.
5. Use the Quick Pressure Release method to bring the pot's pressure back to normal, but do not open the cooker
6. Set the pot aside for 10 minutes to steam the rice. Unlock and open the cooker. Transfer the pork pieces to four serving plates; spoon the rice and beans around them.

Pulled Pork Taco Dinner

(Prep + Cook Time: 50 Minutes | **Servings:** 2)

Ingredients:
- 4 lbs. boneless pork shoulder, cut in two pieces
- 2 cups barbecue sauce; divided
- Pinch of black pepper
- 2 tbsp. olive oil
- Pinch of Cayenne pepper
- 1/2 cup water

Instructions:
1. Preheat the Foodi by selecting Sauté function.
2. Brown the pork on both sides with the oil 2 to 3 minutes per side. Once browned, set aside.
3. Mix 1 cup barbecue sauce and 1/2 cup water into the Foodi. Stir to combine and add the pork back into the Foodi and the rest of the seasoning
4. Cook on High Pressure for 45 minutes. To get 45 minutes cook time, press *Pressure* and use the *Time Adjustment* button to adjust the cook time to 45 minutes.
5. When cooking is complete, select cancel and use Natural Release about 15 minutes.
6. Remove the pork from the Foodi and shred with two forks
7. Strain the cooking juice through a sieve and set aside 1/2 cup of the juice.
8. Select sauté function, put the shredded pork back into Foodi \and add the 1 cup barbecue sauce and the 1/2 cup of cooking juice and bring it back to a simmer and mix well
9. Put the Foodi on *Sautéing/Browning* put the shredded pork back into Foodi and add the 1 cup barbecue sauce and the 1/2 cup of cooking juice and bring it back to a simmer and mix well

10. Serve on warm taco shells with your favorite toppings or on toasted rolls. For the remaining Jus you can save it and turn it into a gravy for your next meal.

BBQ Pork with Ginger Coconut and Sweet Potatoes

(**Prep + Cook Time:** 35 minutes | **Servings:** 4)

Ingredients:
- 4 frozen uncooked boneless pork chops (8 oz. each)
- 3 sweet potatoes, peeled, cut in 1-inch cubes
- 1/2 cup unsweetened coconut milk
- 1 tsp. Chinese five spice powder
- 1/2 stick (1/4 cup) butter
- 1 tbsp. fresh ginger, peeled, minced
- 1/4 cup hoisin sauce
- 1/3 cup honey
- 1 ½ tbsp. soy sauce
- 1 tsp. kosher salt
- 1/2 tsp. white pepper

Instructions:
1. Place potatoes and coconut milk into the pot. Place reversible rack inside pot over potatoes, making sure rack is in the higher position
2. Place pork chops on rack. Assemble pressure lid, making sure the PRESSURE RELEASE valve is in the SEAL position. Select PRESSURE and set to HIGH. Set time to 4 minutes. Select START/STOP to begin
3. While pork chops and potatoes are cooking, whisk together hoisin sauce, honey, soy sauce, and Chinese five spice powder
4. When pressure cooking is complete, quick release the pressure by moving the PRESSURE RELEASE valve to the VENT position. Carefully remove lid when unit has finished releasing pressure
5. Remove rack with pork from pot. Mash sweet potatoes with butter, ginger, and salt, using a mashing utensil that won't scratch the nonstick surface of the pot
6. Place rack with pork back in pot and brush top of pork generously with 1/2 of sauce mixture.
7. Close crisping lid. Select BROIL and set time to 15 minutes. Select START/STOP to begin. After 5 minutes, open lid, flip pork chops, then brush them with remaining sauce.
8. Close lid to resume cooking. Check after 10 minutes and remove if desired doneness is achieved. If not, cook up to 5 more minutes, checking frequently. When cooking is complete, remove pork from rack and allow to rest for 5 minutes before serving with mashed potatoes

Honey Pork Chops

(**Prep + Cook Time:** 30 Minutes | **Servings:** 4)

Ingredients:
- 4 pork chops (boneless or bone-in)
- 1/4 cup ghee
- 1/2 cup local honey
- 1/2 cup balsamic vinegar
- 1 tsp. dried parsley
- 1 tbsp. minced garlic
- 3/4-inch thick
- Sea salt and pepper to taste

Instructions:
1. Season your pork chops with sea salt and pepper. Melt ghee in the stainless steel pot of your Pressure Cooker using the Sauté feature. Sear the pork chops on each side for 1 minute. Add in the remaining ingredients, press the Keep Warm button and stir
2. Secure the lid, close the pressure valve and press the *Pressure* button cook on High pressure for, 15 minutes. Allow the cooking cycle to complete. Quick-release the pressure valve and remove the lid when safe to do so. Serve warm

Delicious Braised Pork Neck Bones

(Prep + Cook Time: 40 minutes | Servings: 6)

Ingredients:
- 3 lb Pork Neck Bones
- 4 tbsp. Olive Oil
- 1 White Onion, sliced
- 1/2 cup Red Wine
- 2 cloves Garlic, smashed
- 1 tbsp. Tomato Paste
- 1 tsp. dried Thyme
- 1 cup Beef Broth
- Salt and Black Pepper to taste

Instructions:
1. Open the lid and select Sear/Sauté mode. Warm the olive oil.
2. Meanwhile season the pork neck bones with salt and pepper. After, place them in the oil to brown on all sides. Work in batches.
3. Each batch should cook in about 5 minutes. Then, remove them onto a plate.
4. Add the onion and season with salt to taste. Stir with a spoon and cook the onions until soft, for a few minutes. Then, add garlic, thyme, pepper, and tomato paste. Cook them for 2 minutes, constant stirring to prevent the tomato paste from burning.
5. Next, pour the red wine into the pot to deglaze the bottom. Add the pork neck bones back to the pot and pour the beef broth over it
6. Close the lid, secure the pressure valve, and select Pressure mode on High pressure for 10 minutes. Press Start/Stop to start cooking.
7. Once the timer has ended, let the pot sit for 10 minutes before doing a quick pressure release. Close the crisping lid and cook on Broil mode for 5 minutes, until nice and tender.
8. Dish the pork neck into a serving bowl and serve with the red wine sauce spooned over and a right amount of broccoli mash

Pulled Pork Chipotle Salad Bowl

(Prep + Cook Time: 2 hours | Servings: 6)

Ingredients:
- 4 lb. pork shoulder butt OR 7 lb. shoulder on the bone
- 1 pinch dried oregano leaves
- 4 tbsp. coconut oil OR other GAPS approved fat (like chicken grease or bacon fat)
- 2 cups chicken stock
- 1 tsp. smoked paprika powder; optional
- 1 tsp. garlic powder
- 1 tsp. black pepper
- 6 cloves garlic
- 2 tsp. sea salt

Instructions:
1. Remove the rind from the pork and then cut the meat from the bone, slicing them into large-sized chunks.
2. Trim the fat off the meat, do not worry too much about this since the fat will dissolve while cooking.
3. Press the *Sauté* key of the Foodi. Put the oil in the pot and let heat
4. When the oil is hot, layer the chunks of meat in the bottom of the pot and sauté for a couple of minutes until nicely browned in spots, this will take about 30 minutes, about how long the *Sauté* function will last.
5. While the meat is browning, peel the garlic cloves and cut into small-sized chunks
6. When the meat is browned, transfer into a large-sized bowl. Pour in a few tbsp. of chicken stock in the pot to deglaze
7. Scrape the browned bits off from the bottom of the using a wooden spoon.
8. Transfer the browned bits into the bowl with the browned meat and continue cooking the rest of the meat chunks.
9. If not all the meat chunks are browned after 30 minutes, simply press the *Sauté* key again and continue cooking

10. When all the meat is browned and transferred into the bowl, put the garlic, oregano leaves, smoked paprika, garlic powder, black pepper, and sea salt to the bowl with the meat.
11. Put all the chicken stock in the pot to deglaze the pot, scraping the browned bits off from the bottom and bring to a simmer.
12. When simmering, return the browned meat and browned bits into the pot
13. Stir to combine. Press the *Cancel* key to stop the *Sauté* function. Cover and lock the lid. Turn the steam valve to Sealing.
14. Press the MEAT key, set the pressure to HIGH, and set the timer for 42 minutes
15. When the Foodi timer beeps, quick release the pressure
16. Unlock and carefully open the lid. Remove the meat from the pot and shred using 2 forks.
17. Put the meat in a bowl. Pour the cooking liquid separator or simply skim the fat off from the top of the cooking liquid.
18. Pour in some of the de-fatted broth in the bowl with the shredded meat
19. Save the leftover broth and use it to add to stews or soup. Top each serving with lime guacamole and salsa over salad greens.

Pork Belly

(Prep + Cook Time: 70 Minutes | **Servings:** 4)

Ingredients:
- 1 lb. pork belly
- ½ to 1 cup white wine
- Rosemary sprig
- 1 garlic clove
- 1 tbsp. olive oil to coat the bottom
- Salt to taste
- Black pepper to taste

Instructions:
1. Put oil in your Foodi and turn to the *Sauté* setting
2. When hot, add pork and sear 2 to 3 minutes on each side until golden and crispy.
3. Pour in wine, about a quarter inch. Season pork with salt, pepper, and garlic.
4. Add garlic clove. Turn on the cooker to *Sauté* to boil the liquid
5. When boiling, lock the lid. Select *Pressure* and cook at HIGH pressure for 40 minutes.
6. If you want the pork to be more like steak, cook for 30 minutes
7. When time is up, hit *Cancel* and wait for the pressure to go down on its own. When the pork is room-temperature, slice and season to taste with more salt.

Classic Red Cooked Pork

(Prep + Cook Time: 50 Minutes | **Servings:** 4)

Ingredients:
- 2 lb. fatty pork belly, cut into 1 ½-inch cubes
- 1 piece (1-inch) ginger; peeled and then smashed
- 2 tbsp. coconut aminos (or soy sauce)
- 1/3 cup water OR bone broth
- 1 tsp. sea salt
- 1 tbsp. blackstrap molasses
- 2 tbsp. maple syrup
- 3 tbsp. sherry
- A couple sprigs coriander OR cilantro leaves; to garnish

Instructions:
1. Put the pork cubes in the pot and pour in enough water to cover the pork cubes
2. Select *Sauté* mode and press the More option.
3. Bring to a boil and boil the pork cubes for 3 minutes
4. When boiled, press the *Cancel* setting. Drain the pork cubes and rinse off any impurities of scum off the meat.
5. Put the pork cubes in a colander and set aside in the sink to drain.
6. Clean and dry the inner pot of the Foodi.
7. Pour the maple syrup in the pot and press the *Sauté* key and heat.

8. Add the pork cubes and brown the meat for about 10 minutes. Add the rest of the ingredients in the pot.
9. Bring to a boil and then press the *Cancel* key to stop the *Sauté* function. Cover and lock the lid.
10. Select *Pressure* and cook at HIGH pressure for 25 minutes
11. When the Foodi timer beeps, release the pressure naturally for 10 to 15 minutes or until the valve drops. Turn the steam valve to Venting to release remaining pressure. Unlock and carefully open the lid.
12. Press the *Sauté* key and bring the contents to a simmer
13. Cook until the sauce is reduced and thick to your liking
14. Serve with cilantro or coriander leaves to garnish. Serve the pork cubes with Boston lettuce leaves to wrap them with.

Simple Spare Ribs with Wine

(Prep + Cook Time: 30 minutes | **Servings:** 4)

Ingredients:
- 1 lb. pork spare ribs, cut into pieces
- 1 tbsp. corn starch
- 1 tbsp. oil

Black Bean Marinade:
- 3 cloves garlic, minced
- 1 tsp. sesame oil
- 1 tsp. sugar
- 1 tbsp. Shaoxing wine
- 1 – 2 tsp. water
- Green onions as garnish
- 1 tsp. fish sauce (optional)
- 1 tbsp. ginger, grated
- 1 tbsp. black bean sauce
- 1 tbsp. light soy sauce
- A pinch of white pepper

Instructions:
1. Marinate the pork spare ribs with Black Bean Marinade in an oven-safe bowl. Then, sit it in the fridge for 25 minutes.
2. First, mix 1 tbsp. of oil into the marinated spare ribs. Then, add 1 tbsp. of cornstarch and mix well. Finally, add 1 – 2 tsp. of water into the spare ribs and mix well
3. Add 1 cup of water into the Foodi Multi-cooker. Place steam rack in the Foodi Multi-cooker. Then, put the bowl of spare ribs on the rack.
4. High pressure for 15 minutes. Lock the lid on the Foodi Multi-cooker and then cook for 15 minutes.
5. To get 15 minutes' cook time, press *Pressure* Button and then adjust the time
6. Pressure Release. Let the pressure to come down naturally for at least 15 minutes, then quick release any pressure left in the pot
7. Finish the dish. Close crisping lid. Select *Air Crisp*, set temperature to 375°F and set time to 10 minutes. Check after 5 minutes, cooking for an additional 5 minutes if dish needs more browning.
8. Taste and add one tsp. of fish sauce and green onions as garnish if you like. Serve immediately

Pork Roast with Spicy Peanut Sauce

(Prep + Cook Time: 30 minutes | **Servings:** 6)

Ingredients:
- 3 lb Pork Roast
- 1 large Red Bell Pepper, seeded and sliced
- 1 cup Hot Water
- 1 large White Onion, sliced
- 1 tbsp. Lime Juice
- 1 tbsp. Garlic Powder
- 1 tsp. Ginger Puree
- 1/2 cup Soy Sauce
- 1 tbsp. Plain Vinegar
- 1/2 cup Peanut Butter
- Salt and Pepper to taste
- 2 Chilies, deseeded, chopped.
- Chopped Peanuts, Chopped Green Onions, Lime Wedges to garnish

Instructions:
1. Add the soy sauce, vinegar, peanut butter, lime juice, garlic powder, chilies, and ginger puree, to a bowl. Whisk together and even
2. Add a few pinches of salt and pepper, and mix it. Open the Foodi lid, and place the pork in the inner pot. Pour the hot water and peanut butter mixture over it.
3. Close the lid, secure the pressure valve, and select Pressure mode on High pressure for 15 minutes. Press Start/Stop to start cooking. Once the timer has stopped, do a quick pressure release
4. Use two forks to shred it, inside the pot, and close the crisping lid. Cook on Broil mode for 4 - 5 minutes, until the sauce thickens.
5. On a bed of cooked rice, spoon the meat with some sauce and garnish it with the chopped peanuts, green onions, and the lemon wedges

Pork Loin Chops with Pears

(Prep + Cook Time: 17 Minutes | **Servings:** 4)

Ingredients:
- 4 (3/4 to 1-inch)-thick boneless center-cut pork loin chops (5 to 7 oz. each)
- 2 medium yellow onions; peeled and cut into 8 wedges each
- 2 large, firm Bosc pears, peeled, cored, and cut into 4 wedges each
- 1/2 cup unsweetened pear cider
- 1/2 tsp. ground allspice
- Several dashes of hot red pepper sauce
- 2 tbsp. unsalted butter
- 1/2 tsp. salt
- 1/2 tsp. ground black pepper

Instructions:
1. Melt 1 tbsp. butter in the Foodi turned to the *Sautéing/Browning* function. Season the chops with the salt and pepper, then brown two of them in the cooker, about 4 minutes, turning once. Transfer to a large plate, melt the remaining tbsp. of butter in the pot, and repeat with the remaining chops
2. Add the onions and pears; cook, stirring occasionally, until the pears are lightly browned, about 3 minutes. Pour in the cider and stir in the allspice and red pepper sauce. Nestle the chops into the sauce, placing them as evenly as possible to make neat but not compact layers. Pour any juices from the plate over them.
3. Lock the lid onto the cooker. Set the Foodi to cook at High pressure for 12 minutes. To get 12 minutes' cook time, press *Pressure* button
4. Turn off the Foodi or unplug it; set aside for 5 minutes. Use the Quick Pressure Release method to bring the pressure back to normal. Unlock and open the lid. Serve the chops with the pears and sauce ladled on each.

Pulled Pork with Crispy Biscuits

(Prep + Cook Time: 1 hour 10 minutes | **Servings:** 8)

Ingredients:
- 2 ½ –3 lb. uncooked boneless pork shoulder, fat trimmed, cut in 2-inch cubes
- 3 tbsp. barbecue seasoning
- 2 tsp. kosher salt
- 1 cup apple cider vinegar
- 1 tbsp. garlic powder
- 1 can (6 oz.) tomato paste
- 1 tube (16.3 oz.) refrigerated biscuit dough

Instructions:
1. Place pork, spices, and vinegar in the pot. Assemble pressure lid, making sure the PRESSURE RELEASE valve is in the SEAL position. Select PRESSURE and set to HIGH. Set time to 35 minutes. Select START/STOP to begin.
2. When pressure cooking is complete, quick release the pressure by moving the PRESSURE RELEASE valve to the VENT position. Carefully remove lid when unit has finished releasing pressure.
3. Select SEAR/SAUTÉ and set to MD:HI. Select START/STOP to begin. Add tomato paste and stir to incorporate. Allow pork to simmer for 10 minutes, or until the liquid has reduced by half. Stir occasionally, using a wooden spoon or silicone tongs to shred the pork

4. Tear each uncooked biscuit so that it is in two halves, like a hamburger bun. Place biscuit halves evenly across the surface of the pork.
5. Close crisping lid. Select BAKE/ROAST, set temperature to 350°F, and set time to 10 minutes. Check after 8 minutes, cooking for an additional 2 minutes if biscuits need more browning. When cooking is complete, serve immediately.

Cilantro Pork Tacos

(Prep + Cook Time: 45 Minutes | **Servings:** 6)

Ingredients:
- 10 oz. ground pork
- 7 oz. corn tortilla
- 1 tsp. paprika
- 1 tbsp. cilantro
- 1 tbsp. tomato paste
- 1 red onion
- 1 tsp. salt
- 1 tsp. basil
- 1 tbsp. butter
- 1 cup lettuce

Instructions:
1. Combine the ground pork, salt, cilantro, paprika, and basil together in the mixing bowl
2. Add butter and tomato paste. Stir the mixture well.
3. After this, place the ground pork mixture in the Foodi and close the lid
4. Cook the dish at the MEAT mode for 27 minutes.
5. Meanwhile, chop the lettuce and peel the onion. Slice the onion
6. When the meat is cooked; remove it from the Foodi and transfer in the corn tortillas.
7. Then add chopped lettuce and sliced onion. Wrap the tacos. Serve the dish immediately.

Tandoori BBQ Pork Ribs

(Prep + Cook Time: 30 Minutes | **Servings:** 2 to 4)

Ingredients:
- 2 lb. Pork Short-Ribs (also called Baby Back Ribs)
- 1" (3cm) ginger; roughly chopped
- 3 cups water; or as needed
- 5 garlic cloves
- 4 tbsp. Tandoori Spice Mix (or your favorite dry rub)
- 2 bay leaves
- 1½ tsp. salt ½ cup BBQ Sauce (your favorite kind)

Instructions:
1. Slice rib slabs to fit in the Foodi and position them in the cooker as flat as possible (this means you'll use the least amount of water, it will pressure cook faster and concentrate the flavors)
2. Add bay leaves, ginger, garlic, salt and two tbsp. of the spice mix
3. Pour-in enough water to cover the meat (about 4 cups).
4. Close and lock the lid of the Foodi. Cook for 22 minutes at High pressure. To get 22 minutes' cook time, press *Pressure* button and use the Cook Time Selector button to adjust the cook time to 22 minutes
5. When time is up, open the Foodi with the Natural release method
6. Carefully lift the tender ribs out of the Foodi and lay them on a cutting board. Cover with foil and let them cool down further for another 5 minutes
7. Pat dry and paint on the BBQ Sauce (or spice paste). Make ahead: Stop here and wrap the meat tightly, refrigerate for up to three days. Grill, broil or barbecue for about 5 minutes per side. Serve immediately.

Tasty Ranch Pork Chops

(Prep + Cook Time: 25 minutes | **Servings:** 4)

Ingredients:
- 4 Pork Loin Chops
- 1/2 cup Chicken Broth
- 1 (15 oz.) can Mushroom Soup Cream
- 1 oz. Ranch Dressing and Seasoning Mix
- Chopped Parsley to garnish

Instructions:
1. Add pork, mushroom soup cream, ranch dressing and seasoning mix, and chicken broth, inside the inner pot of your Foodi.
2. Close the lid, secure the pressure valve, and select Pressure mode on High pressure for 10 minutes. Press Start/Stop
3. Once the timer has ended, do a natural pressure release for 10 minutes, then a quick pressure release to let the remaining steam out.
4. Close the crisping lid and cook for 5 minutes on Broil mode, until tender. Serve with well-seasoned sautéed cremini mushrooms, and the sauce

Honey Mustard Pork Tenderloin Recipe

(Prep + Cook Time: 30 minutes | **Servings:** 4)

Ingredients:
- 2 lb Pork Tenderloin
- 1 tbsp. Worcestershire Sauce
- 1/2 tbsp. Cornstarch
- 1/2 cup Chicken Broth
- 1/4 cup Balsamic Vinegar
- 1 clove Garlic, minced
- 2 tbsp. Olive Oil
- 1/4 cup Honey
- 1 tsp. Sage Powder
- 1 tbsp. Dijon Mustard
- 4 tbsp. Water
- Salt and Black Pepper to taste

Instructions:
1. Put the pork on a clean flat surface and pat dry using paper towels. Season with salt and pepper. Select Sear/Sauté mode.
2. Heat the oil and brown the pork on both sides, for about 4 minutes in total. Remove the pork onto a plate and set aside
3. Add in honey, chicken broth, balsamic vinegar, garlic, Worcestershire sauce, mustard, and sage. Stir the ingredients and return the pork to the pot.
4. Close the lid, secure the pressure valve, and select Pressure mode on High for 15 minutes. Once the timer has ended, do a quick pressure release. Remove the pork with tongs onto a plate and wrap it in aluminum foil
5. Next, mix the cornstarch with water and pour it into the pot. Select Sear/Sauté mode, stir the mixture and cook until it thickens. Then, turn the pot off after the desired thickness is achieved.
6. Unwrap the pork and use a knife to slice it with 3 to 4-inch thickness. Arrange the slices on a serving platter and spoon the sauce all over it. Serve with a syrupy sautéed Brussels sprouts and red onion chunks

Amazing Pork Chops with Applesauce

(Prep + Cook Time: 30 minutes | **Servings:** 4)

Ingredients:
- 2 to 4 pork loin chops (we used center cut, bone-on)
- 2 gala apples, thinly sliced
- 1 tsp. cinnamon powder
- 1 tbsp. honey
- 1/2 cup unsalted homemade chicken stock or water
- 1 tbsp. grapeseed oil or olive oil
- 1 small onion, sliced
- 3 cloves garlic, roughly minced
- 2 tbsp. light soy sauce
- 1 tbsp. butter
- Kosher salt and ground black pepper to taste
- 2 pieces whole cloves (optional)
- 1 ½ tbsp. cornstarch mixed with 2 tbsp. water (optional)

Instructions:
1. Make a few small cut around the sides of the pork chops so they will stay flat and brown evenly
2. Season the pork chops with a generous amount of kosher salt and ground black pepper.
3. Heat up your Foodi Multi-cooker. Add grapeseed oil into the pot. Add the seasoned pork chops into the pot, then let it brown for roughly 2 – 3 minutes on each side. Remove and set aside.
4. Add the sliced onions and stir. Add a pinch of kosher salt and ground black pepper to season if you like. Cook the onions for roughly 1 minute until softened. Then, add garlic and stir for 30 seconds until fragrance
5. Add in the thinly sliced gala apples, whole cloves (optional) and cinnamon powder, then give it a quick stir. Add the honey and partially deglaze the bottom of the pot with a wooden spoon.
6. Add chicken stock and light soy sauce, then fully deglaze the bottom of the pot with a wooden spoon. Taste the seasoning and add more salt and pepper if desired
7. Place the pork chops back with all the meat juice into the pot
8. High pressure for 10 minutes. Lock the lid on the Foodi Multi-cooker and then cook for 10 minutes.
9. To get 10 minutes' cook time, press *Pressure* button and use the Time Adjustment button to adjust the cook time to 10 minutes.
10. Pressure Release. Let it fully natural release (roughly 10 minutes). Open the lid carefully
11. Finish the dish. Close crisping lid. Select *Air Crisp*, set temperature to 375°F and set time to 10 minutes. Check after 10 minutes, cooking for an additional 5 minutes if dish needs more browning
12. Remove the pork chops and set aside. Turn the Multi-cooker to the Sauté setting. Remove the cloves and taste the seasoning one more time.
13. Add more salt and pepper if desired. Add butter and stir until it has fully dissolved into the sauce
14. Mix the cornstarch with water and mix it into the applesauce one third at a time until desired thickness
15. Drizzle the applesauce over the pork chops and serve immediately with side dishes!

Pork with Apple Juice

(Prep + Cook Time: 40 Minutes | **Servings:** 3)

Ingredients:
- 4 (6 oz.) pork tenderloins
- 1 (16 oz.) package sauerkraut; drained
- 6 fluid oz. apple juice
- 2 tsp. fennel seed
- 12 red new potatoes; halved
- 1 tbsp. vegetable oil
- 1 cup water

Instructions:
1. Heat oil in the Foodi, using Sauté button; brown pork tenderloins in the hot oil, about 5 minutes per side. Distribute sauerkraut around the pieces of pork and pour in water and apple juice; sprinkle with fennel seeds
2. Cover the Foodi and cook on High Pressure for 15 minutes. To get 15 minutes' cook time, press *Pressure* button.

3. Use Natural Release Method
4. Place potatoes into the cooker, cover the Foodi and cook on High Pressure for 5 more minutes. To get 5 minutes' cook time, press *Pressure* button and use the *Time Adjustment* button to adjust the cook time to 5 minutes.
5. Release pressure, using the Natural Release Method. Serve.

Pork and Egg Fried Rice

(Prep + Cook Time: 40 Minutes | **Servings:** 4)

Ingredients:
- 1/2 cup frozen peas
- 8 oz. sliced pork loin chop (1/2-inch pieces)
- 1 peeled and finely-chopped carrot
- 3 cups + 2 tbsp. water
- 2 cups long-grain white rice
- 1 beaten egg
- 1 finely-chopped onion
- 3 tbsp. soy sauce
- 3 tbsp. veggie oil
- Salt and pepper to taste

Instructions:
1. Preheat the cooker to *Sauté* function and add 1 tbsp. of oil. Stir the onion and carrot for about 2 minutes.
2. Add pork after seasoning with salt and pepper. Cook for 5 minutes or until the meat is cooked all the way through.
3. Press *Cancel* and take out the onion, carrot, and pork. Pour in water and deglaze, scraping up any bits.
4. Pour in rice, salt, and seal the lid. Select RICE and cook for default time
5. When time is up, press *Cancel* and wait 10 minutes for a natural release. Then Quick Pressure Release any leftover steam.
6. Create a hole in the rice, and pour in the rest of the olive oil before hitting *Sauté*. Add egg and scramble.
7. When the egg is just about ready, add the peas, onion, carrot, and pork
8. Keep stirring for a few minutes until everything is mixed in well. Serve with soy sauce!

Pork Chops with Mushroom Gravy

(Prep + Cook Time: 35 minutes | **Servings:** 4)

Ingredients:
- 4 Pork Chops
- 8 oz. Cremini Mushrooms, sliced
- 1 small Onion, chopped.
- 1 tsp. Garlic Powder
- 1 (10 oz.) can Mushroom Soup
- 1 cup Beef Broth
- 1 sprig Fresh Thyme
- 1 tbsp. Olive Oil
- 3 cloves Garlic, minced
- Salt and Pepper, to taste
- Chopped Parsley to garnish

Instructions:
1. Select Sear/Sauté mode. Add oil, mushrooms, garlic, and onion. Sauté them, stirring occasionally with a spoon, until nice and translucent, for 3 minutes
2. Season the pork chops with salt, garlic powder, and pepper, and add them to the pot followed by the thyme and broth. Seal the lid and select Pressure mode on High pressure for 10 minutes. Press Start/Stop to start cooking
3. Once the timer has ended, do a natural pressure release for about 10 minutes, then a quick pressure release to let the remaining steam out
4. Close the crisping lid and cook on Broil mode for 5 minutes. When ready, add the mushroom soup. Stir it until the mixture thickens a little bit. Dish the pork and gravy into a serving bowl and garnish with parsley.
5. Serve with a side of creamy sweet potato mash

Pulled Pork Tacos

(Prep + Cook Time: 70 Minutes | **Servings:** 8)

Ingredients:
For the pork:
- 1 piece (4 lb.) pork shoulder (a.k.a pork butt, bone out or in)
- 1 yellow onion; large-sized, peeled and thinly sliced
- 1 cup chicken broth; OR beef broth
- 1 tsp. freshly ground pepper
- 1/2 tsp. garlic powder
- 1 ½ tsp. sea salt
- 1/2 tsp. chipotle chili powder
- 1/2 tsp. cumin
- Your favorite or preferred tortillas

Garnish:
- Purple cabbage; sliced
- Cilantro, chopped
- Lime

Instructions:
1. In a bowl, combine all of the spices until well mixed.
2. Put the onion in the Foodi and pour in the broth
3. Rub all the sides of the pork with the spice mixture and then put the spice-rubbed pork into the pot. Cover and lock the lid
4. Press the MEAT key and set the timer for 60 minutes
5. When the Foodi timer beeps, press the *Cancel* key and unplug the Foodi. Turn the steam valve to quick release the pressure. Unlock and carefully open the lid
6. Transfer the meat into a cutting board, discard the onion and the cooking liquid.
7. With 2 forks, shred the meat, discarding the fat in the process
8. Use the shredded meat to make tacos, garnishing with sliced purple cabbage and chopped cilantro. Top with your favorite guacamole and salsa.

Pulled Pork Burgers

(Prep + Cook Time: 55 Minutes | **Servings:** 2)

Ingredients:
- 1 lb. pork shoulder
- 1 onion; roughly chopped
- 2 brioche buns
- 2 tbsp. mayonnaise (1tbsp. per burger)
- 2 slices of cheddar cheese (or any other cheese)
- 1 apple, grated
- 1/2 tsp. ground cumin
- 1/2 tsp. ground coriander
- 1/2 tsp. paprika
- 2 tbsp. tomato ketchup
- 1 tsp. Worcester sauce (or soy sauce as a substitute)
- 1 tbsp. brown sugar
- 1 cup (8 fl oz.) apple juice
- Salt and pepper; to taste

Instructions:
1. Place the onion, cumin, coriander, paprika, ketchup, Worcester or soy sauce, brown sugar, apple juice, salt, and pepper into the Pressure Cooker, stir to combine
2. Place the pork shoulder and onion into the pot
3. Secure the lid onto the pot and press the *Pressure* button cook on High pressure for 45 minutes.
4. Once the pot beeps, Quick Pressure Release the pressure and remove the lid
5. Place the pork onto a board to rest while you heat a skillet or fry pan
6. Once the pan is hot, place the pork skin-side down onto the pan and fry until golden and crispy.
7. Simmer the leftover liquid in the Pressure Cooker on the SAUTÉ function until reduced and thick.
8. With 2 forks, shred the pork meat into pieces
9. Grill the brioche buns under the grill in the oven, or place them cut-side down on a hot, oiled skillet.

10. Spread the buns with mayonnaise, then place a generous pile of pulled pork on top, then a sprinkle of grated apple, then the cheese (you could also grill the cheese onto the bun if you want it to be extra melted).
11. Drizzle some of the reduced liquid from the Pressure Cooker over onto the burger before serving!

Note: Place the Pork Burgers in your ninja foodi cook and crisp basket and lock the lid. Then Press AIR-CRISP button and set the temperature 380°F for 2 – 3 minutes.

Asian Pork

(Prep + Cook Time: 40 Minutes | **Servings:** 2)

Ingredients:
- 1/4 cup hoisin sauce
- 3/4 lb. pork shoulder; trimmed of as much visible fat as possible, cut into 2-inch cubes
- 4 slider buns or soft dinner rolls
- 2 tbsp. rice vinegar
- 1 tbsp. minced fresh ginger
- 2 tsp. minced garlic
- 1 tsp. Asian chili-garlic sauce; plus, additional as desired

Instructions:
1. In the Foodi, stir together the hoisin sauce, rice vinegar, ginger, garlic, and chili-garlic sauce until thoroughly mixed. Add the pork, and toss to coat
2. Lock the lid in place, and bring the pot to High pressure. Cook at High pressure for 35 minutes. To get 35 minutes' cook time, press *Pressure* button.
3. Use the natural Pressure release method
4. Unlock and remove the lid. Pour the pork and sauce through a coarse sieve; set the pork aside to cool. Return the sauce to the cooker, and let it sit for 1 to 2 minutes so any fat rises to the surface. Skim or blot off as much fat as possible and discard.
5. Turn the Foodi to *Sautéing/Browning* and simmer the sauce for about 5 minutes, or until it's the consistency of a thick tomato sauce
6. While the sauce thickens, shred the pork, discarding any fat or gristle. Add the shredded pork to the sauce, and heat through. Serve on buns or over rice.

Delicious Pork Carnitas in Lettuce Cups

(Prep + Cook Time: 30 minutes | **Servings:** 6)

Ingredients:
- 3 lb Pork Shoulder
- 1 small head Butter Lettuce, leaves removed, washed and dried
- 2 tbsp. Olive Oil
- 1 tsp. Cumin Powder
- 1 tsp. Garlic Powder
- 1 tsp. White Pepper
- 2 tsp. dried Oregano
- 1/2 tsp. Cayenne Pepper
- 1/2 tsp. Coriander Powder
- 1 tsp. Red Pepper Flakes
- 2 Limes, cut in wedges
- 2 Carrots, grated
- 1 ½ cup Water
- 1 Onion, chopped.
- Salt to taste

Instructions:
1. In a bowl, add onion, cayenne, coriander, garlic, cumin, white pepper, dried oregano, red pepper flakes, and salt. Mix them well with a spoon.
2. Drizzle over the pork and rub to coat. Then, wrap the meat in plastic wrap and refrigerate overnight.
3. On the next day, open the Foodi lid, and select Sear/Sauté mode. Pour 2 tbsp. of olive oil in the pot and while heating, take the pork out from the fridge, remove the wraps and place it in the pot
4. Brown it on both sides for 6 minutes and then pour the water. Close the lid, secure the pressure valve, and select Pressure mode on High pressure for 15 minutes. Press Start/Stop to start cooking.
5. Once the timer has stopped, do a quick pressure release. Use two forks to shred the pork, inside the pot. Close the crisping lid, and select Bake/Roast mode. Set for 10 minutes at 350°F

6. When ready, turn off the heat and begin assembling.
7. Arrange double layers of lettuce leaves on a flat surface, make a bed of grated carrots in them, and spoon the pulled pork on them
8. Drizzle a sauce of choice (I used mustardy sauce) over them, and serve with lime wedges for freshness.

Pulled Pork Lettuce Wraps

(Prep + Cook Time: 100 Minutes | **Servings:** 6)

Ingredients:
- 4 lb. pork roast
- 2 lime wedges
- 1 chopped onion
- 1 head washed and dried butter lettuce
- 2 grated carrots
- 2 tbsp. oil
- 1 tbsp. salt
- 2 to 3 cups water

Spice Mix:
- 1 tbsp. unsweetened cocoa powder
- 1 tsp. cumin
- 1/8 tsp. cayenne
- 1/8 tsp. coriander
- 2 tsp. oregano
- 1 tsp. red pepper flakes
- 1 tsp. garlic powder
- 1 tsp. white pepper

Instructions:
1. Marinate the pork the night before by mixing all the ingredients in the second list and rubbing into the pork. Store in the fridge.
2. The next day, turn your Foodi to *Sauté*. When warm, brown roast all over.
3. Pour in 2 to 3 cups water, so the roast is almost totally submerged. Close and seal the lid
4. Select *Pressure* and cook at HIGH pressure for 55 minutes.
5. When time is up, press *Cancel* and let the pressure release naturally.
6. When ready, take out the meat and pull with two forks.
7. Turn the cooker back to *Sauté* and reduce the liquid by half
8. Strain and skim off any excess fat. If you want crispy pork, fry in a pan with some oil until it becomes light brown.
9. Mix pork with the cooking liquid before serving in the lettuce with grated carrots, a squirt of lime, and any other toppings.

Pork Loin and Apples

(Prep + Cook Time: 43 minutes | **Servings:** 8)

Ingredients:
- 1 (3 lb.) boneless pork loin roast
- 1 large red onion, halved and thinly sliced
- 2 medium tart green apples, such as Granny Smith, peeled, cored and thinly sliced
- 1/2 cup moderately sweet white wine, such as Riesling
- 2 tbsp. unsalted butter
- 1/4 cup chicken broth
- 4 fresh thyme sprigs
- 2 bay leaves
- 1/2 tsp. salt
- 1/2 tsp. ground black pepper

Instructions:
1. Melt the butter in the Foodi Multi-cooker, set on the *Sauté* function. Add the pork loin and brown it on all sides, turning occasionally, about 8 minutes in all. Transfer to a large plate.
2. Add the onion to the pot; cook, often stirring, until softened, about 3 minutes. Stir in the apple, thyme and bay leaves. Pour in the wine and scrape up any browned bits on the bottom of the pot
3. Pour in the broth; stir in the salt and pepper. Nestle the pork loin into this apple mixture; pour any juices from the plate into the pot.
4. High pressure for 30 minutes. Lock the lid on the Foodi Multi-cooker and then cook for 30 minutes.
5. To get 30 minutes' cook time, press *Pressure* button and adjust the time

6. Pressure Release. Use the quick release method to bring the pot's pressure to normal
7. Finish the dish. Close crisping lid and select Broil, set time to 7 minutes
8. Transfer the pork to a cutting board; let stand for 5 minutes while you dish the sauce into serving bowls or onto a serving platter. Slice the loin into 1/2-inch-thick rounds and lay these over the sauce

Shoulder Ribs with Barbecue Rub and Sauce

(**Prep + Cook Time:** 80 Minutes | **Servings:** 6 to 8)

Ingredients:
- 3 lb. pork shoulder western ribs (or cut a pork shoulder into 1 ½, inch thick strips, or pork shoulder chops)
- 1/2 cup barbecue sauce for the cooker; plus 1/2 cup barbecue sauce to stir in at the end
- 2 tsp. Diamond Crystal kosher salt or 1 ½ tsp. table salt
- 1 tsp. barbecue rub
- 1/2 cup water

Instructions:
1. Sprinkle the ribs evenly with the kosher salt and the barbecue rub
2. Pour the 1/2 cup water into the Foodi, add the ribs, and then pour 1/2 cup of barbecue sauce over the ribs. (Don't stir, we want the sweet barbecue sauce to float on top to keep it from burning.)
3. Lock the lid on the Foodi and cook at High pressure for 45 minutes. To get 45 minutes cook time, press *Pressure* and use the *Time Adjustment* button to adjust the cook time to 45 minutes
4. Let the Pressure release naturally
5. Remove the ribs to a platter. Spoon 1/2 cup of the liquid from the pot into a measuring cup.
6. Stir 1/2 cup of barbecue sauce into the juices in the measuring cup. Serve and Enjoy.

Sausage and Cheesy Mashed Potatoes

(**Prep + Cook Time:** 35 Minutes | **Servings:** 2)

Ingredients:
For the potatoes:
- 4 floury potatoes, large-sized, peeled and then cut into 1½ -inch sized cubes
- 1 knob butter
- 2 oz. double Gloucester or mature cheddar cheese; grated, use more, if desired
- 1/2 cup milk
- 1 tsp. mustard powder OR 2 tsp. whole-grain or Dijon mustard
- Salt and pepper to taste

For the sausages:
- 6 pork sausages; thick pieces (prick each sausage with a sharp knife once)
- 1/2 cup sticky onions (about 6 rounded tablespoon), see notes
- 1/2 cup red wine
- 1 tbsp. corn flour mixed with 1 tbsp. cold water
- 2 tsp. olive oil
- 1½ cup water
- Salt and black pepper to taste

Instructions:
1. Put the potatoes in the Foodi and pour in 1 cup of water. Cover and lock the lid
2. Press the *Pressure* key, set the pressure to HIGH, and set the timer for 4 minutes.
3. When the Foodi timer beeps, turn the steam valve to quick release the pressure
4. Unlock and carefully open the lid. Drain the potatoes in a colander. Let sit for a couple of minutes.
5. Discard the cooking water. Dry the inner pot and return to the housing
6. Press the *Sauté* key and press the More option. Put the oil in the pot and let heat.
7. Add the sausages and cook, stirring occasionally, until all the sides of the sausage are nicely colored.
8. When the sausages are browned, add the onion. Immediately follow with the wine and then 1/2 cup of water.
9. Press the *Cancel* key to stop the *Sauté* function. Cover and lock the lid
10. Press the *Pressure* key, set the pressure to HIGH, and set the timer for 8 minutes.

11. Meanwhile, heat the milk in a saucepan until hot. Stir in the butter, mustard, and seasoning.
12. Mash the potatoes and mix in the milk mixture into the mashed potatoes until desired texture is achieved.
13. Stir in the cheese and tightly cover with a foil
14. When the Foodi timer beeps, turn the steam valve to Venting to quick release the pressure.
15. Unlock and carefully open the lid. Press the *Sauté* key. While stirring the contents of the pot, pour the corn flour mix in the pot.
16. Bring to a bubble for a few minutes until the sauce is thick to desired consistency. Season to taste and serve over the mash

Notes: To make sticky onions, cook finely sliced onions in a knob of butter and a little oil until translucent and soft in very low heat for about 30 minutes in a saucepan with the lid on. After 30 minutes, take the lid off, sprinkle the onion with a bit of brown sugar and balsamic vinegar, and then generously season with pepper and salt. Cook until the liquid has evaporated and the onions are nice and sticky.

Pork Chops

(Prep + Cook Time: 20 Minutes | **Servings:** 6)

Ingredients:
- 3 to 4 Pork Chops 1/2 to 3/4 inch thick
- Onions chopped as much as you like; 1/2 cup maybe
- 2 to 4 Garlic cloves, squashed and chopped
- Butter, 1 tbsp.
- Oil 1 to 2 tbsp. or orange/ginger coconut oil
- 1 egg, beaten
- Flour
- Salt and Pepper
- Bread Crumbs

Instructions:
1. Turn on the Foodi to the Sauté setting, then wait for it to boil. Heat the oil and butter to very hot.
2. Make sure your pork chops are at room temperature. Dredge them in flour, dip into beaten egg, and dredge them in bread crumbs. Brown them lots on both sides in the hot Foodi. When well browned on both sides, remove and put on plate
3. Throw in the onions, swish them around for a minute until softer looking, then throw in the garlic and swish around.
4. Leave the onions, garlic and drippings in the pot. Add about two to three tbsp. of water. Put steamer in pot, place browned pork chops on steamer above the water and drippings
5. Lock the lid on the Foodi and then cook On High pressure for 5 minutes. To get 5 minutes' cook time, press *Pressure* button and use the *Time Adjustment* button to adjust the cook time to 5 minutes.
6. Pressure Release Let the pressure to come down naturally for at least 15 minutes, then quick release any pressure left in the pot
7. Remove from the pot. Perfect, juicy pork chops you may use the 'juice' in the pot to pour over the pork chops or you can add a little polenta (or flour) and water, Sauté and make it like a gravy. Serve and enjoy!

Pork with Hominy

(Prep + Cook Time: 40 Minutes | Servings: 6)

Ingredients:
- 1¼ lb. pork shoulder, boneless and cut into medium pieces
- 30 oz. canned hominy; drained
- 4 cups chicken stock
- Avocado slices; for serving
- Lime wedges, for serving
- 2 tbsp. vegetable oil
- 2 tbsp. chili powder
- 4 garlic cloves; peeled and minced
- 1 white onion; peeled and chopped
- 1/4 cup water
- 2 tbsp. cornstarch
- Salt and ground black pepper; to taste

Instructions:
1. Set the Foodi on *Sauté* mode, add 1 tbsp. oil and heat it up. Add the pork, salt, and pepper, brown on all sides, and transfer to a bowl. Add the rest of the oil to the Foodi and heat it up. Add the garlic, onion, and chili powder, stir, and sauté for 4 minutes. Add half of the stock, stir, and cook for 1 minute. Add the rest of the stock and return pork to pot, stir
2. Cover, and cook on the *Pressure* setting for 30 minutes. Release the pressure naturally for 10 minutes, transfer the pork to a cutting board, and shred with 2 forks. Add the cornstarch mixed with water to the Foodi and set on *Sauté* mode. Add the hominy, more salt and pepper, and shredded pork, stir, and cook for 2 minutes. Divide among bowls, and serve with avocado slices on top and lime wedges on the side.

Peppers and Pork Stew

(Prep + Cook Time: 18 minutes | Servings: 4)

Ingredients:
- 1 large yellow or white onion, chopped.
- 1 large green bell pepper, stemmed, cored and cut into 1/4-inch-thick strips
- 1 lb. boneless center-cut pork loin chops, cut into 1/4-inch-thick strips
- 1 large red bell pepper, stemmed, cored and cut into 1/4-inch-thick strips
- 1 (14 oz.) can diced tomatoes, drained (about 1 3/4 cups)
- 2 tsp. minced, seeded fresh jalapeño chile
- 2 tsp. dried oregano
- 2 tbsp. olive oil
- 2 tsp. minced garlic
- 2 ½ cups canned hominy drained and rinsed
- 1 cup chicken broth

Instructions:
1. Heat the oil in a Foodi Multi-cooker, turned to the Sauté function. Add the onion and both bell peppers; cook, often stirring, until the onion softens, about 4 minutes.
2. Add the garlic, jalapeño and oregano; stir well until aromatic, less than 20 seconds. Add the hominy, tomatoes, broth and pork; stir over the heat for 1 minute
3. High pressure for 12 minutes. Lock the lid on the Foodi Multi-cooker and then cook for 12 minutes.
4. To get 12 minutes' cook time, press *Pressure* button and use the Time Adjustment button to adjust the cook time to 12 minutes.
5. Pressure Release. Use the quick release method to bring the pot's pressure back to normal. Unlock and open the cooker. Stir well before serving

Pork Loin with Vegetable Sauce

(Prep + Cook Time: 35 minutes | **Servings:** 4)

Ingredients:
- 2 lb Pork Loin Roast
- 1 tbsp. Cornstarch
- 3 Carrots, chopped.
- 1 cup Chicken Broth
- 2 tbsp. Worcestershire Sauce
- 1 medium Onion, diced
- 2 tbsp. Butter
- 3 stalks Celery, chopped.
- 2 tsp. dried Basil
- 2 tsp. dried Thyme
- 3 cloves Garlic, minced
- 1 tsp. Yellow Mustard
- 1/4 cup Water
- 1/2 tbsp. Sugar
- Salt and Pepper, to taste

Instructions:
1. Select Sear/Sauté mode, and heat oil. Season the pork with salt and pepper. Sear the pork to golden brown on both sides. Takes about 4 minutes
2. Then, add the garlic and onions, and cook them until soft, for about 4 minutes.
3. Top with the celery, carrots, chicken broth, Worcestershire sauce, mustard, thyme, basil, and sugar.
4. Close the lid, secure the pressure valve, and select Pressure mode on High pressure for 15 minutes. Press Start/Stop to start cooking
5. Once the timer is off, do a quick pressure release. Next, add the cornstarch to the water, in a bowl, and mix with a spoon, until nice and smooth.
6. Add it to the pot, close the crisping lid, and cook on Broil mode, for 3 - 5 minutes, until the sauce becomes a slurry with a bit of thickness, and the pork is nice and tender
7. Adjust the seasoning, and ladle to a serving platter. Serve with a side of steamed almond garlicky rapini mix.

Pulled Pork

(Prep + Cook Time: 1 hour 33 minutes | **Servings:** 10)

Ingredients:
- 1 (4- to 4½ lb.) bone in skinless pork shoulder, preferably pork butt
- Up to 1 ½ cups light-colored beer, preferably a pale ale or amber lager
- 1/2 tsp. garlic powder
- 1/2 tsp. ground cloves
- 1/2 tsp. ground cinnamon
- 2 tbsp. smoked paprika
- 2 tbsp. packed dark brown sugar
- 1 tbsp. ground cumin
- 1/2 tbsp. dry mustard
- 1 tsp. ground coriander
- 1 tsp. dried thyme
- 1 tsp. onion powder
- 1 tsp. salt
- 2 tsp. ground black pepper

Instructions:
1. Mix the smoked paprika, brown sugar, cumin, pepper, mustard, coriander, thyme, onion powder, salt, garlic powder, cloves and cinnamon in a small bowl. Massage the mixture all over the pork.
2. Set the pork in the Foodi Multi-cooker. Pour 1cup beer into the electric cooker without knocking the spices off the meat
3. High pressure for 80 minutes. Lock the lid on the Foodi Multi-cooker and then cook for 80 minutes.
4. To get 80 minutes' cook time, press *Pressure* button and use the Time Adjustment button to adjust the cook time to 80 minutes.
5. Pressure Release. Let its pressure fall to normal naturally, 25 to 35 minutes
6. Finish the dish. Close crisping lid and select Broil, set time to 7 minutes
7. Transfer the meat to a large cutting board. Let stand for 5 minutes. Use a spoon to skim as much fat off the sauce in the pot as possible
8. Set the *Sauté* function. Bring the sauce to a simmer, stirring occasionally; continue boiling the sauce, often stirring, until reduced by half, 7 to 10 minutes.

9. Use two forks to shred the meat off the bones; discard the bones and any attached cartilage. Pull any large chunks of meat apart with the forks and stir the meat back into the simmering sauce to reheat. Serve and Enjoy!

Tasty Crispy Pork Carnitas

(**Prep + Cook Time:** 1 hour 12 minutes | **Servings:** 10)

Ingredients:
- 2 ½-lb. trimmed, boneless pork shoulder blade roast
- 3/4 cup reduced-sodium chicken broth
- 2 - 3 chipotle peppers in adobo sauce (to taste)
- 1/2 tsp. sazon
- 1/4 tsp. dry oregano
- 1/4 tsp. dry adobo seasoning
- 1/2 tsp. garlic powder
- 2 bay leaves
- 6 cloves garlic, cut into sliver
- 1 ½ tsp. cumin
- 2 tsp. kosher salt
- black pepper, to taste

Instructions:
1. Season pork with salt and pepper. Bring the cooker to high pressure by pressing the Sauté button and brown pork on all sides on high heat for about 5 minutes. Remove from heat and allow to cool.
2. Using a sharp knife, insert blade into pork about 1-inch deep and insert the garlic slivers, you'll want to do this all over. Season pork with cumin, sazon, oregano, adobo and garlic powder all over
3. Pour chicken broth, add chipotle peppers and stir, add bay leaves and place pork in the Foodi Multi-cooker
4. High pressure for 50 minutes. Lock the lid on the Foodi Multi-cooker and then cook for 50 minutes.
5. To get 50 minutes' cook time, press *Pressure* button and use the Time Adjustment button to adjust the cook time to 50 minutes.
6. Pressure Release. Use natural release method. Close crisping lid and select Broil, set time to 7 minutes. Serve and Enjoy!

Pork Tenderloin Braised Apples

(Prep + Cook Time: 50 minutes | **Servings:** 4)

Ingredients:
- 1/2 cup Diamond Crystal kosher salt or 1/4 cup fine table salt
- 1/4 cup granulated sugar

For The Pork and Apples
- 1 (1 lb.) pork tenderloin, trimmed of silver skin and halved crosswise
- 1 medium Granny Smith apple or another tart apple, peeled and cut into 1/4-inch slices
- Kosher salt, for salting and seasoning
- 2 tbsp. unsalted butter
- 2 cups very hot tap water
- 2 cups ice water
- For The Brine (optional)
- 1 cup thinly sliced onion
- 3/4 cup apple juice, cider or hard cider
- 1/2 cup low sodium chicken broth
- 2 tbsp. heavy (whipping) cream
- 1 tsp. Dijon mustard, plus additional as needed

Instructions:

To make the brine (if using)
1. In a large stainless steel or glass bowl, dissolve the salt and sugar in hot water; then stir in the ice water. Submerge the pork in the brine and refrigerate for 2 to 3 hours. Drain and pat dry.

To make the pork and apples
2. If you choose not to brine the pork, sprinkle it liberally with kosher salt. Set to *Sauté/browning* heat the butter just until it stops foaming.
3. Add the pork halves, browning on all sides, about 4 minutes' total. Transfer to a plate or rack and set aside.
4. Add the onion slices to the cooker and cook, stirring, for 2 to 3 minutes or until they just start to brown. Add the apple slices and cook for 1 minute. Add the apple juice and scrape the browned bits from the bottom of the pot.
5. Bring to a simmer and cook for 2 to 3 minutes or until the juice has reduced by about one-third. Add the chicken broth and return the pork tenderloin to the cooker, placing the pieces on top of the apples and onions
6. High pressure for 45 minutes. Lock the lid on the Foodi Multi-cooker and then cook for 45 minutes.
7. To get 45 minutes' cook time, press *pressure* button and use the adjust button to adjust the cook time to 45 minutes
8. Pressure Release. Use the quick release method.
9. Finish the dish. Close crisping lid. Discard the bay leaves. Select *Air Crisp*, set temperature to 375°F and set time to 10 minutes. Check after 5 minutes, cooking for an additional 5 minutes if dish needs more browning.
10. Transfer the pork to a plate or rack and tent it with aluminum foil while you finish the sauce.
11. Turn the Foodi Multi-cooker to *Sauté*, simmer for about 6 minutes or until the liquid is reduced by about half. Stir in the heavy cream and mustard and taste, adding kosher salt or more mustard as needed.
12. Slice the pork into 3/4-inch pieces and place on a serving platter. Spoon the apples, onions and sauce over the pork and serve

Beef & Lamb

Round Roast and Veggies

(Prep + Cook Time: 40 Minutes | **Servings:** 6)

Ingredients:
- 2 to 3 lb. round roast (top or bottom)
- 1 lb. potatoes; quartered or cubed
- 2 to 3 cups sliced mushrooms
- 1 large white onion; sliced or diced however you prefer to eat them
- 3 cups vegetable or beef broth
- 1 tbsp. thyme
- 2 tbsp. minced garlic
- 2 tbsp. olive oil
- Generous pinch of salt and pepper

Instructions:
1. Add all wet ingredients and spices to the Foodi and stir to combine
2. Add in meat and veggies, excluding potatoes
3. Seal the lid and set the timer for 15 minutes on HIGH pressure.
4. Do a quick release and add in potatoes.
5. Cook for another 10 minutes on HIGH pressure
6. Do another quick release. Remove and enjoy!

Seasoned Italian Beef

(Prep + Cook Time: 1 hour 55 Minutes | **Servings:** 6)

Ingredients:
- 3 lb. of grass-fed chuck roast
- 1/4 cup apple cider vinegar
- 6 garlic cloves
- 1 cup beef broth
- 2 tsp. garlic powder
- 1 tsp. marjoram
- 1 tsp. basil
- 1/2 tsp. ground ginger
- 1 tsp. oregano
- 1 tsp. onion powder
- 1 tsp. Himalayan pink salt

Instructions:
1. Cut a series of slits in the meat, and press the garlic cloves inside
2. In a bowl, mix the onion powder, garlic powder, salt, ginger, basil, oregano, and marjoram.
3. Rub into the meat and put in your Foodi. Pour in the apple cider vinegar and broth.
4. Close and lock the lid. Press *Pressure* and cook at HIGH pressure for 90 minutes.
5. When time is up, press *Cancel* and wait for a natural release
6. When all the pressure is gone, open the lid and shred the beef on a plate. Serve over salad, cauliflower rice, cooked sweet potatoes, and so on

Lamb Steaks with Feta and Potatoes

(Prep + Cook Time: 30 Minutes | **Servings:** 2)

Ingredients:
- 2 medium-large potatoes, skin on, cut into cubes
- 5 oz. feta cheese; crumbled
- 3 garlic cloves; sliced
- 2 lamb steaks
- Olive oil
- 1/2 tsp. dried mixed herbs
- Salt and pepper, to taste

Instructions:
1. Pour 2 cups of water into the Pressure Cooker and place the steaming basket into the pot. Place the potato cubes into the steaming basket and sprinkle with salt
2. High pressure for 3 minutes. Secure the lid onto the pot and press the *Pressure* button, adjust the time to 3 minutes

3. Once the pot beeps, Quick Pressure Release the pressure and remove the lid.
4. Take the basket of potatoes out of the pot and set aside, discard any leftover water from the pot.
5. Drizzle some olive oil into the Pressure Cooker and press the SAUTÉ button, adjust the temperature to HIGH.
6. Sprinkle the lamb with salt, pepper, and herbs, and once the oil is hot, add the steaks to the pot and cook for about 1 minute each side, (or more if you prefer more well-done meat)
7. Remove the lamb steaks from the pot and place on a board to rest. Don't wash the pot, just leave it as it is.
8. Place the garlic into the pot and adjust the temperature to LOW (the pot should still be on the SAUTÉ function), sauté the garlic for about 30 seconds
9. Add the steamed potatoes to the pot and stir to coat in oil and garlic, sauté for about 5 minutes until crispy and golden, don't worry if they get a bit mushy, that's part of the charm! Before serving, stir the feta cheese into the potatoes.

Cheesy Beef Pasta

(Prep + Cook Time: 30 Minutes | **Servings:** 8)

Ingredients:
- 1 ¼ lb. ground beef
- 1 lb. elbow macaroni
- 8 oz. sharp cheddar
- 1 packet onion soup mix
- 3 ½ cups hot water
- 3 beef bouillon cubes

Instructions:
1. Press the *Sauté* key of the Foodi. Add the beef and sauté until browned
2. While the beef is cooking, combine the bouillon cubes with the hot water, and onion soup mix in a bowl and stir until well mixed.
3. When the beef browned, add the liquid mixture and the pasta in the pot and stir well to combine. Cover and lock the lid
4. Press the *Pressure* key, set the pressure to HIGH, and set the timer for 5 minutes.
5. When the Foodi timer beeps press the *Cancel* key. Turn the steam valve to quick release the pressure. Unlock and carefully open the lid
6. Add the shredded cheese, press the *Sauté* key, and sauté for about 1 to 2 minutes or until the cheese is melted. Serve immediately.

Balsamic Maple Beef

(Prep + Cook Time: 55 Minutes | **Servings:** 6)

Ingredients:
- 3 lb. chuck steak; boneless, fat trimmed, sliced into 1/2-inch strips
- 1/2 cup balsamic vinegar
- 1 cup maple syrup
- 1 cup bone broth
- 2 tbsp. avocado oil OR olive oil
- 1 tsp. ground ginger
- 1 tsp. garlic; finely chopped
- 1 ½ tsp. salt

Instructions:
1. Trim the fat off from the joint the beef and slice the meat into 1/2-inch thin strips. In a bowl, mix the ground ginger with the salt. Season the meat with the ginger mix
2. Press the *Sauté* key of the Foodi. Put the oil in the pot and heat
3. When the oil is hot and shimmery, but not smoking, add the beef and cook until all sides are browned; you will have to cook in batches.
4. Transfer the browned beef into a plate and set aside. Put the garlic in the pot and sauté for about 1 minute.
5. Add the broth, maple syrup, and balsamic vinegar. Stir to mix. Return the browned beef into the pot
6. Press the *Cancel* key to stop the *Sauté* function. Cover and lock the lid
7. Press the *Pressure* key, set the pressure to HIGH, and set the timer for 35 minutes.

8. When the Foodi timer beeps turn the steam valve to venting to quick release the pressure.
9. Unlock and carefully open the lid. If desired, you can thicken the sauce. Press the *Sauté* key
10. Mix 4 tbsp. arrowroot or tapioca starch with 4 tbsp. water until smooth and then add into the pot; cook for about 5 minutes or until the sauce is thick. Serve!

Awesime Beef Roast

(Prep + Cook Time: 70 Minutes | **Servings:** 8)

Ingredients:
- 4 lb. beef chuck roast; cut into cubes (2 inches)
- 5 minced garlic cloves
- 1 thumb of grated ginger
- 1/2 cup soy sauce
- 1 peeled and chopped Granny Smith apple
- 1 cup beef broth
- Juice of one big orange
- 2 tbsp. olive oil
- Salt and pepper to taste

Instructions:
1. Season the roast with salt and pepper. Turn on your Foodi to *Sauté*. When hot, pour in the olive oil and brown the roast all over
2. Move the meat to a plate
3. Pour in the beef broth and scrape any stuck bits of meat.
4. Pour in soy sauce and stir
5. Put the roast back into the pot.
6. Arrange the cut apple, garlic, and ginger on top.
7. Pour in the orange juice. Close the pressure cooker lid
8. Select *Pressure* and cook for 45 minutes at HIGH pressure. Press *Cancel* and Quick Pressure Release the pressure when the timer beeps. Serve!

Stuffed Rigatoni

(Prep + Cook Time: 45 Minutes | **Servings:** 6)

Ingredients:
- 1/2 lb. ground beef
- 1 lb. rigatoni; cooked
- 1/2 lb. hot sausage
- 32 oz. of your favorite sauce
- 16 oz. mozzarella
- 16 oz. ricotta cheese
- 2 eggs
- 1 tbsp. parsley
- 1 tbsp. garlic powder

Equipment:
- Spring-form pan

Instructions:
1. In a large-sized bowl, mix the ricotta cheese with the mozzarella cheese, 2 eggs, parsley, and garlic powder. Set aside
2. Press the *Sauté* key of the Foodi
3. Brown the sausage and the ground beef in the pot, breaking up the sausages in the process.
4. Add into the bowl with the sauce and mix well. Turn off the pot for the time being
5. Coat the bottom of the spring-form pan with the meat-sauce mix. In a standing up position, place the pasta in the pan.
6. Spoon the cheese mix into a plastic bag. Poke a hole in one corner of the plastic bag and squeeze the cheese mix inside each rigatoni. Top the sauce mix with additional mozzarella cheese
7. Set a trivet in the Foodi and pour in 1 cup of water. Place the spring-form pan in the trivet. Cover and lock the lid.
8. Press the *Pressure* key, set the pressure to HIGH, and set the timer for 20 minutes
9. When the Foodi timer beeps, turn the steam valve to quick release the pressure
10. Unlock and carefully open the lid. Let the pan sit in the pot for 10 minutes or until the dish settles. Serve!

Pressure Cooker Chili

(Prep + Cook Time: 25 Minutes | **Servings:** 4)

Ingredients:
- 1 lb. ground beef
- 2 cans (15 oz.) red kidney beans drained and rinsed
- 1 can (28 oz.) crushed tomatoes
- 1 can (15 oz.) sweet corn drained
- 1 cup chicken stock
- 3 tbsp. tomato paste
- 1 tsp. unsweetened cocoa powder
- 1 tbsp. oil
- 2 cloves garlic minced
- 1 medium onion diced
- 1 tbsp. ground chipotle chili powder
- 1 to 2 tsp. chili powder
- 1 tbsp. cumin seed ground
- 1 tsp. dried oregano
- Brown sugar
- Kosher salt
- Black pepper

Instructions:
1. In a small bowl combine chicken stock, tomato paste, and unsweetened cocoa powder. Set aside.
2. Press *Sauté* button, when hot add oil and diced onion. Sauté for about 5 minutes until caramelized. Add minced garlic and sauté for 1 more minute
3. Add ground beef, chipotle chili powder, chili powder, ground cumin, and oregano. Use a
4. Wooden spoon to break the meat up into small pieces and Sauté until brown and slightly crispy.
5. Add stock mix and deglaze the pot. Then add kidney beans and mix
6. Pour the crushed tomatoes on top but don't mix
7. Cover and cook for 10 minutes at High pressure. To get 10 minutes cook time, press *Pressure* button.
8. Then natural release
9. Add sweet corn and season with brown sugar, salt, and black pepper to taste. Serve.

Lamb Shanks

(Prep + Cook Time: 55 Minutes | **Servings:** 4)

Ingredients:
- 4 lamb shanks
- 1 beef bouillon cube
- 3 carrots; peeled and chopped
- 1 yellow onion, peeled and diced
- 2 garlic cloves; peeled and minced
- 4 oz. red wine
- 2 tbsp. extra virgin olive oil
- 2 tbsp. white flour
- 2 tbsp. tomato paste
- 1 tsp. dried oregano
- 1 tomato; cored and chopped
- 2 tbsp. water
- Salt and ground black pepper, to taste

Instructions:
1. In a bowl, mix the flour with salt and pepper. Add the lamb shanks and toss to coat. Set the Foodi on *Sauté* mode, add the oil and heat it up. Add the lamb, brown on all sides, and transfer to a bowl. Add the onion, oregano, carrots, and garlic to the Foodi, stir and cook for 5 minutes. Add the tomato, tomato paste, water, wine, and bouillon cube, stir and bring to a boil. Return the lamb to pot, stir
2. Cover, and cook on *Pressure* mode for 25 minutes. Release the pressure, uncover the Foodi, divide the lamb among plates, pour cooking sauce all over, and serve

Corned Beef and Cabbage

(Prep + Cook Time: 1 hour 35 Minutes | **Servings:** 6)

Ingredients:
- 3 lb. cabbage, cut into eight wedges
- 1 ½ lb. new potatoes; quartered
- 1 lb. carrots; peeled and cut to 2.5 inches in length
- 1 quartered onion
- 1 corned beef spice packet
- 1 quartered celery stalk
- 4 cups water

Instructions:
1. Rinse the beef. Put in the Foodi along with onion and celery
2. Add in the spice packet and pour in water. Close and seal the lid
3. Press *Pressure* and cook for 90 minutes at HIGH pressure
4. When time is up, press *Cancel* and very carefully Quick Pressure Release the pressure.
5. Plate beef and keep celery and onion in the pot.
6. Add potatoes, carrots and cabbage in the pot. Close and seal lid again.
7. Select *Pressure* and cook for 5 minutes at HIGH pressure
8. When time is up, turn off cooker and Quick Pressure Release. Move veggies to plate with the corned beef.
9. Pour pot liquid through a gravy strainer. Serve beef and veggies with a bit of broth on top, and the rest in a gravy boat.

Korean Style Braised Short Ribs

(Prep + Cook Time: 55 Minutes | **Servings:** 4 to 6)

Ingredients:
- 4 lb. beef short ribs; about 3 inches thick, cut into 3 rib portions
- 2 green onions cut into 1-inch lengths
- 3 cloves garlic; smashed
- 3 quarter-sized slices of ginger
- 1/2 cup water
- 1/2 cup soy sauce
- 1/4 cup rice wine (or dry sherry)
- 1/4 cup pear juice (or apple juice)
- 1 tsp. vegetable oil
- 2 tsp. sesame oil
- Minced green onions
- Gochujang sauce

Instructions:
1. Heat the vegetable oil in the Foodi using the *Sauté* function, until the oil is shimmering. Add the green onion, garlic, and ginger, and sauté for 1 minute, or until you can smell garlic. Add the short ribs, water, soy sauce, rice wine, pear juice and sesame oil. Stir until the ribs are completely coated
2. Lock the lid on the Foodi and then cook for 45 minutes On High pressure. To get 45 minutes' cook time, press *Pressure* button and use the *Time Adjustment* button to adjust the cook time to 45 minutes.
3. Pressure Release Let the pressure to come down naturally for at least 15 minutes, then quick release any pressure left in the pot
4. Remove the short ribs from the pot with a slotted spoon. Serve the ribs with the degreased sauce.

Texas Beef Chili

(Prep + Cook Time: 55 Minutes | **Servings:** 4)

Ingredients:
- 1 lb. beef, grass-fed, organic
- 26 oz. tomatoes; finely chopped
- 1 green bell pepper; seeds removed and diced
- 4 carrots, large-sized, chopped into small pieces
- 1 onion; large-sized, diced
- 1 tbsp. fresh parsley, chopped
- 1 tbsp. Worcestershire sauce
- 1 tsp. garlic powder
- 1 tsp. onion powder
- 1 tsp. paprika
- 1 tsp. sea salt
- 1/2 tsp. ground black pepper
- 4 tsp. chili powder
- Pinch cumin

For serving, optional:
- Jalapenos, sliced
- Onions; diced
- Sour cream, dairy-free

Instructions:
1. Press the *Sauté* key. Add the ground beef into the Foodi and cook until browned
2. Add the remaining ingredients and mix well to combine. Lock the lid and close the steam valve.
3. Press *Cancel* to stop the *Sauté* function. Press *Meat/ Stew* key. It will automatically be set for 35 minutes
4. When the timer beeps, let the pressure release naturally.

Beef Chili

(Prep + Cook Time: 50 Minutes | **Servings:** 6)

Ingredients:
- 1½ lb. ground beef
- 1 sweet onion; peeled and chopped
- 16 oz. mixed beans, soaked overnight and drained
- 28 oz. canned diced tomatoes
- 17 oz. beef stock
- 12 oz. beer
- 6 garlic cloves; peeled and chopped
- 7 jalapeño peppers, diced
- 1 bay leaf
- 4 carrots; peeled and chopped
- Salt and ground black pepper, to taste
- 2 tbsp. vegetable oil
- 3 tbsp. chili powder
- 1 tsp. chili powder

Instructions:
1. Set the Foodi on *Sauté* mode, add half of the oil and heat it up
2. Add the beef, stir, brown for 8 minutes and transfer to a bowl. Add the rest of the oil to the Foodi and heat it up. Add the carrots, onion, jalapeños and garlic, stir, and sauté for 4 minutes. Add the beer and tomatoes and stir
3. Add the beans, bay leaf, stock, chili powder, chili powder, salt, pepper, and beef, stir, cover and cook on the Pressure setting for 25 minutes. Release the pressure naturally, uncover the Foodi, stir chili, transfer to bowls, and serve

Beef Tacos with Chili Sauce

(Prep + Cook Time: 1 hour 15 Minutes | **Servings:** 6)

Ingredients:
- 3 lb. beef short ribs or beef chuck roast, boneless, cut into 1-inch strips
- 1 dried chipotle chili; stemmed, seeded, and rinsed or
- 3 dried guajillo chilies, stemmed, seeded, and rinsed (or 2 more ancho chilies)
- 1 onion; large-sized, sliced
- 1 canned chipotle en adobo
- 3 cloves garlic; peeled
- 2 dried ancho chilies, stemmed, seeded, and rinsed
- 1/2 cup beer (preferably Negra Modelo) OR water
- 1 tbsp. Worcestershire sauce
- 1 tbsp. soy sauce
- 1 ½ tsp. kosher salt (I used Diamond Crystal)

Instructions:
1. Season the short ribs with salt and stack them in the Foodi
2. Top with the garlic, onions, and peppers.
3. Pour in the beer, Worcestershire sauce, and soy sauce. Cover and lock the lid.
4. Press the *Pressure* key, set the pressure to HIGH, and set the timer for 40 minutes
5. When the Foodi timer beeps, release the pressure naturally for 10 to 15 minutes or until the valve drops. Turn the steam valve to Venting to release remaining pressure. Unlock and carefully open the lid.
6. With a slotted spoon or with tongs, transfer the beef into a plate and set aside
7. Pour the cooking liquid through a strainer set on a fat separator. Transfer the solids; garlic, onions, and pepper in blender.
8. When the fat surfaces, pour the de-fatted cooking liquid in the blender
9. Starting from low power, blend the cooking liquid; slowly increasing to the highest speed, blending for 1 minute or until the sauce is very smooth.
10. Shred the beef and pour in the sauce.
11. Toss to coat the beef with the sauce. Taste and adjust salt as needed

Braised Beef Shank in Soybean Paste

(Prep + Cook Time: 60 Minutes | **Servings:** 6 to 8)

Ingredients:
- 2 (2½ lb.) beef shank
- 2 green onions chopped to 2-inch length
- 5 to 6 cloves garlic crushed
- 2 tbsp. olive oil
- 1 tbsp. chili bean paste
- 1 tbsp. sweet soybean paste
- 1 tsp. Ginger sliced fresh
- 1 tsp. Chinese cooking wine
- 1 tbsp. light soy sauce
- 1 tbsp. dark soy sauce
- 3 to 4 tbsp. water
- 2 tsp. sugar
- 1/3 tsp. salt

Instructions:
1. Soak beef in cold water for 30 minutes and then drain. Dice the beef into 1-inch pieces. Heat 1 tbsp. of olive oil in the Foodi on the *Sauté* setting and add beef
2. Sauté for a few minutes until water evaporates and beef turns brown. Transfer beef in a bowl and set aside.
3. Add another 1 tbsp. of olive oil in the pot. Sauté chili bean paste and sweet soybean paste for about 30 seconds.
4. Add chopped green onion, ginger and garlic; continue to sauté for 30 seconds
5. Put the beef back into the pot, and sauté for 1 minute, then add the cooking wine, both soy sauces, sugar, salt, and water.
6. Press the *Cancel* key to stop *Sauté* function

7. Cover the lid and place the pressure valve in sealing position. Select *Pressure* and cook at HIGH pressure for 38 minutes. When the program is done, wait another 5 minutes
8. Slowly release the pressure then open the lid. Select *Sauté* and set temperature to More, stir occasionally until the sauce is reduced to 1/3 its volume. Transfer the braised beef shank into to a serving bowl, serve immediately over rice.

Beef and Pasta Casserole

(Prep + Cook Time: 30 Minutes | **Servings:** 4)

Ingredients:
- 1 lb. ground beef
- 1 celery stalk; chopped
- 17 oz. pasta
- 1 yellow onion; peeled and chopped
- 1 carrot, peeled and chopped
- 13 oz. mozzarella cheese; shredded
- 16 oz. tomato puree
- 1 tbsp. red wine
- 2 tbsp. butter
- Salt and ground black pepper; to taste

Instructions:
1. Set the Foodi on *Sauté* mode, add the butter and melt it. Add the carrot, onion, and celery, stir, and cook for 5 minutes
2. Add the beef, salt and pepper, and cook for 10 minutes. Add the wine, stir and cook for 1 minute. Add the pasta, tomato puree, and water to cover pasta, stir
3. Cover and cook on the *Pressure* setting for 6 minutes. Release the pressure, uncover the Foodi, add the cheese, stir, divide everything among plates, and serve.

Lamb Shanks with Pancetta

(Prep + Cook Time: 1hour 15 Minutes | **Servings:** 4)

Ingredients:
- 1 (6 oz.) pancetta chunk, chopped
- 2 cups dry; light white wine, such as Sauvignon Blanc
- 4 (12 oz.) lamb shanks
- 1 small yellow onion, chopped
- 1 (28 oz.) can diced tomatoes; drained (about 3½ cups)
- 1 oz. dried mushrooms; preferably porcini, crumbled
- 2 tbsp. olive oil
- 3 tbsp. packed celery leaves, minced
- 2 tbsp. minced chives
- 2 tbsp. all-purpose flour
- 1/2 tsp. ground black pepper

Instructions:
1. Heat the oil in the Foodi, turned to the *Sautéing/Browning* function. Add the pancetta and brown well, about 6 minutes, stirring often. Use a slotted spoon to transfer the pancetta to a large bowl
2. Add two of the shanks to the cooker; brown on all sides, turning occasionally, about 8 minutes. Transfer them to the bowl and repeat with the remaining shanks
3. Add the onion to the pot; cook, stirring often, until softened, about 4 minutes. Stir in the tomatoes, dried mushroom crumbles, celery leaves, and chives. Cook until bubbling, about minutes, stirring often.
4. Whisk the wine, flour, and pepper in a medium bowl until the flour dissolves; stir this mixture into the sauce in the pot. Cook until thickened and bubbling, about 1 minute
5. Return the shanks, pancetta, and their juices to the cooker
6. Close the lid and the pressure valve and then cook On High pressure for 60 minutes. To get 60 minutes' cook time, press *Pressure* button and use the *Time Adjustment* button to adjust the cook time to 60 minutes.
7. Turn off the Foodi or unplug it so it doesn't jump to its keep-warm setting.
8. Let its pressure return to normal naturally, 20 to 30 minutes
9. Unlock and open the cooker. Transfer a shank to each serving bowl. Skim any surface fat from the sauce with a flatware spoon. Ladle the sauce and vegetables over the lamb shanks

Marinated Steak

(Prep + Cook Time: 45 Minutes | **Servings:** 4)

Ingredients:
- 2 lb. flank steak
- 2 tbsp. onion soup mix; dried
- ¼ cups apple cider vinegar
- 1/2 cups olive oil
- 1 tbsp. Worcestershire sauce

Instructions:
1. Press the *Sauté* key of the Foodi. Put the flank steak in the pot and cook each side until browned.
2. Add the Worcestershire sauce, vinegar, onion soup mix, and olive oil
3. Press the *Cancel* key to stop the *Sauté* function. Cover and lock the lid
4. Press the MEAT/ STEW key, and set the timer for 35 minutes.
5. When the Foodi timer beeps turn the steam valve to quick release the pressure. Unlock and carefully open the lid. Serve!

Easy Osso Bucco

(Prep + Cook Time: 25 Minutes | **Servings:** 4)

Ingredients:
- 4 veal or lamb shanks cut to size for the Foodi
- 2 medium carrots chopped in large chunks
- 2 stalks celery cut into large chunks
- 1 medium to large onion chopped
- 2 cloves crushed garlic
- 1 to 2 cups chicken broth (keep in mind of the size of the Foodi)
- 2 lbs. red potatoes (washed)
- 1/4 cup flour
- 1/2 tsp. black pepper
- 1/2 tsp. salt
- 1/2 tsp. garlic powder
- 1/2 tsp. onion powder
- 1 tsp. thyme
- 1 tsp. rosemary
- 1/4 cup olive oil
- 1 tbsp. butter
- 2 tbsp. butter

Instructions:
1. Add the flour and the seasonings to a large bowl. Use a wire whisk to blend everything together.
2. Rinse the shanks and dry with a paper towel. Roll each shank in the flour mix and set aside on a plate Preheat a large skillet. Add the oil and bring to almost smoking. Place the shanks in the skillet and brown turning each shank to brown all sides of the shank. Once they are browned, set aside. Add the flour to the remaining oil and make a rue. Once the rue is made add the broth to loosen the rue into a sauce
3. Pour ½ of the sauce on the Foodi and place each shank into the sauce standing upright. Fill in the gaps with the vegetables. Pour the remaining sauce over the shanks and vegetables.
4. Seal the Foodi and cook On High pressure for approximately 90 minutes. To get 90 minutes' cook time, press Pressure button and use the COOK *Time Adjustment* button to adjust the cook time to 90 minutes
5. Turn off the Foodi or unplug it. Allow its pressure to fall to normal naturally, 15 to 20 minutes.
6. Boil the red potatoes (skin on) until tender. Mash the potatoes adding 2 tbsp. of butter. Salt and pepper to taste
7. Serve a lamb shank on a bed of potatoes. Add a large spoon of the vegetables. Ladle on some of the sauce from the cooker over the shank, vegetables and potatoes.

Lamb Stew with Brussels Sprouts

(Prep + Cook Time: 35 Minutes | **Servings:** 6)

Ingredients:
- 2½ lb. boneless leg of lamb, well trimmed and cut into 2-inch pieces
- 1 lb. small Brussels sprouts, stemmed and halved
- 1 large yellow onion; halved and sliced into thin half-moons
- 3 medium garlic cloves; slivered
- 1 cup chicken broth
- 1 cup packed dried apples; chopped
- 1/4 cup shelled unsalted pistachios
- 2 tsp. ground coriander
- 1/2 tbsp. ground cinnamon
- 1 tsp. ground cumin
- 1 tsp. ground black pepper
- 1/2 tsp. ground ginger
- 1/2 tsp. salt
- 2 tbsp. olive oil
- 1 tbsp. honey

Instructions:
1. Mix the coriander, cinnamon, cumin, pepper, ginger, and salt in a large bowl. Add the lamb and stir until evenly and well coated in the spices; set aside
2. Heat the oil in the Foodi turned to the *Sautéing/Browning* mode. Add the onion and cook, stirring often, until softened, about 5 minutes
3. Add the meat and every drop of spice from the bowl, as well as the garlic. Cook, stirring occasionally, until the meat has browned a bit, about 5 minutes. Add the broth, dried apples, pistachios, and honey; stir to scrape up any browned bits on the pot's bottom.
4. Lock the lid in place. Set the Foodi to cook at High pressure for 30 minutes. To get 30 minutes' cook time, press *Pressure* button and use the *Time Adjustment* button to adjust the cook time to 30 minutes
5. Use the Quick Pressure Release method
6. Unlock and open the cooker. Stir in the Brussels sprouts.
7. Lock the lid back onto the pot. Set the Foodi to cook once again at High pressure for 8 minutes To get 8 minutes' cook time, press *Pressure* button and use the *Time Adjustment* button to adjust the cook time to 8 minutes.
8. Drop the pot's pressure back to normal with the Quick Pressure Release method. Unlock and open the cooker. Stir well before serving.

Goulash

(Prep + Cook Time: 30 Minutes | **Servings:** 4)

Ingredients:
- 1½ lb. beef chuck roast, trimmed of excess fat and cut into 1½-inch cubes
- 1/2 lb. small red potatoes; left whole if less than 1½ inches in diameter, halved if larger
- 1 (14 oz.) can diced tomatoes; drained
- 2 large carrots, peeled and cut into 1-inch rounds (about 1½ cups)
- 2 medium red bell peppers; cut into 1-inch pieces (about 1½ cups)
- 1/4 cup sweet paprika
- 2 cups sliced onions
- 2 garlic cloves, minced (about 2 teaspoons)
- Sour cream; for garnish (optional)
- 2 tbsp. olive oil; divided
- 2 tsp. caraway seeds
- 2 tsp. dried marjoram or oregano
- 3 cups Beef Stock or low-sodium broth
- Kosher salt, for seasoning

Instructions:
1. Set the Foodi to *Sautéing/Browning* heat 1 tbsp. of olive oil until it shimmers and flows like water. Add the beef, and sear on two sides, working in batches if necessary so as not to crowd the pan. Remove the beef from the cooker, and set aside
2. Add the remaining 1 tbsp. of olive oil to the pan; then add the onions and garlic, and sprinkle with a pinch or two of kosher salt. Cook, stirring, for about 3 minutes, or until the onions and garlic soften.

Add the paprika, caraway seeds, and marjoram. Stir to coat the onions. Cook for about 1 minute, or until fragrant.
3. Pour the Beef Stock into the Foodi, and stir to dissolve the spices. Return the beef to the pot. Add the tomatoes, carrots, red bell peppers, and red potatoes
4. Lock the lid in place, and bring the pot to High pressure. Cook at High pressure for 25 minutes. To get 25 minutes' cook time, press *Pressure* button and use the COOK *Time Adjustment* button to adjust the cook time to 25 minutes.
5. When the timer goes off, turn the cooker off. ("warm" setting, turn off).
6. After cooking, use the natural method to release pressure
7. Unlock and remove the lid. Let the goulash sit for 1 minute to allow any fat to rise to the surface. Spoon or blot off as much as possible.

Tender Pot Roast

(Prep + Cook Time: 50 Minutes | **Servings:** 6)

Ingredients:
- 2 to 3 lb. beef, chuck roast
- 4 carrots; chopped
- 4 potatoes; large-sized, cut into large cubes
- 1 onion
- 2 stalks celery; chopped
- 1 cup beef broth
- 1 cup red wine
- 3 tbsp. steak sauce; optional
- 3 cloves garlic
- 2 tbsp. olive oil
- 2 tbsp. Italian Seasonings

Instructions:
1. Press the *Sauté* key of your Foodi. Pour in the olive oil. Add the roast beef and cook each side for about 1 to 2 minutes or until browned. Transfer the browned beef into a plate
2. Put the celery, carrots, and potatoes in the pot. Top with the garlic and onion
3. Pour the beef broth and the wine in the pot. Put the roast on top of the vegetables
4. Spread the seasonings over the top of the roast and then spread with the steak sauce. Press the *Cancel* key to stop the *Sauté* function. Cover and lock the lid
5. Press the *Pressure* key, set the pressure to HIGH, and set the timer for 35 minutes
6. When the Foodi timer beeps, release the pressure naturally for 10 to 15 minutes or until the valve drops.
7. Turn the steam valve to release remaining pressure. Unlock and carefully open the lid. Serve!

Classic Brisket with Veggies

(Prep + Cook Time: 1 hour 20 minutes | **Servings:** 4 to 6)

Ingredients:
- 2 lb. or larger regular brisket, rinsed and patted dry
- 2 ½ cup homemade beef broth or make from Knorr Beef Base
- 2 tbsp. olive oil
- 5 or 6 red potatoes
- 2 cup large chunks carrots
- 3 tbsp. Worcestershire Sauce
- 4 bay leaves
- Granulated garlic
- Knorr Demi-Glace sauce
- 1/2 cup dehydrated onion
- 2 stalks celery in 1 chunks
- Fresh ground black pepper
- 3 tbsp. heaping chopped garlic
- 1 large yellow onion
- 5 or 6 red potatoes

Instructions:
1. Put the Foodi Multi-cooker on the sauté setting. Put in 1 tbsp. (more if needed) of the oil and caramelize the onions. Once golden, remove from pot, put in a bowl and set aside. But keep the Foodi Multi-cooker on the *Sauté* setting.

2. Rub the freshly ground pepper on both sides of the brisket. Do the same with the granulated garlic. Add 1 tbsp. olive oil (or more) and only lightly sear the brisket on all sides
3. Add back the onions, garlic, Worcestershire sauce, bay leaves, dehydrated onion and beef broth
4. High pressure for 50 minutes. Close the lid and the pressure valve and then cook for 50 minutes
5. To get 50 minutes' cook time, press *Pressure* button and use the Time Adjustment button to adjust the cook time to 50 minutes
6. While the meat is cooking, peel and cut up all the veggies. When the meat is done, use the quick pressure release feature and then remove the lid. Add all of the veggies, replace the lid and cook at high pressure for to 10 minutes.
7. To get 10 minutes' cook time, press *Steam* button
8. Pressure Release. When the time is up, turn the pot off, use the quick release again and remove the lid.
9. Finish the dish. Close crisping lid. Select ""BROIL"" and set time to 8 minutes. Check after 5 minutes, cooking for an additional 3 minutes if dish needs more browning
10. Use a platter to remove the veggies and meat. Use the *Sauté* setting and bring the broth to a boil, then add the Knorr Demi-Glace mixing with a Wisk.
11. Adjust seasonings as needed. Serve with Cole Slaw or other salad, homemade rolls or Italian garlic bread. Be sure to remove the bay leaves before serving. Serve and Enjoy

Beef Bourguignon

(**Prep + Cook Time:** 25 Minutes | **Servings:** 4)

Ingredients:
- 3/4 lb. beef chuck roast, trimmed of excess fat and cut into 2-inch chunks
- 1/2 cup frozen pearl onions; thawed
- 2 bacon slices; sliced crosswise into ½-inch pieces
- 1/2 cup "Sautéed" Mushrooms
- 1 cup dry red wine (preferably Pinot Noir); divided
- 1/2 cup low-sodium beef broth
- 1 very small onion, cut into eighths
- 1 medium carrot; peeled and cut into 1/4-inch slices (about 1/2 cup)
- 1 tsp. unsalted butter
- 2 tsp. tomato paste
- 1 bay leaf
- 1 fresh thyme sprig
- 1 tbsp. fresh minced parsley
- 1 garlic clove; smashed
- 1/2 tsp. kosher salt
- Freshly ground black pepper

Instructions:
1. Season the beef with the kosher salt.
2. Set the Foodi to *Sautéing/Browning* add the butter and bacon. Cook, stirring, for about 4 minutes, or until the bacon renders most of it's fat and is crisp. Remove the bacon, and set aside. Blot the beef chunks dry, and add them to the Foodi. Brown on all sides, about 10 minutes total, working in batches if necessary so as not to crowd the pan. Remove the beef from the pot, and set aside
3. Add the tomato paste to the pot, and cook, stirring, for about 1 minute, or until the paste has darkened slightly. Add 1/2 cup of red wine, and cook, stirring, to release the browned bits from the bottom of the pan. Add the remaining 1/2 cup of red wine and the beef broth, onion, carrot, garlic, bay leaf, and thyme. Return the beef to the pot, and stir to combine.
4. Lock the lid in place, and bring the pot to High pressure. Cook at High pressure for 40 minutes. To get 40 minutes' cook time, press *Pressure*.
5. After cooking, use the natural method to release pressure
6. Unlock and remove the lid. Using tongs, remove the beef chunks to a bowl while you finish the sauce. Pour the sauce and vegetables through a strainer or colander into a fat separator. Discard the vegetables, bay leaf, and thyme sprig. When the fat has risen to the top of the separator, pour the defatted sauce back into the cooker, and add the pearl onions. Turned to *Sautéing/Browning* simmer the sauce for about 3 minutes, or until slightly thickened. Stir in the reserved bacon. Add the "Sautéed" Mushrooms and parsley, and season with pepper.

Easy Sausage and Peppers

(Prep + Cook Time: 25 minutes | **Servings:** 5 to 6)

Ingredients:
- 2 ½ lb. sweet Italian sausages in their casings
- 1 medium red onion, halved and thinly sliced
- 2 medium garlic cloves, slivered
- 1 cup red (sweet) vermouth
- 4 large red bell peppers, stemmed, seeded and cut into strips
- 2 tbsp. olive oil
- 2 tbsp. balsamic vinegar
- 1/4 tsp. grated nutmeg

Instructions:
1. Heat the oil in a Foodi Multi-cooker, turned to the sauté function. Prick the sausages with a fork, add them to the pot and brown on all sides, about 6 minutes. Transfer to a large bowl
2. Add the peppers and onion; cook, stirring almost constantly, just until the pepper strips glisten, about 2 minutes.
3. Add the garlic, cook a few seconds and then stir in the vermouth, vinegar and nutmeg. Nestle the sausages into the mixture
4. High pressure for 10 minutes. Lock the lid on the Foodi Multi-cooker and Cook for 10 minutes.
5. To get 10 minutes' cook time, press the *Pressure* button and adjust the time
6. Pressure Release. Use the quick release method to bring the pot's pressure back to normal
7. Remove the lid from the Foodi Multi-cooker. Close crisping lid. Select *Air Crisp*, set temperature to 390°F and set time to 10 minutes.
8. Check after 8 minutes, cooking for an additional 2 minutes if dish needs more browning. Stir well before serving

Pasta with Meat Sauce

(Prep + Cook Time: 15 Minutes | **Servings:** 4)

Ingredients:
- 1 ½ lb. ground beef
- 24 oz. pasta sauce
- 8 oz. dried pasta
- 12 oz. water
- Italian seasoning to taste

Instructions:
1. Turn your cooker to *Sauté*
2. Add ground beef to brown, breaking it up with a spatula as it cooks
3. When browned, press *Cancel* and pour in pasta, sauce, and water. You'll probably have to break the pasta in half.
4. Close and lock the lid. Select *Pressure* and cook at HIGH pressure for 5 minutes
5. When time is up, press *Cancel* and use a quick release. Season with Italian seasoning to taste and serve!

Steaks with Garlic Cream Sauce

(Prep + Cook Time: 25 Minutes | Servings: 4)

Ingredients:
- 1/4 cup dry white wine
- 3/4 cup heavy cream
- Olive oil
- 4 garlic cloves; finely chopped
- 1/2 tsp. fresh oregano; finely chopped
- 2 steaks, room temperature
- Salt and pepper, to taste

Instructions:
1. Press the SAUTÉ button on your Pressure Cooker and adjust the temperature to HIGH, drizzle some olive oil into the pot
2. Once the oil is very hot, carefully place the steaks into the pot and cook according to your preference (rare, medium, well done), turn the steak and cook the other side
3. Remove the steaks from the pot and leave on a board to rest, and sprinkle the steaks with salt and pepper at this stage.
4. Don't wash the Pot before you make the sauce, the leftover steak juices will add lovely flavor to the sauce.
5. Keep the Foodi on the SAUTÉ function, but adjust the temperature to NORMAL.
6. Add the garlic, herbs, and wine to the pot, sauté until the wine has reduced and the smell of alcohol has disappeared.
7. Add the cream, salt, and pepper to the pot and stir to combine
8. Simmer the sauce for about 5 minutes until thick and creamy. Serve the steak with a generous helping of creamy garlic sauce spooned over the top.

Lamb Skewers with Pita Bread and Eggplant Dip

(Prep + Cook Time: 30 Minutes | Servings: 2)

Ingredients:
- 2 lamb steaks; cut into cubes
- 3 garlic cloves, finely chopped
- 1 large eggplant; cut into chunks
- 1/2 cup plain Greek yogurt
- 2 pita breads (store bought is fine)
- Olive oil
- 1/2 tsp. ground cumin
- 1/2 tsp. chili powder
- Salt and pepper

Instructions:
1. Press the SAUTÉ button on your Foodi and adjust the temperature to HIGH, drizzle some olive oil into the pot
2. Coat the lamb with salt, pepper, cumin, and chili powder.
3. Once the oil is very hot, add the lamb cubes and sauté for about 5 minutes, turning a few times so the lamb cubes are golden and brown on all sides.
4. Take the lamb cubes out of the pot and leave aside, don't wash the pot (the lamb juices and leftover spices will flavor the eggplant!)
5. Keep the Pressure Cooker on the sauté function, adjust the temperature to LOW.
6. Drizzle some more olive oil into the Pressure Cooker and add the garlic, cook for about 20 seconds until the garlic is soft
7. Add the eggplant and keep stirring as the eggplant sautés and becomes soft and mushy.
8. Remove the eggplant and place into a small bowl, add the yogurt, salt, and pepper, stir to combine.
9. Toast the pita breads and fill with eggplant filling, lamb cubes, and any other fillings you desire (baby spinach is a great match!).

Beef Chili & Cornbread Casserole

(Prep + Cook Time: 60 minutes | **Servings:** 8)

Ingredients:
- 2 lb. uncooked ground beef
- 3 cans (14 oz. each) kidney beans, rinsed, drained
- 1 can (28 oz.) crushed tomatoes
- 1 cup beef stock
- 1 large white onion, peeled, diced
- 1 green bell pepper, diced
- 1 jalapeño pepper, diced, seeds removed
- 4 cloves garlic, peeled, minced
- 2 tbsp. kosher salt
- 1 tbsp. ground black pepper
- 2 tbsp. ground cumin
- 1 tbsp. onion powder
- 1 tbsp. garlic powder
- 2 cups Cheddar Corn Bread batter, uncooked
- 1 cup shredded Mexican cheese blend
- Sour cream, for serving

Instructions:
1. Place beef, beans, tomatoes, and stock into the pot, breaking apart meat. Assemble pressure lid, making sure the PRESSURE RELEASE valve is in the SEAL position. Select PRESSURE and set to HIGH. Set time to 15 minutes. Select START/STOP to begin.
2. When pressure cooking is complete, quick release the pressure by moving the PRESSURE RELEASE valve to the VENT position. Carefully remove lid when unit has finished releasing pressure
3. Select SEAR/SAUTÉ. Set temperature to MD, Select START/STOP. Add onion, green bell pepper, jalapeño pepper, garlic, and spices; stir to incorporate. Bring to a simmer and cook for 5 minutes, stirring occasionally.
4. Dollop corn bread batter evenly over the top of the chili. Close crisping lid. Select BAKE/ROAST, set temperature to 360°F, and set time to 26 minutes. Select START/STOP to begin.
5. After 15 minutes, open lid and insert a wooden toothpick into the center of the corn bread. If corn bread is not done, close lid to resume cooking for another 8 minutes.
6. When corn bread is done, sprinkle it with cheese and close lid to resume cooking for 3 minutes, or until cheese is melted. When cooking is complete, top with sour cream and serve.

Mongolian Beef

(Prep + Cook Time: 25 Minutes | **Servings:** 4)

Ingredients:
- 1½ lb. Flank steak
- 1 garlic clove; minced
- 1 green onion, sliced, for garnish
- 1 carrot; shredded
- 1/2 cup brown sugar
- 1 tbsp. olive oil
- 3/4 cup soy sauce
- 1/2 tsp. fresh ginger; minced
- 1/4 cup water

To thicken the sauce:
- 3 tbsp. water
- 3 tbsp. cornstarch

Instructions:
1. Slice the flank into the strips. In a bowl, combine the soy sauce with the oil, garlic, ginger, sugar, and water.
2. Pour the sauce in the Foodi
3. Add the shredded carrot and beef strips, and mix until the beef is coated with the sauce. Cover and lock the lid
4. Press the *Pressure* key, set the pressure to HIGH, and set the timer for 8 minutes.
5. When the Foodi timer beeps press the *Cancel* key and unplug the Foodi
6. Let the pressure release naturally for 10 to 15 minutes or until the valve drops. Turn the steam valve to release remaining pressure. Unlock and carefully open the lid.
7. In a small-sized bowl, combine the cornstarch with the water until there are no more lumps

8. Press the *Sauté* key and pour cornstarch mixture into the pot. Boil for about 1 to 2 minutes or until the sauce is thick. Serve on a platter and garnish with chopped green onions.

BBQ Pulled Beef Sandwiches

(Prep + Cook Time: 1 hour | **Servings:** 2 to 4)

Ingredients:
- 2 lb. Beef of choice
- 4 cups finely shredded Cabbage (the secret ingredient and you'll never know it's in there.)
- 2 cups Water
- 1/2 cup of your favorite BBQ Sauce
- 1 cup Ketchup
- 1/3 cup Worcestershire Sauce
- 1 tbsp. mustard
- 1 tbsp. Horse Radish

Instructions:
1. Add and stir in ingredients to your Foodi Multi-cooker.
2. High pressure for 35 minutes. Lock the lid on the Foodi Multi-cooker and then cook for 35 minutes.
3. To get 35 minutes' cook time, press *Pressure* button and adjust the time.
4. Pressure Release. Use natural release method. Finish the dish. Remove the lid from the Foodi Multi-cooker. Close crisping lid. Select *Air Crisp*, set temperature to 390°F and set time to 15 minutes.
5. Check after 10 minutes, cooking for an additional 5 minutes if dish needs more browning.
6. Set the beef aside. Set the Foodi Multi-cooker to a *Sauté* mode, Sauté the sauce until it reaches the desired consistency. Serve and Enjoy

Cold Beef Noodle Salad

(Prep + Cook Time: 20 Minutes | **Servings:** 2)

Ingredients:
- 10 oz. dried rice noodles (flat or vermicelli, any kind works)
- 1 scallion; finely chopped
- 1 large sirloin steak (about 1 lb)
- 1 fresh red chili; finely chopped (seeds removed if you don't want too much spice)
- 1 fresh lime
- Handful of fresh coriander; finely chopped
- 1 tsp. brown sugar
- 1 tsp. sesame oil (if you have it)
- 2 tsp. fish sauce (if you have it, you can use soy sauce as a substitute)
- Olive oil
- Salt and pepper, to taste

Instructions:
1. Bring a pot of water to the boil and add the rice noodles, cook until soft (or follow the packet Directions if they need alternate cooking methods, some are pre-cooked and just need to be soaked in hot water), run cold water over the noodles until they are cold, then leave aside
2. Press the SAUTÉ button on your Pressure Cooker and adjust the temperature to HIGH, drizzle some olive oil into the pot
3. Once the oil is hot, add the steak to the pot and cook for about 2 minutes on both sides, or longer if you want your steak well done.
4. Remove the steak from the pot and place on a board to rest, sprinkle with salt and pepper.
5. In a large salad bowl, add the scallions, coriander, chili, juice of one lime, brown sugar, sesame oil, and fish or soy sauce, stir to combine.
6. Add the cooked noodles and toss to coat in the dressing. Slice the steak into thin strips and scatter over the noodle salad before serving

Shredded Barbecue Skirt Steak

(Prep + Cook Time: 25 Minutes | **Servings:** 4)

Ingredients:
- 3 lb. beef skirt steak, cut into 6-inch-long pieces
- Up to 3 canned chipotles in adobo sauce; stemmed, seeded, and chopped
- 1 medium shallot, chopped
- 1/4 cup unsweetened apple juice
- 1/4 cup fresh lime juice
- 1 tbsp. minced garlic
- 1 tbsp. packed fresh oregano leaves; finely chopped
- 1 tbsp. ground cumin
- 1/2 tsp. salt
- 1/4 tsp. ground cloves
- 4 juniper berries (optional)
- 2 tbsp. rendered bacon fat

Instructions:
1. Place the apple juice, lime juice, chipotles, shallot, garlic, oregano, cumin, salt, cloves, and juniper berries, if using, in a large blender or food processor; cover and blend or process until smooth, stopping the machine a couple of times to scrape down the inside of the canister
2. Melt the bacon fat in the Foodi turned to the *Sautéing/Browning* function. Add one or two of the steaks and brown on both sides, about 4 minutes, turning once. Transfer to a plate and continue browning until you've worked your way through all the steak pieces
3. Return the meat and any juices on its plate to the cooker. Pour the pureed sauce over the beef; stir well.
4. Lock the lid onto the pot. Set the pot to cook at High pressure for 42 minutes. To get 42 minutes' cook time, press Pressure button and use the COOK *Time Adjustment* button to adjust the cook time to 42 minutes
5. Reduce the pressure
6. Turn off the Foodi or unplug it. Allow its pressure to fall to normal naturally, 15 to 20 minutes.
7. Unlock and open the lid. Transfer the meat to a large cutting board; shred with two forks. Return the meat to the sauce in the cooker; stir well before serving. Serve.

Shredded Pepper Steak

(Prep + Cook Time: 1 hour 40 Minutes | **Servings:** 6)

Ingredients:
- 3 to 4 lb. beef (cheap steak or roast cuts will all work)
- 1 (16 oz.) jar Mild Pepper Rings (banana peppers or pepperoncini)
- 1/2 cup salted beef broth
- 1 tbsp. garlic powder
- Red chili flakes to taste

Instructions:
1. Season beef with garlic powder and red chili flakes before adding to cooker.
2. Pour peppers (including juice) and broth into cooker, too. Seal the lid
3. Select *Pressure* and cook at HIGH pressure for 70 minutes
4. When the timer beeps, press *Cancel* and wait for a natural pressure release. When safe, open the cooker and shred the meat. Serve!

Notes: The jarred peppers can typically be found in the Italian* foods section of your grocery store.

Beef and Bean Pasta Casserole

(Prep + Cook Time: 20 Minutes | **Servings:** 4)

Ingredients:
- 1 lb. lean ground beef
- 1 (15 oz.) can of drained and rinsed kidney beans
- 1 (12 oz.) bottle brown ale
- 8 oz. pasta shells
- 1 chopped yellow onion
- 1 seeded and chopped green bell pepper
- 1 (28 oz.) can of diced tomatoes
- 2 cups corn kernels
- 1 tbsp. minced garlic
- 2 tbsp. sweet paprika
- 1 tbsp. olive oil
- 1 tsp. ground cumin
- 1 tsp. dried oregano
- 1/2 tsp. chipotle pepper
- 1/2 tsp. salt

Instructions:
1. Heat your oil in the Foodi on the *Sauté* setting
2. When hot, add garlic, bell pepper, and onion. Stir until the onion becomes clear.
3. Add the ground beef, breaking it up with a spatula if necessary.
4. Keep stirring and browning, which should take about 4 minutes
5. Add the corn, tomatoes, beans, and seasonings. Pour in the beer. Stir until the beer foam has gone down.
6. Add the pasta and stir so it becomes coated. Close and seal the lid
7. Select *Pressure* and cook at HIGH pressure for 8 minutes. When time is up, hit *Cancel* and carefully Quick Pressure Release the pressure. Stir the casserole before serving.

Braised Short Ribs

(Prep + Cook Time: 1 hour 5 minutes | **Servings:** 4 to 6)

Ingredients:
- 4 lb. beef short ribs, about 3 inches thick, cut into 3 rib portions
- 1/4 cup rice wine (or dry sherry)
- 1/4 cup pear juice (or apple juice)
- 2 green onions cut into 1-inch lengths
- 3 cloves garlic, smashed
- 3 quarter-sized slices of ginger
- 1 tsp. vegetable oil
- 1/2 cup water
- 1/2 cup soy sauce
- 2 tsp. sesame oil
- Minced green onions
- Gochujang sauce

Instructions:
1. Heat the vegetable oil in the Foodi Multi-cooker using the *Sauté* function, until the oil is shimmering. Add the green onion, garlic and ginger and sauté for 1 minute or until you can smell the garlic
2. Add the short ribs, water, soy sauce, rice wine, pear juice and sesame oil. Stir until the ribs are completely coated.
3. High pressure for 45 minutes. Lock the lid on the Foodi Multi-cooker and then cook for 45 minutes.
4. To get 45 minutes' cook time, press *Meat/Chicken* button and use the "ADJUST" button to adjust the cook time to 45 minutes
5. Pressure Release. Let the pressure to come down naturally for at least 15 minutes, then quick release any pressure left in the pot
6. Finish the dish. Close crisping lid. Select "BROIL" and set time to 8 minutes. Check after 5 minutes, cooking for an additional 3 minutes if dish needs more browning.
7. Remove the short ribs from the pot with a slotted spoon. Serve the ribs with the degreased sauce

Pot Roast

(Prep + Cook Time: 1 hour 50 minutes | **Servings:** 4 to 6)

Ingredients:
- 1 (3- to 3½ lb.) boneless beef chuck roast
- 1 ½ lb. small white or yellow potatoes
- 1/2 oz. dried mushrooms, preferably porcini
- 1 tbsp. olive oil
- 1 large yellow onion, chopped.
- 2 tsp. minced garlic
- 1 ½ cups beef broth
- 3 tbsp. tomato paste
- 1 (4-inch) rosemary sprig
- 1 tsp. salt
- 1/2 tsp. ground black pepper

Instructions:
1. Heat the oil in the Foodi Multi-cooker. Turn on the Multi-cooker to the Sauté setting then wait for it to boil
2. Season the roast with the salt and pepper; brown it on both sides, turning once, about 10 minutes. Transfer the meat to a large bowl
3. Add the onion; cook, often stirring, until translucent, about 4 minutes. Add the garlic; cook, stirring constantly, until aromatic, about 30 seconds. Pour 1 ¼ cup broth in the Foodi Multi-cooker
4. Add the tomato paste and stir well until dissolved. Tuck the rosemary into the sauce and crumble in the mushrooms. Nestle the meat into the sauce, adding any juices in the bowl.
5. High pressure for 60 minutes. Close the lid and the pressure valve and then cook for 60 minutes.
6. To get 60 minutes' cook time, press *Pressure* button and use the Time Adjustment button to adjust the cook time to 60 minutes.
7. Pressure Release. Use the quick release method
8. Unlock and open the cooker; sprinkle the potatoes around the meat
9. High pressure for 30 minutes. Close the lid and the pressure valve again and cook for 30 minutes.
10. To get 30 minutes' cook time, press *Pressure* button.
11. Pressure Release. Use the natural release method 20 to 30 minutes
12. Finish the dish. Close crisping lid. Select "BROIL" and set time to 8 minutes. Check after 5 minutes, cooking for an additional 3 minutes if dish needs more browning.
13. Transfer the roast to a cutting board; set aside for 5 minutes. Discard the rosemary sprig
14. Slice the meat into 2-inch irregular chunks and serve these in bowls with the vegetables, mushrooms and broth. Serve

Red Beef Curry

(Prep + Cook Time: 1 hour 10 minutes | **Servings:** 6 to 8)

Ingredients:
- 8 oz. can bamboo shoots, drained
- 2 lb. flat iron steak (or chuck blade steak), cut into 2 inches by 1/2-inch strips
- 1 medium onion, peeled and sliced into 1/2-inch wedges
- 1 red bell pepper, cored, stemmed and sliced into 1/2-inch strips
- Cream from the top of a (13.5 oz.) can coconut milk
- 1 tbsp. vegetable oil
- 3 cloves garlic, crushed
- 1/2-inch piece of ginger, peeled and crushed
- 4 tbsp. red curry paste (a whole 4 oz. can)
- 1 tbsp. fish sauce (plus more to taste)
- 1 tbsp. soy sauce (plus more to taste)
- 1/2 cup chicken stock or water
- Juice of 1 lime
- Minced cilantro
- Minced basil (preferably Thai basil)
- Lime wedges
- Jasmine rice
- 1 tsp. Diamond Crystal kosher salt or 2 tsp. fine sea salt

Instructions:
1. Heat the vegetable oil in the Foodi Multi-cooker using the *Sauté* function, until the oil is shimmering. Stir in the onion, red bell pepper, garlic and ginger and sauté until the onion starts to soften about 3 minutes.
2. Fry the curry paste: Scoop the cream from the top of the can of coconut milk and add it to the pot, then stir in the curry paste. Cook, often stirring, until the curry paste darkens, about 5 minutes.
3. Sprinkle the beef with the kosher salt. Add the beef to the pot and stir to coat with curry paste. Stir in the rest of the can of coconut milk, bamboo shoots, chicken stock, fish sauce and soy sauce
4. High pressure for 12 minutes. Lock the lid on the Foodi Multi-cooker and then cook for 12 minutes
5. To get 12 minutes' cook time, press *Pressure* button and adjust the cook time
6. Pressure Release. Let the pressure to come down naturally for at least 20 minutes, then quick release any pressure left in the pot.
7. Finish the dish. Remove the lid from the Foodi Multi-cooker. Close crisping lid. Select "BROIL" and set time to 8 minutes. Check after 5 minutes, cooking for an additional 3 minutes if dish needs more browning
8. Stir in the lime juice and then taste the curry for seasoning, adding more fish sauce or brown sugar as needed.
9. Ladle the curry into bowls, sprinkle with minced cilantro and basil and serve with Jasmine rice. Serve and Enjoy!

Delightful Lamb Shanks with Pancetta

(Prep + Cook Time: 1 hour 15 minutes | **Servings:** 4)

Ingredients:
- 1 (28 oz.) can diced tomatoes, drained (about 3 ½ cups)
- 4 (12 oz.) lamb shanks
- 1 (6 oz.) pancetta chunk, chopped.
- 2 cups dry, light white wine, such as Sauvignon Blanc
- 1 oz. dried mushrooms, preferably porcini, crumbled
- 2 tbsp. olive oil
- 1 small yellow onion, chopped.
- 3 tbsp. packed celery leaves, minced
- 2 tbsp. minced chives
- 2 tbsp. all-purpose flour
- 1/2 tsp. ground black pepper

Instructions:
1. Heat the oil in the Foodi Multi-cooker, turned to the *Sauté* function. Add the pancetta and brown well, about 6 minutes, stirring often. Use a slotted spoon to transfer the pancetta to a large bowl

2. Add two of the shanks to the cooker; brown on all sides, turning occasionally, about 8 minutes. Transfer them to the bowl and repeat with the remaining shanks.
3. Add the onion to the pot; cook, often stirring, until softened, about 4 minutes. Stir in the tomatoes, dried mushroom crumbles, celery leaves and chives. Cook until bubbling, about minutes, stirring often
4. Whisk the wine, flour and pepper in a medium bowl until the flour dissolves; stir this mixture into the sauce in the pot. Cook until thickened and bubbling, about 1 minute
5. Return the shanks, pancetta and their juices to the cooker.
6. High pressure for 60 minutes. Close the lid and the pressure valve and then cook for 60 minutes
7. To get 60 minutes' cook time, press *Pressure* button and use the Time Adjustment button to adjust the cook time to 60 minutes
8. Turn off the Foodi Multi-cooker or unplug it, so it doesn't jump to its keep-warm setting
9. Pressure Release. Let its pressure return to normal naturally, 20 to 30 minutes
10. Finish the dish. Remove the lid from the Foodi Multi-cooker. Close crisping lid. Select *Air Crisp*, set temperature to 375°F and set time to 18 minutes. Check after 10 minutes, cooking for an additional 8 minutes if dish needs more browning.
11. Transfer a shank to each serving bowl. Skim any surface fat from the sauce with a flatware spoon. Ladle the sauce and vegetables over the lamb shanks

Chili Con Carne

(Prep + Cook Time: 45 Minutes | **Servings:** 4)

Ingredients:
- 1 lb. ground beef
- 4 oz. kidney beans; soaked overnight and drained
- 1 yellow onion; peeled and chopped
- 4 tbsp. extra virgin olive oil
- 8 oz. canned diced tomatoes
- 1 bay leaf
- 1 tsp. tomato paste
- 1 tbsp. chili powder
- 1/2 tsp. cumin
- 5 oz. water
- 2 garlic cloves; peeled and minced
- Salt and ground black pepper, to taste

Instructions:
1. Set the Foodi on *Sauté* mode, add 1 tbsp. oil and heat it up. Add the meat, brown for a few minutes and transfer to a bowl
2. Add the rest of the oil to the Foodi and also heat it up. Add the onion and garlic, stir, and cook for 3 minutes. Return the beef to pot, add the bay leaf, beans, tomato paste, tomatoes, chili powder, cumin, salt, pepper, and water, stir
3. Cover, and cook on the Pressure setting for 18 minutes. Release the pressure, uncover the Foodi, discard bay leaf, divide chili among bowls, and serve.

BBQ Baby Back Ribs

(Prep + Cook Time: 52 minutes | **Servings:** 4)

Ingredients:
- 1 (4 lb.) rack baby back ribs, cut into 2 or 3 sections to fit in the cooker
- 1/4 cup canned tomato paste
- 2 tbsp. cider vinegar
- 1 tbsp. sweet paprika
- 1/2 tbsp. coriander seeds
- 1/2 tbsp. fennel seeds
- 1 tsp. onion powder
- 1 tsp. dried thyme
- 1/2 tsp. ground allspice
- 1/4 tsp. celery seeds
- 1/2 tsp. salt
- 1/2 tsp. ground black pepper

Instructions:

1. Whisk the tomato paste, vinegar, paprika, coriander and fennel seeds, onion powder, thyme, allspice, salt, pepper and celery seeds with 3/4 cup water in an electric Multi-cooker until the tomato paste dissolves.
2. Add the ribs; toss to coat thoroughly and evenly in the sauce.
3. High pressure for 32 minutes. Lock the lid on the Foodi Multi-cooker and then cook for 32 minutes.
4. To get 32 minutes' cook time, press *Pressure* button and use the Time Adjustment button to adjust the cook time to 32 minutes
5. Pressure Release. Let the pressure to come down naturally for at least 15 minutes, then quick release any pressure left in the pot.
6. Finish the dish. Remove the lid from the Foodi Multi-cooker. Close crisping lid. Select *Air Crisp*, set temperature to 400°F and set time to 15 minutes. Check after 10 minutes, cooking for an additional 5 minutes if dish needs more browning.
7. Transfer the rib rack sections to a large rimmed baking sheet. Set the electric one to its browning function. Bring the sauce to a simmer. Cook, stirring occasionally, until the sauce has thickened, 3 to 5 minutes.
8. Position the oven rack 4 to 6 inches from the broiler; heat the broiler. Brush a light coating of the sauce onto the ribs, then broil until glazed and hot, 6 to 8 minutes, turning once
9. Slice the racks between the bones to make individual ribs. Serve with the extra sauce on the side

Beef Barley Mushroom Stew with Sour Cream

(**Prep + Cook Time:** 25 Minutes | **Servings:** 4)

Ingredients:
- 1/2 to 1 lb. stew beef cut into chunks (decide how much or how little meat you want)
- 1/2 cup uncooked pearl barley
- 1 cup sour cream (allow to stand at room temperature 15 minutes before adding.)
- 1 small yellow onion chopped
- 1 garlic clove minced
- 3 cups beef broth (unsalted or low salt preferred)
- 1 cup sliced fresh mushrooms
- 1/2 tsp. salt
- 1/8 tsp. black pepper; coarse ground
- 1 bay leaf
- 1 fresh thyme sprig (replace with dried if necessary)
- 1 tbsp. tomato paste
- 1 tbsp. Worcestershire sauce
- 1 tbsp. chopped parsley, chopped (optional)

Instructions:
1. Place all the ingredients into Foodi. Brown the beef in oil or butter together with the chopped onion using the *Sauté* mode
2. Lock the lid on the Foodi and then cook On High pressure for 35 minutes. To get 35 minutes' cook time, press *Pressure* button
3. Use Natural Pressure Release Method. Remove bay leaf and thyme spring. Taste and adjust salt and pepper accordingly.
4. Add 3/4 cup of sour cream and mix well
5. Use remaining sour cream to add a dollop on top before serving. Serve.

Chinese Beef Stew

(Prep + Cook Time: 42 Minutes | **Servings:** 4 to 6)

Ingredients:

- 2 lb beef round; cubed into one inch pieces
- 1/2 cup broth, preferably beef
- 2 medium onions sliced
- 1 to 2 Tsps. oil
- 1/2 tsp. sugar
- 2 tsps. Rice wine or sherry
- 1 tbsp. soy sauce
- 1 tbsp. Worcestershire sauce
- 1 can of mushrooms
- 1 to 2 tsps. Fresh ginger chopped finely
- 1 to 2 tsps. Cornstarch slurry if needed
- 2 tsps. Cornstarch
- Pinch of smoked Paprika
- 1 to 2 tsp. garlic powder
- Salt and pepper

Instructions:

1. Place sugar, rice wine and soy sauce into Power Pressure Cooker using the *Sauté* mode fry for 30 seconds.
2. Add beef broth and Worcestershire sauce, stir and close the lid
3. Lock the lid on the Foodi and then cook On High pressure for 30 minutes. To get 30 minutes' cook time, press *Pressure* button and use the *Time Adjustment* button to adjust the cook time to 30 minutes.
4. Leave on keep warm for 3 minutes.
5. Release pressure using the Natural Release Method.
6. when meat is done; add chopped ginger, mushrooms (optional) and more salt and pepper (if needed).
7. Sauté for another minute
8. Add cornstarch slurry to thicken to desired taste (if needed). Serve with rice and stir fried greens or fresh cut veggies.

Lamb, Rice, And Chickpea Casserole

(Prep + Cook Time: 40 Minutes | **Servings:** 6)

Ingredients:

- 2 lb. boneless leg of lamb, well trimmed and cut into 1½-inch pieces
- 1 (15 oz.) can chickpeas; drained and rinsed (about 1¾ cups)
- 1 cup long-grain white rice; such as white basmati rice
- 1 medium yellow onion, halved
- 2 tsp. whole allspice berries
- 2 tsp. whole cloves
- 1 tsp. black peppercorns
- 8 green cardamom pods
- 2 bay leaves
- 2 tbsp. olive oil
- 1 large yellow onion; halved and sliced into thin half-moons
- 1 tbsp. minced garlic
- 1/2 tsp. ground allspice
- 1/2 tsp. ground ginger
- Up to ½ tsp. saffron threads
- 1 tbsp. salt

Instructions:

1. Combine the lamb, onion halves, salt, allspice berries, cloves, peppercorns, cardamom pods, and bay leaves in the Foodi. Add enough tap water to cover all the ingredients
2. Lock the lid onto the pot. Set the Foodi to cook at High pressure for 15 minutes. To get 15 minutes' cook time, press *Pressure* button.
3. Use the Quick Pressure Release method.
4. Unlock and open the cooker. Cool for 5 minutes. Transfer the meat from the pot to a large bowl. Set a large bowl underneath a colander and drain the contents of the pot through the colander, catching the broth below. Discard the solids. Rinse out the cooker
5. Turn the Foodi to its *Sautéing/Browning* mode. Add the oil, then the onion. Cook, stirring often, until softened, about 4 minutes. Stir the garlic; cook for just 30 seconds or so. Add the chickpeas, rice, allspice, ginger, and saffron; stir over the heat for 1 minute. Return the meat and any juices to the pot; pour in 2¼ cups of the reserved cooking liquid and stir well

6. Lock the lid onto the pot again. Set the Foodi to cook at High pressure for 15 minutes. To get 15 minutes' cook time, press *Pressure* button.
7. Use the Quick Pressure Release method to return the pot's pressure to normal, but do not remove the lid. Set the cooker aside for 5 minutes. Unlock and open the cooker. Stir well before serving.

Beef Stuffed Peppers

(Prep + Cook Time: 40 minutes | **Servings:** 6)

Ingredients:
- 1 lb. uncooked ground beef
- 1 tbsp. garlic powder
- 4 large bell peppers, seeds and stems removed, tops chopped.
- 1 tsp. black pepper
- 3 tbsp. paprika
- 1 ½ tsp. ground cumin
- 1 cup brown rice
- 1 cup chicken stock
- 1/4 cup dry white wine
- 1 cup whole cashews, chopped.
- 1 tbsp. ground cinnamon
- 1/2 tsp. ground cloves
- 1 ½ tbsp. kosher salt, divided.
- 1 small onion, peeled, finely chopped.
- 1/2 cup fresh parsley, chopped.

Instructions:
1. In a small mixing bowl, stir together the garlic powder, black pepper, cinnamon, cloves, 1 ½ tsp. salt, paprika, and cumin; set aside
2. Add beef, onion, rice, stock, wine, and 2 tbsp. spice mix to the pot, breaking apart meat. Assemble pressure lid, making sure the PRESSURE RELEASE valve is in the SEAL position. Select PRESSURE and set to HIGH. Set time to 15 minutes. Select START/STOP to begin.
3. When pressure cooking is complete, naturally release the pressure for 10 minutes, then quick release any remaining pressure by moving the PRESSURE RELEASE valve to the VENT position. Carefully remove lid when unit has finished releasing pressure
4. Stir meat mixture, then add chopped pepper tops, cashews, fresh parsley, and remaining salt. Using a rubber or wooden spoon, stuff mixture into the 4 bell peppers.
5. Place stuffed peppers in the pot. Close crisping lid. Select BAKE/ROAST, set temperature to 360°F, and set time to 15 minutes. Select START/STOP to begin. When cooking is complete, serve immediately

Special Lamb Shanks Provençal

(Prep + Cook Time: 1 hour 10 minutes | **Servings:** 5 to 6)

Ingredients:
- 2 large (12 oz.) lamb shanks
- 2 medium plum tomatoes, coarsely chopped. or 1/2 cup diced canned tomatoes, drained
- 1/2 cup dry white wine or dry white vermouth
- 1 cup Chicken Stock or low sodium broth
- Freshly ground black pepper
- 1 tbsp. olive oil
- 1 cup sliced onion
- 2 garlic cloves, finely minced
- 1 bay leaf
- 1/3 cup pitted Kalamata olives
- 2 tbsp. coarsely chopped fresh parsley
- 1 tsp. kosher salt, plus additional for seasoning
- 1 lemon, sliced very thin

Instructions:
1. Sprinkle the lamb shanks with 1 tsp. of kosher salt and several grinds of pepper. The longer ahead of the cooking time you can do this the better.
2. Cover and let sit for 20 minutes to 2 hours at room temperature or refrigerate for up to 24 hours
3. Heat the vegetable oil in the Foodi Multi-cooker using the *Sauté* function, until the oil is shimmering and flows like water. Add the lamb shanks and brown on all sides, about 6 minutes' total.

4. Remove them to a plate. Add the onion and garlic and sprinkle with a pinch or two of kosher salt. Cook, stirring, for about 3 minutes or until the onions just begin to brown. Add the tomatoes and cook until most of their liquid evaporates.
5. Add the white wine and stir, scraping up the browned bits from the bottom of the cooker
6. Cook for 2 to 3 minutes or until the wine reduces by about half; then add the Chicken Stock and bay leaf. Return the lamb shanks to the cooker and place the lemon slices over them.
7. High pressure for 40 minutes. Lock the lid on the Foodi Multi-cooker and then cook for 40 minutes.
8. To get 40 minutes' cook time, press *Pressure* button and adjust the time.
9. Pressure Release. After cooking, use the natural method to release pressure
10. Finish the dish. Remove the lid from the Foodi Multi-cooker. Close crisping lid. Select *Air Crisp*, set temperature to 375°F and set time to 18 minutes. Check after 10 minutes, cooking for an additional 8 minutes if dish needs more browning
11. Transfer the lamb to a cutting board or plate and tent it with aluminum foil. Strain the sauce into a fat separator and let it rest until the fat rises to the surface
12. If you don't have a fat separator, let the sauce sit for a few minutes, then spoon or blot off any excess fat from the top and discard.
13. Pour the defatted sauce back into the cooker along with the strained vegetables. If you want a thicker sauce, simmer the liquid for about 5 minutes or until it reaches the desired consistency
14. Stir in the olives and parsley. Place the shanks in shallow bowls, pour the sauce and vegetables over the lamb and serve
15. Lamb shanks benefit from salting in advance, which makes them much more flavorful and helps them brown beautifully. If you have the time, salt them up to 24 hours in advance. Place them on a tray and refrigerate, covered loosely with foil.

Mouthwatering Beef Stew

(Prep + Cook Time: 25 minutes | **Servings:** 4)

Ingredients:
- 1 ½ lb. lean ground beef (about 93% lean)
- 1 large sweet potato (about 1 lb.), peeled and shredded through the large holes of a box grater
- 1 tbsp. olive oil
- 1 large yellow onion, chopped.
- 1 tsp. ground cinnamon
- 1 tsp. ground cumin
- 1/2 tsp. dried sage
- 1/2 tsp. dried oregano
- 2 ½ cups beef broth
- 2 tbsp. yellow cornmeal
- 2 tbsp. honey
- 1/2 tsp. salt
- 1/2 tsp. ground black pepper

Instructions:
1. Heat the oil in the Foodi Multi-cooker turned to the Sauté function. Crumble in the ground beef; cook, stirring occasionally, until it loses its raw color and browns a bit, about 5 minutes
2. Add the onion; cook, often stirring, until softened, about 3 minutes
3. Stir in the sweet potato, cinnamon, cumin, sage, oregano, salt and pepper
4. Cook for 1 minute, stirring constantly. Stir in the cornmeal and honey; cook for 1 minute, often stirring, to dissolve the cornmeal. Stir in the broth.
5. High pressure for 5 minutes. Lock the lid on the Foodi Multi-cooker and then cook for 5 minutes.
6. To get 5 minutes' cook time, press *Pressure* button and use the Time Adjustment button to adjust the cook time to 5 minutes
7. Pressure Release. Use the quick release method to drop the pot's pressure to normal.
8. Finish the dish. Remove the lid from the Foodi Multi-cooker. Close crisping lid. Select *Air Crisp*, set temperature to 390°F and set time to 20 minutes.
9. Check after 15 minutes, cooking for an additional 15 minutes if dish needs more browning. Stir well and set aside, loosely covered, for 5 minutes before serving.

Beef Stew

(Prep + Cook Time: 1 hour 25 minutes | **Servings:** 4 to 6)

Ingredients:
- 2 lb. beef stew meat
- 5 scrubbed medium-sized potatoes chopped.
- 2 packets McCormick Stew Seasoning (or stew seasoning of your choice for 2 lb. meat)
- 1 cup raw green beans
- 1 cup carrots chopped.
- 1 onion chopped
- 4 stalks celery
- 4 cups water

Instructions:
1. Add the beef Stew meet, McCormick Stew Seasoning Packets and the water to the Foodi Multi-cooker
2. High pressure for 45 minutes. Lock the lid on the Foodi Multi-cooker and then cook for 45 minutes
3. To get 45 minutes' cook time, press *Pressure* button and use the adjust button to adjust the cook time to 45 minutes
4. Pressure Release. Release the pressure using Natural Release
5. Remove the lid and stir.
6. Add vegetables below the maximum fill line, put the lid back on
7. High pressure for 15 minutes. Lock the lid on the Foodi Multi-cooker and cook for 15 minutes
8. To get 15 minutes' cook time, press *Pressure* button and then adjust the time
9. Pressure Release. Use Natural Release Method. Serve and enjoy

Lamb with Enchilada Sauce

(Prep + Cook Time: 1 hour 10 minutes | **Servings:** 3 to 4)

Ingredients:
- 3 lamb shoulder
- 1 (19 oz. can) Old El Paso Enchilada sauce
- 1 Spanish onion
- Cilantro, chopped without the stems
- Corn tortillas (3 to 4 per person)
- 3 garlic cloves, minced
- 2 tbsp. oil
- Salt to taste
- Limes cut into 8ths
- Chipotle-style rice
- Black beans or refried beans

Instructions:
1. Marinate lamb overnight in Old El Paso Enchilada sauce (mild, medium or hot)
2. Turn on the Foodi Multi-cooker to *Sauté* mode. Add oil. Put in the onions and cook until soft, add garlic and cook for 1 minute.
3. Add the lamb and marinade wait until boil
4. High pressure for 45 minutes. Lock the lid on the Foodi Multi-cooker and then cook for 45 minutes.
5. To get 45 minutes' cook time, press *Pressure* button and use the adjust button to adjust the cook time to 45 minutes.
6. Pressure Release. Let the pressure to come down naturally for at least 15 minutes, then quick release any pressure left in the pot
7. Finish the dish. Remove the lid from the Foodi Multi-cooker. Close crisping lid. Select *Air Crisp*, set temperature to 375°F and set time to 15 minutes. Check after 10 minutes, cooking for an additional 5 minutes if dish needs more browning
8. Cut the limes, heat the beans put the hot rice into a serving bowl.
9. Set the Lamb aside. Ladle a generous amount of sauce over it
10. Heat up 3 to 4 corn tortillas. Put the lamb mixture onto a soft warm corn tortilla, sprinkle on cilantro, then squeeze with lime juice. Serve and Enjoy!

Lamb and Bulgur-Stuffed Acorn Squash

(Prep + Cook Time: 40 Minutes | **Servings:** 2)

Ingredients:
- 1 lb. ground lamb
- 1 large egg white, lightly beaten
- 1 medium acorn squash; halved and seeded
- 1 cup water; for steaming
- 1/2 cup finely chopped fresh parsley
- 1/4 cup minced fresh mint
- 1/2 cup medium or coarse bulgur wheat
- 1 tbsp. olive oil
- 1/2 cup chopped onion
- 2 tbsp. minced red or green bell pepper
- 1 tbsp. minced garlic
- 2 tsp. kosher salt; plus, additional for seasoning
- 2 tsp. ground cumin
- 1/2 tsp. ground coriander

Instructions:
1. In a medium bowl, soak the bulgur wheat in very hot tap water for about 15 minutes, or until softened but still slightly chewy
2. Set the Foodi to *Sautéing/Browning* heat the olive oil until it shimmers and flows like water. Add the onion, red bell pepper, and garlic, and sprinkle with a pinch or two of kosher salt. Cook, stirring, for about 2 minutes, or until the vegetables soften.
3. Drain the bulgur, and return it to the bowl. Transfer the cooked vegetables to the bowl. Add the lamb, 2 tsp. of kosher salt, and the cumin, coriander, parsley, mint, and egg white. Stir just to combine; don't overwork the meat, or it may become tough
4. Make sure the two squash halves will sit level and fit in the Foodi in one layer, trimming if necessary. Evenly divide the meat mixture and stuff it into the squash halves.
5. Add the water to the Foodi, and insert the steamer basket or trivet
6. Place the squash halves on the steamer insert.
7. Lock the lid in place, Cook at High pressure for 20 minutes. To get 20 minutes' cook time, press *Pressure* button.
8. Use the Quick Pressure Release method. Unlock and remove the lid. Using a large slotted spatula, carefully remove the squash halves (they'll be quite soft), and serve
9. If you can't find acorn squash, or simply don't like it, you can form the meat mixture into a meatloaf and cook it separately. Use the foil sling as described in the Tomato-Glazed Meatloaf recipe to transfer it in and out of the cooker

Beef Ribs

(Prep + Cook Time: 1 hour 20 minutes | **Servings:** 4 to 6)

Ingredients:
- 4 lb. beef ribs (about 8), ask the butcher to saw or chop them in half
- 1/4 cup rice vinegar (or white balsamic vinegar)
- 1 knob fresh ginger, peeled and finely chopped.
- 2/3 cup salt-free (homemade) beef stock
- 2 cloves garlic, peeled and smashed
- 1 pinch red pepper flakes
- 1/3 cup raw sugar
- 1 tbsp. sesame oil
- 2/3 cup soy sauce
- 1 to 2 tbsp. water
- 2 tbsp. cornstarch

Instructions:
1. Turn on the Foodi Multi-cooker to *Sauté* mode. Add sesame oil garlic, ginger and red pepper flakes and sauté for a minute.
2. Then, de-glaze with vinegar, mix-in the sugar, soy sauce and beef stock - mix well
3. Add the ribs to the Foodi Multi-cooker coating them with the mixture
4. High pressure for 60 minutes. Close and lock the lid of the Foodi Multi-cooker, cook at high pressure for 60 minutes

5. To get 60 minutes' cook time, press *Pressure* button and use the Time Adjustment button to adjust the cook time to 60 minutes
6. Pressure Release. Use the Natural release method (20 minutes)
7. Finish the dish. Remove the lid from the Foodi Multi-cooker. Close crisping lid. Select "BROIL" and set time to 10 minutes. Check after 6 minutes, cooking for an additional 4 minutes if dish needs more browning
8. Make a slurry with the cornstarch and water and then mix into the rib cooking liquid in the Foodi Multi-cooker. *Sauté* the mixture until it reaches the desired consistency. Serve and Enjoy!

Moroccan Lamb and Couscous Stew

(Prep + Cook Time: 35 Minutes | **Servings:** 4 to 6)

Ingredients:
- 2 lb. lamb shoulder, cut into 1 1/2-inch (4 cm) pieces
- 1 medium yellow onion, thinly sliced
- 6 medium carrots; cut into 3-inch (7.5 cm) sticks
- 8 dried apricots; coarsely chopped
- 1/4 cup roasted almonds, coarsely chopped
- 3/4 cup couscous
- 1/4 cup chopped fresh cilantro
- 1 tsp. kosher salt
- 1/2 tsp. freshly ground black pepper
- 3 cloves garlic; finely chopped
- 1 tbsp. extra-virgin olive oil
- 2 tsp. paprika
- 1 ½ tsp. ground cumin
- 1/2 tsp. ground cinnamon
- 1 tbsp. finely grated fresh ginger
- 1/2 cup water
- 1 lemon

Instructions:
1. Turn the Foodi on to (Sauté). Heat the olive oil. Season the lamb with the salt and pepper. In batches, cook the lamb until browned on all sides, about 5 minutes. Transfer to a plate
2. Add the onion to the pot and cook, stirring, for 2 minutes. Add the garlic, paprika, cumin, and cinnamon, and cook, stirring, for 1 minute. Add the carrots, ginger, and water. Using a vegetable peeler, peel 3 strips of lemon zest from the lemon and add to the pot. Add the lamb
3. Lock the lid in place, Cook at High pressure for 25 minutes. To get 25 minutes' cook time, press *Pressure* button and use the *Time Adjustment* button to adjust the cook time to 25 minutes
4. Use the "Quick Release" method to vent the steam, then open the lid. Stir in the couscous and apricots. Lock the lid and let stand for 10 minutes.

Tex-Mex Meatloaf Recipe

(Prep + Cook Time: 45 minutes | **Servings:** 8)

Ingredients:
- 1 lb. uncooked ground beef
- 1 tbsp. garlic powder
- 2 tsp. ground cumin
- 2 tsp. chili powder
- 1 tsp. cayenne pepper
- 1 egg
- 1 bell pepper, diced
- 2 tsp. kosher salt
- 1/4 cup fresh cilantro leaves
- 1/4 barbecue sauce, divided.
- 1/2 jalapeño pepper, seeds removed, minced
- 1 small onion, peeled, diced
- 3 corn tortillas, roughly chopped.
- 1 cup water
- 1 cup corn chips, crushed

Instructions:
1. Stir together beef, egg, bell pepper, jalapeño pepper, onion, tortillas, spices, cilantro, and tbsp. barbecue sauce in a large mixing bowl.
2. Place meat mixture in the 8 ½-inch loaf pan and cover tightly with aluminum foil

3. Pour water into pot. Place the loaf pan on the reversible rack, making sure rack is in the lower position. Place rack with pan in pot. Assemble the pressure lid, making sure the PRESSURE RELEASE valve is in the SEAL position
4. Select PRESSURE and set to HIGH. Set time to 15 minutes. Select START/STOP to begin
5. When pressure cooking is complete, quick release the pressure by moving the PRESSURE RELEASE valve to the VENT position. Carefully remove lid when unit has finished releasing pressure
6. Carefully remove foil from loaf pan and close crisping lid. Select BAKE/ROAST, set temperature to 360°F, and set time to 15 minutes. Select START/STOP to begin.
7. While the meatloaf is cooking, stir together the crushed corn chips and 2 tbsp. barbecue sauce in a bowl.
8. After 7 minutes, open lid and top meatloaf with the corn chip mixture. Close lid to resume cooking. When cooking is complete, remove meatloaf from pot and allow to cool for 10 minutes before serving

Sausage and Chard Pasta Sauce

(**Prep + Cook Time:** 18 minutes | **Servings:** 5 to 6)

Ingredients:
- 1 lb. mild Italian pork sausage meat, any casings removed
- 3 small hot chiles, such as cherry peppers or Anaheim chiles, stemmed, seeded and chopped.
- 1 medium red onion, chopped.
- 1/2 cup dry red wine, such as Syrah
- 1/2 cup canned tomato paste
- 1/4 cup chicken broth
- 4 cups stemmed and chopped Swiss chard
- 2 tbsp. olive oil
- 1 tbsp. minced garlic
- 1 tbsp. dried basil
- 2 tsp. dried oregano

Instructions:
1. Heat the oil in a Foodi Multi-cooker, turned to the sauté function
2. Add the onion and cook, often stirring, until softened, about 4 minutes. Add the chiles and garlic; cook until aromatic, stirring all the while, about 1 minute.
3. Crumble in the sausage meat, breaking up any clumps with a wooden spoon.
4. Stir until it loses its raw color. Stir in the wine, tomato paste, broth, basil and oregano until the tomato paste dissolves. Add the chard and stir well.
5. High pressure for 6 minutes. Lock the lid onto the cooker, set the machine's timer to cook at high pressure for 6 minutes
6. To get 6 minutes' cook time, press the *Pressure* button and use the Time Adjustment button to adjust the cook time to 6 minutes
7. Pressure Release. Use the quick release method to drop the pressure back to normal.
8. Finish the dish. Remove the lid from the Foodi Multi-cooker. Close crisping lid. Select "BROIL" and set time to 5 minutes
9. Check after 4 minutes, cooking for an additional 4 minutes if dish needs more browning. Stir well before serving

Garlic Teriyaki Beef

(Prep + Cook Time: 55 Minutes | **Servings:** 4)

Ingredients:
- 2 cloves garlic, finely chopped

For the teriyaki sauce:
- 1/4 cup maple syrup; preferably organic grade B or higher
- 1/4 cup coconut aminos OR soy sauce instead
- 1 piece (2 lb.) flank steak
- 2 tbsp. fish sauce
- 1 tbsp. raw honey
- 1 ½ tsp. ground or fresh ginger, optional

Instructions:
1. Slice the flank steak into 1/2-inch strips
2. In a bowl, put all of the teriyaki sauce and mix until combined
3. Put the steak strips and the sauce in the Foodi; there is no need to brown the meat. Add garlic. Cover and lock the lid.
4. Press the *Pressure* key, set the pressure to HIGH, and set the timer for 40 minutes.
5. When the Foodi timer beeps, turn the steam valve to quick release the pressure. Unlock and carefully open the lid. Serve and enjoy!

Delicious Lamb Casserole

(Prep + Cook Time: 1 hour 5 minutes | **Servings:** 6 to 8)

Ingredients:
- 1-lb. rack of lamb
- 1 lb. of baby potatoes
- 2 carrots
- 1 large onion
- 2 stalks of celery
- 2 medium size tomatoes
- 1 to 2 tsp. of salt depending on the salt content of the chicken stock
- 2 cups of chicken stock
- 2 tsp. of Paprika
- 2 tbsp. of ketchup
- 2 tsp. of cumin powder
- 3 tbsp. of sherry or red wine
- A splash of beer if you have one in hand
- 3 to 4 large cloves of garlic
- A pinch of dried rosemary
- A pinch of dried oregano leaves

Instructions:
1. Dice the tomatoes, onion and garlic, cut potatoes and carrots, cut the rack of lamb into two halves. Put all the ingredients, in the Foodi Multi-cooker.
2. High pressure for 35 minutes. Lock the lid on the Foodi Multi-cooker and then cook for 35 minutes.
3. To get 35 minutes' cook time, press *Pressure* button and adjust the time
4. Pressure Release. Use Natural-Release Method for 10 minutes and then Quick Release
5. Remove the lid from the Foodi Multi-cooker. Close crisping lid. Select *Air Crisp*, set temperature to 400°F and set time to 15 minutes.
6. Check after 10 minutes, cooking for an additional 5 minutes if dish needs more browning. Serve and Enjoy!

Easy Short Ribs and Root Vegetables

(Prep + Cook Time: 1 hour 15 minutes | **Servings:** 6)

Ingredients:
- 6 uncooked bone-in beef short ribs (about 3 lb.), trimmed of excess fat and silver skin
- 2 tsp. kosher salt, divided.
- 3 carrots, peeled, cut in 1-inch pieces
- 3 parsnips, peeled, cut in 1-inch pieces
- 2 tsp. black pepper, divided.
- 3 cloves garlic, peeled, minced
- 1 onion, peeled, chopped.
- 1/4 cup Marsala wine
- 1/4 cup beef broth
- 2 tbsp. brown sugar
- 2 tbsp. fresh thyme, minced, divided.
- 2 tbsp. olive oil, divided.
- 1 cup pearl onions
- 1/4 cup fresh parsley, minced

Instructions:
1. Season short ribs on all sides with 1 tsp. salt and 1 tsp. pepper. Select SEAR/SAUTÉ and set to HIGH. Select START/STOP to begin. Heat 1 tbsp. oil in the pot for 3 minutes.
2. After 3 minutes, add short ribs to pot and cook until browned on all sides, about 10 minutes
3. Add onion, wine, broth, brown sugar, garlic, 1 tbsp. thyme, 1/2 tsp. salt, and 1/2 tsp. pepper to pot. Assemble pressure lid, making sure the PRESSURE RELEASE valve is in the SEAL position. Select PRESSURE and set to HIGH. Set time to 40 minutes. Select START/STOP to begin.
4. Toss carrots, parsnips, and pearl onions with remaining oil, thyme, salt, and pepper
5. When pressure cooking is complete, quick release the pressure by moving the PRESSURE RELEASE valve to the VENT position. Carefully remove lid when unit has finished releasing pressure
6. Place the reversible rack inside pot over ribs, making sure rack is in the higher position. Place vegetable mixture on rack. Close crisping lid. Select BAKE/ROAST, set temperature to 350°F, and set time to 15 minutes. Select START/STOP to begin
7. Once vegetables are tender and roasted, transfer them and the ribs to a serving tray and tent loosely with aluminum foil to keep warm.
8. Select SEAR/SAUTÉ and set to HIGH. Bring liquid in pot to simmer for 5 minutes. Transfer to bowl and let sit for 2 minutes, then spoon off top layer of fat. Stir in parsley. When cooking is complete, serve sauce with vegetables and ribs

Teriyaki Beef

(Prep + Cook Time: 45 Minutes | **Servings:** 4 to 6)

Ingredients:
- 1 lb. stewing beef cubes
- 1 tbsp. cornstarch
- 1 cup water; plus 1 tbsp.
- 1/4 cup sodium-reduced soy sauce
- 2 green onions; sliced
- 1 small onion, sliced into sticks
- 1 small red pepper, sliced
- 1 small yellow pepper, sliced
- 3 cloves garlic; crushed
- 2 tbsp. brown sugar
- 1/2 tsp. pepper, plus more
- 1 tbsp. extra virgin olive oil
- 1-inch fresh ginger; grated
- Salt to taste

Instructions:
1. Whisk together the 1 cup of water, the soy sauce, brown sugar, garlic, ginger and 1/2 tsp. pepper (no salt); set aside
2. Set your Foodi to *Sauté* and add in the olive oil, when it's hot add the onion and peppers; season with salt and pepper.
3. Sauté for 2 to 3 minutes, just until the veggies start to soften and then set the veggies aside in a bowl.
4. Add the beef to the Foodi to brown (with the setting still on *Sauté*) working in batches if needed; season with salt and pepper
5. Give the soy mixture a quick mix and then add it to the pot, gently scraping the bottom of the pot to release any yummy bits.

6. Cover with the lid and lock it. Select *Pressure* and cook at HIGH pressure for 45 minutes. Use a quick release
7. Whisk together the 1 tbsp. water and the cornstarch until completely smooth, it should look like white water.
8. Take the lid off the pot, set the pot back to *Sauté* and when the liquid comes to a boil add in the cornstarch/water slurry; let it bubble until the sauce thickens.
9. Turn the pot off and add in the reserved peppers, onion and the green onion; mix well.
10. Taste and adjust seasoning before serving. Serve on your favorite rice or noodles

Notes: Use any combination of peppers you'd like. Feel free to add in more veggies of your choosing

Mini Pork Roast

(Prep + Cook Time: 35 Minutes | **Servings:** 2)

Ingredients:
- Small pork loin (approximately 1 lb), sprinkled with salt and pepper
- 1 cup stock (veggie or chicken)
- 1/2 cup apple juice
- 1 apple; cut into 5 pieces
- Olive oil

Instructions:
1. Pour the apple juice and stock into the Pressure Cooker. Place the apple chunks and pork loin into the pot (it will sit in the liquid)
2. Secure the lid onto the pot and press the *Pressure* button, adjust the time to 20 minutes and cook on High pressure
3. Once the pot beeps, Quick Pressure Release the pressure and remove the lid.
4. Place the pork loin onto a board to rest as you heat a skillet or fry pan with a drizzle of oil.
5. Once the fry pan is very hot, place the cooked pork loin into the pan and fry on all sides for a minute or so, or until crispy and golden.
6. You can utilize the leftover liquid in the Pressure Cooker by pressing the SAUTÉ button and simmering the liquid until reduced (on LOW heat)
7. Serve with your favorite vegetables and a drizzle of reduced liquid. Any leftover meat will make an amazing sandwich!

Meatballs with Artichokes

(Prep + Cook Time: 25 Minutes | **Servings:** 4)

Ingredients:
- 1½ lb. lean ground beef (preferably 93% lean)
- 1 medium shallot; peeled and shredded through the large holes of a box grater
- 1 (28 oz.) can diced tomatoes (about 3½ cups)
- 1 (9 oz.) box frozen artichoke heart quarters; thawed (about 2 cups)
- 1/2 cup rosé wine; such as Bandol
- 1/4 cup loosely packed fresh basil leaves, minced
- 2 tbsp. loosely packed fresh oregano leaves, minced
- 1/2 cup dried orzo
- 1 tbsp. minced fresh dill fronds
- 2 tsp. finely grated lemon zest
- 1 tsp. minced garlic
- 1 large egg; at room temperature
- 2 tbsp. olive oil
- 1/2 tsp. salt
- 1/2 tsp. ground black pepper

Instructions:
1. Mix the ground beef, orzo, shallot, dill, lemon zest, garlic, and egg in a large bowl until uniform. Form into twelve 2-inch balls.
2. Heat the oil in the Foodi set to the *Sautéing/Browning* function. Add the meatballs, just as many as will fit without crowding. Brown on all sides, turning occasionally, about 8 minutes. Transfer to a bowl and repeat with the rest of the meatballs

3. Add the tomatoes, artichokes, wine, basil, oregano, salt, and pepper to the cooker; stir well to get any browned bits off the bottom of the pot. Return the meatballs and their juices to the sauce.
4. Lock the lid onto the pot. Switch the Foodi to cook at High pressure for 8 minutes. To get 8 minutes' cook time, press *Pressure* button and use the COOK *Time Adjustment* button to adjust the cook time to 8 minutes
5. Use the Quick Pressure Release method to drop the pot's pressure back to normal.
6. Unlock and open the pot. Stir gently before scooping the meatballs into serving bowls; ladle the sauce over them.

Mexican Beef

(**Prep + Cook Time:** 45 Minutes | **Servings:** 4)

Ingredients:
- 2½ lb. boneless beef short ribs, beef brisket, or beef chuck roast cut into 1½- to 2-inch cubes
- 1/2 cup minced cilantro (optional)
- 2 radishes; thinly sliced (optional)
- 6 garlic cloves; peeled and smashed
- 1/2 cup roasted tomato salsa
- 1/2 cup bone broth
- 1 tbsp. chili powder
- 1½ tsp. kosher salt (Diamond Crystal brand)
- 1 tbsp. ghee or fat of choice
- 1 medium onion; thinly sliced
- 1 tbsp. tomato paste
- 1/2 tsp. Red Boat Fish Sauce
- Freshly ground black pepper

Instructions:
1. Combine cubed beef, chili powder, and salt in a large bowl
2. Set the Foodi to the *Sauté* Function, and add the ghee to the cooking insert. Once the fat's melted, add the onions and sauté until translucent.
3. Stir in the tomato paste and garlic, and cook for 30 seconds or until fragrant
4. Toss in the seasoned beef and pour in the salsa, stock, and fish sauce.
5. Lock the lid on the Foodi, bring it up to High pressure, and cook at High pressure for 40 minutes. Press the *Pressure* button to switch to the pressure-cooking mode, 40 Minutes.
6. When the stew is finished cooking, the Foodi will switch automatically to a *Keep Warm* mode.
7. Use the Natural Pressure Release Method for 15 minutes, then quick release the pressure
8. Unlock the lid and season to taste with salt and pepper. Serve.

Poultry

Chicken Leg Quarters with Rosemary

(Prep + Cook Time: 23 Minutes | **Servings:** 4 to 6)

Ingredients:
- 8 medium garlic cloves
- 4 chicken leg-and-thigh quarters (3 to 3½ lb. total weight); skin removed
- 3/4 cup chicken broth
- 2 tbsp. olive oil
- 2 tbsp. loosely packed fresh rosemary leaves; minced
- 1 tbsp. mild paprika
- 1 tsp. salt
- 1/2 tsp. ground black pepper

Instructions:
1. Make a paste from the olive oil, rosemary, paprika, salt, and pepper by stirring it in a small bowl with a fork. Rub this paste into the quarters
2. Pour the broth into the Foodi; set the quarters in the pot, overlapping only as necessary. Tuck the garlic cloves around the quarters
3. Lock the lid onto the pot. Set the Foodi to cook at High pressure for 18 minutes. To get 18 minutes' cook time, press the *Pressure* button and use the *Time Adjustment* button to adjust the cook time to 18 minutes.
4. Use the Natural Pressure Release method, 12 to 15 minutes. Unlock and open the pot. Transfer the chicken to serving plates; stir the sauce and spoon over the meat

Moroccan Chicken

(Prep + Cook Time: 35 Minutes | **Servings:** 4)

Ingredients:
- 6 chicken thighs
- 2 tbsp. extra virgin olive oil
- 10 cardamom pods
- 1 cup green olives
- 1 cup chicken stock
- 1/4 cup dried cranberries
- 1/2 cup parsley; diced
- 2 bay leaves
- 1/2 tsp. coriander
- 1 tsp. cloves
- 1/2 tsp. cumin
- 1/2 tsp. ground ginger
- 1/2 tsp. turmeric
- 1/2 tsp. ground cinnamon
- 1 tsp. paprika
- 2 yellow onions; peeled and chopped
- 2 tbsp. tomato paste
- 5 garlic cloves; peeled and chopped
- 1/4 cup white wine
- Juice of 1 lemon

Instructions:
1. In a bowl, mix the bay leaf with the cardamom, cloves, coriander, ginger, cumin, cinnamon, turmeric, and paprika and stir. Set the Foodi on *Sauté* mode, add the oil and heat up
2. Add the chicken thighs, brown for a few minutes, and transfer to a plate. Add the onion to the Foodi, stir, and cook for 4 minutes. Add the garlic, stir and cook for 1 minute. Add the wine, tomato paste, and spices from the bowl, stock, and chicken. Stir
3. Cover and cook on the "Poultry" setting for 15 minutes. Release the pressure, discard bay leaf, cardamom, and cloves, add the olives, cranberries, lemon juice, and parsley, stir, divide the chicken mixture among plates, and serve.

Cacciatore Chicken

(Prep + Cook Time: 25 Minutes | **Servings:** 4)

Ingredients:
- 8 chicken drumsticks
- 1 bay leaf
- 1 yellow onion; peeled chopped
- 1 cup chicken stock
- 28 oz. canned crushed tomatoes
- 1 tsp. dried oregano
- 1/2 cup black olives; pitted and sliced
- 1 tsp. garlic powder
- Salt, to taste

Instructions:
1. Set the Foodi on *Sauté* mode, add the stock, bay leaf, and salt and stir. Add the chicken, garlic powder, onion, oregano, and crushed tomatoes, stir
2. Cover the Foodi and cook on the "Poultry" setting for 15 minutes. Release the pressure naturally, uncover the Foodi, discard the bay leaf, divide the cacciatore chicken among plates, drizzle cooking liquid on top, sprinkle with the olives, and serve

Lemon and Garlic Chicken

(Prep + Cook Time: 25 Minutes | **Servings:** 4)

Ingredients:
- 1 lemon, large-sized, juiced, or more to taste
- 1 to 2 lb. chicken; thighs or breasts
- 1/2 cup chicken broth; organic or homemade
- 5 garlic cloves; minced
- 1/4 cup white cooking wine
- 3 to 4 tsp. arrowroot flour; or more
- 1 onion, diced
- 1 tbsp. avocado oil; OR ghee, OR lard
- 1 tsp. dried parsley
- 1 tsp. sea salt
- 1/4 tsp. paprika

Instructions:
1. Press the *Sauté* key of the Foodi. Put the cooking fat and the diced onion into the pot
2. Cook for about 5 minutes or until the onions are softened, or you can cook until they begin to brown.
3. Except for the arrowroot flour, add the rest of the ingredients into the pot. Cover and lock the lid.
4. Press the "POULTRY" key let cook on preset cooking time.
5. When the Foodi timer beeps, press the *Cancel* key and unplug the Foodi
6. Turn the steam valve to quick release the pressure. Unlock and carefully open the lid
7. If you want a thick sauce, remove about 1/4 cup of the sauce, add the arrowroot flour in the cup and stir to make slurry.
8. Pour the slurry back into the pot. Stir until thicken. Serve immediately.

Sesame Ginger Chicken

(Prep + Cook Time: 35 Minutes | **Servings:** 6)

Ingredients:
- 1½ lb. boneless, skinless chicken thighs, cut into large pieces
- 2 tbsp. soy sauce
- 1 tbsp. minced garlic
- 1 tbsp. Truvia
- 1 tbsp. rice vinegar
- 1 tbsp. sesame oil
- 1 tbsp. minced fresh ginger

Instructions:
1. Put the chicken in a heatproof bowl. Add the soy sauce, sesame oil, ginger, garlic, Truvia, and vinegar. Stir to coat the chicken. Cover the bowl with aluminum foil or a silicone lid. Pour 2 cups of water into the inner cooking pot of the Pressure Cooker, then place a trivet in the pot. Place the bowl on the trivet

2. Lock the lid into place. Pressure Cook and adjust the pressure to High. Cook for 10 minutes. When the cooking is complete, let the pressure release naturally for 10 minutes, then Quick Pressure Release any remaining pressure. Unlock the lid
3. Remove the chicken and shred it, then mix it back in with the liquid in the bowl. Serve as is, over zoodles, or in a salad, as shown on the opposite page, with crushed peanuts and Easy Asian Peanut Dressing.

Chinese Chicken and Rice

(Prep + Cook Time: 60 Minutes | **Servings:** 4)

Ingredients:
- 6 to 8 chicken drumsticks; marinated
- 3 cups jasmine rice rinsed
- 6 shiitake mushrooms dried; marinated
- Ginger shredded, for garnish
- Green onions sliced; for garnish
- 1 tsp. salt
- 1½ cups water

Marinade:
- 1 tsp. dark soy sauce
- 1 tbsp. light soy sauce
- 1/2 tsp. sugar
- 1/2 tsp. corn starch
- 1 tsp. Shaoxing rice wine
- 1 tbsp. Ginger shredded
- Dash white pepper powder
- 1 tsp. five spice powder

Instructions:
1. Place the dried shiitake mushrooms in a small bowl. Rehydrate them with cold water for 20 minutes.
2. Chop the drumsticks into 2 pieces. Then, marinate the chicken and mushrooms with the marinade sauce for 20 minutes
3. Rinse rice under cold water by gently scrubbing the rice with your fingertips in a circling motion. Pour out the milky water, and continue to rinse until the water is clear. Then, drain the water
4. Add the rice, 1 tsp. of salt, marinated chicken and mushrooms, and 1½ cups of water in the Foodi.
5. Close the lid. Select *Pressure* and cook at HIGH pressure for 9 minutes. When time is up, use natural pressure release for 15 minutes. Serve immediately

Lemongrass Chicken

(Prep + Cook Time: 20 Minutes | **Servings:** 5)

Ingredients:
- 1 bunch lemongrass, bottom removed and trimmed
- 10 chicken drumsticks
- 1-inch ginger root; peeled and chopped
- 4 garlic cloves; peeled and crushed
- 1 cup coconut milk
- 1 yellow onion; peeled and chopped
- 2 tbsp. fish sauce
- 3 tbsp. coconut aminos
- 1 tsp. Chinese five spice powder
- 1 tsp. butter
- 1/4 cup cilantro, diced
- 1 tbsp. lime juice
- Salt and ground black pepper, to taste

Instructions:
1. In a food processor, mix the lemongrass with the ginger, garlic, aminos, fish sauce, and five spice powder, and pulse well. Add the coconut milk and pulse again. Set the Foodi on *Sauté* mode, add the butter and melt it. Add the onion, stir, and cook for 5 minutes
2. Add the chicken, salt, and pepper, stir, and cook for 1 minute. Add the coconut milk and lemongrass mix, stir,
3. Cover, set on "Poultry" mode, and cook for 15 minutes. Release the pressure, uncover, and add more salt and pepper and lime juice, stir, divide among plates, and serve with cilantro sprinkled on top.

Turkey Mix and Mashed Potatoes

(Prep + Cook Time: 50 Minutes | **Servings:** 3)

Ingredients:
- 2 turkey quarters
- 5 Yukon gold potatoes; cut into halves
- 1 cup chicken stock
- 3.5 oz. cream
- 1 yellow onion; peeled and chopped
- 1 carrot, peeled and chopped
- 3 garlic cloves; peeled and minced
- 1 celery stalk, chopped
- 3 tbsp. cornstarch mixed with 2 tbsp. water
- 2 tbsp. Parmesan cheese; grated
- 2 tbsp. butter
- 2 tbsp. extra virgin olive oil
- Dried rosemary
- 2 bay leaves
- Dried sage
- Dried thyme
- White wine
- Salt and ground black pepper, to taste

Instructions:
1. Season the turkey with salt and pepper. Put 1 tbsp. oil into the Foodi, set the Foodi on *Sauté* mode, and heat it up. Add the turkey, brown the pieces for 4 minutes, transfer them to a plate set aside. Add 1/2 cup stock to the Foodi and stir well. Add the 1 tbsp. oil and heat it up. Add the onion, stir, and cook for 1 minute. Add the garlic, stir, and cook for 20 seconds. Add the salt and pepper, carrot and celery, stir and cook for 7 minutes
2. Add the bay leaves, thyme, sage, and rosemary, stir and cook everything 1 minute. Add the wine, turkey and the rest of the stock. Put the potatoes in the steamer basket and also introduce it in the Foodi
3. Cover and cook for 20 minutes on Egg mode. Release the pressure for 10 minutes, uncover the Foodi, transfer the potatoes to a bowl and mash them. Add the salt, pepper, butter, Parmesan cheese, and cream and stir well. Divide the turkey quarters to plates and set the Foodi on *Sauté* mode
4. Add the cornstarch mixture to pot, stir well, and cook for 2 to 3 minutes. Drizzle the sauce over the turkey, add the mashed potatoes on the side, and serve.

Turkey Meatballs

(Prep + Cook Time: 50 Minutes | **Servings:** 8)

Ingredients:
- 1 lb. turkey meat, ground
- 3 dried shiitake mushrooms; soaked in water, drained, and chopped
- 1 yellow onion, peeled and minced
- 1/4 cup Parmesan cheese; grated
- 1/2 cup panko bread crumbs
- 4 garlic cloves; peeled and minced
- 1/4 cup parsley, chopped
- 12 cremini mushrooms; chopped
- 1 cup chicken stock
- 2 tbsp. extra virgin olive oil
- 2 tbsp. butter
- Sherry
- 2 tbsp. cornstarch mixed with 2 tbsp. water
- 1 tsp. dried oregano
- 1 egg; whisked
- 1/4 cup milk
- 2 tsp. soy sauce
- 1 tsp. fish sauce
- Salt and ground black pepper, to taste

Instructions:
1. In a bowl, mix the turkey meat with Parmesan cheese, salt, pepper, onion, garlic, bread crumbs, parsley, oregano, egg, milk, fish sauce, and 1 tsp. soy sauce, stir well, and shape 16 meatballs. Heat up a pan with 1 tbsp. oil over medium-high heat, add the meatballs, brown them for 1 minutes on each side, and transfer them to a plate. Pour the chicken stock into the pan, stir, and take off heat
2. Set the Foodi on *Sauté* mode, add 1 tbsp. oil, 2 tbsp. butter, and heat them up. Add the cremini mushrooms, salt, and pepper, stir, and cook for 10 minutes. Add the dried mushrooms, sherry, and the rest of the soy sauce and stir well

3. Add the meatballs, cover the Foodi and cook on the *Pressure* setting for 6 minutes. Release the pressure, uncover the Foodi, add the cornstarch slurry, stir well, divide everything between plates, and serve.

Salsa Chicken

(Prep + Cook Time: 35 Minutes | Servings: 5)

Ingredients:
- 1 lb. chicken breast; skinless and boneless
- 1 cup chunky salsa
- 3/4 tsp. cumin
- Dried oregano
- Salt and ground black pepper, to taste

Instructions:
1. Season the chicken with salt and pepper to taste and add it to the Foodi. Add the oregano, cumin, and the salsa, stir
2. Cover, set the Foodi on "Poultry" mode and cook for 25 minutes. Release the pressure, transfer the chicken and salsa to a bowl, shred meat with a fork, and serve with some tortillas on the side

Chicken BBQ

(Prep + Cook Time: 30 Minutes | Servings: 6)

Ingredients:
- 4 to 5 lb. chicken thighs, bone-in or boneless, skinless, fat trimmed off
- 1 onion; medium-sized, chopped
- 2 garlic cloves; chopped
- 1/8 tsp. pepper; or more to taste
- 1/2 cup barbecue sauce (use your favorite)
- 1/2 cup PLUS 1½ tbsp. water, divided
- 1 tbsp. olive oil
- 1½ tbsp. cornstarch
- 1/4 tsp. salt, or more to taste

Instructions:
1. Press the *Sauté* key of the Foodi. Add the oil and heat
2. Add the garlic and onion and sauté for about 1 to 2 minutes or until soft
3. Stir in the 1/2 cup of water and barbecue sauce.
4. With the meaty side faced up, add the chicken in the pot. Press the *Cancel* key to stop the *Sauté* function. Cover and lock the lid
5. Press the *Pressure* key, set the pressure to HIGH, and set the timer for 10 minutes.
6. When the Foodi timer beeps let the pressure release naturally. Turn the steam valve to release remaining pressure
7. Unlock and carefully open the lid. Preheat the broiler. Grease a broiler pan and transfer the chicken into the greased pan
8. Generously season both sides with salt and pepper. Arrange the chicken in the pan with the meaty side faced down. Set aside
9. Press the *Sauté* key of the Foodi. Bring the cooking liquid in pot to a boil. In a small-sized bowl, combine the cornstarch with 1 ½ tbsp. of water until smooth
10. When the cooking liquid is boiling, add about ½ of the cornstarch mix into the pot; stir until the sauce is thick.
11. Add more cornstarch mix, if needed. Simmer the sauce until thick. Taste the sauce and, if needed, season with salt and pepper to taste.
12. Turn off the Foodi. Brush the top of the chicken with the sauce.
13. Turn the Foodi setting to broil, and preheat the broiler 10 to 15 minutes before cooking
14. Place the pan 6 inches from the heat source and broil for about 2 to 3 minutes or until the chicken is glazed.
15. Remove the pan from the Foodi, flip the chicken, and brush the other side with the sauce
16. Return the pan to the Foodi and broil for 2 to 3 minutes more or until the other side is glazed. Serve the chicken barbecue while it's still hot. Serve the remaining sauce on the side

Filipino Chicken Adobo

(Prep + Cook Time: 55 Minutes | **Servings:** 4)

Ingredients:
- 6 chicken drumsticks or two lb. of chicken
- 1 tbsp. oil
- Green onions chopped for garnish

Sauce:
- 1/4 cup Filipino soy sauce
- 1/4 cup Filipino vinegar
- 1/2 cup light soy sauce
- 1 tbsp. sugar
- 1 tbsp. fish sauce

Spice:
- 10 cloves garlic crushed
- 1 red chili dried
- 4 bay leaves dried
- 1 small onion minced
- 1 tsp. black peppercorn ground
- 1 tsp. cornstarch mixed with 1 tbsp. water, optional

Instructions:
1. Combine Filipino soy sauce, light soy sauce, Filipino vinegar, fish sauce and sugar in a medium mixing bowl.
2. Press the *Sauté* function. Add oil to the Foodi and brown the chicken for 1 to 2 minutes with the skin side down first. Then, remove the chicken from the pot
3. Sauté garlic and onion in the pot until fragrant and golden in color. Then, add ground black peppercorn, red chili, and bay leaves to the pot and sauté for 30 seconds
4. Add the Sauce mixture and deglaze the pot.
5. Cook on the *Pressure* Setting at HIGH pressure for 9 minutes, and then use a natural release.
6. Optional: remove the chicken from the pot. Simmer the sauce using the *Sauté* function and add cornstarch mixture until the sauce is reduced
7. Optional: Brown the chicken underneath a broiler with the skin side up for 5 minutes.
8. Place the chicken on serving plate, pour in the Sauce mixture, and add chopped green onions for garnish. Serve and enjoy!

Chicken Sandwiches

(Prep + Cook Time: 25 Minutes | **Servings:** 8)

Ingredients:
- 6 chicken breasts, skinless and boneless
- 12 oz. orange juice
- 8 hamburger buns
- 15 oz. canned peaches with juice
- 20 oz. canned pineapple with juice; chopped
- 8 grilled pineapple slices; for serving
- 2 tbsp. lemon juice
- 1 tsp. soy sauce
- 1 tbsp. cornstarch
- 1/4 cup brown sugar

Instructions:
1. In a bowl, mix the orange juice with the soy sauce, lemon juice, canned pineapple, peaches, and sugar and stir well. Pour half of this mixture into the Foodi, add the chicken and pour the rest of the sauce over meat
2. Cover the Foodi and cook on the "Poultry" setting for 15 minutes. Release the pressure, take out the chicken and put it on a cutting board. Shred the meat and set the dish aside. In a bowl, mix the cornstarch with 1 tbsp. cooking juice and stir well
3. Transfer the sauce to a pot, add the cornstarch mix and chicken, stir, and cook for a few minutes. Divide this chicken mix onto hamburger buns, top with grilled pineapple pieces, and serve.

Sweet and Tangy Chicken

(Prep + Cook Time: 20 Minutes | **Servings:** 4)

Ingredients:
- 2 lb. chicken thighs, boneless and skinless
- 1/4 cup extra virgin olive oil
- 1/2 cup fish sauce
- 1 cup lime juice
- 2 tbsp. coconut nectar
- 1 tsp. fresh mint; chopped
- 1 tsp. ginger; grated
- 2 tsp. cilantro, diced

Instructions:
1. Put chicken thighs into the Foodi. In a bowl, mix the lime juice with the fish sauce, olive oil, coconut nectar, ginger, mint, and cilantro and whisk well. Pour this over the chicken; cover the Foodi
2. Cook on the Pressure setting for 10 minutes. Release the pressure, divide the chicken among plates, and serve

Chicken in Tomatillo Sauce

(Prep + Cook Time: 25 Minutes | **Servings:** 6)

Ingredients:
- 1 lb. chicken thighs, skinless and boneless
- 15 oz. canned tomatillos; chopped
- 1 yellow onion; peeled and sliced thinly
- 1 garlic clove, peeled and crushed
- 4 oz. canned chopped green chilies
- 1/2 cup cilantro; diced
- 5 oz. canned garbanzo beans, drained
- 15 oz. rice; already cooked
- 5 oz. tomatoes; cored and chopped
- 15 oz. cheddar cheese, grated
- 4 oz. black olives; pitted and chopped
- 2 tbsp. extra virgin olive oil
- Salt and ground black pepper, to taste

Instructions:
1. Set the Foodi on *Sauté* mode, add the oil, and heat it up. Add the onions, stir, and cook for 5 minutes. Add the garlic, stir, and cook for 15 seconds. Add the chicken, chilies, salt, pepper, cilantro, and tomatillos, stir
2. Cover the Foodi, and cook on *Pressure* mode for 8 minutes. Release the pressure, uncover the Foodi, take the chicken out and shred it
3. Return the chicken to pot, add rice, beans, set the Foodi on *Sauté* mode, and cook for 1 minute. Add the cheese, tomatoes, and olives, stir, cook for 2 minutes, divide among plates, and serve.

Chicken Congee

(Prep + Cook Time: 1 hour 5 Minutes | **Servings:** 7 cups)

Ingredients:
- 5 to 6 chicken drumsticks
- 1 rice measuring cup (180 ml) Jasmine rice
- 7 cups water (using standard 250 ml cup)
- Green onions for garnish
- 1 tbsp. ginger, sliced into strips
- Salt to taste

Instructions:
1. Rinse rice in the pot under cold water by gently scrubbing the rice with your fingertips in a circling motion. Pour out the milky water, and continue to rinse until water is clear. Drain well
2. Add Rice, 7 cups of water (using standard 250 ml cup) and ginger into the Foodi.
3. Close lid and cook at High pressure for 15 minutes in the Foodi. To get 15 minutes' cook time, press *Pressure* button.
4. Natural release for 5 minutes, then Quick Release. Be careful as you do quick release
5. Open the lid, Do Not Stir. Add the chicken drumsticks into the Foodi, then close the lid again.
6. Cook at High pressure for another 20 minutes, to get 20 minutes' cook time, press Pressure button.
7. Then natural release for 15 minutes, and quick release after.
8. Heat up the pot (press *Sauté* button), season with salt and stir until desired consistency.

9. Use tongs and fork to separate the chicken meat from the bones (they literally fall off the bone) and remove the chicken bones.
10. Remove congee from heat and garnish with green onions

Chicken And Rice

(Prep + Cook Time: 20 Minutes | **Servings:** 2 to 4)

Ingredients:
- 6, 8 chicken drumsticks, marinated
- 1½ cup water
- 2 rice measuring cups Jasmine rice; rinse
- 6 dried shiitake mushrooms; marinated
- 1 tsp. Salt
- 1 tbsp. ginger, shredded
- Green onions for garnish

Marinade:
- 1 tbsp. light soy sauce
- 1 tsp. dark soy sauce
- 1/2 tsp. sugar
- 1/2 tsp. corn starch
- 1 tsp. Shaoxing rice wine
- A dash of white pepper powder
- 1 tbsp. ginger; shredded
- 1 tsp. five spice powder

Instructions:
1. Place the dried shiitake mushrooms in a small bowl. Rehydrate them with cold water for 20 minutes.
2. Chop the drumsticks into 2 pieces. Then, marinate the chicken and mushrooms with the marinade sauce for 20 minutes
3. Rinse rice under cold water by gently scrubbing the rice with your fingertips in a circling motion. Pour out the milky water, and continue to rinse until the water is clear. Then, drain the water
4. Add the rice, 1 tsp. of salt, and marinated chicken and mushrooms, and 1½ cup of water in the Foodi.
5. Lock the lid on the Foodi and then cook On High pressure for 10 minutes. To get 10 minutes' cook time, press *Pressure* button
6. Pressure Release Let the pressure to come down naturally for at least 15 minutes, then quick release any pressure left in the pot. Serve immediately.

Chicken Romano

(Prep + Cook Time: 25 Minutes | **Servings:** 4)

Ingredients:
- 6 chicken thighs, boneless and skinless and cut into medium chunks
- 1/2 cup white flour
- 1 yellow onion; peeled and chopped
- 1 cup Romano cheese; grated
- 10 oz. tomato sauce
- 1 tsp. white wine vinegar
- 4 oz. mushrooms; sliced
- 2 tbsp. vegetable oil
- 1 tbsp. sugar
- 1 tbsp. dried oregano
- 1 tsp. garlic; minced
- 1 tsp. dried basil
- 1 tsp. chicken bouillon granules
- Salt and ground black pepper; to taste

Instructions:
1. Set the Foodi on *Sauté* mode, add the oil and heat it up. Add the chicken pieces, stir, and brown them for 2 minutes. Add the onion and garlic, stir, and cook for 3 minutes. Add the salt, pepper, flour, and stir well. Add the tomato sauce, vinegar, mushrooms, sugar, oregano, basil and bouillon granules, stir
2. Cover, and cook on the *Pressure* setting for 10 minutes. Release the pressure for 10 minutes, uncover the Foodi, add the cheese, stir, divide among plates, and serve

Chicken Korma

(Prep + Cook Time: 25 Minutes | **Servings:** 6)

Ingredients:
- 1 lb. chicken breasts and/or legs, boneless and skinless or with bones, as you prefer

For the Sauce:
- 1 oz. cashews raw; or substitute with almonds if you prefer
- 1/2 green Serrano pepper Jalapeño, or Thai chili pepper
- 5 cloves garlic
- 1 small onion chopped
- 1/2 cup tomatoes diced
- 1 tsp. cumin-coriander powder
- 1/2 tsp. cayenne pepper adjust to your preference
- 1/2 cup water (use this to slosh about in the blender jar and then pour it into the pressure cooker)
- 1 tsp. Ginger minced
- 1 tsp. turmeric
- 1 tsp. salt
- 1 tsp. garam masala

For Finishing:
- 1/4 cup cilantro chopped
- 1/2 cup coconut milk full fat; add more if you'd like
- 1 tsp. garam masala

Instructions:
1. Blend together all ingredients listed under "For the Sauce" (all ingredients excluding chicken, garam masala, coconut milk and cilantro)
2. Pour the sauce into the Foodi. Place the chicken on top. If your chicken is frozen, just push it down into the sauce a little
3. Cook on the *Pressure* Setting at HIGH pressure for 10 minutes. When time is up, wait 15 minutes for a natural pressure release
4. Open the lid and carefully take out the chicken and cut into bite size pieces. Add coconut milk and garam masala into the pot and stir
5. Put the chicken back in, serve and garnish with cilantro if you'd like.

Chipotle Chicken, Rice, and Black Beans

(Prep + Cook Time: 30 Minutes | **Servings:** 6)

Ingredients:
- 1 lb. chicken thighs or breasts; boneless, skinless, cut into bite sized pieces
- 1 tbsp. chipotle peppers; in adobo sauce
- 4 cups diced tomatoes in juice
- 1/2 cup water; filtered
- 1/2 lime, juiced
- 1 onion; small-sized, chopped
- 1 can black beans; organic, drained and rinsed
- 1 cup Jasmine Rice, uncooked
- 1/2 tsp. black pepper; finely ground
- 2 tbsp. butter, ghee, or coconut oil
- 2 tsp. real salt, OR sea salt

Instructions:
1. Put the chicken, butter, pepper, salt, rice, lime juice, water, chipotle peppers, tomatoes with its juices, and onion in the Foodi, stir and combine. Cover and lock the lid
2. Press the *Pressure* key, set the pressure to HIGH, and set the timer for 6 minutes
3. When the Foodi timer beeps, press the *Cancel* key and unplug the Foodi. Turn the steam valve to quick release the pressure.
4. Unlock and carefully open the lid
5. Add the black beans into the pot and stir to combine.
6. Taste and, if needed, season with pepper and salt to taste. Divide between serving bowls and garnish each serving with sour cream, shredded cheese, and guacamole

Chicken Piccata

(Prep + Cook Time: 45 Minutes | **Servings:** 4 to 6)

Ingredients:

- 1½ lb. boneless chicken breasts, trimmed (6 breasts)
- 1/2 cup all purpose flour plus 1 tablespoon; divided
- 2 tsp. kosher salt, divided
- 3 oz. capers; drained
- 3/4 cup chicken broth
- 1/3 cup fresh lemon juice
- 1/4 cup sour cream
- Lemon slices for garnish
- 2 tbsp. olive oil
- 3 cloves garlic; minced
- 2 tbsp. cooking sherry
- 1 tsp. dried basil
- 1 tsp. dried oregano

Instructions:

1. Place 1/2 cup flour and 1 tsp. salt in a large zip-top bag
2. Place the chicken breasts in the bag and shake to coat in flour. Shake off any excess flour and transfer to a plate.
3. Heat your Foodi to Sauté for 30 minutes. When the pot comes to temperature coat the bottom of the pot with olive oil. Working 2 pieces at a time brown the chicken breasts on both sides. When browned, transfer to a clean plate
4. When all the chicken is browned add the garlic to the pot and cook until softened (about1 minute) stirring constantly. Add in the chicken broth, lemon juice, sherry, basil and oregano. Add the chicken back to the pot and nestle into the liquid. Top with the capers.
5. Place the lid on the pot and set to pressure cook on High for 10 minutes. To get 10 minutes' cook time, press *Pressure* button
6. While the chicken is cooking mix together the sour cream and remaining 1 tbsp. of flour in a separate bowl. Set aside
7. Use Quick-release method. Remove the chicken from the pot placing on a serving platter
8. Whisk in the sour cream to the liquid and cook for 1 minute. The liquid will be very hot, you don't need to heat the pot. Pour the sauce over the chicken and serve warm over pasta if desired.

Turkey Chili

(Prep + Cook Time: 20 Minutes | **Servings:** 4)

Ingredients:

- 1 lb. turkey meat, ground
- 12 oz. vegetable stock
- 15 oz. chickpeas; already cooked
- 1 yellow onion; peeled and chopped
- 1 yellow bell pepper; seeded and chopped
- 3 garlic cloves, peeled and chopped
- 5 oz. water
- 1½ tsp. cumin
- 2½ tbsp. chili powder
- Cayenne pepper
- Salt and ground black pepper; to taste

Instructions:

1. Put the turkey meat into the Foodi. Add the water, stir, cover and cook on the "Poultry" setting for 5 minutes. Release the pressure, uncover the Foodi and add the chickpeas, bell pepper, onion, garlic, chili powder, cumin, salt, pepper, cayenne pepper, and stock. Stir
2. Cover the Foodi, and cook on the *Pressure* setting for 5 minutes. Release the pressure for 10 minutes, uncover the Foodi again, stir the chili, divide it among plates, and serve

Chicken with Cherries & Pumpkin Seed Wild Rice

(Prep + Cook Time: 55 Minutes | **Servings:** 4 to 6)

Ingredients:
- 1/2 cup pumpkin seeds toasted
- 12 chicken thighs
- 2 plum tomatoes diced
- 4 cups vegetable stock low sodium
- 1 cup balsamic vinegar
- 1/2 cup evaporated palm sugar
- 1 tbsp. molasses
- 1/4 cup butter melted
- 1 orange peeled and quartered
- 4 sprigs rosemary
- 2 cups Bing Cherries pitted and halved fresh
- 1/4 tsp. sea salt
- 1 ⅓ cups wild rice rinsed
- 1/4 cup butter
- 1 onion minced
- 1 onion julienned
- Sea salt to taste

Instructions:
1. In the inner pot of the Foodi add the balsamic vinegar, evaporated palm sugar, molasses, butter, orange and onion. Mix well
2. Add the chicken, salt and rosemary. Stir to coat
3. Add 1½ cups of cherries. Place the lid on the pressure cooker and lock into place. Press the *Pressure* button; adjust pressure cooking time to 25 minutes.
4. When done and pressure has naturally released, remove the lid
5. While the chicken is cooking: Bring veggie stock to boil in a medium saucepan on the stove top. Add rinsed wild rice. Cover and simmer for 50 minutes.
6. In a large sauté pan, heat the butter. Sauté onion until caramelized.
7. Add tomato and sauté for 3 to 4 minutes. Add onions and tomato to the rice.
8. Add 1/2 cup of cherries to the sauté pan and sauté for 3 to 4 minutes until soft and juicy
9. Add cherries and toasted pumpkin seeds to the rice. Stir to incorporate. Add salt if needed
10. Place wild rice on a serving platter and top with chicken. Pour juices from the chicken over the entire platter and garnish with rosemary

Chicken Alfredo Pasta

(Prep + Cook Time: 5 Minutes | **Servings:** 3)

Ingredients:
- 8 oz. fettuccine
- 1 cup cooked + diced chicken
- 1 (15 oz.) jar of Alfredo sauce
- 2 tsp. chicken seasoning
- 2 cups water

Instructions:
1. Break your pasta in half so it fits in the cooker
2. Add pasta, water, and chicken seasoning to Foodi.
3. Seal the lid. Select STEAM and cook at HIGH pressure for 3 minutes
4. When the timer beeps, press *Cancel* and use a quick release
5. Drain the pasta and add to serving bowl. Mix in Alfredo sauce and chicken. Serve!

Baked Chicken

(Prep + Cook Time: 50 Minutes | **Servings:** 8)

Ingredients:
- 2 tsp. sand ginger dried, Kaempferia Galanga or Zeodary Powder
- Dash white pepper optional; ground
- 1¼ tsp. kosher salt
- 1/4 tsp. five spice powder

Instructions:
1. Season the chicken legs by placing the chicken legs in a large mixing bowl. Pour in 2 tsp. of dried sand ginger, 1¼ tsp. of kosher salt, and 1/4 tsp. of five spice powder. Mix well
2. Place the seasoned chicken legs on a large piece of parchment paper (Do NOT use aluminum foil). Wrap it up tightly and place it on a shallow dish with the opening side facing upwards. Do not stack more than 2 levels of chicken legs.
3. Place a steamer rack in the pressure cooker and pour in 1 cup of water. Carefully place the chicken legs dish onto the rack
4. Close the lid and cook on the *Pressure* Setting at HIGH Pressure for 18 to 26 minutes, then natural release for 20 minutes (turn off the heat and do NOT touch it). Open the lid carefully. Remove the dish from the pressure cooker and unwrap the parchment paper carefully

Fall Off the Bone Chicken

(Prep + Cook Time: 45 Minutes | **Servings:** 10)

Ingredients:
- 4 lb. preferably organic
- 1½ cups chicken bone broth
- 1 whole chicken; about
- 1/4 tsp. black pepper; fresh ground
- 2 tbsp. fresh squeezed lemon juice
- 6 cloves garlic, peeled
- 1 tbsp. coconut oil; organic virgin
- 1 tsp. dried thyme
- 1 tsp. paprika
- 1/2 tsp. sea salt

Instructions:
1. In a small-sized bowl, combine the pepper, salt, thyme, and paprika. Rub the outside of the chicken with the spice mix
2. Press the *Sauté* key of the Foodi. Put the oil in the pot and heat until shimmering.
3. With the breast side faced down, put the chicken in the pot and cook for 6 to 7 minutes. Rotate the chicken.
4. Add the broth, garlic cloves, and lemon juice. Cover and lock the lid
5. Press the *Pressure* key, set the pressure to HIGH, and set the timer for 25 minutes
6. When the timer beeps, let the pressure release naturally. Turn the steam valve to Venting to release any remaining pressure. Carefully open the lid
7. Transfer the chicken into a large plate and let stand for 5 minutes. Carve and serve.

Turkey Thighs

(Prep + Cook Time: 1 hour 45 Minutes | **Servings:** 4)

Ingredients:
- 2 turkey thighs (about 1 lb.), excess fat removed
- 1 cup sliced Portobello mushrooms
- 1 cup chicken broth plus 1 tbsp. red-wine vinegar
- 1 cup thinly sliced onions
- 3 tbsp. flour
- 2 tsp. minced garlic
- 1/2 tsp. each dried rosemary, sage, thyme, salt and pepper

Instructions:
1. Set Foodi to *Sauté* and brown the turkey thighs. Add the rest of the ingredients and close the lid, Lock the lid on the Foodi and then cook On High pressure for 30 minutes. To get 30 minutes' cook time, press Pressure button
2. Use a Quick Pressure Release Method; check for done-ness, if meat is not fork tender add 15 minutes and resume cooking on Poultry setting
3. When meat is done, remove turkey thighs to cutting board and cover loosely with foil.
4. In a small bowl, whisk flour and water until well blended. Whisk flour mixture into liquid, onions and mushrooms in cooker, mixing well
5. Turn cooker to Keep-warm and simmer gravy for 15 minutes or until thickened.
6. Cut meat in large pieces from both sides of each thigh bone to give you 4 pieces. Arrange on serving plates; spoon on some gravy.

Filipino Chicken

(Prep + Cook Time: 25 Minutes | **Servings:** 4)

Ingredients:
- 5 lb. chicken thighs
- 4 garlic cloves; minced
- 1/2 cup white vinegar
- 3 bay leaves
- 1/2 cup soy sauce
- 1 tsp. black peppercorns; crushed
- Salt and ground black pepper, to taste

Instructions:
1. Set the Foodi on "Poultry" mode, add the chicken, vinegar, soy sauce, salt, pepper, garlic, peppercorns, and bay leaves, stir
2. Cover, and cook on the *Pressure* setting for 15 Minutes. Release the pressure for 10 minutes, uncover the Foodi, discard the bay leaves, stir, divide the chicken between plates, and serve

Lemon Garlic Chicken

(Prep + Cook Time: 30 Minutes | **Servings:** 2)

Ingredients:
- 1 to 2 lb. chicken breasts or thighs
- 1 large lemon juiced (or more to taste)
- 1/2 cup organic chicken broth or homemade
- 3 - 4 tsp. (or more) arrowroot flour
- 1/4 tsp. paprika
- 1/4 cup white cooking wine
- 1 onion; diced
- 1 tbsp. avocado oil, lard, or ghee
- 1 tsp. dried parsley
- 5 garlic cloves; minced
- 1 tsp. sea salt

Instructions:
1. Set the Foodi to the *Sauté* function. Add the diced onion and cooking fat.
2. Sauté the onions for 5 to 10 minutes or until softened
3. Add in the remaining ingredients except for the arrowroot flour and secure the lid on your Foodi.
4. Close lid and cook at High pressure for 15 minutes in the Foodi. To get 15 minutes' cook time, press *Pressure* button

5. Use Quick-release method
6. At this point you may thicken your sauce by making a slurry. To do this remove about 1/4 cup sauce from the pot, add in the arrowroot flour, and then reintroduce the slurry into the remaining liquid. Stir and serve right away.

Delicious Chicken Dinner

(Prep + Cook Time: 45 Minutes | **Servings:** 4)

Ingredients:
- 2 lb. boneless chicken thighs
- 1/4 cup coconut aminos (or soy sauce)
- 1/4 cup honey
- 1/4 cup coconut oil
- 3 tbsp. organic ketchup
- 2 tsp. garlic powder
- 1 ½ tsp. sea salt
- 1/2 tsp. black pepper

Instructions:
1. Put everything in your Foodi. Stir, so the chicken becomes completely coated. Close and seal the lid.
2. Press *Pressure* and adjust time to 18 minutes. For frozen chicken, 40 minutes
3. When time is up, hit *Cancel* and Quick Pressure Release
4. Take out the chicken and hit *Sauté*.
5. Simmer for 5 minutes until the sauce has thickened nicely. Serve with a vegetable side dish!

Turkey Sausage and Macaroni Casserole

(Prep + Cook Time: 15 Minutes | **Servings:** 4 to 6)

Ingredients:
- 1 lb. turkey sausage, such as sweet Italian turkey sausage, cut into 1-inch pieces
- 8 oz. dried elbow macaroni
- 1½ cups shredded Swiss cheese (about 6 oz.)
- 1 cup shelled fresh peas; or frozen peas, thawed
- 1½ cups regular or low-fat evaporated milk
- 1½ cups chicken broth
- 1½ tbsp. all-purpose flour
- 1 tsp. dried sage
- 2 tbsp. unsalted butter
- 1/2 small red onion; chopped
- 1/4 tsp. salt
- 1/4 tsp. ground black pepper

Instructions:
1. Whisk the milk, broth, flour, and sage in a large bowl until the flour has dissolved; set aside.
2. Melt the butter in the Foodi turned to the *Sautéing/Browning* function. Add the onion and cook, stirring occasionally, just until softened, about 2 minutes
3. Add the sausage pieces; cook, stirring occasionally, until browned, about 4 minutes. Stir in the milk mixture until smooth, then add the macaroni and toss well
4. Lock the lid onto the pot. Set the Foodi to cook at High pressure for 8 minutes. To get 8 minutes' cook time, press *Pressure* button and use the *Time Adjustment* button to adjust the cook time to 8 minutes
5. Use the Quick Pressure Release method
6. Unlock and open the pot. Stir in the cheese, peas, salt, and pepper. Set the lid loosely over the pot and set aside for 5 minutes to melt the cheese and warm through. Stir well before serving.

Turkey Gluten Free Gravy

(Prep + Cook Time: 55 minutes | **Servings:** 6)

Ingredients:
- 1 (4 - 5 lb.) bone in, skin on turkey breast
- 2 tbsp. ghee or butter (use coconut oil for AIP)
- 1 medium onion, cut into medium dice
- 1 large carrot, cut into medium dice
- 1 celery rib, cut into medium dice
- 1 garlic clove, peeled and smashed
- 1 ½ cups bone broth (preferably from chicken or turkey bones)
- Black pepper (omit for AIP)
- 2 tsp. dried sage
- 1/4 cup dry white wine
- 1 bay leaf
- 1 tbsp. tapioca starch (optional)
- Salt to taste

Instructions:
1. Set the *Sauté* function. Pat turkey breast dry and generously season with salt and pepper. Melt cooking fat in the Foodi Multi-cooker.
2. Brown turkey breast, skin side down, about 5 minutes and transfer to a plate, leaving fat in the pot
3. Add onion, carrot and celery to pot and cook until softened, about 5 minutes. Stir in garlic and sage and cook until fragrant, about 30 seconds.
4. Pour in wine and cook until slightly reduced about 3 minutes. Stir in broth and bay leaf. Using a wooden spoon, scrape up all browned bits stuck on the bottom of pot
5. Place turkey skin side up in the pot with any accumulated juices
6. High pressure for 35 minutes. Lock the lid on the Foodi Multi-cooker and then cook for 35 minutes.
7. To get 35 minutes' cook time, press *Pressure* button and use the Time Adjustment button to adjust the cook time to 35
8. Pressure Release. Use quick release method and carefully remove lid
9. Finish the dish. Close crisping lid. Select *Air Crisp*, set temperature to 375°F and set time to 10 minutes. Check after 5 minutes, cooking for an additional 5 minutes if dish needs more browning.
10. Transfer turkey breast to carving board or plate and tent loosely with foil, allowing it to rest while you prepare the gravy.
11. Use an immersion blender or carefully transfer cooking liquid and vegetables to blender and puree until smooth. Return to heat and cook until thickened and reduced to about 2 cups. Adjust seasoning to taste. Slice turkey breast and serve with hot gravy. Enjoy!

Honey Barbecue Chicken Wings

(Prep + Cook Time: 35 Minutes | **Servings:** 4)

Ingredients:
- 2 lb. chicken wings
- 1/2 cup apple juice
- 1/2 cup brown sugar
- 3/4 cup honey barbecue sauce
- Cayenne pepper
- 1 tsp. red pepper flakes
- 2 tsp. paprika
- 1/2 cup water
- 1/2 tsp. dried basil
- Salt and ground black pepper, to taste

Instructions:
1. Put the chicken wings into the Foodi. Add the barbecue sauce, apple juice, salt, pepper, red pepper, paprika, basil, sugar, and water. Stir
2. Cover, and cook on the "Poultry" setting for 10 minutes. Release the pressure, uncover the Foodi, transfer chicken to a baking sheet, add the sauce all over, place under a preheated broiler, broil for 7 minutes, turn the chicken wings, broil for 7 minutes, divide among plates, and serve

Stuffed Chicken Breasts

(Prep + Cook Time: 40 Minutes | **Servings:** 2)

Ingredients:
- 2 chicken breasts; skinless, boneless, and butterflied
- 16 bacon strips
- 4 mozzarella cheese slices
- 1-piece ham; cut in half and cooked
- 6 asparagus spears
- 2 cup water
- Salt and ground black pepper; to taste

Instructions:
1. In a bowl, mix the chicken breasts with salt and 1 cup water, stir, cover, and keep in the refrigerator for 30 minutes. Pat chicken breasts dry and place them on a working surface. Add 2 slices of mozzarella, 1-piece ham, and 3 asparagus pieces onto each. Add salt and pepper and roll up each chicken breast
2. Place 8 bacon strips on a working surface, add the chicken and wrap them in bacon. Repeat this with the rest of the bacon strips and the other chicken breast. Put rolls in the steamer basket of the Foodi, add 1 cup water to the Foodi
3. Cover and cook on the *Pressure* setting for 10 minutes. Release the pressure, pat dry rolls with paper towels and leave them on a plate. Set the Foodi on *Sauté* mode, add the chicken rolls and brown them for a few minutes. Divide among plates, and serve.

Crack Chicken

(Prep + Cook Time: 40 Minutes | **Servings:** 4)

Ingredients:
- 2 lb. chicken breast, boneless
- 1 packet ranch seasoning
- 4 oz. cheddar cheese
- 8 oz. cream cheese
- 6 to 8 bacon slices; cooked
- 3 tbsp. cornstarch
- 1 cup water

Instructions:
1. Put the chicken breasts and cream cheese in the Foodi. Sprinkle the top of the chicken and cream cheese with the ranch seasoning.
2. Pour in 1 cup of water. Cover and lock the lid
3. Press the *Pressure* key, set the pressure to HIGH, and set the timer for 25 minutes.
4. When the Foodi timer beeps, turn the steam valve to venting to quick release the pressure.
5. Carefully open the lid. Transfer the chicken into a large plate and shred the meat.
6. Press the *Sauté* key of the Foodi and select LESS. Whisk in the cornstarch. Add the cheese and the shredded chicken into the pot. Stir in the bacon. Serve

Shredded Chicken Breast

(Prep + Cook Time: 30 Minutes | **Servings:** 4)

Ingredients:
- 1 ½ to 2 lbs boneless chicken breasts
- 1/2 cup chicken broth
- 1/2 tsp. salt
- 1/2 tsp. garlic salt
- 1/8 tsp. pepper

Instructions:
1. Place chicken in your Foodi Season both sides of chicken with garlic salt and pepper.
2. Pour the chicken broth
3. Seal Foodi, making sure your valve is set to sealing. Press *Pressure* button. Once done, wait for Foodi to depressurize on it's own, known as natural release
4. Note: If you are wanting to use the quick release method, I suggest adding 5 extra minutes to the Foodi cooking timer.
5. Place chicken on a cutting board and shred with 2 forks, OR slice chicken breast.

Cilantro Chicken Meatballs

(Prep + Cook Time: 30 Minutes | **Servings:** 4)

Ingredients:
- 1 lb. ground pastured chicken
- 1/4 cup avocado oil, olive oil or preferred cooking fat
- 1/4 cup water
- 1/2 cup fresh cilantro; chopped
- 1/2 onion; minced
- 2 tbsp. apple cider vinegar
- 2 tbsp. sesame oil
- 1 egg
- 1/4 cup coconut aminos
- 1 tsp. sea salt
- 1/2 tsp. garlic powder

Instructions:
1. To assemble the meatballs, begin by combining all of the ingredients, except for the cooking fat and water, in a mixing bowl. Use your hands to make sure the ingredients are incorporated well with each other
2. Plug in your Pressure Cooker, pour the 1/4 cup (60 ml) cooking fat into the stainless steel basin and press the Sauté button. Shape your meatballs until they are a couple of inches (5 cm) in diameter and place them into the hot oil. Cook the meatballs on all sides until they begin to brown, around 5 minutes, and then press the Start/Stop button
3. High pressure for 3 minutes. Add the water into the bottom of the stainless bowl. Secure the lid to the POT, close off the pressure valve and press the *Pressure* button cook on high for 3 minutes
4. Allow the meatballs to cook. Once complete, Quick Pressure Release the pressure valve and remove the lid once safe to do so. Transfer the meatballs onto a towel-lined plate and serve warm.

Braised Chicken with Capers and Parsley

(Prep + Cook Time: 45 Minutes | **Servings:** 4)

Ingredients:
- 4 chicken breasts, skinless, bone-in
- 1 can (14.5 oz.) chicken broth
- 1 onion; large-sized, minced
- 1/2 cup flat-leaf parsley; minced, plus more for garnish
- 1/3 cup salted capers, soaked well in several changes of water
- 1/3 cup white wine vinegar
- 1 tbsp. cornstarch
- 1 tbsp. water
- 2 tbsp. olive oil; divided
- Freshly ground black pepper
- Salt to taste

Instructions:
1. Season the chicken with salt and pepper generously.
2. Press the *Sauté* key of the Foodi. Put 1 tbsp. olive oil in the pot and heat
3. Cooking in 2 batches, cook the chicken in the pot until both sides are browned. Transfer the browned chicken onto a platter.
4. Put the remaining 1 tbsp. olive oil in the pot
5. When hot, add the onion; cook, stirring, for about 5 minutes or until soft.
6. Add the capers and parsley and cook for 1 minute. Stir in the broth.
7. Add the vinegar. Return the chicken, along with any accumulated juices, into the pot. Cover and lock the lid.
8. Press the *Pressure* key, set the pressure to HIGH, and set the timer for 13 minutes.
9. When the Foodi timer beeps, turn the steam valve to Venting to quick release the pressure. Unlock and carefully open the lid
10. Transfer the chicken onto a platter using tongs. Cover the platter with foil to keep warm. In a small-sized bowl, mix the cornstarch with the water.
11. Press the *Sauté* key. Bring the broth in the pot to a boil
12. Add the cornstarch mix, constantly stirring until the sauce is thick. Turn off the Foodi.
13. Season the salt and pepper to taste. Spoon the sauce over the cooked chicken. Garnish with parsley and serve.

Chicken Pina Colada

(Prep + Cook Time: 35 Minutes | **Servings:** 4)

Ingredients:
- 2 lb. chicken thighs, organic, cut into 1-inch chunks
- 1/2 cup coconut cream; full fat
- 1/2 cup green onion; chopped, for garnish
- 1 cup pineapple chunks; frozen or fresh
- 1/8 tsp. salt
- 1 tsp. cinnamon
- 2 tbsp. coconut aminos (or soy sauce)

Optional:
- 1 tsp. arrowroot starch
- 1 tbsp. water.

Instructions:
1. Except for the green onions, put all of the ingredients in the Foodi. Cover and lock the lid
2. Press the "POULTRY" key and cook on preset HIGH pressure and 15 minutes cooking time.
3. When the Foodi timer beeps, press the *Cancel* key and turn off the Foodi
4. Let the pressure release naturally for 10 to 15 minutes or until the valve drops.
5. Turn the steam valve to Venting to release remaining pressure. Unlock and carefully open the lid. Stir to mix.
6. If you want a thick sauce, stir in 1 tsp. arrowroot starch with 1 tbsp. water
7. Press the *Sauté* key of the Foodi.
8. Add the arrowroot starch mixture into the pot and cook until thick to preferred thickness.
9. Turn the Foodi off. Serve garnished with green onions

Notes:
To make your own coconut cream, simply place a can of full fat coconut milk in the fridge overnight. When ready to use, open can from bottom and drain out coconut water (you can drink it or discard it). You will be left with pure coconut cream in the can.

Chicken with Soy Sauce

(Prep + Cook Time: 40 Minutes | **Servings:** 8)

Ingredients:
- 1 small piece of ginger minced
- 1 green onion minced
- 1 medium size chicken
- 2 tbsp. sugar
- 1 tbsp. cooking wine or 2 tbsp. wine
- 2 tsp. salt
- 2 tsp. soy sauce

Instructions:
1. Mix the 2 tsp. salt, 2 tbsp. sugar and seasoned the outside/inside chicken with them evenly
2. Add one tsp. salt and cover the bottom of the Foodi
3. Put seasoned chicken, soy sauce, wine into Foodi.
4. High pressure for 15 minutes. Press the *Pressure* button and wait till it is done.
5. Turn the chicken over then press the *Pressure* button again
6. Use the Quick Pressure Release method
7. Then the delicious chicken, retaining flavor and nutrition, is ready to be served.
8. Cut the chicken into pieces.
9. Mix ginger and green onion with chicken oil to make a dipping sauce. Serve

Cordon Blue Chicken Casserole

(Prep + Cook Time: 50 Minutes | **Servings:** 8)

Ingredients:
- 1 lb. chicken breast, boneless, skinless, sliced into thin strips
- 1 lb. ham; cubed
- 8 oz. Gouda cheese
- 8 oz. heavy cream
- 16 oz. Rotini pasta
- 16 oz. Swiss cheese
- 2 cups chicken broth
- 1 cup panko bread crumbs
- 1 tbsp. spicy mustard
- 2 tbsp. butter

Instructions:
1. Put the uncooked pasta in the Foodi. Cover the pasta with 2 cups of chicken broth.
2. Put the chicken strips and ham cubes on top. Cover and lock the lid
3. Press the *Pressure* key, set the pressure to HIGH, and set the timer for 25 minutes.
4. When the Foodi timer beeps press the *Cancel* key and unplug the Foodi. Turn the steam valve to quick release the pressure. Unlock and carefully open the lid
5. Pour the mustard and heavy cream in the pot. Add both the cheeses in the pot and stir until smooth and creamy. In a small-sized pan, add the butter and melt.
6. When the butter is melted, add the bread crumbs and stir for about 2 to 3 minutes or until golden and toasty. Serve the pasta mixture sprinkled with the toasted bread on top

Easy Turkey Drumsticks

(Prep + Cook Time: 45 Minutes | **Servings:** 6)

Ingredients:
- 6 turkey drumsticks
- 2 packed tsp. brown sugar
- 1/2 cup soy sauce
- 1 tbsp. Diamond Crystal kosher salt
- 1 tsp. fresh ground black pepper
- 1/2 tsp. garlic powder
- 1/2 cup water

Instructions:
1. Mix the salt, brown sugar, pepper, and garlic powder, breaking up any clumps of brown sugar. Sprinkle evenly over the turkey drumsticks
2. Pour the water and soy sauce into the Foodi, then add the drumsticks.
3. Lock the lid and cook at High pressure for 25 minutes. To get 25 minutes' cook time, press *Pressure* button and use the *Time Adjustment* button to adjust the cook time to 25 minutes
4. Use Natural Pressure Release method for 15 minutes, and then use Quick Pressure Release.
5. Lift the drumsticks out of the pot with tongs, be careful, they are fall-apart tender.
6. Let the fat float to the top, and pass the de-fatted liquid at the table as a sauce. Serve.

Chicken and Potatoes

(Prep + Cook Time: 30 Minutes | **Servings:** 4)

Ingredients:
- 2 lb. red potatoes; peeled, and cut into quarters
- 2 lb. chicken thighs, skinless and boneless
- 3/4 cup chicken stock
- 1/4 cup lemon juice
- 2 tbsp. extra virgin olive oil
- 3 tbsp. Dijon mustard
- 2 tbsp. Italian seasoning
- Salt and ground black pepper; to taste

Instructions:
1. Set the Foodi on *Sauté* mode, add the oil, and heat it up. Add the chicken thighs, salt, and pepper, stir, and brown for 2 minutes. In a bowl, mix the stock with mustard, Italian seasoning, and lemon juice, and stir well. Pour this over the chicken, add the potatoes, stir

2. Cover the Foodi and cook on the "Poultry" setting for 15 minutes. Release the pressure, uncover the Foodi, stir the chicken, divide among plates, and serve

Duck and Vegetables

(Prep + Cook Time: 50 Minutes | **Servings:** 8)

Ingredients:
- 1 duck; chopped into eight pieces
- 1 cucumber; chopped
- 1-inch ginger piece, peeled and chopped
- 1 tbsp. wine
- 2 carrots; peeled and chopped
- 2 cups water
- Salt and ground black pepper, to taste

Instructions:
1. Put the duck pieces into the Foodi. Add the cucumber, carrots, wine, water, ginger, salt, and pepper, stir
2. Cover, and cook on "Poultry" mode for 40 minutes. Use the Natural Release Method, divide the mix among plates, and serve.

Asian Chicken

(Prep + Cook Time: 20 Minutes | **Servings:** 6)

Ingredients:
- 6 chicken thighs, boneless, skinless
- 1/3 cup white wine
- 1/2 cup soy sauce
- 5 garlic cloves; minced
- 1½ cups water
- 3 tbsp. scallions; chopped
- 1 tsp. sesame seeds
- 1 tbsp. Sriracha Hot Chili Sauce
- 1 tbsp. olive oil
- 1 ½ tsp. fresh ginger, grated
- 1 ½ tbsp. honey

Instructions:
1. Season both sides of the chicken thighs with garlic powder and pepper. Press the *Sauté* key and select the More option. Add the olive oil and heat
2. When the oil is hot, add the chicken and cook until both sides are browned; do not overcrowd the Foodi. You will need to cook in batches
3. While the chicken is browning, mix the Sriracha with the water, honey, soy sauce, wine, ginger, and garlic in a bowl
4. When the last batch of the chicken is browned, return all the browned chicken in the pot. Pour the Sriracha mixture in the pot.
5. Press the *Cancel* key to stop the *Sauté* function. Cover and lock the lid.
6. Press the *Pressure* key, set the pressure to HIGH, and set the timer for 5 minutes
7. When the Foodi timer beeps, turn the steam valve to quick release the pressure. Unlock and carefully open the lid.
8. Transfer the chicken into a serving platter and tent with foil to keep warm
9. Press the *Sauté* key and select the More option. Boil the sauce for 10 minutes. Pour the sauce over the chicken and top with scallions and sesame seeds.
10. Serve with broccoli and cauliflower rice. You can pour some of the sauce over the broccoli and the cauliflower rice.

Chicken Rogan Josh Curry

(Prep + Cook Time: 60 Minutes **| Servings:** 8)

Ingredients:
- 5-lb. boneless, skinless chicken thighs
- 1/3 lb. curry paste
- 2 coarsely chopped large tomatoes
- 4 oz. baby spinach leaves
- 4 oz. coriander leaves
- 1½ cups Greek Yogurt
- 1 tbsp. vegetable oil
- 1 onion, cut into wedges

Instructions:
1. First, combine the yogurt and the curry paste in a large bowl
2. Add the chicken and pour over with the mixture.
3. The chicken should be completely coated in the yogurt and curry mixture.
4. Leave the chicken in the bowl and cover with plastic wrap. Place the bowl in your refrigerator for about 30 minutes.
5. Press *Sauté* mode and heat the vegetable oil in your Foodi.
6. Add the onion and cook until it is golden brown. This should take about 8 to 10 minutes.
7. Add the onion and the diced tomatoes to the marinated chicken
8. Combine the ingredients and then pour into the Foodi
9. Close the lid. Press the *Pressure* key, set the pressure to HIGH, and set the timer for 15 minutes.
10. When the Foodi timer beeps. Allow the pressure to release naturally and then serve over rice or steamed vegetables.

Crispy Chicken Thighs with Carrots and Rice Pilaf

(Prep + Cook Time: 25 minutes **| Servings:** 4)

Ingredients:
- 4 uncooked boneless skin-on chicken thighs
- 1 box (6 oz.) rice pilaf
- 2 tbsp. honey, warmed
- 1/2 tsp. smoked paprika
- 1 3/4 cups water
- 1 tbsp. butter
- 4 carrots, peeled, cut in half, lengthwise
- 2 tsp. kosher salt, divided.
- 1 tbsp. extra-virgin olive oil
- 2 tsp. poultry spice
- 1/2 tsp. ground cumin

Instructions:
1. Place rice pilaf, water, and butter into pot; stir to incorporate
2. Place reversible rack in the pot, making sure rack is in the higher position. Place carrots in center of rack. Arrange chicken thighs, skin side up, around the carrots. Assemble pressure lid, making sure the PRESSURE RELEASE valve is in the SEAL position. Select PRESSURE and set to HIGH. Set time to 4 minutes. Select START/STOP to begin.
3. While chicken and rice are cooking, stir together warm honey, smoked paprika, cumin, and 1 tsp. salt. Set aside
4. When pressure cooking is complete, quick release the pressure by moving the PRESSURE RELEASE valve to the VENT position. Carefully remove lid when unit has finished releasing pressure.
5. Brush carrots with seasoned honey. Brush chicken with olive oil, then season evenly with poultry spice and remaining salt
6. Close crisping lid. Select BROIL and set time to 10 minutes. Select START/STOP to begin. When cooking is complete, serve chicken with carrots and rice.

Bone Broth

(Prep + Cook Time: 1 hour 40 Minutes | Servings: 8)

Ingredients:
- 2 to 3 lb. bones (2 to 3 lb. lamb, beef, pork, or non-oily fish, or 1 carcass of whole chicken)
- Assorted veggies (1/2 onion, a couple carrots, a couple stalks celery, and fresh herbs, if you have them on hand)
- Filtered water
- 1 tsp. unrefined sea salt
- 1 to 2 tbsp. apple cider vinegar

Instructions:
1. Put the bones in the Foodi. Top with the veggies. Add the salt and apple cider vinegar.
2. Pour in enough water to fill the pot 2/3 full. If you have enough time, let the pot sit for 30 minutes to allow the vinegar to start pulling the minerals out of the bones
3. Cover and lock the lid. Press the *Pressure* button, set the pressure to LOW, and set the timer for 120 minutes
4. When the Foodi timer beeps, press the *Cancel* key and unplug the Foodi. Let the pressure release naturally for 10 to 15 minutes or until the valve drops.
5. Unlock and carefully open the lid. Strain the broth
6. Discard the veggies and bones. Pour the broth into jars. Store in the refrigerator or freeze

Chicken Salad

(Prep + Cook Time: 1 hour 5 Minutes | Servings: 2)

Ingredients:
- 1 chicken breast, skinless and boneless
- 3 garlic cloves; peeled and minced
- Mixed salad greens
- A handful cherry tomatoes; cut into halves
- 3 cups water
- 1 tbsp. mustard
- 1 tbsp. balsamic vinegar
- 1 tbsp. honey
- 3 tbsp. extra virgin olive oil
- Salt and ground black pepper, to taste

Instructions:
1. In a bowl, mix 2 cups water with a pinch of salt. Add the chicken to the mixture, stir, and keep in the refrigerator for 45 minutes. Add the remaining water to the Foodi, place the chicken breast in the steamer basket of the Foodi
2. Cover and cook on the *Pressure* setting for 5 minutes. Release the pressure naturally, set the chicken breast aside to rest, then cut into thin strips. In a bowl, mix the garlic with salt and pepper, mustard, honey, vinegar, and olive oil and whisk well. In a salad bowl, mix chicken strips with the salad greens and tomatoes. Drizzle the vinaigrette on top, and serve.

Ginger Garlic Drumsticks

(Prep + Cook Time: 45 Minutes | Servings: 4)

Ingredients:
- 6 - 8 chicken drumsticks, skin on

For the sauce:
- 1/4 cup water
- 1/2 onion; chopped
- 1/2 cup soy sauce
- 2 tbsp. rice wine vinegar
- 2 tbsp. honey
- 2 tbsp. brown sugar
- 2 cloves garlic; minced
- 1 tsp. fresh ginger, minced

Instructions:
1. In a bowl, mix all of the sauce ingredients until well combined. Pour the sauce in the Foodi.

2. Add the chicken in the pot and push them down to submerge them in the sauce; they do not have to be covered completely with sauce. Cover and lock the lid
3. Press the *Pressure* key, set the pressure to HIGH, and set the timer for 15 minutes.
4. When the Foodi timer beeps, let the pressure release naturally for 15 minutes. Turn the steam valve to release remaining pressure. Unlock and carefully open the lid
5. Press the *Sauté* key and boil until the sauce is reduced.
6. Remove the drumsticks and transfer them into a parchment paper lined cookie sheet.
7. Turn the oven setting to broil, and preheat the broiler 10 to 15 minutes before cooking. Broil each side of the chicken for 2 minutes.
8. Meanwhile, let the sauce cook in the Foodi until reduced more.
9. Remove the chicken from the oven and put on a serving platter. Pour the sauce over the chicken. Serve and enjoy!

Curried Lemon Coconut Chicken

(Prep + Cook Time: 40 Minutes | **Servings:** 6)

Ingredients:
- About 4 lbs. chicken, breasts, thighs, or a combo (whatever you have)
- 1 can full fat coconut milk
- 1/4 Cup lemon juice
- 1 tbsp. curry powder
- 1 tsp. turmeric
- 1/2 tsp. salt
- Optional: 1/2 to 1 tsp. lemon zest

Instructions:
1. Mix the coconut milk, lemon juice and spices together in a bowl or glass measuring cup.
2. Pour a little bit on the bottom of the Foodi
3. Add the chicken.
4. Pour in the rest, including the coconut cream chunk if you've got one, on top of the chicken.
5. Lock in the lid and close the valve. Turn the Foodi to "poultry" which should be 15 minutes at High pressure
6. If working with frozen chicken breasts, add 10 minutes to the cook time and you should be fine.
7. Use the Quick Pressure Release method.
8. Test chicken for doneness by cutting open and observing the center
9. Use 2 forks to shred the chicken up in the pot.
10. Add 1/2 to 1 tsp. lemon zest after cooking. Serve with steamed or roasted veggies or over rice.

Thai Lime Chicken

(Prep + Cook Time: 20 Minutes | **Servings:** 4 to 6)

Ingredients:
- 2 lbs. boneless skinless chicken thighs
- 1 tsp. grated fresh ginger
- 1 tsp. chopped fresh mint
- 2 tsp. chopped fresh cilantro
- 1 Cup lime juice
- 1/2 Cup fish sauce
- 1/4 Cup olive oil
- 2 tbsp. coconut nectar

Instructions:
1. Place the Chicken in bottom of the Foodi. Combine all remaining ingredients in a mason jar and shake well
2. Pour over chicken
3. Cook at High pressure for 10 minutes, to get 10 minutes' cook time, press *Pressure* button.
4. Use Quick Pressure Release method. Serve

Turkey Legs

(Prep + Cook Time: 40 Minutes | **Servings:** 2 to 4)

Ingredients:
- 2 turkey legs
- 1 small onion; sliced
- 3 cloves garlic; roughly minced
- 1 celery stalk, chopped
- 1 cup unsalted homemade chicken stock
- 1 tbsp. light soy sauce
- 1 tbsp. olive oil
- 2 bay leaves
- A pinch of rosemary
- A pinch of thyme
- A dash of sherry wine
- Kosher salt and ground black pepper to taste

Instructions:
1. Season the turkey legs with generous amount of kosher salt and ground black pepper.
2. Heat up your Foodi, press *Sauté* button
3. Add 1 tbsp. of olive oil into the pot. Ensure to coat the oil over the whole bottom of the pot. Add the seasoned turkey legs into the pot, then let it brown for roughly 2, 3 minutes per side. Remove and set aside.
4. Add the sliced onion and stir. Add a pinch of kosher salt and ground black pepper to season if you like. Cook the onions for roughly one minute until soften. Add garlic, and then stir for 30 seconds until fragrance.
5. Add in chopped celery and cook for roughly one minute
6. Add in a dash of sherry wine, deglaze the bottom of the pot with a wooden spoon. Allow it to cook for a moment for the alcohol to evaporate. Add chicken stock and light soy sauce, then taste the seasoning. Add in more salt and pepper if desired
7. Place the turkey legs into the Foodi, then close lid. Pressure cook at High pressure for 20 minutes. To get 20 minutes' cook time, press *Pressure* button
8. Use Natural Pressure Release method for 10 minutes and then Quick Pressure Release. Serve.

Chicken and Sausage Stew

(Prep + Cook Time: 20 Minutes | **Servings:** 6)

Ingredients:
- 2 lb. boneless skinless chicken thighs, trimmed
- 3/4 lb. smoked pork or turkey sausage; such as kielbasa, cut into 2-inch pieces
- 1 medium celery stalk, chopped
- 1 large globe or beefsteak tomato, chopped
- 8 small red potatoes; halved
- 1 small yellow onion, chopped
- 1/2 cup dry white wine; such as Pinot Grigio
- 1/2 cup chicken broth
- 1 tbsp. minced garlic
- 1 tsp. dried oregano
- 1 tsp. finely grated orange zest
- 1 tsp. smoked paprika
- 1/2 tsp. fennel seeds
- 1/2 tsp. salt
- 1/2 tsp. ground black pepper
- Up to ½ tsp. saffron threads
- 2 tsp. olive oil

Instructions:
1. Mix the chicken, garlic, oregano, zest, smoked paprika, fennel seeds, salt, pepper, and saffron in a large bowl until the meat is evenly coated in the spices. Cover and refrigerate for 4 to 6 hours
2. Heat the oil in the Foodi turned to the *Sautéing/Browning* function. Add half the chicken thighs and brown well, turning once, about 6 minutes. Transfer to a large, clean bowl and repeat with the remainder of the chicken
3. Add the onion and celery to the pot; cook, stirring often, until the onion turns translucent, about 4 minutes. Add the tomato and stir just until it begins to break down, about 2 minutes. Pour in the wine and broth; scrape up any browned bits in the bottom of the cooker.

4. Return the chicken to the cooker, adding any juices in the bowl and every last speck of the spices. Nestle the sausage and potatoes into the sauce
5. Lock the lid onto the cooker. Set the Foodi to cook at High pressure for 15 minutes. To get 15 minutes' cook time, press *Pressure* button
6. Use the Quick Pressure Release method. Stir well before serving.

Sweet Chipotle Chicken Wings

(**Prep + Cook Time:** 25 minutes | **Servings:** 2)

Ingredients:
- 3 tbsp. Mexican hot sauce (such as Valentina brand)
- 1 tsp. minced canned chipotle in adobo sauce
- 1 cup water, for steaming
- 2 tbsp. honey

Instructions:
1. If using whole wings, cut off the tips and discard. Cut the wings at the joint into two pieces each the *drumette and the flat.
2. Add the water and insert the steamer basket or trivet. Place the wings on the steamer insert
3. High pressure for 10 minutes. Close the lid and the pressure valve and then cook for 10 minutes.
4. To get 10 minutes' cook time, press *Pressure* button and the time selector
5. Pressure Release. Use the quick release method. Finish the dish. While the wings are cooking, make the sauce. In a large bowl, whisk together the hot sauce, honey and minced chipotle.
6. Close crisping lid. Select *Air Crisp*, set temperature to 390°F and set time to 10 minutes. Select START/STOP to begin. Serve!

Instant Penne with Chicken

(**Prep + Cook Time:** 10 minutes | **Servings:** 4)

Ingredients:
- 1/2 lb. penne or similar pasta shape
- 3 (4 oz.) boneless, skinless chicken thighs
- Parmigiano Reggiano or similar cheese, for garnish
- 3 garlic cloves, minced or pressed (about 1 tbsp.)
- 1 small green bell pepper, seeded and cut into 1-inch chunks (about 1 ½ cups)
- 1 ½ cups Quick Marinara Sauce or plain tomato sauce
- 1/2 tsp. dried Italian herbs, divided. (or 1/4 tsp. dried oregano and 1/4 tsp. dried basil)
- 3 cups arugula or baby spinach
- 2 tbsp. minced sun dried tomatoes (optional)
- 1 tbsp. all purpose flour
- 1 tsp. kosher salt, divided.
- 1/8 tsp. granulated garlic or garlic powder
- 1/8 tsp. freshly ground black pepper
- 1 tbsp. olive oil
- 1 cup thinly sliced onion
- 1/2 cup dry white or red wine
- 1 3/4 cups water

Instructions:
1. In a small bowl or jar with a shaker top, mix the flour, 1/2 tsp. of kosher salt the granulated garlic, 1/4 tsp. of Italian herbs and the pepper. Sprinkle the flour mixture over both sides of the chicken thighs, coating as evenly as possible.
2. Set Foodi Multi-cooker to *Sauté*, heat the olive oil until it shimmers and flows like water. Add the chicken thighs and cook for 5 minutes or until golden brown
3. Turn the thighs over and cook the other side for 5 minutes more or until that side is also golden brown. Remove the thighs to a rack or cutting board and cool for 3 minutes.
4. With the Foodi Multi-cooker on *Sauté* add the onion, green bell pepper and garlic. Cook for about 3 minutes, stirring until the onions just start to brown

5. Pour in the wine and scrape the bottom of the pan to release the browned bits, cooking until the wine is almost completely evaporated
6. Add the Quick Marinara Sauce the remaining 1/2 tsp. of kosher salt the sun dried tomatoes (if using) the remaining 1/4 tsp. of Italian herbs the water the chicken and the penne.
7. High pressure for 5 minutes. Lock the lid on the Foodi Multi-cooker and then cook for 5 minutes.
8. To get 5 minutes' cook time, press *Pressure* button and use the Time Adjustment button to adjust the cook time to 5 minutes
9. Pressure Release. Use the quick release method.
10. Finish the dish. Unlock and remove the lid. The penne should be almost done and the sauce will be a little thin
11. Add the arugula and stir. With the Foodi Multi-cooker set to *Sauté*, cook for 3 to 4 minutes or until the pasta is done to your liking the arugula is wilted and the sauce has thickened. Serve topped with grated Parmigiano Reggiano.

Chicken and Green Chile Stew

(**Prep + Cook Time:** 20 Minutes | **Servings:** 4 to 6)

Ingredients:
- 6 boneless skinless chicken thighs (about 1½ lb.), trimmed and halved
- 1 large yellow onion; chopped
- 3 (4½ oz.) cans chopped mild green chiles (about 1½ cups)
- 2 cups chicken broth
- 6 small white potatoes (about 1¼ lb.); halved
- 1/4 cup loosely packed fresh cilantro leaves, chopped
- 2 tbsp. peanut oil
- 1 tbsp. minced garlic
- 1/2 tbsp. ground cumin
- 1 tsp. dried oregano

Instructions:
1. Heat the oil in the Foodi turned to the *Sautéing/Browning* function. Add the chicken and cook until lightly browned, about 6 minutes, stirring occasionally. Transfer the chicken pieces to a large bowl
2. Add the onion to the pot; cook, stirring often, until softened, about 4 minutes. Stir in the chiles, garlic, cumin, and oregano; cook until aromatic, less than a minute. Pour in the broth and stir well to get any browned bits up off the bottom of the pot. Return the chicken and any juices to the cooker, add the potatoes, and stir well.
3. Lock the lid onto the pot. Set the Foodi to cook at High pressure for 15 minutes. To get 15 minutes' cook time, press *Pressure* button
4. Use the Quick Pressure Release method. Unlock and open the pot. Stir in the cilantro before serving. Serve.

Chicken with Mushrooms

(**Prep + Cook Time:** 30 Minutes | **Servings:** 4)

Ingredients:
- 6 boneless skinless chicken (cut into bite-sized chunks)
- 1 cup Romano cheese
- 1 (10 oz.) can tomato sauce
- 1 (4 oz.) can, I have used fresh sliced mushrooms
- 1/2 cup flour (all-purpose)
- 2 tbsp. oil
- 1 onion minced
- 1 tsp. vinegar
- 1 tbsp. sugar
- 1 tsp. garlic, minced
- 1 tbsp. dried oregano
- 1 tsp. dried basil
- 1 tsp. chicken bouillon granules
- 1/2 tsp. salt
- 1/2 tsp. pepper

Instructions:
1. Turn your Foodi onto the *Sauté* feature and place the chicken in oil until chicken starts to brown.
2. Add onion and garlic and cook until they start to become translucent
3. Add remaining ingredients except Romano cheese. Stir to combine ingredients
4. Close the Foodi lid. Cook at High pressure for 10 minutes. To get 10 minutes' cook time, press *Pressure* button
5. After cooking, use "keep warm" mode for 10 minutes. Use Quick Pressure Release Method.
6. Remove lid and add Romano cheese and stir.
7. Add the butter-flour paste-mixture to thicken sauce. Serve.

Honey Sriracha Chicken Wings

(Prep + Cook Time: 20 Minutes | **Servings:** 4)

Ingredients:
- 1 lb. pasture-raised chicken wings (or drummettes)
- 2 tbsp. cooking fat (ghee, olive oil, avocado oil)
- 1/2 tsp. garlic powder
- 1/4 cup local honey
- 2 tsp. Sriracha
- 1/4 cup water
- 1/2 tsp. sea salt

Instructions:
1. Start by patting your chicken wings dry with a towel. Sprinkle them with the sea salt and garlic powder. In a bowl, whisk together the honey and Sriracha. Now baste the wings with half of the honey-Sriracha mixture
2. Turn your Pressure Cooker on and select the Sauté feature. Pour in your cooking fat and situate the chicken wings in the basin. The browning step is your only opportunity to seal in the juices and crisp the skin, so brown them on both sides (about 2 minutes on each side, being cautious not to burn), and then pour in the water and secure the lid
3. High pressure for 5 minutes. Close off the pressure valve and press the Keep Warm button. Now select the *Pressure* button cook on High pressure for 5 minutes. Once the cooking is complete, Quick Pressure Release the pressure valve and remove the lid when safe. Remove the wings and drizzle with the remaining Sriracha mixture. Serve warm.

Whole Chicken Recipe

(Prep + Cook Time: 30 Minutes | **Servings:** 8)

Ingredients:
- 1 medium-sized; whole chicken
- 1 minced piece of ginger
- 1 minced green onion
- 2 tbsp. sugar
- 1 tbsp. cooking wine
- 2 to 3 cups water or chicken broth
- 2 tsp. soy sauce
- 2 tsp. salt

Instructions:
1. Season the chicken thoroughly with salt and sugar.
2. Sprinkle 1 tsp. of salt into the bottom of the Foodi
3. Pour the wine, water or broth and soy sauce into the cooker, and add the chicken.
4. Choose "POULTRY" and cook on HIGH pressure for 15 minutes
5. When time is up, flip the chicken, and push "POULTRY" again
6. Let the pressure come down naturally before opening the cooker. Serve chicken pieces with green onion on top and any side dishes you'd like.

Turkey Chili

(Prep + Cook Time: 40 Minutes | **Servings:** 4)

Ingredients:
- 1 lb. 85% lean ground turkey
- 15 oz. chick peas (or your favorite white bean), previously cooked in your Foodi
- 1 yellow bell pepper diced (you can add another yellow bell pepper)
- 1 medium onion diced
- 12 oz. water with vegetable stock or 12 oz. vegetable stock
- 4 to 5 oz. water
- 2 to 3 cloves garlic peeled and not chopped 2.5 tbsp. chili powder
- 1.5 tsp. cumin
- 1/8 tsp. cayenne
- 2 cans original rotel
- 1 (5.5 oz.) can V8

Instructions:
1. Add lean ground turkey and water into Foodi.
2. Lock the lid on the Foodi and then cook On High pressure for 5 minutes. To get 5 minutes' cook time, press *Pressure* button and use the *Time Adjustment* button to adjust the cook time to 5 minutes
3. Use Natural Pressure Release method for 10 minutes, then Quick Pressure Release.
4. Open the Foodi and break up the ground turkey add the remaining ingredients
5. Lock the lid on the Foodi and then cook On High pressure for 5 minutes. To get 5 minutes' cook time, press *Pressure* button and use the *Time Adjustment* button to adjust the cook time to 5 minutes
6. Use Natural Pressure Release method for 10 minutes, then Quick Pressure Release. Stir, Serve and enjoy.

Now and Later Butter Chicken

(Prep + Cook Time: 55 Minutes | **Servings:** 4)

Ingredients:
- 1 (14.5 oz.) can diced tomatoes, undrained
- 1 lb. boneless; skinless chicken breasts or thighs
- 1/2 cup unsalted butter, cut into cubes, or 1/2 cup coconut oil
- 1/2 cup heavy (whipping) cream or full-fat coconut milk
- 1/4 to 1/2 cup chopped fresh cilantro
- 4 cups Cauliflower Rice or cucumber noodles
- 5 or 6 garlic cloves; minced
- 1 tbsp. minced fresh ginger
- 1 tsp. ground turmeric
- 1 tsp. cayenne
- 1 tsp. smoked paprika
- 2 tsp. Garam Masala; divided
- 1 tsp. ground cumin
- 1 tsp. salt

Instructions:
1. Put the tomatoes, garlic, ginger, turmeric, cayenne, paprika, 1 tsp. of garam masala, cumin, and salt in the inner cooking pot of the Pressure Cooker. Mix thoroughly, then place the chicken pieces on top of the sauce.
2. Lock the lid into place. Select Manual and adjust the pressure to High. Cook for 10 minutes. When the cooking is complete, let the pressure release naturally. Unlock the lid. Carefully remove the chicken and set aside
3. Using an immersion blender in the pot, blend together all the ingredients into a smooth sauce. (Or use a stand blender, but be careful with the hot sauce and be sure to leave the inside lid open to vent.) After blending, let the sauce cool before adding the remaining ingredients or it will be thinner than is ideal. Add the butter cubes, cream, remaining 1 tsp. of garam masala, and cilantro. Stir until well incorporated. The sauce should be thick enough to coat the back of a spoon when you're done
4. Remove half the sauce and freeze it for later or refrigerate for up to 2 to 3 days.
5. Cut the chicken into bite-size pieces. Add it back to the sauce

6. Preheat the Pressure Cooker by selecting Sauté and adjust to Less for low heat. Let the chicken heat through. Break it up into smaller pieces if you like, but don't shred it. Serve over cauliflower rice or raw cucumber noodles.

Stuffed Chicken Recipe

(Prep + Cook Time: 30 minutes | **Servings:** 4)

Ingredients:
- 4 Chicken Breasts, skinless
- 1 cup Baby Spinach, frozen
- 1/2 cup crumbled Feta Cheese
- 2 tbsp. Olive Oil
- 2 tsp dried Parsley
- 1/2 tsp dried Oregano
- 1/2 tsp Garlic Powder
- Salt and Black Pepper to taste
- 1 cup Water

Instructions:
1. Wrap the chicken in plastic and put on a cutting board. Use a rolling pin to pound flat to a quarter inch thickness. Remove the plastic wrap
2. In a bowl, mix spinach, salt, and feta cheese and scoop the mixture onto the chicken breasts. Wrap the chicken to secure the spinach filling in it.
3. Use toothpicks to secure the wrap firmly from opening. Gently season the chicken pieces with oregano, parsley, garlic powder, and pepper
4. Select Sear/Sauté mode on Foodi. Heat the oil, add the chicken, and sear to golden brown on each side. Work in 2 batches.
5. Remove the chicken onto a plate and set aside. Pour the water into the pot and use a spoon to scrape the bottom of the pot to let loose any chicken pieces or seasoning that is stuck to the bottom of the pot. Fit the reversible rack into the pot with care as the pot will still be hot
6. Transfer the chicken onto the rack. Seal the lid and select Pressure mode on High pressure for 10 minutes. Press Start/Stop.
7. Once the timer has ended, do a quick pressure release. Close the crisping lid and cook on Bake/Roast mode for 5 minutes at 370 F
8. Plate the chicken and serve with a side of sautéed asparagus, and some slices of tomatoes.

Mozzarella Marinara Chicken

(Prep + Cook Time: 35 Minutes | **Servings:** 4)

Ingredients:
- 4 large chicken breasts, boneless, skinless
- 1 cup low-fat Mozzarella, grated
- 1 cup water
- 2 cloves garlic; crushed or pressed
- 1 can (14 oz.) crushed tomatoes in puree
- 1 tbsp. olive oil
- 1 tsp. dried basil
- 1/4 tsp. red pepper flakes
- 1/4 tsp. salt

Instructions:
1. Season the chicken breast with salt and pepper.
2. Add the oil into the Foodi, press the *Sauté* key, and heat the oil.
3. Cooking in 2 batches, cook the chicken breast until browned. Transfer onto a plate. If needed, add more oil in the pot
4. Add the garlic; sauté for 1 minute. Add the water, tomatoes, red pepper flakes, basil, or salt. Stir until combined.
5. Return the chicken into the Foodi. Cover and lock the lid.
6. Press the *Pressure* key, set the pressure to HIGH, and set the timer for 5 minutes
7. When the Foodi timer beeps, turn the steam valve to Venting to quick release the pressure. Unlock and carefully open the lid.
8. Check the chicken to make sure the meat is cooked and the middle is no longer pink. Preheat the broiler.

9. Grease a small-sized glass casserole with nonstick cooking spray
10. Put the chicken in the dish. Press the *Sauté* key of the Foodi. Bring the sauce in the pot to a simmer and cook until thick to your preferred consistency.
11. Pour the thickened sauce over the chicken in the dish. Sprinkle grated mozzarella cheese over the chicken.
12. Put the dish in the broiler and broil until the cheese starts to brown lightly and melted. Watch carefully because the cheese can brown quickly

Chicken Breasts with White Wine

(Prep + Cook Time: 25 minutes | **Servings:** 4)

Ingredients:
- 4 (12 oz.) bone in, skin on chicken breasts
- 1 (4-inch) fresh rosemary sprig
- 1/2 cup fresh orange juice
- 1/2 cup dry but light white wine, such as Sauvignon Blanc
- 1/2 tbsp. potato starch or cornstarch
- 1 tbsp. honey
- 3 tbsp. unsalted butter
- 1/2 tsp. salt
- 1/2 tsp. ground black pepper

Instructions:
1. Melt the butter in a Foodi Multi-cooker, turned to the sauté function. Season the chicken with the salt and pepper, then add two breasts skin side down to the cooker.
2. Brown well, turning once, about 5 minutes; transfer to a large bowl. Brown the remaining breasts and leave them in the cooker
3. Return the first two breasts to the cooker, arranging them so that all are skin up but overlapping only as necessary, thinner parts over thick. Pour the orange juice and wine over the chicken. Tuck in the rosemary and drizzle everything with honey
4. High pressure for 18 minutes. Lock the lid on the Foodi Multi-cooker and then cook for 18 minutes.
5. To get 18 minutes' cook time, press *Pressure* button and use the Time Adjustment button to adjust the cook time to 18 minutes.
6. Pressure Release. Use the quick release method to bring the pot's pressure back to normal.
7. Finish the dish. Unlock and open the pot. Discard the rosemary sprig. Use kitchen tongs to transfer the chicken breasts to individual serving plates or a serving platter
8. Dissolve the potato starch or cornstarch with 1/2 tbsp. water in a small bowl. Turn the Foodi to its sauté function; bring the sauce to a simmer
9. Add this slurry and cook, stirring all the time, until thickened, about 20 seconds. Ladle the sauce over the chicken to serve.

Chicken Ragú

(Prep + Cook Time: 12 Minutes | **Servings:** 4 to 6)

Ingredients:
- 2 lb. boneless skinless chicken thighs; trimmed and finely chopped
- 1/2 cup dry; oaky white wine, such as Chardonnay
- 1 lb. dried spaghetti; cooked and drained
- 1 (8 oz.) pancetta chunk, chopped
- Up to 1/2 tsp. grated nutmeg
- 1/4 cup tomato paste
- 1 medium yellow onion; diced
- 1 medium carrot; diced
- 1 tbsp. unsalted butter
- 2 tbsp. olive oil
- 1½ cups chicken broth
- 6 tbsp. golden raisins
- 2 tbsp. loosely packed fresh sage leaves; minced
- 1/2 tsp. ground cloves
- 1/2 tsp. ground black pepper

Instructions:
1. Melt the butter in the oil in the Foodi turned to the *Sautéing/Browning* function. Add the pancetta, onion, and carrot; cook, stirring often, until the onion softens, about 5 minutes

2. Add the chicken and cook, stirring occasionally, until it has lost its raw color, about 4 minutes. Pour in the wine and scrape up any browned bits on the bottom of the pot as it comes to a simmer. Add the broth, raisins, tomato paste, sage, cloves, pepper, and nutmeg; stir until the tomato sauce dissolves.
3. Lock the lid onto the pot. Set the Foodi to cook at High pressure for 7 minutes. To get 7 minutes' cook time, press *Pressure* button and use the *Time Adjustment* button to adjust the cook time to 7 minutes.
4. Use the Quick Pressure Release method
5. Unlock and open the pot. Turn the Foodi to its *Sautéing/Browning* function. Bring the sauce to a simmer; cook, stirring often, until slightly thickened, about 5 minutes. Serve over the cooked spaghetti in bowls.

Delicious Chicken and Coconut Curry

(Prep + Cook Time: 35 minutes | **Servings:** 4)

Ingredients:
- 4 Chicken Breasts
- 2 cup Green Beans, cut in half
- 2 Red Bell Pepper, seeded and cut in 2-inch sliced
- 2 Yellow Bell Pepper, seeded and cut in 2-inch slices
- 1/2 cup Chicken Broth
- 2 cups Coconut Milk
- 4 tbsp. Red Curry Paste
- 4 tbsp. Sugar
- 2 tbsp. Lime Juice
- Salt and Black Pepper to taste

Instructions:
1. Add the chicken, red curry paste, salt, pepper, coconut milk, broth and sugar, in the Foodi inner pot
2. Close the pressure lid, secure the pressure valve, and select Pressure mode on High for 15 minutes. Press Start/Stop.
3. Once the timer has ended, do a quick pressure release, and open the lid
4. Remove the chicken onto a cutting board and close the crisping lid. Select Broil mode. Add the bell peppers, green beans, and lime juice.
5. Stir the sauce with a spoon and cook for 4 minutes
6. Slice the chicken with a knife, pour the sauce and vegetables over and serve warm.

Texas Trail Chili

(Prep + Cook Time: 20 minutes | **Servings:** 8)

Ingredients:
- 1 ½ lb. ground beef, turkey or chicken
- 2 Cups favorite Bloody Mary mix (spicy preferred)
- 4 tbsp. (or more if you like) favorite chili powder, divided.
- 2 Cans (14 oz. each) kidney beans, drained and rinsed well
- 2 Cans (14 oz. each) diced tomatoes with green chilies (or 28 oz. can diced tomatoes with juice)
- 2 tbsp. canola oil
- 1 large onion, peeled, chopped.
- 1 ½-Cups Water
- Corn chips
- Shredded cheese
- Sliced green onions
- Sour cream

Instructions:
1. In the Foodi Multi-cooker pot, heat the oil. Use *Sauté* Function. Add the onion and Sauté about 8 minutes until it becomes lightly golden brown. Add the meat and cook until it browns, breaking it up as it cooks.
2. When meat is done, remove turkey thighs to a cutting board and cover loosely with foil
3. Stir in the Bloody Mary mix and heat, stirring and scraping up any browned bits on the bottom of the pan.
4. Add the tomatoes, beans and 2 tbsp. of the chili powder. Stir well. Bring to just a boil; add the water

5. High pressure for 5 minutes. Lock the lid on the Foodi Multi-cooker and then cook for 5 minutes
6. To get 5 minutes' cook time, press *Pressure* button and use the Time Adjustment button to adjust the cook time to 5 minutes
7. Pressure Release. Use the Quick Release method.
8. Finish the dish. Just before serving stir in tbsp. of the chili powder then let it stand 5 minutes.
9. Ladle into bowls and garnish as desired

Turkey Meatballs in Tomato Sauce

(Prep + Cook Time: 15 minutes | **Servings:** 4)

Ingredients:
- 1 lb. ground turkey
- 1 large egg, at room temperature and beaten in a small bowl
- 1 (28 oz.) can whole tomatoes, drained and roughly chopped. (about 3 ½ cups)
- 1 medium yellow onion, chopped.
- 2 medium celery stalks, thinly sliced
- 1/2 cup plain dried breadcrumbs
- 1/4 cup finely grated Parmesan cheese (about 1/2 oz.)
- 2 tbsp. unsalted butter
- 1/2 cup chicken broth
- 1 tbsp. packed fresh oregano leaves, minced
- 1/4 tsp. grated nutmeg
- 1/4 cup heavy cream
- 1/2 tsp. dried oregano
- 1/2 tsp. dried rosemary
- 1/2 tsp. ground black pepper
- 1/2 tsp. salt

Instructions:
1. Mix the ground turkey, egg, breadcrumbs, cheese, oregano, rosemary, pepper and 1/4 tsp. salt in a large bowl until well combined. Form the mixture into 12 balls.
2. Melt the butter in the Foodi Multi-cooker turned to the sauté function. Add the onion and celery; cook, often stirring, until the onion turns translucent, about 3 minutes.
3. Stir in the tomatoes, broth, oregano and the remaining 1/4 tsp. salt. Drop the meatballs into the sauce.
4. High pressure for 10 minutes. Lock the lid on the Foodi Multi-cooker and then cook for 10 minutes.
5. To get 10 minutes' cook time, press *Pressure* button and use the Time Adjustment button to adjust the cook time to 10 minutes
6. Pressure Release. Use the quick release method to drop the pot's pressure to normal
7. Finish the dish. Unlock and open the cooker. Turn the Foodi Multi-cooker to its sauté function.
8. Stir in the cream and nutmeg; simmer, stirring all the while, for 1 minute to reduce the cream a little and blend the flavors.

Green Chicken Curry

(Prep + Cook Time: 25 minutes | **Servings:** 6 to 8)

Ingredients:
- 3 lb. boneless skinless chicken thighs, cut into 1/2-inch by 2 inch lengths
- 12 oz. green beans, trimmed and cut into 2 inch pieces
- Cream from the top of a (13.5 oz.) can coconut milk
- 1 tsp. Diamond Crystal kosher salt or 3/4 tsp. fine sea salt
- The rest of the (13.5 oz.) can coconut milk
- 4 tbsp. green curry paste (a whole 4 oz. can)
- 1 tbsp. fish sauce (plus more to taste)
- 1 tbsp. soy sauce (plus more to taste)
- 1 tbsp. brown sugar (plus more to taste)
- 1 tbsp. vegetable oil
- 1 medium onion, peeled and sliced thin
- 3 cloves garlic, crushed
- 1/2- inch piece of ginger, peeled and crushed
- 1 cup chicken stock or water
- Juice from 1 lime
- Minced basil (preferably Thai basil)
- Minced cilantro
- Jasmine rice
- Lime wedges

Instructions:
1. Heat the vegetable oil in the Foodi Multi-cooker until shimmering, use Sauté mode. Stir in the onion, garlic and ginger and Sauté until the onion starts to soften, about 3 minutes.
2. Fry the curry paste: Scoop the cream from the top of the can of coconut milk and add it to the pot, then stir in the curry paste. Cook, often stirring, until the curry paste darkens, about 5 minutes
3. Sprinkle the chicken with the kosher salt. Add the chicken to the pot and stir to coat with curry paste. Stir in the rest of the can of coconut milk, chicken stock, fish sauce, soy sauce and brown sugar.
4. High pressure for 10 minutes. Lock the lid on the Foodi Multi-cooker and then cook for 10 minutes.
5. To get 10 minutes' cook time, press *Pressure* button and use the Time Adjustment button to adjust the cook time to 10 minutes
6. Pressure Release. Use the quick release method to bring the pot's pressure back to normal
7. Finish the dish. Close crisping lid. Select *Air Crisp*, set temperature to 390°F and set time to 15 minutes. Check after 10 minutes, cooking for an additional 5 minutes if dish needs more browning.
8. Finish the curry: Remove the lid from the Foodi Multi-cooker, then set Sauté mode. Stir in the lime juice and the green beans and simmer the curry until the green beans are crisp tender, about 4 minutes
9. Taste the curry for seasoning, adding more soy sauce (to add salt) or brown sugar (to add sweet) as needed. Ladle the curry into bowls, sprinkle with minced cilantro and basil and serve with Jasmine rice.

Turkey Breast

(**Prep + Cook Time:** 1 hour 10 minutes | **Servings:** 4)

Ingredients:
- 1 frozen turkey breast with frozen gravy packet
- 1 whole onion

Instructions:
1. Place frozen turkey breast, rozen gravy packet and whole onion in the Foodi Multi-cooker
2. High pressure for 30 minutes. Lock the lid on the Foodi Multi-cooker and then cook for 30 minutes.
3. To get 30 minutes' cook time, press *Pressure* button and use the Time Adjustment button to adjust the cook time to 30 minutes.
4. Pressure Release. Use natural release method
5. Remove lid, turn turkey breast over
6. High pressure for 30 minutes. Replace lid on the Foodi Multi-cooker and then cook for 30 minutes.
7. To get 30 minutes' cook time, press *Pressure* button
8. and use the Time Adjustment button to adjust the cook time to 30 minutes.
9. Pressure Release. Use natural release method, again.
10. Finish the dish. Close crisping lid. Select *Air Crisp*, set temperature to 360°F and set time to 10 minutes. Check after 5 minutes, cooking for an additional 5 minutes if dish needs more browning
11. Remove mesh. Remove turkey and slice. Places slices and turkey gravy into serving dish.

Awesome Turkey Sloppy Joes

(**Prep + Cook Time:** 35 minutes | **Servings:** 2)

Ingredients:
- 1 large or 2 small turkey thighs (1 ½ lb. total), skin removed
- 1/4 small red or green bell pepper, chopped. (about 2 tbsp.)
- 1 tbsp. cider or wine vinegar, plus additional as needed
- 2 tsp. ancho or New Mexico chili powder
- 1 tsp. Dijon mustard
- 1/2 tsp. Worcestershire sauce
- 1 tbsp. olive oil
- 1/4 cup chopped onion
- 1 garlic clove, minced or pressed
- Kosher salt
- 2/3 cup tomato sauce
- 1/4 cup beer or water
- 1 tbsp. packed brown sugar
- 2 hamburger buns

Instructions:
1. Set the Foodi Multi-cooker to *Sauté*, heat the olive oil until it shimmers and flows like water. Add the onion, bell pepper and garlic and sprinkle with a pinch or two of kosher salt. Cook for about 5 minutes, stirring, until the onions just begin to brown.
2. Add the tomato sauce, beer, cider vinegar, brown sugar, chili powder, mustard and Worcestershire sauce. Bring to a simmer. Stir to make sure the brown sugar is dissolved. Place the turkey thigh in the cooker
3. High pressure for 30 minutes. Lock the lid on the Foodi Multi-cooker and then cook for 30 minutes
4. To get 30 minutes' cook time, press *Pressure* button and use the Time Adjustment button to adjust the cook time to 30 minutes
5. Pressure Release. Use the natural release.
6. Unlock and remove the lid; transfer the turkey to a plate or cutting board to cool.
7. Finish the dish. Set the Foodi Multi-cooker to *Sauté* and simmer the sauce for about 5 minutes or until it's the consistency of a thick tomato sauce.
8. Skim any visible fat from the surface and discard. Taste and adjust the seasoning. Serve on the hamburger buns.

Chicken with Mushrooms and Artichoke Hearts

(**Prep + Cook Time:** 18 minutes | **Servings:** 6)

Ingredients:
- 2 (8 oz.) or 4 (4 oz.) bone in, skin on chicken thighs
- 4 oz. white button or cremini mushrooms, trimmed and quartered
- 1 tbsp. olive oil
- 1/2 cup frozen artichoke hearts, thawed
- 1/3 cup low sodium chicken broth
- 1/4 cup sliced onion
- 1/2 cup dry white wine
- 1 bay leaf
- 1/4 tsp. dried thyme
- Freshly ground black pepper
- 1/2 tsp. kosher salt

Instructions:
1. Using 1/2 tsp. of kosher salt, sprinkle the chicken thighs on both sides.
2. In the Foodi Multi-cooker set to *Sauté*, heat the olive oil until it shimmers and flows like water. Add the chicken thighs, skin sidedown and cook, undisturbed, for about 6 minutes or until the skin is dark golden brown and most of the fat under the skin has rendered
3. Turn the thighs to the other side and cook for about 3 minutes more or until that side is light golden brown. Remove the thighs
4. Carefully pour off almost all the fat, leaving just enough (about 1 tbsp.) to cover the bottom of the Foodi Multi-cooker with a thick coat. Add the onion and mushrooms and cook for about 5 minutes or until softened. Add the white wine and cook for 3 to 5 minutes or until reduced by half
5. Add the bay leaf, thyme, artichokes and chicken broth and bring to a simmer. Return the chicken to the pot, skin side up.
6. High pressure for 12 minutes. Lock the lid on the Foodi Multi-cooker and then cook for 12 minutes.
7. To get 12 minutes' cook time, press *Pressure* button and use the Time Adjustment button to adjust the cook time to 12 minutes
8. Pressure Release. After cooking, use the natural method to release pressure
9. Finish the dish. Unlock and remove the lid. Remove the chicken thighs from the pan and set aside. Remove the bay leaf.
10. Strain the sauce into a fat separator and let it rest until the fat rises to the surface. If you don't have a fat separator, let the sauce sit for a few minutes; then spoon or blot off any excess fat from the top and discard.
11. Pour the defatted sauce back into the cooker and add the chicken thighs and the solids from the sauce. If you prefer a thicker sauce, turn the Foodi Multi-cooker to the *Sauté* function and simmer the sauce for several minutes until it's reduced to the consistency you like
12. Adjust the seasoning, adding more salt if necessary and several grinds of pepper and serve.

Cranberry Braised Turkey Wings

(Prep + Cook Time: 35 Minutes | **Servings:** 2 to 4)

Ingredients:
- 1 cup Dry Cranberries or "Crasins" (soaked in boiling water for 5 minutes) or 1½ cup Fresh Cranberries or 4 Turkey wings (2 to 3 lbs.)
- 1 cup of canned cranberries; rinsed
- 1 cup Freshly Squeezed Orange juice (or prepared juice with no added sugar)
- 1 medium Onion; roughly sliced
- 1 cup shelled Walnuts
- 2 tbsp. Butter
- 2 tbsp. Oil
- Salt and Pepper, to taste
- 1 bunch Fresh Thyme

Instructions:
1. Set the Foodi to *Sauté*, melt the butter and swirl the olive oil
2. Brown the turkey wings on both sides adding salt and pepper to taste. Make sure that the skin side is nicely colored.
3. Remove the wings briefly from the Foodi and add the onion, then on top of that add the wings, cranberries, walnuts, a little bundle of Thyme
4. Pour the orange juice over the turkey
5. Close and lock the Foodi. Cook for 20 minutes at High pressure. To get 20 minutes' cook time, press *Pressure* button.
6. Use the Natural method.
7. Remove the thyme bundle and carefully remove the wings to a serving dish. Slide the serving dish under the broiler for about 5 minutes or until the wings are sufficiently caramelized
8. In the meantime, reduce the cooking liquid to about half. Pour the reduced liquid, walnuts, onions and cranberries over the wings and serve

Yummy Spicy Turkey Chili

(Prep + Cook Time: 55 minutes | **Servings:** 4)

Ingredients:
- 1 lb. ground turkey
- 1/4 cup your favorite hot sauce
- 1 (15 oz.) can fire roasted diced tomatoes
- 1 (15 oz.) can kidney beans, including their liquid
- 1 medium yellow onion, diced
- 2 green bell peppers, seeded and diced
- 2 fresh cayenne peppers, chopped. (seeds included)
- 4 cloves garlic, chopped.
- 1 cup grated Monterey Jack cheese
- 1 tbsp. olive oil
- 1 tsp. ground cumin
- 1/2 tsp. dried oregano leaves
- 1/4 cup chopped cilantro

Instructions:
1. Set the Foodi Multi-cooker to its *Sauté* setting and add the oil. Add the onions, peppers and garlic and sauté until the onions soften and begin to brown, about 10 minutes. Add the cumin and oregano and sauté two more minutes, until aromatic.
2. Add the ground turkey, breaking it up with a spoon or spatula. Sauté until opaque and cooked through, about 5 minutes
3. Add the hot sauce, canned tomatoes and kidney beans and stir to combine.
4. High pressure for 45 minutes. Lock the lid on the Foodi Multi-cooker and then cook for 45 minutes.
5. To get 45 minutes' cook time, press *pressure* button and use the adjust button to adjust the cook time to 45 minutes.
6. Pressure Release. Use natural release method
7. Finish the dish. Top with grated cheese and cilantro and serve with rice or cornbread, if desired.

Olive and Lemon Ligurian Chicken

(Prep + Cook Time: 35 minutes | **Servings:** 6 to 8)

Ingredients:

- 3.5 oz. (100g) Black Gourmet Salt-Cured Olives (Taggiesche, French or Kalamata)
- 3 sprigs of Fresh Rosemary (two for chopping, one for garnish)
- 1 whole chicken, cut into parts or package of bone in chicken pieces, skin removed (or not) 1/2 cup (125ml) dry white wine
- 2 garlic cloves, chopped.
- 2 sprigs of Fresh Sage
- 1/2 bunch of Parsley Leaves and stems
- 3 lemons, juiced (about a 3/4 cup or 180ml)
- 4 tbsp. extra virgin olive oil
- 1 tsp. sea salt
- 1/4 tsp. pepper
- 1 fresh lemon, for garnish (optional)

Instructions:

1. Prepare the marinade by finely chopping together the garlic, rosemary, sage and parsley. Place them in a container and add the lemon juice, olive oil, salt and pepper. Mix well and set aside.
2. Remove the skin from the chicken (save it for a chicken stock)
3. In the preheated Foodi Multi-cooker, with the lid off, add a swirl of olive oil and brown the chicken pieces on all sides for about 5 minutes.
4. De-glaze cooker with the white wine until it has almost all evaporated (about 3 minutes)
5. Add the chicken pieces back in this time being careful with the order. Put all dark meat (wings, legs, thighs) first and then the chicken breasts on top so that they do not touch the bottom of the Foodi Multi-cooker.
6. Pour the remaining marinade on top. Don't worry if this does not seem like enough liquid the chicken will also release its juices into the cooker, too
7. High pressure for 10 minutes. Lock the lid on the Foodi Multi-cooker and then cook for 10 minutes.
8. To get 10 minutes' cook time, press *Pressure* button and adjust the time.
9. Pressure Release. When time is up, open the cooker by releasing the pressure using the Quick Release Method
10. Finish the dish. Close crisping lid. Select *Air Crisp*, set temperature to 390°F and set time to 10 minutes. Check after 5 minutes, cooking for an additional 5 minutes if dish needs more browning
11. Take the chicken pieces out of the cooker and place on a serving platter tightly covered with foil.
12. Reduce the cooking liquid in the Foodi Multi-cooker, if necessary, with the lid off to 1/4 of its amount or until it becomes thick and syrupy
13. Put all of the chicken pieces back into the Foodi Multi-cooker to warm up. Mix and spoon the thick glaze onto the chicken pieces and simmer it in the glaze for a few minutes before serving.
14. Sprinkle with fresh rosemary, olives and lemon slices. When serving, caution your guests that the olives still have their pits!

Delicious Frozen Chicken Dinner

(Prep + Cook Time: 50 minutes | **Servings:** 2)

Ingredients:

- 2 frozen chicken breasts (8 - 10 oz. each)
- 2 tbsp. olive oil, divided.
- 1 small onion, peeled, diced
- 3/4 cup chicken stock
- 1 bag (12 oz.) green beans, trimmed
- 1 tsp. black pepper, divided.
- 1/4 cup fresh parsley, chopped.
- 1 cup wild rice blend
- 3 tsp. kosher salt, divided.
- 1 tbsp. Moroccan seasoning "Ras el Hanout"
- 1/4 cup honey mustard sauce

Instructions:
1. Select SEAR/SAUTÉ and set to HIGH. Allow to preheat for 5 minutes.
2. After 5 minutes, add 1 tbsp. oil and onion. Cook, stirring occasionally, for 3 minutes, until onions are fragrant. Add wild rice, 2 tsp. salt, and Moroccan seasoning. Cook, stirring frequently, until the rice is coated with oil and very shiny. Add chicken stock and stir to incorporate
3. Place frozen chicken breasts on reversible rack, making sure rack is in the higher position. Place rack inside pot over rice mixture.
4. Assemble pressure lid, making sure the PRESSURE RELEASE valve is in the SEAL position. Select PRESSURE and set to HIGH. Set time to 22 minutes. Select START/STOP to begin
5. While chicken and rice are cooking, toss green beans in a bowl with the remaining oil, salt, and pepper
6. When pressure cooking is complete, allow pressure to naturally release for 10 minutes. After 10 minutes, quick release any remaining pressure by turning the PRESSURE RELEASE valve to the VENT position. Carefully remove lid when unit has finished releasing pressure.
7. Lift reversible rack out of the pot. Stir parsley into rice, then add green beans directly on top of the rice
8. Brush chicken breasts on all sides with honey mustard sauce, then return the reversible rack to the pot over rice and green beans. Close crisping lid. Select BROIL and set time to 10 minutes. Select START/STOP to begin.
9. Cooking is complete when internal temperature reaches 165°F. Serve chicken with green beans and rice.

Enchilada Chicken Breasts

(Prep + Cook Time: 30 minutes | **Servings:** 4)

Ingredients:
- 4 (6 to 8 oz.) boneless skinless chicken breasts
- 1/2 cup light-colored beer, preferably a Pilsner or an IPA
- 1 (8 oz.) can tomato sauce (1 cup)
- 1 tsp. packed dark brown sugar
- 1 tsp. ground cumin
- 1 tsp. smoked paprika
- 1/2 tsp. onion powder
- 1/4 tsp. garlic powder
- 2 tbsp. olive oil
- 2 tbsp. chili powder
- 2 tbsp. fresh lime juice
- 1/2 tsp. salt
- 1/2 tsp. ground black pepper

Instructions:
1. Mix the brown sugar, cumin, smoked paprika, salt, pepper, onion powder and garlic powder in a medium bowl. Massage the spice rub onto the chicken breasts.
2. Heat the oil in the Foodi Multi-cooker using the *Sauté* function. Set the breasts in the cooker and brown well, turning once, about 6 minutes
3. Mix the tomato sauce, beer, chili powder and lime juice in the bowl the spices were in; pour the sauce over the breasts.
4. High pressure for 15 minutes. Close the lid and Cook for 15 minutes.
5. To get 15 minutes' cook time, press the *Pressure* Button and adjust the time
6. Pressure Release. Use the quick release method to bring the pot's pressure back to normal
7. Close crisping lid. Select *Air Crisp*, set temperature to 390°F and set time to 9 minutes. Check after 6 minutes, cooking for an additional 3 minutes if dish needs more browning. Serve the chicken with the sauce ladled on top.

Herbed Whole Roasted Chicken

(Prep + Cook Time: 50 minutes | **Servings:** 4)

Ingredients:
- 1 whole uncooked chicken (4 ½ - 5 lb.)
- 1 tbsp. whole black peppercorns
- 2 tbsp. plus 2 tsp. kosher salt, divided.
- 1/4 cup hot water
- 1/4 cup honey
- Juice of 2 lemons (1/4 cup lemon juice)
- 5 sprigs fresh thyme
- 5 cloves garlic, peeled, smashed
- 1 tbsp. canola oil
- 2 tsp. ground black pepper

Instructions:
1. Rinse chicken and tie legs together with cooking twine.
2. In a small bowl, mix together lemon juice, hot water, honey, and 2 tbsp. salt. Pour mixture into the pot. Place whole peppercorns, thyme, and garlic in the pot
3. Place chicken into the Cook & Crisp basket and place basket in pot. Assemble pressure lid, making sure the pressure release valve is in the SEAL position. Select PRESSURE and set to HIGH. Set time to 22 minutes. Select START/STOP to begin
4. When pressure cooking is complete, allow pressure to naturally release for 5 minutes. After 5 minutes, quick release remaining pressure by moving the pressure release valve to the VENT position. Carefully remove lid when unit has finished releasing pressure.
5. Brush chicken with canola oil or spray with cooking spray. Season with salt and pepper
6. Close crisping lid. Select AIR CRISP, set temperature to 400°F, and set time to 8 minutes. Select START/STOP to begin. Cook until desired level of crispness is reached, adding up to 10 additional minutes
7. Cooking is complete when internal temperature reaches 165°F. Remove chicken from basket using 2 large serving forks. Let rest for 5 to 10 minutes before serving.

Delicious Chicken Pot Pie Recipe

(Prep + Cook Time: 35 minutes | **Servings:** 6)

Ingredients:
- 2 lb. uncooked boneless skinless chicken breasts, cut in 1-inch cubes
- 1/2 stick (1/4 cup) unsalted butter
- 1/2 large onion, peeled, diced
- 1 large carrot, peeled, diced
- 2 cloves garlic, peeled, minced
- 1 stalk celery, diced
- 1/2 cup frozen peas
- 1 ½ tsp. fresh thyme, minced
- 2 tsp. kosher salt
- 1/2 tsp. black pepper
- 1/2 cup heavy cream
- 1 cup chicken broth
- 1 tbsp. fresh Italian parsley, minced
- 1/4 cup all-purpose flour

Instructions:
1. Select SEAR/SAUTÉ and set to MD:HI. Select START/STOP to begin. Allow to preheat for 5 minutes. After 5 minutes, add butter to pot. Once it melts, add onion, carrot, and garlic, and SAUTÉ until softened, about 3 minutes
2. Add chicken and broth to the pot. Assemble pressure lid, making sure the PRESSURE RELEASE valve is in the SEAL position. Select PRESSURE and set to HIGH. Set time to 5 minutes. Select START/STOP to begin
3. When pressure cooking is complete, quick release the pressure by moving the PRESSURE RELEASE valve to the VENT position. Carefully remove lid when unit has finished releasing pressure.
4. Select SEAR/SAUTÉ and set to MD:HI. Select START/STOP to begin. Add remaining ingredients to pot, except pie crust. Stir until sauce thickens and bubbles, about 3 minutes
5. Lay pie crust evenly on top of the filling mixture, folding over edges if necessary. Make a small cut in center of pie crust so that steam can escape during baking. Close the crisping lid. Select BROIL and set time to 10 minutes. Select START/STOP to begin.

6. When cooking is complete, remove pot from unit and place on a heat-resistant surface. Let rest 10 to 15 minutes before serving

Aromatic Turkey Breast

(**Prep + Cook Time:** 1 hour 20 minutes | **Servings:** 8)

Ingredients:
- 6.5 lb. bone in, skin on turkey breast
- 1 (14 oz.) can turkey or chicken broth
- 1 large onion, quartered
- 1 stock celery, cut in large pieces
- 1 sprig thyme
- 3 tbsp. cornstarch
- 3 tbsp. cold water
- Salt and pepper, to taste

Instructions:
1. Season turkey breast liberally with salt and pepper. Put trivet in the bottom. Add chicken broth, onion, celery and thyme. Add the turkey to the cooking pot breast side up.
2. High pressure for 45 minutes. Lock the lid on the Foodi Multi-cooker and then cook for 45 minutes.
3. To get 45 minutes' cook time, press *Pressure* button and use the adjust button to adjust the cook time to 45 minutes
4. Pressure Release. Use a natural pressure release for 10 minutes, then do a quick pressure release
5. Check if the turkey is done. If it isn't, lock the lid in place and cook it for a few more minutes.
6. Finish the dish. Close crisping lid. Select *Air Crisp*, set temperature to 360°F and set time to 10 minutes. Check after 5 minutes, cooking for an additional 5 minutes if dish needs more browning. Carefully remove turkey and place on large plate. Cover with foil
7. Strain and skim the fat off the broth. Whisk together cornstarch and cold water; add to broth in cooking pot. Select Sauté and stir until broth thickens
8. Add salt and pepper to taste. Slice the turkey and serve immediately.

Sweet Soy Chicken Wings

(Prep + Cook Time: 40 minutes | **Servings:** 2 to 4)

Ingredients:
- 1 ½ lb. chicken wings
- Chicken Wing Marinade
- 1/2 large shallot or 1 small shallot, roughly minced
- 4 cloves garlic, roughly minced
- 2 tbsp. light soy sauce
- 1 tbsp. ginger, sliced
- 1 tbsp. honey
- 1 tbsp. dark soy sauce
- 1 tbsp. Shaoxing wine
- 1 to 2-star anise
- 1/2 cup warm water
- 1 tbsp. peanut oil
- 1 ½ tbsp. cornstarch
- 1 tsp. sugar
- 1/4 tsp. salt

Instructions:
1. Marinate the chicken wings with the Chicken Wing Marinade for 20 minutes.
2. Heat the Foodi Multi-cooker using the *Sauté* function
3. Add 1 tbsp. of peanut oil into the pot. Add the marinated chicken wings into the pot. Then, brown the chicken wings for roughly 30 seconds on each side. Flip a few times as you brown them as the soy sauce and sugar can be burnt easily. Remove and set aside.
4. Add the minced shallot, star anise and sliced ginger, then stir for roughly a minute. Add the minced garlic and stir until fragrant (roughly 30 seconds)
5. Mix 1 tbsp. of honey with 1/2 cup of warm water, then add it into the pot and deglaze the bottom of the pot with a wooden spoon
6. Place all the chicken wings with all the meat juice and the leftover chicken wing marinade into the pot.
7. High pressure for 5 minutes. Lock the lid on the Foodi Multi-cooker and then cook for 5 minutes.
8. To get 5 minutes' cook time, press *Pressure* button and use the Time Adjustment button to adjust the cook time to 5 minutes
9. Pressure Release. Let the pressure to come down naturally for at least 10 minutes, then quick release any pressure left in the pot.
10. Finish the dish. Close crisping lid. Select *Air Crisp*, set temperature to 390°F and set time to 10 minutes. Check after 10 minutes, cooking for an additional 5 minutes if dish needs more browning
11. Open the lid carefully and taste one of the honey soy chicken wings and the honey soy sauce. Season with more salt or honey if desired.
12. Remove all the chicken wings from the pot and set aside. Turn the Foodi Multi-cooker to its sauté function. Mix 1 ½ tbsp. of cornstarch with 1 tbsp. of cold running tap water. Keep mixing and add it into the honey soy sauce one third at a time until desired thickness.
13. Turn off the heat and add the chicken wings back into the pot. Coat well with the honey soy sauce and serve immediately!

Fish & Seafood

Salmon with Bok Choy

(Prep + Cook Time: 15 minutes | **Servings:** 4)

Ingredients:
- 4 frozen skinless salmon fillets (4 oz. 1-inch thick each)
- 1 cup jasmine rice, rinsed
- 3/4 cup water
- 2 heads baby bok choy, stems on, rinsed, cut in half
- 1/4 cup mirin
- 1 tsp. sesame oil
- 1 tsp. kosher salt
- 2 tbsp. red miso paste
- 2 tbsp. butter, softened
- Sesame seeds, for garnish

Instructions:
1. Place rice and water into the pot. Stir to combine. Place reversible rack in pot, making sure rack is in the higher position
2. Season salmon with salt, then place on rack. Assemble pressure lid, making sure the PRESSURE RELEASE valve is in the SEAL position. Select PRESSURE and set to HIGH. Set time to 2 minutes. Select START/STOP to begin.
3. While salmon and rice are cooking, stir together miso and butter to form a paste. Toss bok choy with mirin and sesame oil
4. When pressure cooking is complete, quick release the pressure by moving the PRESSURE RELEASE valve to the VENT position. Carefully remove lid when unit has finished releasing pressure
5. Gently pat salmon dry with paper towel, then spread miso butter evenly on top of the fillets. Add bok choy to the rack. Close crisping lid. Select BROIL and set time to 7 minutes. Select START/STOP to begin, checking for doneness after 5 minutes.
6. When cooking is complete, remove salmon from rack and serve with bok choy and rice. Garnish with sesame seeds, if desired

Tuna and Capers Tomato Pasts

(Prep + Cook Time: 20 Minutes | **Servings:** 2)

Ingredients:
- 1 can (3.5 oz.) solid tuna packed in vegetable oil
- 1 can (15 oz.) fire-roasted diced tomatoes
- 2 cups pasta; your choice (I used Orecchiette)
- 2 garlic cloves; sliced
- 2 tbsp. olive oil
- 2 tbsp. capers
- Grated parmesan
- Red wine (just enough to fill 1/2 of the tomato can)
- Salt and pepper to taste
- Seasonings: use oregano and dried chilies

Instructions:
1. Set the Foodi to *Sauté* and wait until hot. Add the garlic and sauté until fragrant.
2. Add the pasta, seasonings, and tomatoes. Fill the empty can of tomatoes with red wine until 1/2 full and then pour enough water into the can until full
3. Pour the wine mix in the Foodi. Lock the lid and turn the steam valve to Sealing.
4. Select *Pressure* and cook at HIGH pressure for 6 minutes. When the timer beeps, turn the steam valve to quick release the pressure
5. Carefully open the capers and tuna. Gently add into the pot and stir. Divide the pasta into serving bowls.

Tuna and Buttery Crackers Casserole

(Prep + Cook Time: 25 Minutes | **Servings:** 8)

Ingredients:
- 8 oz. fresh tuna
- 2 cups pasta (I have used elbow mac)
- 1/4 cup heavy cream
- 1 cup celery
- 1 cup buttery crackers; crushed
- 1 cup onion
- 1 cup frozen peas
- 1 cup cheddar; shredded
- 3 tbsp. butter
- 3 tbsp. all-purpose flour
- 3 ½ cups chicken stock
- 2 tsp. salt
- Fresh ground black pepper

Instructions:
1. Press *Sauté* to preheat the Foodi. When hot, put the celery and onion.
2. Sauté until the onion is translucent. Pour the chicken stock and pasta, and season with salt and pepper.
3. Stir to combine for a bit. Put the fresh tuna on top of the pasta mix. Press *Cancel* to stop the *Sauté* function. Close and lock the lid
4. Select *Pressure* and cook at HIGH pressure for 5 minutes. Meanwhile, heat the sauté pan over medium-high
5. Put the butter in the pan and melt. Add the flour and stir, cook for 2 minutes. Remove the pan from the heat and set aside.
6. When the timer beeps, turn the steam valve to Venting to quick release the pressure. Transfer the tuna onto a plate and set aside
7. Pour the butter mix into the Foodi. Press the *Sauté* key. Stir until the mixture is thick. Turn off the Foodi. Add the heavy cream, peas, tuna and stir.
8. Cover the mix with the crackers and then with the grated cheese. Cover and let stand for 5 minutes. Serve.

Trout-Farro Salad

(Prep + Cook Time: 25 Minutes | **Servings:** 4)

Ingredients:
- 12 oz. skinned and chopped cooked trout
- 1 large, shaved fennel bulb
- 1/2 cup low-fat mayonnaise
- 1/4 cup low-fat sour cream
- 1 cup semi-pearled Farro
- 1 tsp. white sugar
- 1 tsp. ground black pepper
- 3 tbsp. lemon juice
- 2 tbsp. Dijon mustard
- Water as needed

Instructions:
1. Put the farro in your Foodi and pour in just enough water so the grain is covered by two inches. Close and seal the lid
2. Select *Pressure* and cook at HIGH pressure for 17 minutes.
3. When time is up, press *Cancel* and Quick Pressure Release the pressure.
4. Shave your fennel and put in a colander. Pour farro right on top of it, draining.
5. Toss fennel and farro together, and set aside for about 30 minutes
6. When you're just about ready to serve, mix the mayo, sour cream, lemon juice, Dijon, white sugar, and pepper together. Add the farro, fish and fennel. Serve right away.

Seafood Paella

(Prep + Cook Time: 35 Minutes | **Servings:** 4)

Ingredients:
- 4 white fish heads
- 1 Medium Yellow Onion; diced
- 1 Red Bell Pepper, diced
- 1 Green Bell Pepper, diced
- Large pinch saffron threads
- 2 Cups short-grain rice
- 1 Cup of seafood (squid, meaty white fish, scallops)
- 2 Cups of mixed shellfish (clams, mussels, shrimp)
- 2 carrots
- 1 Celery
- 1 Bay leaf
- Bunch of parsley with stems
- 6 Cups of water
- 4 tbsp. EVOO
- 1¾ Cups Vegetable Stock or Seafood Stock
- 1/8 Tsp Ground Turmeric
- 2 Tsp Sea Salt

Instructions:
1. Add all the ingredients to Foodi. Set on High for 5 minutes. When timer goes off, use Natural-release.
2. Set Foodi on *Sauté* and heat EVOO
3. When the oil gets hot, add onions and peppers and Sauté until onions soften, about 4 minutes.
4. Stir in the saffron, rice, and seafood and sauté everything together for 2 minutes.
5. Then add stock, turmeric, salt, and mix well.
6. Arrange the shellfish on top and do not mix further.
7. Close and lock the lid of the Foodi. Cook at High pressure for 6 minutes. To get 6 minutes' cook time, press *Pressure* button and use the *Time Adjustment* button to adjust the cook time to 6 minutes.
8. When timer is up, use natural Pressure release. method
9. Open the lid when the vent valve opens and mix the paella well, cover and let stand for 1 minute before serving.

Pernod Mackerel and Vegetables Recipe

(Prep + Cook Time: 25 minutes + 2 hours for marinating | **Servings:** 6)

Ingredients:
- 1 lb. Asparagus, trimmed
- 3 large Whole Mackerel, cut into 2 pieces
- 1 Carrot, cut into sticks
- 1 Orange Bell Pepper, seeded and cut into sticks
- 1 Celery stalk, cut into sticks
- 1/2 cup Butter, at room temperature
- 6 medium Tomatoes, quartered
- 1 large Brown Onion, sliced thinly
- 2 ½ tbsp. Pernod
- 3 cloves Garlic, minced
- 2 Lemons, cut into wedges
- 1 ½ cups Water
- Salt and Black Pepper to taste

Instructions:
1. Cut out 6 pieces of parchment paper a little longer and wider than a piece of fish with kitchen scissors. Then, cut out 6 pieces of foil slightly longer than the parchment papers.
2. Lay the foil wraps on a flat surface and place each parchment paper on each aluminium foil
3. In a bowl, add tomatoes, onions, garlic, bell pepper, Pernod, butter, asparagus, carrot, celery, salt, and pepper. Use a spoon to mix them.
4. Place each fish piece on the layer of parchment and foil wraps. Spoon the vegetable mixture on each fish. Then, wrap the fish and place the fish packets in the refrigerator to marinate for 2 hours. Remove the fish to a flat surface.
5. Open the Foodi, pour the water in, and fit the reversible rack at the bottom of the pot. Put the packets on the trivet. Seal the lid and select Steam mode on High pressure for 3 minutes. Press Start/Stop to start cooking

6. Once the timer has ended, do a quick pressure release, and open the lid. Remove the trivet with the fish packets onto a flat surface. Carefully open the foil and using a spatula. Return the packets to the pot, on top of the rack
7. Close the crisping lid and cook on Air Crisp for 3 minutes at 300°F. Then, remove to serving plates. Serve with lemon wedges

Special Farro with Fennel and Smoked Trout

(Prep + Cook Time: 22 minutes | **Servings:** 4)

Ingredients:
- 1 cup semi perlato farro
- 12 oz. smoked trout; skinned and chopped.
- 1 large fennel bulb; trimmed and shaved into thin strips
- 1/4 cup regular or low fat sour cream
- 1/2 cup regular or low fat mayonnaise
- 3 tbsp. lemon juice
- 1 tsp. sugar
- 2 tbsp. Dijon mustard
- 1 tsp. ground black pepper

Instructions:
1. Pour the farro into the Foodi Multi-cooker; pour in enough water that the grains are submerged by 2 inches.
2. High pressure for 17 minutes. Lock the lid on the Foodi Multi-cooker and then cook for 17 minutes.
3. To get 17 minutes' cook time, press *Pressure* button and use the Time Adjustment button to adjust the cook time to 17 minutes
4. Pressure Release. Use the quick release method to drop the pot's pressure to normal.
5. Finish the dish. Unlock and open the cooker. Place the fennel strips in a colander set in the sink and drain the farro into the colander over the fennel. Toss well, then let cool for 30 minutes in the colander
6. Whisk the mayonnaise, sour cream, lemon juice, mustard, sugar and pepper in a large serving bowl until creamy. Add the farro, fennel and smoked trout; toss gently to coat well

Coconut Fish Curry

(Prep + Cook Time: 20 Minutes | **Servings:** 2 to 4)

Ingredients:
- 1 to 1 ½ lb. Fish steaks or fillets, rinsed and cut into bite-size pieces (fresh or frozen and thawed)
- 1 Tomato; chopped (or a heaping cup of cherry tomatoes)
- 2 Green Chiles; sliced into strips
- 2 Medium onions, sliced into strips
- 2 Garlic cloves; squeezed
- 3 tbsp. of Curry Powder mix. (instead of the 5 spices noted above)
- 1 tbsp. freshly grated Ginger; or 1/8 tsp. Ginger Powder
- 6 Curry leaves, or Bay Laurel Leaves; or Kaffir Lime Leaves, or Basil
- 2 cups or (500ml) un-sweetened Coconut Milk
- 1 tbsp. ground Coriander
- 2 tsp. ground Cumin
- 1/2 tsp. ground Turmeric
- 1 tsp. Chili Powder, or 1 tsp. of Hot Pepper Flakes
- 1/2 tsp. Ground Fenugreek (Methi)
- Lemon juice to taste (I have used the juice from ½ lemon)
- Salt to taste (I used about 2 tsp.)

Instructions:
1. In the preheated Foodi, add a swirl of oil and then drop in the curry leaves and lightly fry them until golden around the edges (about 1 minute)
2. Then add the onion, garlic and ginger and Sauté until the onion is soft.
3. Add all of the ground spices: Coriander, Cumin, Turmeric, Chili Powder and Fenugreek and Sauté them together with the onions until they have released their aroma (about 2 minutes)
4. De-glaze with the coconut milk making sure to un-stick anything from the bottom of the cooker and incorporate it in the sauce.

5. Add the Green Chiles, Tomatoes and fish pieces. Stir to coat the fish well with the mixture.
6. Lock the lid on the Foodi and then cook On High pressure for 3 minutes. To get 3 minutes' cook time, press *Pressure* button and use the *Time Adjustment* button to adjust the cook time to 3 minutes.
7. Use the "Quick Release" method to vent the steam, then open the lid
8. Add salt to taste and spritz with lemon juice just before serving. Serve alone, or with steamed rice.

Tomatillo and Shrimp Casserole

(Prep + Cook Time: 30 minutes | **Servings:** 4)

Ingredients:
- 1 ½ lb. medium shrimp (about 30 per pound); peeled and deveined
- 1/4 cup loosely packed fresh cilantro leaves; chopped.
- 1 ½ lb. fresh tomatillos; husked and chopped.
- 1/2 cup bottled clam juice
- 1 cup shredded Monterey jack cheese (about 4 oz.)
- 2 tbsp. olive oil
- 1 medium yellow onion; chopped.
- 1 small fresh jalapeño chile; stemmed; seeded and minced
- 2 tsp. minced garlic
- 2 tbsp. fresh lime juice

Instructions:
1. Heat the oil in the Foodi Multi-cooker turned to the *Browning* function. Add the onion and cook, often stirring, until translucent, about 3 minutes.
2. Add the jalapeño and garlic; cook until aromatic, stirring all the while, less than a minute.
3. Stir in the tomatillos, clam juice and lime juice.
4. High pressure for 9 minutes. Lock the lid on the Foodi Multi-cooker and then cook for 9 minutes.
5. To get 9 minutes' cook time, press *Pressure* button and use the Time Adjustment button to adjust the cook time to 9 minutes.
6. Pressure Release Use the quick release method
7. Finish the dish. Unlock and open the pot. Turn the Foodi Multi-cooker to its *Sauté* function. Stir in the shrimp and cilantro; cook for 2 minutes, stirring frequently.
8. Sprinkle the cheese over the top of the casserole. Close crisping lid and select Broil, set time to 5 minutes. Press Start/Stop button to begin. Serve and enjoy

Cod Fillets with Almonds and Peas

(Prep + Cook Time: 10 Minutes | **Servings:** 4)

Ingredients:
- 1 lb. frozen cod fish fillet
- 10 oz. frozen peas
- 2 halved garlic cloves
- 1 cup chicken broth
- 1/2 cup packed parsley
- 2 tbsp. fresh oregano
- 2 tbsp. sliced almonds
- 1/2 tsp. paprika

Instructions:
1. Take the fish out of the freezer. In a food processor stir together garlic, oregano, parsley, paprika, and 1 tbsp. almonds
2. Turn your Foodi to *Sauté* and heat a bit of olive oil
3. When hot, toast the rest of the almonds until they are fragrant.
4. Take out the almonds and put on a paper towel.
5. Pour the broth in the cooker and add your herb mixture
6. Cut the fish into 4 pieces and put in the steamer basket.
7. Lower into the cooker and close the lid.
8. Select *Pressure* and cook at HIGH pressure for 3 minutes.
9. Press *Cancel* and quick release the pressure.
10. The fish is done when it is solid, not translucent
11. Add the frozen peas and close the lid again.

12. Cook at HIGH pressure for 1 minute. Use a quick release. Serve with the toasted almonds on top.

Notes: If you want a thicker sauce, remove the fish before mixing 1 tbsp. of cornstarch with 1 tbsp. of cold water, and pouring into the cooker. Turn the cooker to *Sauté* and bring to a simmer until thickened

Caramelized Haddock

(Prep + Cook Time: 55 Minutes | **Servings:** 4)

Ingredients:
- 1 lb. of haddock
- 1/4 cup white sugar
- 1 cup of coconut water
- 3 garlic cloves, chopped
- 1 minced red chili
- 1 minced spring onion
- 1/3 cup water
- 3 tbsp. fish sauce
- 2 tsp. black pepper

Instructions:
1. Marinate the fish in garlic, fish sauce, and pepper for at least 30 minutes. Put the sugar and water in the Foodi and heat on *Sauté* mode until the sugar has browned into a caramel
2. Add fish and coconut water to the cooker. Close and seal lid
3. Select *Pressure* and cook at HIGH pressure for 10 minutes
4. When time is up, press *Cancel* and let the pressure release naturally. Serve with chili and onion.

Lemon Dill Cod with Broccoli

(Prep + Cook Time: 5 Minutes | **Servings:** 4)

Ingredients:
- 1 lb. 1-inch thick frozen cod fillet
- 2 cups of broccoli
- Dill weed
- 1 cup water
- Lemon pepper
- Dash of salt

Instructions:
1. Cut the fish into 4 pieces. Season with lemon pepper, salt, and dill weed.
2. Pour 1 cup of water into the Foodi and lower in the steamer basket
3. Put the fish and broccoli florets in the basket. Close the cooker
4. Select *Pressure* and cook for 2 minutes at LOW pressure. (Press Stop when complete 2 Minute).
5. Quick-release the pressure after time is up, and you've turned off the cooker. Serve right away.

Special Fish Filets

(Prep + Cook Time: 15 minutes | **Servings:** 2)

Ingredients:
- 4 White Fish fillets (any white fish)
- 1 lb. Cherry Tomatoes; halved
- 1 cup Black salt-cured Olives (French, Taggiesche or Kalamata)
- 1 bunch of fresh Thyme Olive Oil
- 1 clove of garlic; pressed
- 2 tbsp. Pickled Capers
- Salt and pepper to taste

Instructions:
1. Prepare the base of the Foodi Multi-cooker with 1½ to 2 cups of water and trivet or steamer basket.
2. Line the bottom of the heat-proof bowl with cherry tomato halves (to keep the fish filet from sticking), add Thyme (reserve a few sprigs for garnish)
3. Place the fish fillets over the cherry tomatoes, sprinkle with remaining tomatoes, crushed garlic, a dash of olive oil and a pinch of salt.
4. Insert the dish in the Foodi Multi-cooker - if your heat proof dish does not have handles construct them by making a long aluminum sling.
5. High pressure for 5 minutes. Lock the lid on the Foodi Multi-cooker and then cook for 5 minutes.
6. To get 5 minutes' cook time, press *Pressure* button and then adjust the time

7. Pressure Release. Perform a quick release to release the cooker's pressure.
8. Finish the dish. Close crisping lid and select Broil, set time to 7 minutes
9. Distribute fish into individual plates, top with cherry tomatoes and sprinkle with olives, capers, fresh Thyme, a crackle of pepper and a little swirl of fresh olive oil

Alaskan Cod with Pinto Beans

(Prep + Cook Time: 30 minutes | Servings: 4)

Ingredients:
- 2 (18 oz.) Alaskan Cod, cut into 4 pieces each
- 2 cloves Garlic, minced
- 1/2 cup Olive Brine
- 3 cups Chicken Broth
- Salt and Black Pepper to taste
- 2 small Onions, chopped.
- 1 head Fennel, quartered
- 1 cup Pinto Beans, soaked, drained and rinsed
- 1 cup Green Olives, pitted and crushed
- 1/2 cup Basil Leaves
- 1/2 cup Tomato Puree
- 4 tbsp. Olive Oil
- Lemon Slices to garnish

Instructions:
1. Heat the olive oil and add the garlic and onion. Stir-fry on Sear/Sauté mode until the onion softens. Pour in chicken broth and tomato puree. Let simmer for about 3 minutes.
2. Add fennel, olives, beans, salt, and pepper. Seal the lid and select Steam mode on High pressure for 10 minutes. Press Start/Stop to start cooking
3. Once the timer has stopped, do a quick pressure release, and open the lid. Transfer the beans to a plate with a slotted spoon. Adjust broth's taste with salt and pepper and add the cod pieces to the cooker.
4. Close the lid again, secure the pressure valve, and select Steam mode on Low pressure for 3 minutes. Press Start/Stop.
5. Once the timer has ended, do a quick pressure release, and open the lid.
6. Remove the cod into soup plates, top with the beans and basil leaves, and spoon the broth over them. Serve with a side of crusted bread

Southern Shrimp Chowder

(Prep + Cook Time: 30 Minutes | Servings: 4)

Ingredients:
- 1 (15 oz.) can coconut milk
- 2 cups raw frozen shrimp
- 2 ribs celery; minced
- 1 large onion; diced
- 1 red pepper; diced
- 1 cup cauliflower; riced
- 1 heaping tsp. Cajun seasoning
- 8 oz. Chicken Stock
- 2 tbsp. ghee
- 1/2 tsp. garlic powder
- 1/2 tsp. onion powder
- 3 tbsp. arrowroot; tapioca or cassava flour
- Additional sea salt and pepper; to taste

Instructions:
1. Combine the ghee, celery, onion and red pepper in the stainless steel bowl of your Pressure Cooker. Press the Sauté button and cook for 5 minutes, or until the vegetables begin to soften. Now press the Keep Warm button. Add the remaining ingredients except for the arrowroot and give them a quick stir. Secure the lid and close the pressure valve
2. Now press the Pressure button cook on High Pressure for 10 minutes. Allow the cooking cycle to complete, and then Quick Pressure Release the pressure valve, removing the lid when safe to do so
3. Now remove 1/2 cup (118 ml) of the broth and whisk in your 3 tbsp. (18 g) of arrowroot or preferred starch. Once it is fully incorporated, stir the slurry back into the main pot, allowing the chowder to thicken; this will take just a minute or so while stirring. Now add your sea salt and pepper to taste

Delightful Tuna Noodle

(Prep + Cook Time: 24 minutes | **Servings:** 2)

Ingredients:
- 8 oz. of dry wide egg noodles (uncooked)
- 1 can (14 oz.) diced tomatoes with basil; garlic and oregano(undrained) or any kind you have on hand.
- 1 jar (7.5 oz.) marinated artichoke hearts; drained with saving the liquid, then chop it up
- 1 tbsp. of Oil
- 1/2 cup of chopped red onion
- 1 ¼ cups of water
- 1 can of tuna fish in water; drained
- Crumpled feta cheese
- Fresh chopped parsley or dried
- 1/4 tsp. of salt
- 1/8 tsp. of pepper

Instructions:
1. Sauté the red onion for about 2 minutes. Add the dry noodles, tomatoes, water, salt and pepper.
2. High pressure for 10 minutes. Lock the lid on the Foodi Multi-cooker and then cook for 10 minutes.
3. To get 10 minutes' cook time, press *Pressure* button and adjust the time
4. Pressure Release. Release the pressure using natural release method
5. Turn off the warm setting. Add tuna, artichokes and your reserved liquid from the artichokes and sauté on normal while stirring for about 4 more minutes till hot, top with a feta cheese to your liking.
6. Close crisping lid and select Broil, set time to 7 minutes. Press Start/Stop button. Serve

Mackerel Salad

(Prep + Cook Time: 25 Minutes | **Servings:** 6)

Ingredients:
- 8 oz. mackerel
- 1 big cucumbers
- 1 red onion
- 1 cup lettuce
- 1 tsp. oregano
- 7 oz. tomatoes
- 1 garlic clove
- 1 tbsp. olive oil
- 1/2 tsp. rosemary
- 1/2 cup fish stock
- 1 tsp. salt
- 1 tsp. paprika

Instructions:
1. Wash the lettuce and chop it. Rub the mackerel with the salt, paprika, and rosemary
2. Place the spiced mackerel in the Foodi. Add the fish stock and close the lid. Select *Pressure* and cook at HIGH pressure for 10 minutes.
3. Peel the garlic clove and slice it. Peel the red onion and slice it
4. Combine the sliced red onion with the chopped lettuce. Slice the cucumber and chop tomatoes.
5. Add the vegetables to the lettuce mixture.
6. Once cooking is complete, use a quick release. The mackerel is cooked; remove it from the Foodi and chill it little. Chop the fish roughly
7. Add the chopped fish in the lettuce mixture.
8. Sprinkle the salad with the olive oil and stir it carefully with the help of the fork, do not damage the fish. Serve the cooked salad immediately.

Lemon and Dill Fish

(Prep + Cook Time: 15 minutes | **Servings:** 2)

Ingredients:
- 2 tilapia or cod fillets
- 2 tbsp. butter
- 2 sprigs fresh dill
- 4 slices lemon
- Salt, pepper and garlic powder

Instructions:
1. Layout 2 large squares of parchment paper. Place a fillet in the center of each parchment square and then season with a generous amount of salt, pepper and garlic powder.
2. On each fillet, place in order: 1 sprig of dill, 2 lemon slices and 1 tbsp. of butter
3. For best results, place the rack or trivet at the bottom of your Foodi Multi-cooker
4. Pour 1 cup of water into the cooker to create a water bath
5. Close up parchment paper around the fillets, folding to seal and then place both packets on metal rack inside cooker.
6. High pressure for 5 minutes. Lock the lid on the Foodi Multi-cooker and then cook for 5 minutes.
7. To get 5 minutes' cook time, press *Pressure* button and then adjust the time
8. Pressure Release. Perform a quick release to release the cooker's pressure. Unwrap packets and serve.
9. There is no need to remove the fish from the packets before serving. In fact, it makes a really nice presentation.

Cod Chowder

(Prep + Cook Time: 40 Minutes | **Servings:** 6)

Ingredients:
- 2 lb. cod
- 1 cup onion, chopped
- 1 cup half-and-half OR heavy cream OR 1 can evaporated milk
- 1 cup clam juice
- 4 to 6 bacon slices; optional
- 4 cups potatoes; peeled and diced
- 4 cups chicken broth, organic
- 2 tbsp. butter
- 1/2 mushrooms; sliced
- 1/2 cup flour
- 1 tsp. old bay seasoning (or more)
- Salt and pepper to taste

Instructions:
1. Pour 1 cup of water into the Foodi and set a trivet. Put the cod on the trivet. Close and lock the lid.
2. Press *Pressure*, set the pressure to HIGH, and set the timer for 9 minutes. Once cooking is complete, use a quick release
3. Transfer the cod onto a large-sized plate. With a fork or a knife, cut the fish into large chunks. Set aside.
4. Remove the trivet and pour the liquid out from the inner pot
5. Press the *Sauté* key. Add the butter, onion, and mushrooms; sauté for 2 minutes or until soft.
6. Add the chicken broth and the potatoes.
7. Press the *Cancel* key to stop the *Sauté* function. Close and lock the lid
8. Select *Pressure* and cook at HIGH pressure for 8 minutes.
9. When the timer beeps, turn the steam valve to quick release the pressure.
10. Add and stir the seasoning, pepper, salt, and fish.
11. In a bowl, mix the clam juice with the flour until well blended
12. Pour the mix into the pot. Turn off the Foodi.
13. Add the half-and-half and stir well until blended. Serve with fresh baked buttered rolls.

Notes: If you are using bacon, cook the bacon until crisp and then transfer into a paper towel lined plate. Add the onions and the mushrooms, cooking them in the bacon fat before adding the broth and potatoes.

Pasta with Tuna

(Prep + Cook Time: 5 minutes | **Servings:** 2 to 4)

Ingredients:
- 16 oz. fusilli pasta
- 2 (5.5 oz. cans) Tuna packed in olive oil water to cover
- 3 anchovies
- 1 tbsp. olive oil
- 1 garlic clove
- 2 tbsp. capers
- 2 cups tomato puree
- 1 ½ tsp. salt

Instructions:
1. In the pre-heated Foodi Multi-cookeron *Sauté* mode, add the oil, garlic and anchovies.
2. Sauté until the anchovies begin to disintegrate and the garlic cloves are just starting to turn golden.
3. Add the tomato puree and salt and mix together.
4. Pour in the uncooked pasta and the contents of one tuna can (5 oz.) mixing to coat the dry pasta evenly.
5. Flatten the pasta in an even layer and pour in just enough water to cover
6. High pressure for 3 minutes. Lock the lid on the Foodi Multi-cooker and then cook for 3 minutes.
7. To get 3 minutes' cook time, press *Pressure* button and use the Time Adjustment button to adjust the cook time to 3 minutes.
8. Pressure Release. When time is up, open the cooker by releasing the pressure.
9. Finish the dish. Mix in the last 5 oz. of tuna. Close crisping lid and select Broil, set time to 7 minutes. Sprinkle with capers before serving

Delicious Cuttlefish

(Prep + Cook Time: 40 Minutes | **Servings:** 6)

Ingredients:
- 1 lb. squid
- 1 tsp. onion powder
- 1 tbsp. lemon juice
- 2 tbsp. starch
- 1 tbsp. minced garlic
- 3 tbsp. fish sauce
- 2 tbsp. butter
- 1 tsp. white pepper
- 1 tbsp. chives
- 1 tsp. salt
- 1/4 chili pepper

Instructions:
1. Slice the squid. Combine the minced garlic, onion powder, starch, chives, salt, and white pepper together. Stir the mixture
2. Then chop the chili and add it to the spice mixture
3. Then combine the sliced squid and spice mixture together. Stir it carefully.
4. After this, sprinkle the seafood mixture with the lemon juice and fish sauce. Stir it. Leave the mixture for 10 minutes.
5. Toss the butter in the Foodi and melt it
6. Then place the sliced squid mixture in the Foodi and close the lid. Cook the dish for 13 minutes at the *Pressure* mode.
7. When the dish is cooked; remove it from the Foodi. Sprinkle the dish with the liquid from the cooked squid. Serve.

Monk Fish with Power Greens

(Prep + Cook Time: 25 minutes | **Servings:** 4)

Ingredients:
- 4 (8 oz.) Monk Fish Fillets, cut in 2 pieces each
- 1/2 lb Baby Bok Choy, stems removed and chopped largely
- 2 tbsp. Olive Oil
- 1 cup Kale Leaves
- 1 Lemon, zested and juiced
- 1/2 cup chopped Green Beans
- 2 cloves Garlic, sliced
- Lemon Wedges to serve
- Salt and White Pepper to taste

Instructions:
1. Pour in the coconut oil, garlic, red chili, and green beans. Stir fry for 5 minutes on Sear/Sauté mode. Add the kale leaves, and cook them to wilt, about 3 minutes.
2. Meanwhile, place the fish on a plate and season with salt, white pepper, and lemon zest. After, remove the green beans and kale into a plate and set aside
3. Back to the pot, add the olive oil and fish. Brown the fillets on each side for about 2 minutes and then add the bok choy in
4. Pour the lemon juice over the fish and gently stir. Cook for 2 minutes and then press Start/Stop to stop cooking.
5. Spoon the fish with bok choy over the green beans and kale. Serve with a side of lemon wedges and there, you have a complete meal

Creamy Garlicky Oyster Stew Recipe

(Prep + Cook Time: 15 minutes | **Servings:** 4)

Ingredients:
- 2 cups Heavy Cream
- 3 (10 oz.) jars Shucked Oysters in Liqueur
- 2 cups chopped Celery
- 2 cups Bone Broth
- 3 cloves Garlic, minced
- 3 tbsp. chopped Parsley
- 3 Shallots, minced
- 3 tbsp. Olive Oil
- Salt and White Pepper to taste

Instructions:
1. Add oil, garlic, shallot, and celery. Stir-fry them for 2 minutes on Sear/Sauté mode, and add the heavy cream, broth, and oysters. Stir once or twice
2. Close the lid, secure the pressure valve, and select Steam mode on High pressure for 3 minutes. Press Start/Stop
3. Once the timer has stopped, do a quick pressure release, and open the lid
4. Season with salt and white pepper. Close the crisping lid and cook for 5 minutes on Broil mode. Stir and dish the oyster stew into serving bowls. Garnish with parsley and top with some croutons

Potato Beer Fish

(Prep + Cook Time: 1 hour | **Servings:** 4)

Ingredients:
- 1 lb. fish fillet
- 4 medium size potatoes; peeled and diced
- 1 red pepper sliced
- 1 cup beer
- 1 tbsp. oyster flavored sauce
- 1 tbsp. rock candy
- 1 tbsp. oil
- 1 tsp. salt

Instructions:
1. Put all ingredients into your Foodi Multi-cooker. High pressure for 40 minutes. Lock the lid on the Foodi Multi-cooker and then cook for 40 minutes.

2. To get 40 minutes' cook time, press *Pressure* button and use the Time Adjustment button to adjust the cook time to 40 minutes
3. Pressure Release. Release the pressure using natural release method.
4. Finish the dish. Close the crisping lid. Select "BROIL" and set the time to 5 minutes. Select START/STOP to begin. Cook until top is browned.
5. Then that is it! Simple, fast, delicious, retaining flavour and nutrition, consistent results all the time. Serve and Enjoy!

Cheesy Tuna Helper

(Prep + Cook Time: 15 Minutes | **Servings:** 6)

Ingredients:
- 1 can (5 oz.) tuna; drained
- 16 oz. egg noodles
- 28 oz. canned cream mushroom soup
- 1 cup frozen peas
- 1/4 cup bread crumbs (optional)
- 3 cups water
- 4 oz. cheddar cheese

Instructions:
1. Put the noodles in the Foodi. Pour the water to cover the noodles
2. Add the frozen peas, tuna, and the soup on top of the pasta layer. Cover and lock the lid
3. Select *Pressure* and cook at HIGH pressure for 4 minutes. When the Foodi timer beeps, press the *Cancel* key and unplug the Foodi. Turn the steam valve to quick release the pressure.
4. Unlock and carefully open the lid. Add the cheese and stir
5. If desired, you can pour the pasta mixture in a baking dish, sprinkle the top with bread crumbs, and broil for about 2 to 3 minutes. Serve.

Fish Curry

(Prep + Cook Time: 25 Minutes | **Servings:** 6)

Ingredients:
- 6 fish fillets, cut into medium pieces
- 14 oz. coconut milk
- 2 garlic cloves; peeled and minced
- 2 onions; sliced
- 2 bell peppers, cored and cut into strips
- 1 tomato; chopped
- 2 tbsp. curry powder
- 1 tbsp. coriander
- 1 tbsp. ginger; grated
- 1/2 tsp. fenugreek
- 1 tsp. red pepper flakes
- 2 tbsp. lemon juice
- 1/2 tsp. turmeric
- 2 tsp. cumin
- Salt and ground black pepper, to taste

Instructions:
1. Set the Foodi on *Sauté* mode, add the oil and curry powder, and fry for 1 minute. Add the ginger, onion, and garlic, stir, and cook for 2 minutes. Add the coriander, turmeric, cumin, fenugreek, and red pepper flakes, stir, and cook 2 minutes. Add the coconut milk, tomatoes, fish, and bell peppers, stir.
2. Cover, and cook on Egg mode for 5 minutes. Release the pressure naturally, add the salt and pepper, stir, and divide into bowls. Serve with lemon juice on top.

Green Chili Mahi-Mahi Fillets

(**Prep + Cook Time:** 10 Minutes | **Servings:** 2)

Ingredients:
- 2 Mahi-Mahi fillets, thawed
- 1/4 cup green chili enchilada sauce; homemade or store-brought
- 2 tbsp. butter
- Salt and pepper to taste
- 1 cup water

Instructions:
1. Pour 1 cup of water into the Foodi and set a steamer rack
2. Grease the bottom of each mahi-mahi fillet with 1 tbsp. of butter, spreading the butter from end to end this will prevent the fish from sticking to the rack.
3. Put the fillets on the rack. Spread 1/4 cup of enchilada sauce between each fillet using a pastry brush; cover them well
4. Top with more enchilada sauce, if desired. Season fillets with salt and pepper. Lock the lid and close the steam valve. Press *Pressure*, set the pressure to HIGH, and set the timer for 5 minutes.
5. When the timer beeps, quickly release the pressure and transfer the fillets into serving plates. Serve.

Notes: The cooking time is sufficient to cook the fillets if they are thawed. Test the fish before taking out. If they are not done, close the lid and let cook with the residual heat of the pot for 1 minute

Fish and Vegetable "Tagine" with Chermoula

(**Prep + Cook Time:** 10 Minutes | **Servings:** 2)

Ingredients:
For The Chermoula
- 4 large garlic cloves
- 1 heaping tsp. ground sweet paprika
- 1/4 cup freshly squeezed lemon juice (about 2 lemons)
- 1 cup fresh cilantro leaves
- 1 cup fresh parsley leaves
- 1½ tsp. kosher salt
- 1/4 tsp. ground cumin
- 1/4 tsp. ground cayenne pepper
- 2 tbsp. olive oil

For The Fish and Vegetables
- 2 (7 oz.) tilapia fillets
- 10 oz. Yukon gold potatoes (about 2 medium or 3 small), peeled and sliced 1/4 inch thick
- 1/2 medium red bell pepper, cut into bite-size chunks
- 1/2 medium green bell pepper, cut into bite-size chunks
- 1 large tomato, seeded and diced
- 1/4 tsp. kosher salt
- 1 very small onion, sliced
- 1/4 cup water

Instructions:
To make the chermoula
1. Into the chute of a small running food processor, drop the garlic cloves, one at a time, and process until minced. Add the cilantro, parsley, lemon juice, kosher salt, paprika, cumin, and cayenne pepper, and process until mostly smooth. With the processor still running, slowly drizzle in the olive oil, and process until the sauce is emulsified
2. If you don't have a food processor, finely mince the garlic, cilantro, and parsley. Transfer to a small bowl, and stir in the lemon juice, kosher salt, paprika, cumin, and cayenne pepper. Slowly whisk in the olive oil. The sauce won't be as smooth as if prepared in a food processor, but it will taste good

To make the fish and vegetables
1. Sprinkle both sides of the fish fillets lightly with the kosher salt, and brush with 3 tbsp. of chermoula. Refrigerate the fish
2. Add the potato slices, red bell pepper, green bell pepper, and onion. Pour in 1/3 cup of chermoula, and gently toss the vegetables to coat. Pour the water over the vegetables
3. Lock the lid on the Foodi and then cook On High pressure for 5 minutes. To get 5 minutes' cook time, press *Pressure* button and use the *Time Adjustment* button to adjust the cook time to 5 minutes.

4. Use the Quick Pressure Release method.
5. Unlock and remove the lid. Sprinkle the tomato over the vegetables in the Foodi, and lay the fillets on top. Drizzle with the remaining chermoula
6. Lock the lid in place again; bring the cooker to High pressure by pressing" Pressure" button cook On High pressure for 1 minute and press KEEP WARM.
7. When the timer goes off, turn the cooker off. ("Warm" setting, turn off).
8. After cooking, use the natural method to release pressure for 4 minutes, then the quick method to release the remaining pressure
9. Unlock and remove the lid. Using a large spatula, carefully remove the fish fillets and vegetables and divide them between 2 plates. Spoon any residual sauce over the fish, and serve.

Red Curry Cod with Red Beans

(Prep + Cook Time: 10 Minutes | **Servings:** 4)

Ingredients:
- 1 can (13½ oz, unsweetened coconut milk
- 8 oz. green beans
- 1 ½ lb. cod or halibut fillet; cut into 2-inch (5 cm) pieces
- 1/2 cup fresh cilantro leaves
- 2 scallions (white and light green parts), thinly sliced
- 1 lime, quartered
- 2 tbsp. red Thai curry paste
- 1 tbsp. finely grated fresh ginger

Instructions:
1. To the Foodi, add the coconut milk, curry paste, and ginger, and whisk together
2. Add the cod. Lay the green beans on top
3. Lock the lid on the Foodi and then cook On High pressure for 5 minutes. To get 5 minutes' cook time, press *Pressure* button and use the *Time Adjustment* button to adjust the cook time to 5 minutes
4. Use the "Quick Release" method to vent the steam, then open the lid
5. Top the curry with the cilantro and scallions, and serve with the lime quarters for squeezing.

Lime Saucy Salmon Recipe

(Prep + Cook Time: 15 minutes | **Servings:** 4)

Ingredients:
- 4 (5 oz.) Salmon Filets
- 1 cup Water
- 1 ½ tsp. Paprika
- 2 tbsp. chopped Parsley
- 2 tbsp. Olive Oil
- 1 tbsp. Maple Syrup
- 2 cloves Garlic, minced
- 2 tsp. Cumin Powder
- 2 tbsp. Hot Water
- 1 Lime, juiced
- Salt and Black Pepper to taste

Instructions:
1. In a bowl, add cumin, paprika, parsley, olive oil, hot water, maple syrup, garlic, and lime juice. Mix with a whisk. Set aside.
2. Open the Foodi and pour the water in. Then, fit the rack. Season the salmon with pepper and salt; and place them on the rack
3. Close the lid, secure the pressure valve, and select Steam mode on High pressure for 3 minutes. Press Start/Stop.
4. Once the timer has ended, do a quick pressure release, and open the pot.
5. Close the crisping lid and cook on Air Crisp mode for 3 minutes at 300 °F. Use a set of tongs to transfer the salmon to a serving plate and drizzle the lime sauce all over it. Serve with steamed swiss chard

Shrimp with Risotto Primavera

(Prep + Cook Time: 40 minutes | **Servings:** 5)

Ingredients:
- 2 tbsp. olive oil, divided.
- 16 uncooked jumbo shrimp (fresh or defrosted), peeled, deveined
- 1 small onion, peeled, finely diced
- 5 ½ cups chicken or vegetable stock
- 2 cups Arborio rice
- 4 cloves garlic, peeled, minced, divided.
- 3 tsp. kosher salt, divided.
- 1 tsp. ground black pepper
- 2 tsp. garlic powder
- 2 tbsp. butter
- 1 ½ cups grated Parmesan cheese, plus more for serving
- Juice of 1 lemon
- 1 bunch asparagus, trimmed, cut in 1-inch pieces
- 1/2 tsp. crushed red pepper (optional)

Instructions:
1. Select SEAR/SAUTÉ and set to MD:HI. Select START/STOP to begin. Allow to preheat for 5 minutes.
2. Add 1 tbsp. oil and onion to pot. SAUTÉ until softened, about 5 minutes. Add half the garlic and cook until fragrant, about 1 minute. Season with 2 tsp. salt.
3. Add stock and rice to pot. Assemble pressure lid, making sure the PRESSURE RELEASE valve is in the SEAL position
4. Select PRESSURE and set to HIGH. Set time to 7 minutes. Select START/STOP to begin. While rice is cooking, toss shrimp in the remaining oil, garlic, salt, garlic powder, black pepper, and crushed red pepper in a mixing bowl
5. When pressure cooking is complete, allow pressure to natural release for 10 minutes. After 10 minutes, quick release remaining pressure by moving the PRESSURE RELEASE valve to the VENT position. Carefully remove lid when unit has finished releasing pressure
6. Stir butter, lemon juice, and asparagus into the rice until evenly incorporated.
7. Place reversible rack inside pot over risotto, making sure rack is in the higher position. Place shrimp on rack. Close crisping lid. Select BROIL and set time to 8 minutes. Select START/STOP to begin
8. When cooking is complete, remove rack from pot. Stir Parmesan into the risotto. Top with shrimp and Parmesan and serve immediately

Coconut Fish Curry

(Prep + Cook Time: 45 Minutes | **Servings:** 4)

Ingredients:
- 1½ lb. white fish fillet rinsed and cut into bite sized pieces
- 2 green chilies sliced into stripes
- 2 medium onions sliced into strips
- 2 cloves garlic finely chopped
- 6 curry leaves; bay leaves, basil or kaffir leaves work too
- 2 cups coconut milk unsweetened; about one small can
- 1 heaping cup cherry tomatoes
- 1 tbsp. Ginger freshly grated
- 1 tbsp. ground coriander
- 1 tbsp. ground cumin
- 1/2 tsp. ground turmeric
- 1 tsp. chili powder
- 1/2 tsp. ground fenugreek
- 1 tsp. olive oil
- Salt to taste
- Lemon juice to taste

Instructions:
1. Press *Sauté* to pre-heat the Foodi. When "Hot" appears on the display, add the oil and the curry leaves
2. Lightly fry the leaves until golden around the edges (about 1 minute).
3. Add in the onion, garlic, and ginger. Sauté until the onion is soft
4. Add all of the ground spices: coriander, turmeric, chili powder and fenugreek. Sauté them together with the onions until they have released their aroma (about 1 minute)

5. Deglaze the pot with the coconut milk, scraping everything from the bottom of the pot to incorporate it into the sauce.
6. Add the green chilies, tomatoes and fish. Stir to coat
7. Close and lock the lid. Select *Pressure* and cook at HIGH pressure for 3 minutes. When time is up, use a quick release. Open the lid. Add salt and lemon juice to taste before serving.

Scallops with Butter Caper Sauce

(Prep + Cook Time: 15 minutes | **Servings:** 6)

Ingredients:
- 2 lb Sea Scallops, foot removed
- 4 tbsp. Capers, drained
- 4 tbsp. Olive Oil
- 10 tbsp. Butter, unsalted
- 1 cup Dry White Wine
- 3 tsp. lemon Zest

Instructions:
1. Melt the butter to caramel brown on Sear/Sauté. Use a soup spook to fetch the butter out into a bowl.
2. Next, heat the oil in the pot, once heated add the scallops and sear them on both sides to golden brown which is about 5 minutes.
3. Remove to a plate and set aside
4. Pour the white wine in the pot to deglaze the bottom while using a spoon to scrape the bottom of the pot of any scallop bits
5. Add the capers, butter, and lemon zest. Use a spoon to gently stir the mixture once. After 40 seconds, spoon the sauce with capers over the scallops. Serve with a side of braised asparagus.

Shrimp and Tomatillo Casserole

(Prep + Cook Time: 20 Minutes | **Servings:** 4)

Ingredients:
- 1 ½ lb. peeled and chopped tomatillos
- 1 stemmed; seeded, and minced jalapeno
- 1 ½ lb. peeled and cleaned shrimp
- 1 cup shredded cheddar cheese
- 1 chopped yellow onion
- 1/2 cup clam juice
- 1/4 cup chopped cilantro
- 2 tbsp. lime juice
- 2 tbsp. olive oil
- 2 tsp. minced garlic

Instructions:
1. Heat the oil in your Foodi on the *Sauté* setting
2. When shiny and hot, add the onion and stir until it becomes clear.
3. Add the garlic and jalapeno. Stir until aromatic; this should only take a minute or so.
4. Add tomatillos, lime juice, and clam juice.
5. Close and seal the lid. Select *Pressure* and cook at HIGH pressure for 9 minutes
6. When the timer beeps, press *Cancel* and Quick Pressure Release. Open the lid and press *Sauté* again.
7. Add cilantro and shrimp, and stir for 2 minutes. Add cheese, stir and cover the lid, but don't bring to pressure.
8. Wait 2 minutes for the cheese to melt. Open the lid and stir before serving.

Steamed Fish

(Prep + Cook Time: 20 Minutes | **Servings:** 4)

Ingredients:
- 1 lb. cherry tomatoes, cut into halves
- 1 garlic clove; peeled and minced
- 4 white fish fillets
- 1 cup olives; pitted and chopped
- Thyme; dried
- 1 cup water
- Olive oil
- Salt and ground black pepper, to taste

Instructions:
1. Put the water into the Foodi. Put the fish fillets in the steamer basket of the Foodi. Add the tomatoes and olives on top. Add the garlic, thyme, oil, salt, and pepper.
2. Cover the Foodi and cook on Egg mode for 10 minutes. Release the pressure, uncover the Foodi, divide fish, olives, and tomatoes mix among plates, and serve

Chili Garlic Black Mussels Recipe

(Prep + Cook Time: 45 minutes | **Servings:** 4)

Ingredients:
- 1 ½ lb Black Mussels, cleaned and de-bearded
- 1 White Onion, chopped finely
- 10 Tomatoes, skin removed and chopped.
- 3 large Chilies, seeded and chopped.
- 1 cup Dry White Wine
- 3 cups Vegetable Broth
- 1/3 cup fresh Basil Leaves
- 3 cloves Garlic, peeled and crushed
- 3 tbsp. Olive Oil
- 4 tbsp. Tomato Paste
- 1 cup fresh Parsley Leaves

Instructions:
1. Heat the olive oil on Sear/Sauté mode, and stir-fry the onion, until soft. Add the chilies and garlic, and cook for 2 minutes, stirring frequently.
2. Stir in the tomatoes and tomato paste, and cook for 2 more minutes. Then, pour in the wine and vegetable broth. Let simmer for 5 minutes
3. Add the mussels, close the lid, secure the pressure valve, and press Steam mode on High pressure for 3 minutes. Press Start/Stop to start cooking.
4. Once the timer has ended, do a natural pressure release for 15 minutes, then a quick pressure release, and open the lid
5. Remove and discard any unopened mussels. Then, add half of the basil and parsley, and stir. Close the crisping lid and cook on Broil mode for 5 minutes
6. Dish the mussels with sauce in serving bowls and garnish it with the remaining basil and parsley. Serve with a side of crusted bread

Salmon Steaks with Creamy Mustard Sauce

(Prep + Cook Time: 11 Minutes | **Servings:** 4)

Ingredients:
- 4 (2-inch)-thick salmon steaks (about 8 oz. each)
- 1 small yellow or white onion; minced
- 1/2 cup dry white wine, such as Chardonnay
- 1/2 cup chicken broth
- 4 tbsp. Dijon mustard
- 1/2 tsp. dried dill
- 1/4 tsp. ground black pepper
- 2 tbsp. heavy cream
- 1 tsp. cornstarch or arrowroot

Instructions:
1. Smear one side of each salmon steak with the mustard; sprinkle with the dill and pepper. Pour the wine and broth into a Foodi; stir in the onion. Set a large vegetable steamer in the pot; line the steamer with parchment paper. Lay the fillets coating side up in the steamer

2. Lock the lid onto the pot. Set the Foodi to cook at High pressure for 6 minutes. To get 6 minutes' cook time, press *Pressure* button and use the *Time Adjustment* button to adjust the cook time to 6 minutes.
3. Use the Quick Pressure Release method to drop the pot's pressure back to normal
4. Unlock and open the pot. Lift out the vegetable steamer; transfer the steaks to serving plates or a serving platter
5. Turn the Foodi to its *Sautéing/Browning* function. Whisk the cream and cornstarch or arrowroot in a small bowl until smooth. Once the sauce is boiling, whisk in this slurry. Continue cooking, whisking all the while, until thickened, about 30 seconds. Pour or ladle the sauce over the fillets to serve

Lobster Bisque

(Prep + Cook Time: 20 Minutes | **Servings:** 4)

Ingredients:
- 1 lb. cooked lobster meat (or shrimp or crab meat)
- 1 cup heavy (whipping) cream
- 2 tsp. Ghee or unsalted butter
- 1 onion; chopped
- 2 cups chicken broth
- 1 cup chopped tomatoes
- 3 cups chopped cauliflower
- 1 tbsp. minced garlic
- 1 tbsp. minced fresh ginger
- 2 tbsp. ready-made pesto
- 1 to 2 tsp. freshly ground black pepper
- 1/2 tsp. salt (or more, depending on how salty your pesto and broth are)

Instructions:
1. Preheat the Pressure Cooker by selecting Sauté and adjusting to high heat. When the inner cooking pot is hot, add the ghee and heat until it is shimmering. Add the onion, garlic, and ginger. Sauté until softened, 2 to 3 minutes.
2. Pour in the chicken broth and stir, scraping the bottom of the pan to loosen any browned bits. Add the tomatoes, cauliflower, pesto, salt, and pepper
3. Lock the lid into place. Select Manual or Pressure Cook and adjust the pressure to High. Cook for 4 minutes. When the cooking is complete, let the pressure release naturally for 10 minutes, then Quick Pressure Release any remaining pressure. Unlock the lid
4. Tilting the pot, use an immersion blender to purée the vegetables into a smooth soup. Turn the pot to Sauté and adjust to high heat. Add the lobster meat and cook until it is heated through. Stir in the cream and serve. Ghee is the ideal ingredient to use in this recipe and is a staple of the keto diet. In a pinch, you can use the same amount of butter in a recipe.

Tasty Mahi Mahi Recipe

(Prep + Cook Time: 15 minutes | **Servings:** 4)

Ingredients:
- 4 Mahi Mahi Fillets, fresh
- 4 cloves Garlic, minced
- 1 tbsp. Sriracha Sauce
- 1 ½ tbsp. Maple Syrup
- 1 Lime, juiced
- 1 ¼ -inch Ginger, grated
- Salt and Black Pepper
- 2 tbsp. Chili Powder
- 1 cup Water

Instructions:
1. Place mahi mahi on a plate and season with salt and pepper on both sides.
2. In a bowl, add garlic, ginger, chili powder, sriracha sauce, maple syrup, and lime juice. Use a spoon to mix it.
3. With a brush, apply the hot sauce mixture on the fillet
4. Then, open the Foodi's lid, pour the water it and fit the rack at the bottom of the pot. Put the fillets on the trivet.
5. Close the lid, secure the pressure valve, and select Steam mode on High pressure for 5 minutes. Press Start/Stop to start cooking

6. Once the timer has ended, do a quick pressure release, and open the lid.
7. Use a set of tongs to remove the mahi mahi onto serving plates. Serve with steamed or braised asparagus.
8. For a crispier taste, cook them for 2 minutes on Air Crisp mode, at 300 °F

Clams in White Wine

(Prep + Cook Time: 10 Minutes | **Servings:** 2)

Ingredients:
- 2 lb. live small clams; purged
- 3 garlic cloves, crushed
- 1 small bunch flat-leaf parsley; chopped
- 1 cup dry white wine, plus more as needed
- 1 tbsp. olive oil

Instructions:
1. Arrange the clams in the steamer basket and set aside
2. Heat the Foodi using the "Sauté "mode, add the oil, and heat briefly. Add the garlic and sauté until it just begins to take on some color. Pour in the wine, adding enough to equal your cooker's minimum liquid requirement. Insert the steamer basket full of clams
3. Close and lock the lid of the Foodi. Cook at low pressure for 5 minutes. To get 5 minutes' cook time, press *Pressure* button and use the *Time Adjustment* button to adjust the cook time to 5 minutes
4. When the time is up, open the Foodi with the Natural release method.
5. Invert the cooker cover on your countertop and set the steamer basket on it, shaking the basket as you lift it to allow all the clam liquid to drip down into the cooking liquid. Discard any unopened clams. Cover the steamer basket with aluminum foil and set aside to keep warm, return the cooker base to medium heat and boil the liquid until reduced by half, tumble the clams back into the Foodi and stir to combine well and warm through
6. Spoon the clams and some sauce into individual bowls and sprinkle with the parsley.
7. Purging Clams: Clams and other shellfish that dwell in the muddy bottom of the sea may contain a bit of sand or dirt that would not be welcome in a finished dish and so need to be purged. Mussels do not need purging as they grow on rocks or on ropes that are held vertically in the sea. To purge, place live shellfish in a very large bowl of cold saltwater (make your own using 1/3 cup of salt to a gallon of water). Let them purge for about 30 minutes, drain, and then repeat two or three times until the water is free of sand
8. If not using the shellfish right away, place in a bowl, cover loosely with a damp paper towels, and refrigerate to use the next day.

Carolina Crab Soup Recipe

(Prep + Cook Time: 45 minutes | **Servings:** 4)

Ingredients:
- 2 lb Crabmeat Lumps
- 2 Celery Stalk, diced
- 1 ½ cup Chicken Broth
- 3/4 cup Heavy Cream
- 6 tbsp. Butter
- 6 tbsp. All-purpose Flour
- 1 White Onion, chopped.
- Salt to taste
- 3 tsp. Worcestershire Sauce
- 3 tsp. Old Bay Seasoning
- 3/4 cup Muscadet
- 3 tsp. minced Garlic
- 1/2 cup Half and Half Cream
- 2 tsp. Hot Sauce
- Lemon Juice, Chopped Dill for serving

Instructions:
1. Melt the butter on Sear/Sauté mode, and mix in the all-purpose flour, in a fast motion to make a rue. Add celery, onion, and garlic. Stir and cook until soft and crispy, for 3 minutes
2. While stirring, gradually add the half and half cream, heavy cream, and broth
3. Let simmer for 2 minutes. Add Worcestershire sauce, old bay seasoning, Muscadet, and hot sauce.
4. Stir and let simmer for 15 minutes. Add the crabmeat and mix it well into the sauce.
5. Close the crisping lid and cook on Broil mode for 10 minutes to soften the meat. Dish into serving bowls, garnish with dill and drizzle squirts of lemon juice over
6. Serve with a side of garlic crusted bread

Steamed Salmon with Garlic Citrus

(Prep + Cook Time: 10 Minutes | **Servings:** 4)

Ingredients:
- 2 (1 lb.) skin-on salmon fillets
- 1 tsp. finely grated orange zest
- 1 tsp. finely grated lemon zest
- 4 tbsp. (1/2 stick) unsalted butter; at room temperature
- 2 tsp. minced garlic
- 1/2 tsp. salt
- 1/2 tsp. ground black pepper

Instructions:
1. Mash the butter, garlic, both zests, salt, and pepper in a small bowl until uniform. Pour 2 cups water in the Foodi. Line a large steamer basket with parchment paper; set it in the cooker. Add the fillets skin side down; top with the butter mixture
2. Lock the lid onto the pot. Set the Foodi to cook at High pressure. for 6 minutes. To get 6 minutes' cook time, press *Pressure* button and use the *Time Adjustment* button to adjust the cook time to 6 minutes.
3. Use the Quick Pressure Release method to drop the pot's pressure to normal
4. Unlock and open the pot. Transfer the salmon to a large platter and slice each fillet into two or three pieces to serve.

Soups

Creamy Potato Cheese Soup

(Prep + Cook Time: 10 Minutes | **Servings:** 6 to 8)

Ingredients:
- 4 large potatoes, peeled and cut into 1 inch cubes (2 ½ lbs.)
- 4 small onions; chopped
- 1 ½ cups water
- 3 cups cheddar cheese; grated
- 1 tbsp. parsley; chopped
- 4 cups milk
- 2 tsp. salt
- 1 can chicken stock
- 1/4 tsp. sea salt
- 1/4 tsp. black pepper

Instructions:
1. Put potatoes, onions, salt and chicken stock in Foodi
2. Cook on High for 5 minutes on High pressure. To get 5 minutes' cook time, press *Pressure* button and use the *Time Adjustment* button to adjust the cook time to 5 minutes
3. Once timer goes off, release pressure and carefully remove lid and allow the potatoes to cool
4. Mix the mixture smooth in a blender and return to the Foodi. Add the milk and pepper and cook on Medium and bring to boil, stirring constantly. Add cheese and stir till cheese melts. Serve immediately, garnish with parsley and warm dinner rolls.

Buffalo Chicken Soup

(Prep + Cook Time: 20 Minutes | **Servings:** 4)

Ingredients:
- 2 chicken breasts; boneless, skinless, frozen or fresh
- 2 cups cheddar cheese, shredded
- 1/4 cup diced onion
- 1 cup heavy cream
- 1 clove garlic; chopped
- 1/3 cup hot sauce
- 1/2 cup celery; diced
- 3 cups chicken bone-broth
- 2 tbsp. ghee; OR butter
- 1 tbsp. ranch dressing mix

Instructions:
1. Except for the cheddar cheese and heavy cream, put the rest of the ingredients into the Foodi. Cover and lock the lid
2. Press the *Pressure* key, set the pressure to HIGH, and set the timer for 10 minutes
3. When the Foodi timer beeps, press the *Cancel* key and unplug the Foodi. Turn the steam valve to quick release the pressure. Unlock and carefully open the lid
4. Carefully remove the chicken, shred the meat, and then return the shredded meat into the soup. Add the cheese and cream and stir to combine. Ladle into bowls and serve.

Colombian Chicken Soup

(Prep + Cook Time: 23 Minutes | **Servings:** 4)

Ingredients:
- 3 bone-in chicken breasts (about 2 lb.)
- 1 ½ lb. Yukon gold potatoes, cut into 1/2-inch (13 mm) pieces
- 8 sprigs fresh cilantro
- 1 lime; quartered
- 1 ear corn, cut into 4 pieces
- 1 medium yellow onion; cut in half
- 2 medium carrots, cut in half crosswise
- 2 ribs celery, cut in half crosswise
- 5 cups (1.2 L) water
- 1/4 tsp. freshly ground black pepper
- 1 avocado
- 1 ½ tsp. kosher salt
- 1/4 cup (60 g) sour cream
- 1 tbsp. (9 g) capers; rinsed
- 1 tsp. dried oregano

Instructions:
1. To the Foodi, add the onion, carrots, celery, chicken, water, and salt
2. Lock the lid on the Foodi and then cook On High pressure for 15 minutes. To get 15 minutes' cook time, press *Pressure* button
3. Use the "Quick Release" method to vent the steam, then open the lid. Transfer the chicken to a large bowl. When cool enough to handle, shred into pieces, discarding the skin and bones
4. Discard the onion, carrots, and celery. Add the potatoes and corn to the broth
5. Lock the lid on the Foodi and then cook On High pressure for 2 minutes. To get 2 minutes' cook time, press *Pressure* button.
6. Use the "Quick Release" method to vent the steam, then open the lid
7. Stir in the chicken and pepper.
8. Divide the soup among bowls. Peel, pit, and slice the avocado. Top the soup with the avocado, sour cream, capers, oregano, and cilantro. Serve with the lime quarters for squeezing.

Chicken Noodle Soup

(Prep + Cook Time: 22 Minutes | **Servings:** 6)

Ingredients:
- 2 cups chicken, already cooked and shredded
- 1 yellow onion; peeled and chopped
- 1 tbsp. butter
- 1 celery stalk; chopped
- 4 carrots, peeled and sliced
- 6 cups chicken stock
- Egg noodles; already cooked
- Salt and ground black pepper, to taste

Instructions:
1. Set the Foodi on *Sauté* mode, add the butter and heat it up. Add the onion, stir, and cook 2 minutes. Add the celery and carrots, stir, and cook 5 minutes. Add the chicken and stock, stir
2. Cover the Foodi and cook on the "Soup" Setting for 5 minutes. Release the pressure, uncover the Foodi, add salt and pepper to taste, and stir. Divide the noodles into soup bowls, add the soup over them, and serve

Potato Soup with Leek and Cheddar

(Prep + Cook Time: 25 Minutes | **Servings:** 8)

Ingredients:
- 4 medium gold potatoes, peeled and diced, I used Yukon
- 1½ cups cream or half and half
- 1/3 cup cheddar cheese; grated
- 3 tbsp. leeks; cleaned and thinly sliced, white and light green (reserve 2 for serving)
- 3/4 cup white wine
- 4 cloves garlic; crushed
- 4 sprigs fresh thyme
- 5 cups vegetable broth
- Leeks, and cheese, for topping
- 1½ tsp. dried oregano
- 1 tsp. kosher salt
- 2 bay leaves
- 2 tbsp. unsalted butter

Instructions:
1. Set the Foodi to *Sauté*
2. Put the butter in the pot and melt. When melted, add the leek and season with salt and sauté until soft.
3. Add the garlic and sauté for 30 seconds. Press *Cancel*. Reserve a few portion of the leek and set aside for serving
4. Add the thyme, bay leaves, oregano, broth, white wine, and potatoes into the pot. Stir to mix.
5. Close and lock the lid. Cook on the *Pressure* setting for 10 minutes Set the pressure to HIGH .
6. When the timer beeps, quick release the pressure. Carefully open the pot
7. Add the cream and with an immersion blender, puree the soup until desired consistency. Press the "KEEP WARM" button and heat the soup through. When the soup is hot, sprinkle with the sautéed leeks, and sprinkle with cheese.

Cream of Asparagus Soup

(Prep + Cook Time: 25 Minutes | **Servings:** 4)

Ingredients:
- 2 lb. fresh asparagus, woody ends removed and then cut into 1-inch pieces
- 8 oz. organic sour cream
- 2 garlic cloves; smashed or chopped
- 1 lemon; organic, zested and juiced
- 1 yellow onion; chopped
- 5 cups bone broth; homemade or store-bought
- 3 tbsp. ghee; grass-fed butter or healthy fat of choice
- 1/2 tsp. dried thyme
- 1 tsp. sea salt to taste

Instructions:
1. Press the *Sauté* key of the Foodi. Add your healthy fat of choice.
2. When the fat is melted, add the garlic and onion, and cook for 5 minutes, occasionally stirring, just until the garlic and onions are fragrant and start to caramelize
3. Add the dried thyme and cook, stirring, for 1 minute. Add the broth
4. With a wooden spoon, scrape any caramelized bits in the bottom of the pot.
5. Add the asparagus, lemon juice, lemon zest, and salt. Press the *Cancel* key to stop the *Sauté* function. Lock the lid and close the steam valve
6. Press the *Pressure*, set the pressure to HIGH, and set the timer to 5 minutes.
7. When the timer beeps, press *Cancel* and unplug the pot. Let the pressure release naturally. Open the steam valve and carefully open the lid.
8. With an immersion blender, puree the soup or blend in small batches using a blender until soft.
9. Add the sour cream during blending. Return into the Foodi, if using a blender and reheat if needed. Alternatively, you can reheat in a stockpot
10. Season to taste, as needed. Top each serving with extra sour cream, extra-virgin olive oil, or lemon juice.

Notes: If you want a dairy-free soup, use plain or full-fat coconut milk instead of sour cream. This will change the taste of the soup a bit. You can also use bacon fat or avocado oil instead of ghee. You can store this soup in the refrigerator for 2 days.

Hamburger Soup

(Prep + Cook Time: 13 Minutes | **Servings:** 2)

Ingredients:
- 1 large yellow onion; diced
- 1½ lb. lean ground beef (93% lean or better)
- 1 (14 oz.) can diced tomatoes (about 1¾ cups)
- 2 medium green bell peppers, stemmed, cored, and chopped
- 2 medium celery stalks; thinly sliced
- 2 medium carrots; thinly sliced
- 3 cups beef broth
- 3 tbsp. tomato paste
- 1 large yellow potato (about 12 oz.), such as Yukon Gold, diced
- 1/4 cup loosely packed fresh parsley leaves; finely chopped
- 1 tbsp. loosely packed fresh oregano leaves; finely chopped
- 1/2 tsp. salt
- 1/2 tsp. ground black pepper

Instructions:
1. Whisk the broth, tomatoes, and tomato paste in the Foodi until the tomato paste dissolves. Stir in the onion, bell peppers, celery, carrots, potato, parsley, oregano, salt, and pepper. Crumble in the ground beef in small clumps
2. Lock the lid onto the pot. Set the Foodi to cook at High pressure for 8 minutes. To get 8 minutes' cook time, press *Pressure* button and use the *Time Adjustment* button to adjust the cook time to 8 minutes.
3. Use the Quick Pressure Release method
4. Unlock and open the pot; stir well before serving. (If desired, use a flatware spoon to skim off some or most of the surface fat before serving

Mushroom Barley Soup

(Prep + Cook Time: 35 Minutes | **Servings:** 8)

Ingredients:
- 1 lb. baby Bella mushrooms, sliced
- 1 onion; medium-sized, diced
- 2 carrots; diced
- 2 stalks celery; diced
- 3/4 cup pearl barley (do not use instant)
- 4 garlic cloves, chopped
- 4 thyme sprigs
- 8 cups beef broth or stock
- 1 sage sprig
- 1 tsp. salt
- 1/4 tsp. freshly ground pepper
- 1/4 tsp. garlic powder

Instructions:
1. Pour all of the ingredients in the Foodi and stir to mix. Cover and lock the lid
2. Press the *Pressure* key, set the pressure to HIGH, and set the timer for 20 minutes
3. When the Foodi timer beeps, press the *Cancel* key and unplug the Foodi. Let the pressure release naturally for 10 minutes. Turn the steam valve to release remaining pressure. Unlock and carefully open the lid. Serve and enjoy!

Asian Beef Soup with Rice Noodles

(Prep + Cook Time: 22 Minutes | **Servings:** 4 to 6)

Ingredients:
- 1½ lb. boneless beef sirloin, trimmed and cut against the grain into ¼-inch-thick strips
- 1 small yellow onion; halved and sliced into thin half-moons
- 8 dried shiitake mushrooms; stemmed, the caps broken into small bits
- 4 oz. dried rice stick noodles; about as wide as fettuccini
- 1/2 cup soy sauce
- 6 cups chicken broth
- 2 tbsp. rice vinegar
- 1 tbsp. minced fresh ginger
- Up to 1 tbsp. sambal oelek
- 1/4 cup mirin

Instructions:
1. Mix the broth, beef, soy sauce, onion, mushrooms, rice vinegar, ginger, and sambal in the Foodi.
2. Lock the lid onto the pot. Set the Foodi to cook at High pressure for 15 minutes. To get 15 minutes' cook time, press *Pressure* button
3. Use the Quick Pressure Release method to bring the pot's pressure to normal
4. Unlock and open the pot. Stir in the mirin and rice stick noodles.
5. Lock the lid back onto the pot. Set the Foodi to cook once again at High pressure for 3 minutes. To get 3 minutes' cook time, press *Pressure* button and use the *Time Adjustment* button to adjust the cook time to 3 minutes
6. Use the Quick Pressure Release method. Unlatch and remove the lid; stir the soup before serving.

Carrot Soup

(Prep + Cook Time: 15 Minutes | **Servings:** 2)

Ingredients:
- 1/3 cup coarsely chopped onion
- 8 oz. carrots; peeled and cut into 1/2-inch-thick coins
- 1/4 cup fresh or pasteurized carrot juice
- 1/4 cup dry sherry
- 1½ cups Chicken Stock or low-sodium broth
- 2 tsp. unsalted butter
- 3 tsp. plain, whole-milk yogurt, divided
- 1/4 tsp. kosher salt; plus, additional as needed
- 1/8 tsp. vanilla extract
- Pinch ground cayenne pepper
- 1 tsp. minced fresh chives (optional)

Instructions:
1. Set the Foodi to *Sautéing/Browning* heat the butter until it stops foaming and just starts to brown. Add the onion and carrots, and sprinkle with ¼ tsp. of kosher salt. Cook for 4 to 5 minutes, stirring occasionally, until the onion starts to brown and the carrots begin to soften. Turn the heat to high, and add the sherry. Bring to a boil, and cook for 1 to 2 minutes, or until most of the sherry has evaporated. Add the Chicken Stock
2. Lock the lid in place, and bring the pot to High pressure for 10 minutes. To get 10 minutes' cook time, press *Pressure* button.
3. Use the Quick Pressure Release method
4. Unlock and remove the lid. Stir in the vanilla and cayenne pepper. Remove from the heat, and cool slightly. Using an immersion or standard blender, purée the soup completely. Stir in the carrot juice. Bring just to a simmer, and season with kosher salt, as needed. Ladle into 2 bowls, drizzle each with 1½ tsp. of yogurt, sprinkle with the chives (if using), and serve.

Beef Stock

(Prep + Cook Time: 95 Minutes | **Servings:** 10)

Ingredients:
- 2 lb. beef soup bones
- 3 large carrots
- 3 celery sticks
- 1 large onion; quartered, skin on
- 1 bay leaf
- 2 tbsp. garlic; minced
- 3 tbsp. apple cider vinegar
- Water
- Handful fresh parsley
- 1 tsp. ground Himalayan salt
- 2 tsp. ground pepper

Instructions:
1. Ideally, baking the bones at 375°F (190°C) for 30 minutes prior to pressure cooking them helps draw out the marrow, but if you only have access to your pressure cooker, it will still get the job done. To start the stock, place the bones, veggies and seasonings into the Foodi. Pour in the apple cider vinegar and cover with water. The amount of water will vary based on the size and quantities of your vegetables. You can add in extra greens if you want
2. Lock the lid on the Foodi and then cook On High pressure for 90 minutes. To get 90 minutes' cook time, press *Pressure* button and use the *Time Adjustment* button to adjust the cook time to 90 minutes
3. Pressure Release Once complete, Quick Pressure Release the pressure valve, allowing the steam to escape.

Bean Soup

(Prep + Cook Time: 65 Minutes | **Servings:** 6)

Ingredients:
- 1 white onions
- 1 sweet red pepper
- 1 lb. chicken fillet
- 1 cup cannellini beans
- 7 cups water
- 1 cup dill
- 4 tbsp. salsa
- 1 jalapeno pepper
- 1/3 cup cream
- 2 tsp. salt
- 1 tsp. white pepper
- 1 tsp. soy sauce

Instructions:
1. Place the cannellini beans in the Foodi. Chop the chicken fillet and add it in the Foodi too
2. Add water and cook the beans at the *Pressure* mode on HIGH PRESSURE for 35 minutes.
3. Meanwhile, chop the dill and jalapeno peppers. Slice the onions and chop the sweet red peppers
4. Add the vegetables to bean mixture and close the lid. Press "Soup" Mode and cook the dish for 15 minutes more.
5. Then sprinkle the soup with the cream, salsa, white pepper, and soy sauce. Stir the soup carefully and cook it for 5 minutes more
6. Remove the soup from the Foodi and let it a little chill. Ladle the soup into the serving bowls.

French Onion Soup

(Prep + Cook Time: 40 Minutes | **Servings:** 2 to 4)

Ingredients:

- 1 oz. Gruyère or other Swiss-style cheese, coarsely grated (about 1/3 cup)
- 2 thin slices French or Italian bread
- 2 cups low-sodium chicken broth
- 4 cups thinly sliced white or yellow onions; divided
- 1/2 cup Beef Stock; Mushroom Stock, or low-sodium broth
- 2 tbsp. unsalted butter; divided
- 1/2 tsp. kosher salt; plus, additional for seasoning
- 1/4 cup dry sherry
- 1/2 tsp. Worcestershire sauce
- 1/4 tsp. dried thyme
- 1 tsp. sherry vinegar or red wine vinegar, plus additional as needed

Instructions:

1. Set the Foodi to *Sautéing/Browning* heat 1 tbsp. of butter until it stops foaming, and then add 1 cup of onions. Sprinkle with a pinch or two of kosher salt, and stir to coat with the butter. Cook the onions in a single layer for about 4 minutes, or until browned. Resist the urge to stir them until you see them browning. Stir them to expose the other side to the heat, and cook for 4 minutes more. The onions should be quite browned but still slightly firm. Remove the onions from the pan, and set aside
2. Pour the sherry into the pot, and stir to scrape up the browned bits from the bottom. When the sherry has mostly evaporated, add the remaining 1 tbsp. of butter, and let it melt. Stir in the remaining 3 cups of onions, and sprinkle with 1/2 tsp. of kosher salt.
3. Lock the lid on the Foodi and then cook On High pressure for 25 minutes. To get 25 minutes' cook time, press *Pressure* button and use the *Time Adjustment* button to adjust the cook time to 25 minutes.
4. Pressure Release Use the Quick Pressure Release method
5. Unlock and remove the lid.
6. The onions should be pale and very soft, with a lot of liquid in the pot. Add the chicken broth, Beef Stock, Worcestershire sauce, and thyme.
7. Lock the lid on the Foodi and then cook On High pressure for 10 minutes. To get 10 minutes' cook time, press *Pressure* button and use the *Time Adjustment* button to adjust the cook time to 10 minutes.
8. Pressure Release Use the Quick Pressure Release method
9. Unlock and remove the lid. Stir in the sherry vinegar, and taste. The soup should be balanced between the sweetness of the onions, the savory stock, and the acid from the vinegar. If it seems bland, add a pinch or two of kosher salt or a little more vinegar. Stir in the reserved cup of onions, and keep warm while you prepare the cheese toasts
10. Preheat the broiler. Reserve 2 tbsp. of the cheese, and sprinkle the remaining cheese evenly over the 2 bread slices. Place the bread slices on a sheet pan under the broiler for 2 to 3 minutes, or until the cheese melts.
11. Place 1 tbsp. of the reserved cheese in each of 2 bowls. Ladle the soup into the bowls, float a toast slice on top of each, and serve.

Chicken Soup

(Prep + Cook Time: 27 Minutes | **Servings:** 4)

Ingredients:
- 4 chicken breasts, skinless and boneless
- 16 oz. chunky salsa
- 29 oz. canned diced tomatoes
- 29 oz. chicken stock
- 2 tbsp. extra virgin olive oil
- 1 onion; peeled and chopped
- 3 garlic cloves, peeled and minced
- 2 tbsp. dried parsley
- 1 tsp. garlic powder
- 1 tbsp. onion powder
- 1 tbsp. chili powder
- 15 oz. frozen corn
- 32 oz. canned black beans; drained
- Salt and ground black pepper, to taste

Instructions:
1. Set the Foodi on *Sauté* mode, add the oil, and heat it up. Add the onion, stir, and cook 5 minutes. Add the garlic, stir, and cook for 1 minute. Add the chicken breasts, salsa, tomatoes, stock, salt, pepper, parsley, garlic powder, onion powder, and chili powder, stir
2. Cover, and cook on the "Soup" Setting for 8 minutes. Release the pressure for 10 minutes, uncover the Foodi, transfer the chicken breasts to a cutting board, shred with 2 forks, and return to pot. Add the beans and corn, set the Foodi on Egg mode and cook for 2 to 3 minutes. Divide into soup bowls, and serve.

Cheese Tortellini and Chicken Soup

(Prep + Cook Time: 35 Minutes | **Servings:** 6)

Ingredients:
- 2 whole chicken breast, skinless and boneless
- 1/2 white onion; chopped
- 1 cup celery; chopped

Your choice of spices for chicken:
- 1 tbsp. parsley
- 1 tbsp. garlic; minced
- 1 tbsp. paprika
- 2 cartons (32 oz. each) chicken broth
- 2 small bags frozen cheese tortellini
- 2 cups baby carrots, chopped
- 1 tsp. pepper
- 1 tsp. salt

Instructions:
1. Pour 1 cup of the chicken broth in the Foodi. Add the chicken breast. Sprinkle the top of the chicken with the spices. Lock the pot and close the steam valve
2. Press the *Pressure* key, set the pressure to HIGH, and set the timer to 15 minutes.
3. Meanwhile, prepare the vegetables.
4. When the timer beeps, open the steam valve to quick release the pressure.
5. Remove the chicken from the pot and shred using two forks. Return the shredded meat into the pot.
6. Add the vegetables and the tortellini
7. Add one container of the chicken broth and add 1/2 of the other container in the pot.
8. If desired, add more parsley or spices. Lock the lead and close the steam valve. Press *Pressure*, set the pressure to HIGH and set the timer for 3 minutes
9. When the timer beeps, let the pressure release quickly. Ladle into bowls and enjoy!

Chicken and White Bean Chili with Tomatoes

(Prep + Cook Time: 35 Minutes | **Servings:** 8)

Ingredients:
- 4 oz. canned mild green chilies, diced
- 3 ¾ cups chicken, boneless breasts, diced
- 2 cups chicken broth or stock; reduced fat
- 14 oz. canned tomatoes, diced
- 1 ¼ cups onion; diced
- 3 cups canned great northern beans; drain and rinse
- 1/4 tsp. cayenne pepper
- 1/2 tsp. paprika
- 1/2 tsp. garlic powder
- 1 tbsp. cumin

Instructions:
1. Combine all of the ingredients in the Foodi. Lock the lid and close the steam valve
2. Press the *Pressure* button and adjust the time for 10 minutes
3. When the timer beeps, release the pressure quickly. Serve and enjoy.

Corn Chowder

(Prep + Cook Time: 12 Minutes | **Servings:** 4 to 6)

Ingredients:
- 4 cups salt-free Vegetable Stock
- 3 small unpeeled red potatoes; cubed
- 4 cups fresh or thawed frozen corn kernels
- 6 slices crisp-cooked prosciutto; for serving
- 1 tbsp. olive oil
- 1 medium green bell pepper; stemmed, seeded, and diced
- 1 medium yellow onion; diced
- 1 medium red bell pepper, stemmed, seeded, and diced
- 1/2 tsp. freshly ground black pepper, plus more if desired
- 3 tbsp. unsalted butter
- 3 tbsp. all-purpose flour
- 1 cup whole milk
- 3 tsp. salt

Instructions:
1. Heat the Foodi using the *Sauté* function, add the oil, onion, and red and green bell peppers and sauté, stirring infrequently, until the onion is translucent, about 5 minutes. Stir in the stock, potatoes, and corn
2. Lock the lid on the Foodi and then cook On High pressure for 6 minutes. To get 6 minutes' cook time, press *Pressure* button and use the *Time Adjustment* button to adjust the cook time to 6 minutes
3. Meanwhile, make a blond roux. In a small saucepan over low heat, mix together the butter and flour and cook, stirring constantly, until the butter has melted and the mixture foams and forms a thick paste. Remove from the heat.
4. When the time is up, open the cooker with the Natural release method
5. Stir the roux, milk, salt, and black pepper into the chowder.
6. Return the uncovered cooker using the *Sauté* function, and simmer the soup, stirring occasionally, until it reaches the desired thickness. Serve with a crispy slice of prosciutto in each bowl.

Beef and Rice Soup

(Prep + Cook Time: 25 Minutes | **Servings:** 6)

Ingredients:
- 1 lb. ground beef
- 28 oz. beef stock
- 14 oz. canned crushed tomatoes
- 12 oz. spicy tomato juice
- 15 oz. canned garbanzo beans; rinsed
- 1/2 cup frozen peas
- 2 carrots; peeled and sliced thin
- 3 garlic cloves; peeled and minced
- 1 yellow onion, peeled and chopped
- 1 potato; cubed
- 1/2 cup white rice
- 1 celery stalk; chopped
- 1 tbsp. vegetable oil
- Salt and ground black pepper, to taste

Instructions:
1. Set the Foodi on *Sauté* mode, add the beef, stir, cook until it browns, and transfer to a plate. Add the oil to the Foodi and heat it up. Add the celery and onion, stir, and cook for 5 minutes. Add the garlic, stir and cook for 1 minute. Add the tomato juice, stock, tomatoes, rice, beans, carrots, potatoes, beef, salt, and pepper, stir
2. Cover and cook on the *Pressure* setting for 5 minutes. Release the pressure, uncover the Foodi, and set it on *Sauté* mode. Add more salt and pepper, if needed, and the peas, stir, bring to a simmer, transfer to bowls, and serve hot

Creole White Bean Soup

(Prep + Cook Time: 18 Minutes | **Servings:** 2 to 4)

Ingredients:
- 6 oz. dried navy beans
- 1½ oz. ham; diced (about 1/3 cup)
- 1 small tomato, seeded and diced, or 1/3 cup canned diced tomatoes
- 3 cups Chicken Stock or low-sodium broth; plus, additional as needed
- 1/4 cup chopped scallions
- 3 cups loosely packed arugula
- 1 tbsp. kosher salt
- 1-quart water
- 1 tbsp. olive oil
- 1/3 cup chopped onion
- 1 tbsp. minced garlic (about 3 medium cloves)
- 1 tsp. Creole or Cajun seasoning
- 1/4 tsp. ground cayenne pepper (optional)
- 2 tbsp. Creole or other whole-grain mustard
- 1/2 tsp. hot pepper sauce (such as Tabasco or Crystal), plus additional as needed
- 1 tsp. Worcestershire sauce

Instructions:
1. In a large bowl, dissolve the kosher salt in the water. Add the beans, and soak at room temperature for 8 to 24 hours. Drain and rinse
2. Set the Foodi to *Sautéing/Browning* You can use the Pressure to sauté (there is no browning or sauté button), heat the olive oil until it shimmers and flows like water. Add the ham, and cook for 2 to 3 minutes, or until it just starts to brown. Add the onion and garlic, and cook for about 2 minutes, or until the onion pieces start to separate and the garlic becomes fragrant. Stir in the Creole seasoning and cayenne pepper (if using), and cook for 1 minute, stirring to coat the ham and vegetables
3. Add the Chicken Stock; then pour in the beans
4. Lock the lid on the Foodi and then cook On High pressure for 12 minutes. To get 12 minutes' cook time, press *Pressure* button
5. Use the Quick Pressure Release method
6. Unlock and remove the lid. Turn the Foodi to *Sautéing/Browning* stir in the mustard, hot pepper sauce, and Worcestershire sauce, and simmer for 3 minutes. Taste and adjust the seasoning, adding more hot sauce or Creole seasoning if you want it spicier. If the soup is too spicy or too thick, add more stock. Add the tomato, scallions, and arugula, and simmer for about 4 minutes, or until the arugula is wilted and the tomatoes are heated through. Ladle into bowls, and serve.

Butternut Squash Soup

(Prep + Cook Time: 26 Minutes | Servings: 6)

Ingredients:
- 1½ lb. butternut squash; baked, peeled and cubed
- 29 oz. chicken stock
- 15 oz. canned diced tomatoes
- 1½ cup half and half
- 1 cup chicken meat; already cooked and shredded
- 1/2 cup green onions; chopped
- 3 tbsp. butter
- 1/2 cup carrots; peeled and chopped
- 1/2 cup celery, chopped
- 1 garlic clove; peeled and minced
- 1/2 tsp. Italian seasoning
- 1/8 tsp. red pepper flakes
- 1 cup orzo; already cooked
- 1/8 tsp. nutmeg, grated
- Green onions; chopped, for serving
- Salt and ground black pepper, to taste

Instructions:
1. Set the Foodi on *Sauté* mode, add the butter and melt it. Add the celery, carrots, and onions, stir, and cook for 3 minutes. Add the garlic, stir, and cook for 1 minute. Add the squash, tomatoes, stock, Italian seasoning, salt, pepper, pepper flakes, and nutmeg. Stir
2. Cover the Foodi, and cook on the "Soup" Setting for 10 minutes. Release the pressure, uncover, and puree everything with an immersion blender. Set the Foodi on Egg mode, add the half and half, orzo, and chicken, stir, and cook for 3 minutes. Divide the soup into bowls, sprinkle green onions on top, and serve.

Creamy Tomato Soup

(Prep + Cook Time: 16 Minutes | Servings: 8)

Ingredients:
- 29 oz. chicken stock
- 3 lb. tomatoes; peeled, cored, and cut into quarters
- 1/4 cup fresh basil; chopped
- 1 carrot, peeled and chopped
- 2 celery stalks; chopped
- 2 garlic cloves, peeled and minced
- 1/2 cup Parmesan cheese; shredded
- 1 yellow onion, peeled and chopped
- 1 tbsp. tomato paste
- 1 cup half and half
- 3 tbsp. butter
- Salt and ground black pepper, to taste

Instructions:
1. Set the Foodi on *Sauté* mode, add the butter and melt it. Add the onion, carrots, and celery, stir, and cook for 3 minutes. Add the garlic, stir, and cook for 1 minute. Add the tomatoes, tomato paste, stock, basil, salt, and pepper, stir.
2. Cover, and cook on the "Soup" Setting for 5 minutes. Release the pressure, uncover the Foodi and puree the soup using and immersion blender. Add the half and half and cheese, stir, set the Foodi on *Sauté* mode and heat everything up. Divide the soup into soup bowls, and serve

Roasted Tomato Soup

(Prep + Cook Time: 15 Minutes | **Servings:** 2)

Ingredients:
- 1 (14.5 oz.) can fire-roasted tomatoes
- 1 small roasted red bell pepper; cut into chunks (about 1/4 cup)
- 1/4 cup dry or medium-dry sherry
- 3/4 cup Chicken Stock or low-sodium broth
- 3 tbsp. olive oil
- 1/2 cup sliced onion
- 1 medium garlic clove; sliced or minced
- 1/8 tsp. ground cumin
- 1/8 tsp. freshly ground black pepper
- 1 tbsp. heavy (whipping) cream (optional)
- Kosher salt

Instructions:
1. Set the Foodi to brown, heat the olive oil until it shimmers and flows like water. Add the onions, and sprinkle with a pinch or two of kosher salt. Cook for about 5 minutes, stirring, until the onions just begin to brown. Add the garlic, and cook for 1 to 2 minutes more, or until fragrant
2. Pour in the sherry, and simmer for 1 to 2 minutes, or until the sherry is reduced by half, scraping up any browned bits from the bottom of the pan. Add the tomatoes, roasted red bell pepper, and Chicken Stock to the Foodi
3. Lock the lid on the Foodi and then cook On High pressure for 10 minutes. To get 10 minutes' cook time, press *Pressure* button and use the *Time Adjustment* button to adjust the cook time to 10 minutes.
4. Pressure Release Use the Quick Pressure Release method
5. For a smooth soup, blend using an immersion or standard blender. Add the cumin and pepper, and adjust the salt, if necessary. If you like a creamier soup, stir in the heavy cream.
6. If using a standard blender, be careful. Steam can build up and blow the lid off if the soup is very hot. Hold the lid on with a towel, and blend in batches, if necessary; don't fill the jar more than halfway full

Chops, Rice and Cheese Soup

(Prep + Cook Time: 20 Minutes | **Servings:** 4)

Ingredients:
- 2 pork chops
- 1 can of Campbell's cheddar cheese soup
- 1/2 of an onion; chopped
- 1/2 of a cup or corn; or the kernels from 1 ear
- 1/4 of a tomato, chopped
- 1/2 a cup of Arborio rice
- 1 ¾ cups of water
- 2 tbsp. olive oil
- Salt and pepper

Instructions:
1. Begin by using the *Sauté* setting on the Foodi to sauté the onions and the pork chops until they are light brown in color
2. Add all of the rest of the ingredients to the Foodi, mix it well and lock the lid into place.
3. Cook at High pressure for 8 minutes. To get 8 minutes' cook time, press *Pressure* button and use the *Time Adjustment* button to adjust the cook time to 8 minutes
4. After the timer goes off you will let the food rest for 2 minutes before using the quick release option.
5. Remove the lid and let sit until all of the liquid is absorbed before serving. Top with Parmesan cheese. Serve.

Butternut Squash Sweet Potato Soup

(Prep + Cook Time: 40 Minutes | **Servings:** 4)

Ingredients:
- 1-inch ginger, peeled
- 2 cups sweet potatoes; peeled and cubed
- 2 cups butternut squash, peeled, seeded, and cubed
- 2 cloves garlic; crushed
- 3 cups bone broth or vegetable broth or chicken broth
- 1 onion, small-medium, cubed
- 2 tbsp. coconut oil
- 1/2 tsp. turmeric
- 1/2 tsp. ground nutmeg
- 1 tsp. walnuts; chopped, for garnish, optional
- 1 tsp. or pinch of sea salt
- 1 tsp. fresh parsley; for garnish, optional
- 1 tsp. dried tarragon
- 1 tsp. cinnamon
- 1 ½ tsp. curry powder

Instructions:
1. Press the *Sauté* key of the Foodi.
2. When the pot is hot, add the coconut oil, ginger, garlic, onions, and pinch of salt. Sauté until the onion is slightly soft
3. Add the rest of the ingredients and stir to mix. Lock the lid and close the steam valve. Press *Pressure* and cook at HIGH pressure for 10 minutes.
4. When the timer beeps, let the pressure release naturally. Carefully open the lid
5. With an immersion blender, puree the soup right in the pot
6. Alternatively, transfer the soup in a blender of a food processor, and puree in batches if needed. Be careful because the soup will be hot. Serve immediately and garnish.

Cream of Spinach with Chicken Bites

(Prep + Cook Time: 45 Minutes | **Servings:** 4 to 6)

Ingredients:
- 1 bag of frozen spinach, thawed (If fresh then roughly 4 to 6 bundles depending on bundle size, some supermarkets carry very large farmer bundles, which you will only need 2 bundles)
- 2 medium size chicken breasts; diced
- 2 cans of chicken stock
- 2 shallots; minced
- 1/4 cup flour (only sprinkle if soup not at desired thickness)
- 3 cups of milk
- 3 table spoons of butter
- 1 clove of garlic; minced
- Salt and pepper to taste

Instructions:
1. Add the spinach and chicken stock to Foodi. Lock the lid and cook on High Pressure for 15 minutes. To get 12 minutes' cook time, press *Pressure* button
2. Meanwhile, in a nonstick skillet add a swirl of olive oil and sauté the diced chicken breasts for 5 minutes on medium then add in the butter, garlic and shallots and sauté for another 5 minutes on high or until meat is fully cooked
3. Once your Foodi timer goes off release pressure. Give it a good stir, add in the milk and only add the flour if it's not at desired thickens.
4. Then ladle the spinach soup into blender and blend until incorporated and smooth
5. Add the soup back into pressure cook along with the chicken. Lock the lid and cook on High for another 5 minutes. Set timer. Once timer goes off release pressure
6. Add salt and pepper to taste and serve with crusty bread and lemon wedges on the side.

Split Pea and Ham Soup

(Prep + Cook Time: 15 Minutes | **Servings:** 2)

Ingredients:
- 1/2 lb. dried split peas, rinsed
- 1/2 cup diced onion
- 3/4 cup diced ham
- 1/2 cup diced carrot
- 1 tbsp. olive oil
- 1 garlic clove; minced or pressed
- 1 bay leaf
- 1 or 2 dashes Tabasco sauce
- 1 tbsp. minced fresh parsley
- 1/4 tsp. dried thyme
- 1-quart water
- 1 tsp. kosher salt
- Freshly ground black pepper

Instructions:
1. Set the Foodi to *Sautéing/Browning* heat the olive oil until it shimmers and flows like water. Add the onion and garlic. Cook for about 2 minutes, stirring, until the onions soften
2. Add the split peas, ham, carrot, bay leaf, parsley, thyme, water, and kosher salt to the Foodi
3. Lock the lid in place, and bring the pot to High pressure. Cook at High pressure for 8 minutes. To get 8 minutes' cook time, press *Pressure* button and use the *Time Adjustment* button to adjust the cook time to 8 minutes.
4. Use the natural method to release pressure. Unlock and remove the lid. Stir in the Tabasco sauce and pepper. Taste, adjust the seasoning as needed, ladle into 2 bowls, and serve.

Corn Soup

(Prep + Cook Time: 25 Minutes | **Servings:** 4)

Ingredients:
- 6 ears of corn, kernels cut off, cobs reserved
- 2 bay leaves
- 4 tarragon sprigs; chopped
- 1-quart chicken stock
- Extra virgin olive oil
- 2 leeks; chopped
- 2 tbsp. butter
- 2 garlic cloves; peeled and minced
- 1 tbsp. fresh chives; chopped
- Salt and ground black pepper, to taste

Instructions:
1. Set the Foodi on *Sauté* mode, add the butter and melt it. Add the garlic and leeks, stir, and cook for 4 minutes. Add the corn, corn cobs, bay leaves, tarragon, and stock to cover everything.
2. Cover the Foodi and cook on the "Soup" Setting for 15 minutes. Release the pressure, uncover the Foodi, discard the bay leaves and corn cobs, and transfer everything to a blender. Pulse well to obtain a smooth soup, add the rest of the stock and blend again. Add the salt and pepper, stir well, divide into soup bowls, and serve cold with chives and olive oil on top.

Chicken Stock

(Prep + Cook Time: 70 Minutes | **Servings:** 10 cups)

Ingredients:
- 2 ½ lb. chicken carcasses
- 2 celery stalks; diced
- 2 carrots; diced
- 2 bay leaves
- 2 onions (keep the outer layers too), diced
- 4 garlic cloves; crushed
- 10 cups water
- Your favorite fresh herbs
- 1 tsp. whole peppercorn
- 1 tbsp. apple cider vinegar (optional)

Instructions:
1. Optional step: Brown the chicken carcasses in your Foodi with 1 tbsp. of oil. This will slightly elevate the flavors and result in a brown stock. Then, add water to deglaze the pot with 100 ml of water
2. Add all ingredients in the Foodi.

3. Lock the lid on the Foodi and then cook On High pressure for 60 minutes. To get 60 minutes' cook time, press *Pressure* button and use the TIME ADJUSTMEN button to adjust the cook time to 60 minutes.
4. When the time is up, open the cooker with the Natural Release method
5. Open the lid. Strain the stock through a colander discarding the solids, and set aside to cool. Let the stock sit in the fridge until the fat rises to the top and form a layer of gel. Then, skim off the fat on the surface.
6. You can use the stock immediately, keep it in the fridge, or freeze it for future use
7. Storage: -Silicone Mold, we love freezing our chicken stock with this mold!! After they freeze in the mold, we pop them out and store them in Ziploc freezer bags. It's a great portion for many recipes, thaws quickly, and super convenient

Beef, Barley, And Mushroom Soup

(Prep + Cook Time: 45 Minutes | Servings: 6)

Ingredients:
- 1½ lb. beef shank rounds, trimmed of any large globs of fat
- 1 large yellow onion; chopped
- 2 medium celery stalks; chopped
- 6 cups beef or chicken broth
- 1 cup pearl (perlato) barley
- 1 oz. dried porcini mushrooms
- 1 tbsp. canola; corn, or vegetable oil
- 1 tbsp. stemmed thyme leaves
- 1/2 tsp. ground allspice
- 1 tsp. minced garlic
- 1/2 tsp. salt
- 1/2 tsp. ground black pepper

Instructions:
1. Warm the oil in the Foodi turned to the *Sautéing/Browning* function. Add the meat and brown on all sides, turning occasionally, about 5 minutes. Transfer to a large bowl
2. Add the onion and celery to the cooker; cook, stirring often, until the onion has softened, about 3 minutes. Add the garlic, stir for a few seconds, then stir in the broth, barley, mushrooms, thyme, allspice, salt, and pepper. Return the meat and any juices in its bowl to the cooker
3. Lock the lid onto the pot. Set the Foodi to cook at High pressure for 40 minutes. To get 40 minutes' cook time, press *Pressure*.
4. Turn off the Foodi or unplug it so it doesn't flip to its keep-warm setting. Let the pot's pressure return to normal, 30 to 40 minutes
5. Unlock and open the pot. Transfer the shank or short ribs to a cutting board. Cool for a couple of minutes, then slice the meat off the bones. Discard the bones and tough cartilage. Chop the meat and stir it into the soup before serving.

Poblano and Chicken Soup

(Prep + Cook Time: 30 Minutes | Servings: 8)

Ingredients:
- 2 cups diced cauliflower
- 1½ lb. chicken breast; cut into large chunks
- 1/4 cup chopped fresh cilantro
- 3 poblano peppers; chopped
- 2 oz. cream cheese; cut into small chunks
- 1 cup sour cream
- 1 cup diced onion
- 5 garlic cloves
- 1 tsp. ground coriander
- 1 tsp. ground cumin
- 1 to 2 tsp. salt
- 2 cups water

Instructions:
1. To the inner cooking pot of the Pressure Cooker, add the onion, poblanos, garlic, cauliflower, chicken, cilantro, coriander, cumin, salt, and water

2. Lock the lid into place. Select Manual or Pressure Cook and adjust the pressure to High. Cook for 15 minutes. When the cooking is complete, let the pressure release naturally for 10 minutes, then Quick Pressure Release any remaining pressure. Unlock the lid.
3. Remove the chicken with tongs and place in a bowl. Tilting the pot, use an immersion blender to roughly purée the vegetable mixture. It should still be slightly chunky
4. Turn the Pressure Cooker to Sauté and adjust to high heat. When the broth is hot and bubbling, add the cream cheese and stir until it melts. Use a whisk to blend in the cream cheese if needed.
5. Shred the chicken and stir it back into the pot. Once it is heated through, serve, topped with sour cream, and enjoy.

Chicken Tortilla Soup

(**Prep + Cook Time:** 30 Minutes | **Servings:** 4)

Ingredients:
- 3 chicken breasts
- 2 (6-inch) corn tortillas cut into 1-inch squares
- 15 oz. of black beans
- 1 cup frozen corn
- 3 to 4 cups chicken broth
- 1 big, chopped tomato
- 1 chopped onion
- 2 minced garlic cloves
- 2 tbsp. chopped cilantro
- 1 bay leaf
- 1 tbsp. olive oil
- 2 tsp. chili powder
- 1 tsp. ground cumin
- 1/4 tsp. ground cayenne pepper

Instructions:
1. Turn on the Foodi to *Sauté*
2. Pour in the olive oil and cook the onion while stirring until soft.
3. Add the cilantro, garlic, and tortillas. Stir and wait 1 minute
4. Add the black beans, corn, tomato, 3 cups of broth, chicken, and spices.
5. Turn off the *Sauté* function and close the lid.
6. Switch over to "Soup" Mode and adjust the time to just 5 minutes
7. When time is up, Quick Pressure Release the pressure
8. Carefully take out the chicken and shred before returning back to the pot. Stir everything well. Serve with cilantro, cheese, lime juice, and any other toppings you enjoy.

Butternut Squash Soup with Chicken Orzo

(**Prep + Cook Time:** 25 Minutes | **Servings:** 6)

Ingredients:
- 1 ½ lb. of fresh baked butternut squash; peeled and cubed
- 1 cup chicken breast, seasoned, cooked and diced
- 1 onion; diced
- 1 garlic clove, minced
- 1/2 cup celery; diced
- 1/2 cup carrots, diced
- 2 cans chicken broth
- 1 cup orzo; cooked
- 1 tomato diced
- 3 tbsp. butter
- 2 tbsp. red pepper flakes
- 2 tbsp. dried parsley flakes
- 1/4 tsp. freshly ground black pepper

Instructions:
1. Set the Foodi to brown, and melt butter to sauté the onion, garlic clove, celery and carrots
2. Then add the chicken broth, red pepper flakes, dried parsley flakes, black pepper, baked butternut squash and tomato diced to the Foodi.
3. Lock the lid on the Foodi and then cook On High pressure for 15 minutes. To get 15 minutes' cook time, press *Pressure* button.
4. Pressure Release Use the Quick Pressure Release method

5. Blend/puree until mixture is smooth.
6. Then add it back to your Foodi along with the chicken breast and orzo and cook On High pressure for another 5 minutes. To get 5 minutes' cook time, press *Pressure* button
7. Pressure Release Use the Quick Pressure Release method. Serve with fresh dinner rolls and butter on the side

Split Pea Soup

(Prep + Cook Time: 30 Minutes | Servings: 6)

Ingredients:
- 1 lb. chicken sausage, ground
- 29 oz. chicken stock
- 16 oz. split peas; rinsed
- 1/2 cup half and half
- 2 tbsp. butter
- 1/4 tsp. red pepper flakes
- 1 yellow onion; peeled and chopped
- 1/2 cup carrots; peeled and chopped
- 1/2 cup celery; chopped
- 2 garlic cloves, peeled and minced
- 2 cups water
- Salt and ground black pepper; to taste

Instructions:
1. Set the Foodi on *Sauté* mode, add the sausage, brown it on all sides and transfer to a plate. Add the butter to the Foodi and melt it. Add the celery, onions, and carrots, stir, and cook 4 minutes. Add the garlic, stir and cook for 1 minute. Add the water, stock, peas and pepper flakes, stir
2. Cover and cook on the "Soup" Setting for 10 minutes. Release the pressure, puree the mix using an immersion blender and set the Foodi on *Sauté* mode. Add the sausage, salt, pepper, and half and half, stir, bring to a simmer, and ladle into soup bowls.

Beef and Vegetable Soup

(Prep + Cook Time: 20 Minutes | Servings: 6)

Ingredients:
- 1 lb. boneless beef bottom round; diced
- 1 medium yellow onion; chopped
- 2 medium carrots; diced
- 12 oz. green beans; trimmed and cut into ½-inch pieces
- 1 cup shelled fresh peas; or frozen peas, thawed
- 1 (28 oz.) can diced tomatoes (about 3½ cups)
- 4 cups (1 quart) beef broth
- 1/2 tsp. mild paprika
- 1/2 tsp. dried marjoram
- 1/2 tsp. salt
- 1/2 tsp. ground black pepper

Instructions:
1. Mix the broth, tomatoes, beef, onion, carrots, paprika, marjoram, salt, and pepper in the Foodi
2. Lock the lid onto the pot. Set the Foodi to cook at High pressure for 15 minutes. To get 15 minutes' cook time, press *Pressure* button.
3. Use the Quick Pressure Release method to bring the pressure in the pot back to normal
4. Unlock and open the pot. Stir in the green beans and peas. Cover and lock on the lid; set aside for 5 minutes to warm up and blanch the vegetables. If necessary, use the Quick Pressure Release method once again to bring the pressure back to normal. Open the lid and stir well before serving.

Barbecue Brisket Soup

(Prep + Cook Time: 80 Minutes | **Servings:** 6 to 8)

Ingredients:
- 1 lb. beef brisket, preferably the flat or first cut, cut against the grain into ½-inch-thick slices
- 1 (28 oz.) can diced tomatoes (about 3½ cups)
- 1 (12 oz.) bottle light-colored beer; preferably an amber ale
- 1 large carrot, chopped
- 1 large sweet potato; peeled and chopped into ½-inch pieces
- 1/4 cup packed dark brown sugar
- 1/4 cup apple cider vinegar
- 4 cups (1 quart) beef or chicken broth
- 2 tbsp. Worcestershire sauce
- 1 tsp. ground coriander
- 1/4 tsp. ground cloves
- 1/2 tsp. ground allspice
- 1/2 tsp. dry mustard
- 1/2 tsp. salt
- 1/4 tsp. ground black pepper

Instructions:
1. Combine everything in the Foodi, stirring until the brown sugar dissolves
2. Lock the lid onto the pot Set the Foodi to cook at High pressure for 75 minutes. To get 75 minutes' cook time, press *Pressure* and use the *Time Adjustment* button to adjust the cook time to 75 minutes
3. Turn off the Foodi or unplug it. Let the pot's pressure return to normal naturally, 35 to 40 minutes.
4. Unlock and open the pot. Stir well before serving

Enchilada Soup

(Prep + Cook Time: 35 Minutes | **Servings:** 6)

Ingredients:
- 1 ½ lb. chicken thighs, boneless, skinless
- 1 can (14.5 oz.) fire-roasted crushed tomatoes
- 1 onion; thinly sliced
- 3 cloves garlic, minced
- 1 bell pepper; thinly sliced
- 1 tbsp. chili powder
- 1 tbsp. cumin
- 1 tsp. oregano
- 1/2 cup water
- 1/2 tsp. smoked paprika
- 2 cups bone broth
- 1/2 tsp. ground pepper
- 1/2 tsp. sea salt

For garnish:
- Fresh cilantro
- 1 avocado

Instructions:
1. Except for the garnish ingredients, put all of the ingredients in the pot in the following order: chicken, tomatoes, bell pepper, onion, garlic, broth, water, cumin, chili powder, oregano, paprika, sea salt, pepper. Cover and lock the lid
2. Press the *Pressure* key, set the pressure to HIGH, and set the timer for 20minutes
3. When the Foodi timer beeps, press the *Cancel* key and unplug the Foodi. Turn the steam valve to quick release the pressure.
4. Unlock and carefully open the lid. Using 2 forks, shred the chicken right in the Foodi
5. Ladle into servings bowls and top each serving with fresh cilantro and avocado.

Chicken and Wild Rice Soup

(Prep + Cook Time: 25 Minutes | **Servings:** 6)

Ingredients:
- 2 chicken breasts, skinless, boneless and chopped
- 6 oz. wild rice
- 28 oz. chicken stock
- 4 oz. cream cheese; cubed
- 1 cup celery; chopped
- 1 cup carrots; chopped
- 1 cup milk
- 1 cup half and half
- 1 cup yellow onion, peeled and chopped
- 2 tbsp. butter
- Red pepper flakes
- Salt and ground black pepper; to taste
- 1 tbsp. dried parsley
- 2 tbsp. cornstarch mixed with 2 tbsp. water

Instructions:
1. Set the Foodi on *Sauté* mode, add the butter and melt it. Add the carrot, onion, and celery, stir and cook for 5 minutes. Add the rice, chicken, stock, parsley, salt, and pepper, stir.
2. Cover, and cook on the "Soup" Setting for 5 minutes. Release the pressure, uncover, and add the cornstarch mixed with water, stir, and set the Foodi on *Sauté* mode. Add the cheese, milk, and half and half, stir, heat up, transfer to bowls, and serve

Special Chicken Soup

(Prep + Cook Time: 45 Minutes | **Servings:** 8)

Ingredients:
- 2 frozen boneless skinless chicken breasts
- 1/2 large onion diced
- 3 peeled carrots chopped into similar size as potatoes for even cooking time
- 4 washed medium size diced potatoes (I did not peel you can if you want)
- 4 cups of water and chicken concentrate/bullion of your choice to equal 32 oz. or if you have it, use chicken stock
- Salt and pepper to taste (flavors will intensify while under pressure)

Instructions:
1. Mix the broth, chicken, potatoes, onion, carrots, salt, and pepper in the Foodi
2. the lid on the Foodi and then cook On High pressure for 35 minutes. To get 35 minutes' cook time, press *Pressure* button and use the *Time Adjustment* button to adjust the cook time to 35 minutes
3. Pressure Release Let the pressure to come down naturally for at least 15 minutes, then quick release any pressure left in the pot. Open when all pressure is released stir and enjoy

Cream of Sweet Potato Soup

(Prep + Cook Time: 20 Minutes | **Servings:** 6)

Ingredients:
- 2 lb. sweet potatoes (about 2 large), peeled and cut into 2-inch pieces
- 8 tbsp. (1 stick) unsalted butter; cut into small pieces
- 1/4 tsp. baking soda
- 2½ cups chicken broth
- 1/2 cup heavy cream
- 1/2 tsp. ground cinnamon
- 1/2 tsp. ground ginger
- 1 tsp. salt

Instructions:
1. Melt the butter in a Foodi turned to the browning function. Stir in the sweet potatoes, salt, cinnamon, ginger, and baking soda. Pour 1/2 cup water over everything
2. Lock the lid on the Foodi and then cook On High pressure for 15 minutes. To get 15 minutes' cook time, press *Pressure* button
3. Pressure Release Use the Quick Pressure Release method to bring the pot's pressure back to normal.

4. Unlock and open the pot. Stir in the broth and cream. Use an immersion blender to puree the soup in the pot; or ladle the soup in batches into a blender, remove the knob from the blender's lid, cover the hole with a clean kitchen towel, and blend until smooth.

Beef Stew

(Prep + Cook Time: 90 Minutes | **Servings:** 4)

Ingredients:
- 1 lb. beef stew meat
- 8 oz. mushrooms
- 14 oz. bag frozen pearl onions
- 0.75 lb. potatoes
- 1 lb. carrots
- 2 tbsp. flour
- 2 tbsp. butter
- 2 cups beef broth
- 1 tbsp. Worcestershire sauce
- 1 tbsp. soy sauce
- 1/2 tbsp. brown sugar
- 2 cloves garlic; minced
- 2 tbsp. tomato paste
- 1 tsp. dried rosemary
- 1 tsp. dried thyme
- Salt and pepper

Instructions:
1. Place the stew meat in a bowl and season lightly with salt and pepper. Add the flour and stir to coat.
2. Place the butter in the Foodi and turn on the *Sauté* function. Heat the butter until it is melted and sizzling, and then add the stew meat. Brown the meat on all sides. Don't stir too often, as this will prevent the meat from achieving a nice brown, crispy exterior. The flour may coat the bottom of the pot and that is okay, just don't let it burn
3. Pour the beef broth into the pot and stir to dissolve the browned bits from the bottom of the pot. Once dissolved, add the Worcestershire sauce, soy sauce, brown sugar, minced garlic, tomato paste, rosemary, and thyme.
4. Wash and quarter the mushrooms. Peel and slice the carrots into one-inch sections. Wash the potatoes well, peel if desired, and then chop into one-inch cubes. Add the pearl onions (no need to thaw), mushrooms, carrots, and potatoes to the Pressure Cooker XL. Give all the ingredients in the pot a good stir.
5. Lock the lid on the Foodi and then cook On High pressure for 35 minutes. To get 35 minutes' cook time, *Pressure* button
6. Let the pressure to come down naturally for at least 15 minutes, then quick release any pressure left in the pot.
7. Once the pressure has released, open the steam valve then carefully open the lid. Give the stew a good stir, taste, and adjust the salt if needed. Serve hot with crusty bread.

Chicken and Tomato Soup

(Prep + Cook Time: 20 Minutes | **Servings:** 4)

Ingredients:
- 1 (15.5 oz.) *can navy beans, rinsed and drained
- 1 (14.5 oz.) *can no-salt-added stewed tomatoes
- 1 (14 oz.) *can fat-free; less-sodium chicken broth
- 1 chipotle chile, canned in adobo sauce, finely chopped
- 2 cups chopped cooked chicken breast (about 1/2 lb.)
- 1/2 cup reduced-fat sour cream
- 1/4 cup chopped fresh cilantro
- 1/2 tsp. ground cumin
- 1 tbsp. extra virgin olive oil

Instructions:
1. Select *Sauté* function to heat oil. Sauté the garlic, onion, carrot and celery. Pour in the diced tomatoes with juice
2. Add the bacon, chicken, rosemary and bay leaf. Stir to combine.

3. Pour in the chicken stock. Add the pasta. Lock the lid on the Foodi and then cook On High pressure for 12 minutes. To get 12 minutes' cook time, press *Pressure* button
4. Run quick release.
5. Drain out the chicken. Shred with two forks. Toss back into the soup
6. Taste first. Season with salt if necessary. Sprinkle pepper. Garnish with chopped parsley. Serve immediately with crusty bread if desired.

Chicken Stew

(Prep + Cook Time: 38 Minutes | **Servings:** 6 to 8)

Ingredients:
- 6 chicken thighs (about 3 ½ lb.) or a cut-up whole chicken
- 1/4 lb. baby carrots; cut into 1/2 inch slices
- 1 tsp. vegetable oil
- 2 tsp. kosher salt
- 1 large onion, diced
- 1 stalk celery; diced
- 2 tbsp. tomato paste
- 1/2 tsp. dried thyme
- 1/2 tsp. Diamond Crystal kosher salt
- 1/2 cup white wine
- 2 cups chicken stock; preferably homemade
- 15 oz. can, diced tomatoes
- 3/4 lb. baby carrots
- 1 ½ lb. new potatoes

Instructions:
1. Season the chicken with 2 tsp. salt. Select the *Sautéing/Browning* Mode. Add 1 tsp. of vegetable oil, wait until shimmering. Brown the chicken in 2 batches, three pieces in each batch. Sear the chicken for 4 minutes per side, or until well browned
2. Once all the chicken is browned, pour off all but 1 tbsp. of the fat in the cooker
3. Sauté the aromatics: Add the onion, celery, sliced carrots, tomato paste, and thyme to the pot. Sprinkle with 1/2 tsp. salt. Sauté for 5 minutes, or until the onions are softened. Add the white wine to the pot, bring to a simmer, and scrape the bottom of the pot to loosen any browned bits. Simmer the wine until reduced by half, about 3 minutes
4. Stir in the chicken stock, then add the chicken thighs and any chicken juices from the bowl. Pour the tomatoes on top, but don't stir. Put a steamer basket on top of everything in the pot, don't worry if it's a little submerged, it will be fine, and put the potatoes and carrots in the steamer basket.
5. Lock the lid on the Foodi and then cook On High pressure for 30 minutes. To get 30 minutes' cook time, press Pressure button
6. Use Natural Pressure Release method for 15 minutes, then quick release.
7. Carefully lift the steamer basket of potatoes and carrots out of the pot, then scoop the chicken pieces out with a slotted spoon. Cut the potatoes in half, and then stir the carrots and potatoes back into the stew. Shred the chicken, discarding the skin, bones, and gristle, and stir the shredded chicken meat back into the stew. Taste for seasoning, adding salt and pepper if necessary. Serve.

Chicken Cream Cheese

(**Prep + Cook Time:** 35 Minutes | **Servings:** 6)

Ingredients:
- 1 lb. chicken breasts, boneless skinless
- 1 (1 oz.) package dry ranch seasoning
- 8 oz. of cream cheese
- 1 (15 oz.) can black beans; drained and rinsed
- 1 (15.25 oz.) can corn; undrained
- 1 (10 oz.) can rotel tomato, undrained
- 2 tsp. cumin; or to taste
- 2 tsp. chili powder, or to taste

Instructions:
1. Put all the ingredients in the Foodi. Lock the lid and close the steam valve
2. Press the *Pressure*, set the pressure to HIGH, and set the timer to 20 minutes
3. When the timer beeps, let the pressure release for 10 to 15 minutes.
4. Open the steam valve to release any remaining pressure from the pot. Carefully open the lid.
5. Remove the chicken and shred
6. Break up the cream cheese and stir into the pot. Cover and let the cheese melt.
7. When the cheese is melted, open the lid and return the shredded meat in the pot. Stir everything to mix.

Notes: Serve with tortilla chips or rice.

Snacks, Appetizers & Side Dishes

Lime Carrot Sticks

(Prep + Cook Time: 24 Minutes | **Servings:** 4)

Ingredients:
- 4 carrots, cut into sticks
- 1 tsp. garlic powder
- 3 tbsp. lime juice
- Cooking spray
- Salt and black pepper to the taste

Instructions:
1. In a bowl, mix all the ingredients and transfer to your Foodi's basket
2. Grease the sticks with cooking spray and cook them on Air Crisp at 390°F for 15 minutes.
3. Serve as a snack right away

Parmesan Brussels Sprouts

(Prep + Cook Time: 25 Minutes | **Servings:** 4)

Ingredients:
- 2 pounds Brussels sprouts, halved.
- 1 tbsp. olive oil
- 4 tbsp. parmesan, grated
- Salt and black pepper to the taste

Instructions:
1. In your Foodi's basket, mix all the ingredients except the parmesan, toss and cook on Air Crisp at 370°F for 20 minutes
2. Divide the sprouts between plates, sprinkle the parmesan on top and serve

Garlicky Cauliflower

(Prep + Cook Time: 25 Minutes | **Servings:** 4)

Ingredients:
- 1 big cauliflower head, florets separated.
- 4 tbsp. butter, melted
- 2 tbsp. garlic, minced
- Salt and black pepper to the taste

Instructions:
1. In a bowl, mix the cauliflower florets with all the other ingredients, toss and put the florets in your Foodi's basket
2. Cook on Air Crisp at 390 degrees for 15 minutes, divide between plates and serve

Vegetarian Rigatoni Bolognese

(Prep + Cook Time: 30 Minutes | **Servings:** 6)

Ingredients:
- 4 oz. Mascarpone cheese
- 12 oz. rigatoni pasta
- 1/2 cup onion; chopped fine
- 1/2 cup celery; chopped fine
- 1/2 cup carrots, chopped fine
- 1/2 cup bell peppers, chopped fine
- 1 cup whole milk
- 1 cup red wine
- 1/4 cup Parmesan cheese finely grated
- 3 tbsp. parsley fresh; chopped
- 3 tbsp. olive oil
- 1 tbsp. garlic; minced
- 2 cups mushrooms, chopped
- 1 cup water
- 1 oz. dried porcini mushrooms; chopped
- 1 can crushed tomatoes 28 oz. can
- 1/2 tsp. black pepper
- 1 tsp. salt or to taste
- 1/4 tsp. dried thyme
- 1 tsp. dried oregano
- 1 tsp. dried basil
- 1 tsp. sugar
- 1 tbsp. balsamic vinegar
- 1 tbsp. tomato paste

- 1/2 tsp. crushed red pepper flakes or to taste

Instructions:
1. Press *Sauté* and add olive oil to inner pot of Foodi. Add onions, celery, carrots, bell peppers and garlic and sauté for 3 minutes, stirring frequently
2. Add fresh mushrooms and sauté for 2 minutes. Turn off Foodi by pressing *Cancel*
3. If there's food stuck to the bottom, deglaze pot with 2 tbsp. of water.
4. Add in dried porcini mushrooms, crushed tomatoes, black pepper, salt, thyme, oregano, basil, sugar, balsamic vinegar, tomato paste, crushed red pepper, pasta, milk, wine and water. Stir to combine
5. Close Foodi lid, and make sure steam release handle is in the Sealing position. Select *Pressure* and cook at HIGH pressure for 7 minutes. Use a quick release
6. There might seem to be more liquid than you'd like, but don't worry, the liquid will get absorbed by the pasta.
7. Stir in mascarpone cheese. Let the pasta rest for a few minutes and it will thicken up. Sprinkle each serving with Parmesan and fresh parsley.

Pepper Jack Mac and Cheese

(Prep + Cook Time: 10 Minutes | **Servings:** 4)

Ingredients:
- 2 ½ cups elbow macaroni
- 1 ½ cups mozzarella cheese
- 1 cup heavy cream
- 1/2 cup whole milk
- 2 cups chicken stock
- 1 ½ cups shredded pepper jack cheese
- 1 tbsp. butter
- 1 tsp. salt
- 1 tsp. black pepper

Instructions:
1. Pour chicken stock and cream into the Foodi. Add macaroni, salt, and pepper. Seal and close the lid.
2. Select *Pressure* and cook at HIGH pressure for 7 minutes
3. When time is up, press *Cancel* and use a quick release
4. Mix in butter, milk, and cheese. Stir well and serve!

Crispy Broccoli Side Salad

(Prep + Cook Time: 25 Minutes | **Servings:** 4)

Ingredients:
- 2 broccoli heads, florets separated.
- 2 tbsp. olive oil
- 1/2 tsp. curry powder
- Salt and black pepper to the taste
- 4 tbsp. mayonnaise

Instructions:
1. In your Foodi's basket, mix the broccoli with all the ingredients except the mayonnaise, toss and cook on Air Crisp at 380°F for 15 minutes
2. Mix the crispy broccoli with the mayo, toss and serve as a side dish

Artichokes with Ghee

(Prep + Cook Time: 27 Minutes | Servings: 3)

Ingredients:
- 3 medium sized artichokes
- 1 cup water
- 9 tbsp. melted ghee (or grass-fed butter)
- 1/2 lemon
- Sea salt

Instructions:
1. Start by preparing your artichokes. To do this, cut off the stems to create a flat bottom and cut an inch (3 cm) off the top of each artichoke as well.
2. Pour your water into the Foodi stainless steel basin and lower in the steamer rack
3. Now place your artichokes on the rack, squeeze them with lemon and sprinkle a bit of sea salt on top.
4. Lock the lid, cook on High pressure for 22 minutes. To get 22 minutes' cook time, press *Pressure* button and use the *Time Adjustment* button to adjust the cook time to 22 minutes
5. Allow the artichokes to cook on High pressure and, when complete, Quick Pressure Release the pressure valve
6. Once safe, remove the lid and carefully remove the artichokes from the Foodi Serve with the melted ghee, divided into 3 serving bowls, each holding 3 tablespoons.

Thyme Celeriac Fries

(Prep + Cook Time: 30 Minutes | Servings: 4)

Ingredients:
- 1 big celeriac, cut into fries
- 1 tbsp. olive oil
- 2 tsp. thyme, chopped.
- Salt and black pepper the taste

Instructions:
1. In a bowl, mix all the ingredients and toss well
2. Put the celery fries in your Foodi's basket and cook at 380 degrees on Air Crisp for 20 minutes.
3. Divide between plates and serve as a side dish

Couscous and Vegetable Medley

(Prep + Cook Time: 30 Minutes | Servings: 3)

Ingredients:
- 1/2 large onion chopped
- 1 large red bell pepper chopped
- 1 cup carrot grated
- 1¾ cup couscous Isreali
- 2 bay leaves or Tej Patta
- 1/2 tsp. garam masala
- 1 tbsp. lemon juice
- 1 tbsp. olive oil
- Cilantro to garnish
- 1¾ cup water
- 2 tsp. salt or to taste

Instructions:
1. Heat the Foodi in *Sauté* mode and add olive oil to it. Add the bay leaves and onions. Sauté for 2 minutes
2. Add the bell peppers and carrots. Sauté for one more minute
3. Add the couscous, water, garam masala and salt. Stir well
4. Change the Foodi setting to *Pressure* and cook at HIGH pressure for 2 minutes. When the Foodi beeps, do 10 minutes natural pressure release.
5. Fluff the couscous, it is fully cooked. Mix in the lemon juice. Garnish with cilantro and serve hot
6. Notes: Prepare with vegetables of your choice. I used bell peppers, carrots and onions, which I had at home. Other options are cauliflower, broccoli, edamame and green peas. If you like, you can add more spices.

Italian Potatoes

(Prep + Cook Time: 30 Minutes | **Servings:** 4)

Ingredients:
- 1 lb. gold potatoes, cut into chunks
- 2 tbsp. cheddar, grated
- 3 tbsp. olive oil
- 1 tsp. Italian seasoning
- A pinch of salt and black pepper

Instructions:
1. In a bowl, mix the potatoes with all the ingredients except the cheese, toss and put them in your Foodi's basket
2. Set the machine on Air Crisp, cook the potatoes at 390°F for 20 minutes, divide between plates and serve with cheddar sprinkled on top

Rainbow Fingerling Potatoes

(Prep + Cook Time: 25 Minutes | **Servings:** 4)

Ingredients:
- 2 lb. rainbow fingerling potatoes
- 1/2 cup diced onion
- 2 tbsp. ghee
- 1 tbsp. olive oil
- 1/2 tsp. onion powder
- 1/2 tsp. paprika
- Up to 1 tsp. sea salt
- 1/4 tsp. black pepper

Instructions:
1. Begin by sautéing the onion in your Foodi in the ghee and olive oil for 5 minutes
2. Add in the potatoes and seasonings
3. Lock the lid on the Foodi and then cook for 20 minutes on High pressure
4. Quick-release the pressure valve when complete and carefully remove the lid. Serve warm.

Rigatoni with Meat Sauce

(Prep + Cook Time: 45 Minutes | **Servings:** 4)

Ingredients:
- 1 lb. rigatoni dried
- 1 lb. italian sausage a combo of sweet and hot tastes delicious
- 3.5 oz. white mushrooms; finely chopped (pulse in food processor or chop by hand)
- 1 can tomatoes 28 oz. can
- 1 can tomato puree 14.5 oz. can
- 2 tbsp. olive oil
- 2 to 3 cloves garlic
- 1 onion finely chopped
- 1 tbsp. tomato paste
- 2 tsp. basil dried
- 2 tsp. oregano dried
- Kosher salt to taste
- Black pepper to taste
- 3½ cups water

Instructions:
1. Heat the oil in your Foodi on *Sauté* mode. When display reads "Hot" add in and sauté the onions, mushrooms, garlic and a pinch of kosher salt and a few grinds of black pepper until softened, at least 5 minutes
2. Stir in the oregano, basil and tomato paste and cook another minute, stirring constantly with a wooden spoon.
3. Add in the sausage meat that you have removed from the casings and brown, breaking it up with your spoon, until no pink remains
4. Pour in the water, the tomato puree and, using your hand, squish the tomatoes in to break them up and then pour in all of the liquid from the can.
5. Give the pot a good stir to make sure you get up all of the fond on the bottom of the pot and then add in the dry rigatoni

6. Give it one more good stir, close and lock the lid. Select *Pressure* and cook at HIGH pressure for 6 minutes.
7. When the time is up, quick release the pressure and open the lid.
8. Let it sit for another minute or two, giving it a couple of stirs, to thicken up a bit. If the sauce seems too thin, you can turn the *Sauté* feature back on and simmer it for a couple of minutes as well
9. Serve in big bowls with freshly grated parmesan
10. Variation: When you have the extra time, you can make the sauce right up to the point where you would add in the dry pasta. Instead, close up the Foodi and seal the vent, hit *Pressure* and cook the sauce for 15 minutes on HIGH pressure
11. Release the steam, add in the dry rigatoni at this point, close it back up and then program it for 6 more minutes at HIGH pressure and proceed as instructed. The extra 15 minutes of cook time give even deeper depth of flavor to the sauce.

Simple Potato Salad

(Prep + Cook Time: 15 Minutes | **Servings:** 4)

Ingredients:
- 24 oz. Yukon gold potatoes, peeled and diced
- 1/2 sweet onion; minced
- 1 rib celery; minced
- 1/4 cup + 1 tbsp. high-quality store-bought mayonnaise
- 1 tbsp. organic yellow mustard
- 1/2 tsp. celery salt
- 1/4 tsp. dried or fresh dill; minced
- 1 tsp. apple cider vinegar
- 1/2 cup water
- Pinch ground black pepper
- **Optional:** paprika to garnish

Instructions:
1. Place the diced potatoes and water into the stainless steel bowl of your Foodi.
2. Secure the lid, close the pressure valve and press the *Pressure* button. Cook on High pressure for 10 minutes
3. Allow the potatoes to cook. Quick-release the pressure valve once the cycle is complete
4. Remove the lid once safe to do so. Drain the water from the potatoes (unless you want soupy potato salad) and stir in all the remaining ingredients.
5. Sprinkle a bit of paprika on top to garnish. Serve.

Spaghetti Squash with Garlic and Sage Brown

(Prep + Cook Time: 20 Minutes | **Servings:** 4)

Ingredients:
- 1 spaghetti squash (about 3 ½ lb.), halved crosswise and seeded
- 12 fresh sage leaves
- 1/4 cup (1/2 stick) unsalted butter
- 2 cloves garlic, thinly sliced
- 2 tsp. packed light brown sugar
- 1/4 tsp. kosher salt
- 1/8 tsp. freshly ground black pepper
- 1/8 tsp. crushed red pepper flakes

Instructions:
1. Insert the steam rack into the Foodi. Add 1 ½ cups (350 ml) water. Place the spaghetti squash halves on the steam rack
2. Lock the lid on the Foodi and then cook for 15 minutes on High pressure.
3. Use the "Quick Release" method to vent the steam.
4. In a small bowl, combine the brown sugar, salt, black pepper, and red pepper flakes. Set aside
5. Lift out the squash. Using 2 forks, shred the squash into long strands and place on a large plate
6. Pour out the water and dry the pot. Press (Sauté). Melt the butter in the pot. Add the garlic and cook, stirring constantly, until light golden brown, about 1 ½ minutes. Add the sage and the brown sugar mixture and cook, stirring, until the sage is crisp, about 45 seconds
7. Lift out the inner pot, spoon the sauce over the squash. Serve.

Honey Glazed Carrots with Dill

(Prep + Cook Time: 8 Minutes | Servings: 4)

Ingredients:
- 8 medium carrots (about 1 lb.)
- 1/4 cup fresh orange juice
- 2 tbsp. unsalted butter
- 1/4 tsp. kosher salt
- 1 tbsp. honey
- 1 tbsp. chopped fresh dill

Instructions:
1. Add the orange juice, butter, and salt into the Foodi
2. Slice the carrots at an angle into 1/2-inch-thick (13 mm) slices and add to the pot.
3. Drizzle the carrots with the honey
4. Lock the lid, cook on High pressure for 3 minutes. To get 3 minutes' cook time, press *Pressure* button and use the *Time Adjustment* button to adjust the cook time to 3 minutes
5. Use the "Quick Release" method to vent the steam, then open the lid
6. Press "Cancel", then press *Sauté*. Simmer, stirring often, until the juice thickens and glazes the carrots, about 3 minutes.
7. Serve the carrots sprinkled with the dill.

Vegetables and Rice

(Prep + Cook Time: 21 Minutes | Servings: 4)

Ingredients:
- 2 whole cardamoms
- 3 garlic cloves; peeled and minced
- 2 cups basmati rice
- 1 cup frozen mixed vegetables
- 2 cups water
- 1/2 tsp. canned green chilies; minced
- 1/2 tsp. ginger, grated
- 2 tbsp. butter
- 1 cinnamon stick
- 1 tbsp. cumin seeds
- 2 bay leaves
- 3 whole cloves
- 5 black peppercorns
- 1 tbsp. sugar
- Salt, to taste

Instructions:
1. Put the water into the Foodi. Add the rice, vegetables, chilies, grated ginger, garlic, cinnamon, cloves, butter, cumin seeds, bay leaves, cardamoms, peppercorns, salt, and sugar
2. Stir, cover, and cook on the ""Rice"" setting for 15 minutes. Release the pressure, remove the cinnamon stick, bay leaves, peppercorns, cloves, and cardamoms, divide among plates, and serve

Sushi Rice

(Prep + Cook Time: 33 Minutes | Servings: 18 sushi pieces)

Ingredients:
- 3 tbsp. rice wine vinegar or 1 tbsp. apple cider vinegar and a pinch of sugar
- 1 cup sushi rice
- 1½ cups water

Instructions:
1. Rinse the sushi rice well, rubbing it around in the strainer as the water passes through. Rinse until the water runs clear (about 3 minutes). Measure the rice and cooking water carefully.
2. To the inner pot, add the rinsed rice and water and mix to evenly distribute the rice. Close and lock the lid. Press *Pressure* button and Cook for 7 minutes at HIGH pressure
3. When cooking time is up, count 5 minutes of natural pressure release. Then, quick release the rest of the pressure slowly using the valve. Even if all of the pressure is naturally released before the 5 minutes are up keep the lid closed the entire time. Otherwise, release any remaining pressure slowly using the valve.
4. Stir the rice-wine vinegar into the rice handling it delicately without over-working it

5. Tumble the rice into a large wooden bowl or wooden cutting board and smooth-out into an even layer.
6. Let cool for about 10 minutes, and it's ready to be used to make sushi! Cool the cooked sushi rice by spreading in an even layer in a wooden bowl or cutting-board
7. For making sushi: Slice fresh vegetables for filling into long thin, even strips use avocado, fresh tomatoes, even peppers Layout nonlinear ingredients in a rectangular shape. Use cooked, smoked or pickled fish for filling, only experts should be purchasing and handling raw fish

Coriander Zucchinis

(Prep + Cook Time: 20 Minutes | **Servings:** 4)

Ingredients:
- 4 zucchinis, sliced
- 1 tbsp. olive oil
- 1 yellow onion, chopped.
- 1 tbsp. tomato sauce
- 1 bunch coriander, chopped.
- Salt and black pepper to the taste

Instructions:
1. Set the Foodi on Sauté mode, add the oil, heat it up, add the onion, stir and sauté for 5 minutes
2. Add the rest of the ingredients, toss, put the pressure lid on and cook on High for 10 minutes
3. Release the pressure fast for 5 minutes, divide the mix between plates and serve as a side dish.

Honey Garlic Chicken Lettuce Wraps

(Prep + Cook Time: 70 Minutes | **Servings:** 4)

Ingredients:
- 8 to 10 chicken thighs boneless, skinless
- 1 jalapeno thinly sliced (optional)
- 1 head lettuce
- 1/8 cup honey garlic sauce store bought or recipe below
- 1 medium carrot grated
- 1/2 bell pepper; thinly sliced
- 1 green onion diced
- 1 avocado thinly sliced
- 1/8 cup cashews crushed or chopped
- 2 tbsp. coconut aminos (or soy sauce)
- 1/4 tsp. chilies
- 1 tbsp. onion minced
- 1/2 tsp. salt
- 1 tsp. black pepper

Fermented Honey Garlic Sauce (Optional):
- 1 Fido Jar or a jar with cover
- Cloves garlic peeled
- Raw honey enough to cover the amount of garlic cloves being used

Instructions:
1. Combine coconut aminos (soy sauce), onions, chilies, salt, pepper and honey garlic sauce (if using the recipe below, crush the garlic cloves and include some of the honey) in a bowl
2. Put boneless skinless chicken thighs into the mixture and let marinate for 20 to 40 minutes
3. Put chicken and sauce into the Foodi. Close and lock the lid. Select *Pressure* and cook at HIGH pressure for 6 minutes.
4. While you are waiting for the chicken to cook (likely 10 minutes to reach pressure, 6 minutes cooking time and a 6-8 minute natural pressure release). Prepare the remaining vegetables, chopping and dicing as needed.
5. Prepare the washed lettuce into full leaves. You can use whatever type of lettuce you prefer
6. Once the natural pressure release time readout reaches 6 minutes open up the valve and release any remaining pressure. The chicken should shred easily with a fork. Leave the shredded chicken marinating in the sauce until you are ready to assemble wraps
7. Lay chicken, grated carrot, pepper slices, chopped cashews, green onion, and avocado, in slices inside the lettuce, drizzling sauce over top of the chicken and veggies before rolling the lettuce around ingredients. Serve.

Making the Honey Garlic Sauce
1. In a clean dry jar, place the garlic cloves, you want to leave a little room at the top.

2. Pour the honey into the jar coving the cloves but again making sure there is some space at the top. As the garlic ferments in the honey, it can bubble up
3. Make sure the garlic cloves stay covered with honey, and that you regularly "burp" the lid of the fido jar or covering
4. Let sit for 4 weeks, or 28 days. The garlic will darken, and the honey slightly more liquid, and then you know it is ready!

Smoky Mushrooms + Onions

(Prep + Cook Time: 7 Minutes | **Servings:** 3)

Ingredients:
- 1 (8 oz.) carton button mushrooms, sliced
- 1 tbsp. ghee
- 2 tbsp. coconut aminos
- 1/8 tsp. smoked paprika
- 1 onion; diced
- 1/2 tsp. sea salt

Instructions:
1. Start by melting the ghee in the stainless steel bowl of your Foodi by pressing the Sauté feature.
2. Add the mushrooms, onion and seasonings and allow them to sauté for about 5 minutes
3. Lock the lid on the Foodi and then cook for 3 minutes on High pressure. To get 3 minutes' cook time, press *Pressure* button and use the *Time Adjustment* button to adjust the cook time to 3 minutes
4. Once the cooking cycle completes, Quick Pressure Release the pressure valve and remove the lid once safe to do so. Serve warm.

Spicy Peppers

(Prep + Cook Time: 25 Minutes | **Servings:** 4)

Ingredients:
- 1 ½ pounds mixed bell peppers, cut into strips
- 1 tsp. garlic powder
- 1 tsp. chili powder
- 1 tbsp. olive oil
- Juice of 1 lime

Instructions:
1. In your Foodi, combine all the ingredients, toss, put the pressure lid on and cook on High for 15 minutes
2. Release the pressure naturally for 10 minutes, divide between plates and serve as a side dish

Mix Bean Salad

(Prep + Cook Time: 50 Minutes | **Servings:** 4)

Ingredients:
- 3/4 cup dried kidney beans, rinsed
- 3/4 cup dried cannellini beans; rinsed
- 8 oz. green beans; trimmed and cut into 1/4-inch (6 mm) pieces
- 1/4 cup finely chopped fresh flat-leaf parsley
- 2 ribs celery; finely chopped
- 1/2 medium red onion; finely chopped
- 2 bay leaves
- 1/4 cup fresh lemon juice
- 1/4 cup extra-virgin olive oil
- 1 tsp. chopped fresh rosemary
- 3/4 tsp. kosher salt
- 1/4 tsp. freshly ground black pepper

Instructions:
1. Place the kidney beans, cannellini beans, and bay leaves in the Foodi along with 7cups (1.6 L) water.
2. Lock the lid on the Foodi and then cook for 30 minutes on High pressure
3. While the beans are cooking, in a large bowl, whisk together the lemon juice, olive oil, rosemary, salt, and pepper to make the vinaigrette. Add the celery and onion, and toss to combine
4. Use the "Natural Release" method for 15 minutes, then vent any remaining steam and open the lid. Discard the bay leaves. Add the green beans and let stand for 5 minutes
5. Drain the beans and run them under cold water to cool. Add them to the bowl with the celery and onion. Add the parsley and toss everything in the vinaigrette to combine. Serve.

Carbonara

(Prep + Cook Time: 25 Minutes | **Servings:** 4)

Ingredients:
- 1 lb. pasta dry; rigatoni, penne or cavatappi are great
- 8 oz. bacon pancetta or guanciale
- Pinch kosher salt
- 1 cup Pecorino Romano finely grated; can also use parmesan
- 4 cups water
- 4 large eggs
- Black pepper as much as you like

Instructions:
1. Put the pasta and the water, with a pinch of kosher salt, in the Foodi and program it to cook on *Pressure* for 5 minutes at HIGH pressure
2. While the cooker heats up, crack the eggs in a bowl, add in the cheese and the black pepper, whisk it until it's all mixed together and put aside until you need it.
3. Cook the bacon (pancetta or, if you can find it, the guanciale), in a frying pan over medium heat for a few minutes until it's crispy and has rendered lots of fat and then remove the pan from the heat
4. When the cooking time on the Foodi is up, do a controlled quick release. Pasta can foam up so release with small spurts until you are sure it's not going to spew all over the place and then release it all at once.
5. Put the pan with the bacon/pancetta back on the heat and dump in the pasta and any liquid left in the pot, wait for the water to come to a fierce bubbling up and cook for about 30 seconds until there is just a bit of water left. You want to see some liquid but you don't it to be all soupy
6. Now, remove the pan from the heat again so that you can add in the eggs/cheese and quickly stir it all together until the eggs thicken into a sauce. If you like it super peppery, season with a bit more, more grated cheese if you like and serve right away.

Paprika Potatoes

(Prep + Cook Time: 30 Minutes | **Servings:** 4)

Ingredients:
- 4 red potatoes, cut into wedges
- 1 tbsp. smoked paprika
- 1 tbsp. olive oil
- Salt and black pepper to the taste

Instructions:
1. In a bowl, mix all the ingredients and toss well
2. Put the Foodi's basket in the machine, add the potatoes inside, set the Foodi on Air Crisp and cook for 20 minutes at 390°F
3. Divide between plates and serve as a side dish

Mixed Mushrooms

(Prep + Cook Time: 25 Minutes | **Servings:** 4)

Ingredients:
- 8 big mushrooms, roughly sliced.
- 1 tbsp. sweet paprika
- 1 tbsp. olive oil
- Salt and black pepper to the taste

Instructions:
1. In your Foodi's basket, mix all the ingredients and toss
2. Cook on Air Crisp mode for 20 minutes at 370°F, divide between plates and serve as a side dish

Oregano Chickpeas Spread

(Prep + Cook Time: 30 Minutes | **Servings:** 4)

Ingredients:
- 2 cups canned chickpeas, drained.
- 1 tsp. oregano, dried
- 2 tbsp. veggie stock
- 2 garlic cloves, minced
- Slat and black pepper to the taste
- 2 tbsp. apple cider vinegar

Instructions:
1. In your Foodi, mix all the ingredients, toss, put the pressure lid on and cook on High for 20 minutes
2. Release the pressure naturally for 10 minutes, blend the mix using an immersion blender, divide into bowls and serve as a party spread

Spice Rubbed Cauliflower Steaks

(Prep + Cook Time: 10 Minutes | **Servings:** 4)

Ingredients:
- 1 large head cauliflower (about 2 lb.)
- 1/4 cup chopped fresh cilantro
- 1 lemon, quartered
- 2 tbsp. extra-virgin olive oil
- 2 tsp. paprika
- 2 tsp. ground cumin
- 3/4 tsp. kosher salt

Instructions:
1. Insert the steam rack into the Foodi. Add 1 ½ cups (350 ml) water
2. Remove the leaves from the cauliflower and trim the core so the cauliflower sits flat.
3. Place on the steam rack. In a small bowl, combine the olive oil, paprika, cumin, and salt. Drizzle over the cauliflower and rub to coat
4. Lock the lid, cook on High pressure for 4 minutes. To get 4 minutes' cook time, press *Pressure* button and use the *Time Adjustment* button to adjust the cook time to 4 minutes
5. Quick-release the pressure valve once the cycle is complete
6. Lift the cauliflower onto a cutting board and slice into 1-inch-thick (2.5 cm) steaks.
7. Divide among plates and sprinkle with the cilantro. Serve with the lemon quarters.

Lime Potatoes

(Prep + Cook Time: 25 Minutes | **Servings:** 4)

Ingredients:
- 1 lb. baby potatoes, halved.
- 2 tbsp. lime juice
- 2 tsp. olive oil

Instructions:
1. In a bowl, mix all the ingredients, toss and put the potatoes in the Foodi's basket
2. Cook the potatoes on Air Crisp mode for 20 minutes at 390°F, divide between plates and serve

Cilantro Brussels Sprouts

(Prep + Cook Time: 25 Minutes | **Servings:** 6)

Ingredients:
- 1 lb. Brussels sprouts, halved
- 1 tbsp. olive oil
- 1 tbsp. cilantro, chopped.

Instructions:
1. In your Foodi's basket mix all the ingredients and toss
2. Cook the sprouts on Air Crisp mode at 370°F for 15 minutes, divide between plates and serve as a side dish

Crispy Turkey Bites

(Prep + Cook Time: 30 Minutes | **Servings:** 4)

Ingredients:
- 1 lb. turkey breast, skinless, boneless and cubed.
- 3/4 cup white flour
- 1 egg, whisked
- 1 cup bread crumbs
- Salt and black pepper to the taste
- Cooking spray

Instructions:
1. In a bowl, mix the flour with salt and pepper and stir.
2. Put the egg in another bowl and the breadcrumbs in a third one
3. Dredge the turkey bites in flour, egg and breadcrumbs, arrange all the bites in your Foodi's basket and grease them with some cooking spray
4. Cook on Air Crisp mode at 380°F for 20 minutes, divide into bowls and serve.

Saffron Risotto

(Prep + Cook Time: 20 Minutes | **Servings:** 10)

Ingredients:
- 1½ cups Arborio rice
- 1 cinnamon stick
- 1/2 cup onion; peeled and chopped
- 1/3 cup almonds; chopped
- 1/3 cup dried currants
- 2 tbsp. extra virgin olive oil
- 1/2 tsp. saffron threads; crushed
- 2 tbsp. hot milk
- 3½ cups vegetable stock
- Salt; to taste
- 1 tbsp. honey

Instructions:
1. In a bowl, mix the milk with the saffron, stir and set aside. Set the Foodi on *Sauté* mode, add the oil and heat it up. Add the onions, stir and cook for 5 minutes. Add the rice, stock, saffron and milk, honey, salt, almonds, cinnamon stick, and currants. Stir.
2. Cover the Foodi and cook on the "Rice" setting for 5 minutes. Release the pressure, fluff the rice a bit, discard the cinnamon stick, divide it among plates, and serve

Peas and Walnuts Mix

(Prep + Cook Time: 30 Minutes | **Servings:** 4)

Ingredients:
- 1½ pounds peas
- 1 tomato, cubed
- 1/2 lb. shallots, chopped.
- 1/4 cup walnuts, chopped.
- Salt and black pepper to the taste
- 2 tbsp. butter, melted

Instructions:
1. In your Foodi, combine all the ingredients, toss, put the pressure lid on, cook on High for 20 minutes and release the pressure for 10 minutes
2. Divide between plates and serve as a side dish.

Balsamic Parsnips Chips

(Prep + Cook Time: 30 Minutes | **Servings:** 4)

Ingredients:
- 4 parsnips, thinly sliced.
- 2 tbsp. olive oil
- Salt and black pepper to the taste
- 2 tbsp. balsamic vinegar

Instructions:
1. Put the Foodi's basket inside and mix all the ingredients in it
2. Cook the chips on Air Crisp at 380°F for 20 minutes
3. Divide into cups and serve as a snack.

Coconut Carrot Chips

(Prep + Cook Time: 25 Minutes | **Servings:** 4)

Ingredients:
- 1 lb. carrots, thinly sliced
- 2 cups coconut, shredded.
- 2 eggs, whisked
- Salt and black pepper to the taste

Instructions:
1. Put the coconut in a bowl and the eggs mixed with salt and pepper in another one
2. Dredge the carrot chips in eggs and then in coconut and put them in your Foodi's basket.
3. Cook the chips on Air Crisp at 380°F for 20 minutes and serve as a snack

Buttery Chicken Bites

(Prep + Cook Time: 20 Minutes | **Servings:** 4)

Ingredients:
- 1 lb. chicken breast, skinless, boneless and cubed.
- 2 tsp. garlic powder
- Salt and black pepper to the taste
- 2 tsp. butter, melted

Instructions:
1. In a bowl, mix all the ingredients and transfer to your Foodi's basket
2. Cook the chicken bites on Air Crisp at 380°F for 15 minutes
3. Divide into bowls and serve as a snack.

Broccoli and Bacon Mix

(Prep + Cook Time: 30 Minutes | **Servings:** 4)

Ingredients:
- 1 lb. bacon, chopped.
- 1 big broccoli head, florets separated.
- 1 tsp. canola oil
- 4 tbsp. butter, melted
- 1 cup heavy cream
- Salt and black pepper to the taste

Instructions:
1. Mix all the ingredients in the Foodi, put the pressure lid on and cook on High for 20 minutes
2. Release the pressure naturally for 10 minutes, divide between plates and serve as a side dish

Green Beans and Cherry Tomatoes

(Prep + Cook Time: 20 Minutes | **Servings:** 4)

Ingredients:
- 15 green beans, trimmed and halved.
- 8 cherry tomatoes, halved
- 1/2 tsp. nutmeg, ground
- 2 tbsp. olive oil
- 1 red onion, chopped.
- Salt and black pepper to the taste

Instructions:
1. In your Foodi, combine all the ingredients, toss, put the pressure lid on and cook on High for 15 minutes
2. Release the pressure fast for 5 minutes, divide the mix between plates and serve as a side dish

Zucchini and Dill Spread

(Prep + Cook Time: 20 Minutes | **Servings:** 6)

Ingredients:
- 1/2 cup dill, chopped.
- 2 garlic cloves, minced
- 3 zucchinis, grated
- 2 eggs, whisked
- Cooking spray
- Salt and black pepper to the taste

Instructions:
1. Put the reversible rack in the Foodi, add the baking pan inside and grease it with cooking spray
2. Add all the ingredients inside, set the machine on Baking mode and cook the mix at 370°F for 15 minutes.
3. Divide into cups and serve warm as a spread

Vegan Alfredo Sauce

(Prep + Cook Time: 20 Minutes | **Servings:** 4)

Ingredients:
- 12 oz. cauliflower florets
- Almond milk if needed
- Garlic salt to taste
- 1/2 cup water
- Black pepper to taste

Instructions:
1. Pour water into your Foodi. Put cauliflower florets into your steamer basket and lower into cooker. Seal the lid
2. Select *Pressure* and cook at HIGH pressure for 3 minutes.
3. When the timer beeps, press *Cancel* and wait for a natural pressure release.
4. Remove steamer basket and cool cauliflower for a few minutes
5. Pulse cauliflower with pot liquid in a blender until very smooth. If it isn't quite creamy enough, add a splash of almond milk. Season with garlic salt and black pepper.

Coconut Potatoes

(Prep + Cook Time: 25 Minutes | **Servings:** 4)

Ingredients:
- 1 lb. gold potatoes, cut into wedges
- 1 tbsp. canola oil
- 1 cup coconut cream
- Salt and black pepper to the taste

Instructions:
1. Put the reversible rack in the Foodi, add the baking pan inside and mix all the ingredients into the pan.
2. Set the machine on Baking mode and cook at 380°F for 20 minutes
3. Divide between plates and serve as a side dish

Sweet Potato Wedges

(Prep + Cook Time: 15 Minutes | **Servings:** 4)

Ingredients:
- 2 big sweet potatoes, cut into wedges
- 2 tsp. avocado oil
- 1 tbsp. rosemary, chopped.
- Salt and black pepper to the taste

Instructions:
1. In a bowl, mix all the ingredients and toss
2. Put the wedges in your Foodi's basket, set the machine on Air Crisp and cook at 400°F for 10 minutes.
3. Divide between plates and serve as a side dish

Thyme Baby Carrots

(Prep + Cook Time: 20 Minutes | **Servings:** 4)

Ingredients:
- 1 lb. baby carrots
- 2 tbsp. thyme, chopped.
- 2 tbsp. olive oil
- Salt and black pepper to the taste

Instructions:
1. In your Foodi's basket, mix all the ingredients, toss and cook on Air Crisp at 360°F for 15 minutes.
2. Divide the thyme carrots mix between plates and serve as a side dish

Paprika Potato Chips

(Prep + Cook Time: 30 Minutes | **Servings:** 4)

Ingredients:
- 4 potatoes, thinly sliced.
- 1 tsp. olive oil
- 1/2 tsp. turmeric powder
- Salt and black pepper to the taste

Instructions:
1. In a bowl, mix all the ingredients and toss
2. Put the Foodi's basket inside, put the potato chips in it and cook them on Air Crisp at 380°F for 20 minutes.
3. Serve as a snack

Ginger Mushroom Sauté

(Prep + Cook Time: 25 Minutes | **Servings:** 4)

Ingredients:
- 1 lb. mushrooms, sliced
- 4 garlic cloves, minced.
- 2 tbsp. avocado oil
- 1 tbsp. ginger, grated
- 4 tbsp. soy sauce
- Juice of 1 lemon

Instructions:
1. In your Foodi, combine all the ingredients, toss, put the pressure lid on and cook on High for 15 minutes
2. Release the pressure naturally for 10 minutes, divide between plates and serve

Simple Cilantro Parsnips

(Prep + Cook Time: 25 Minutes | **Servings:** 4)

Ingredients:
- 1 lb. parsnips, cut into matchsticks
- 1 tbsp. cilantro, chopped.
- 1/4 cup veggie stock
- Salt and white pepper to the taste

Instructions:
1. In your Foodi, mix all the ingredients, toss, put the pressure lid on and cook on High for 12 minutes
2. Release the pressure naturally for 10 minutes, divide the parsnips mix between plates and serve

Celeriac Sticks

(Prep + Cook Time: 25 Minutes | **Servings:** 4)

Ingredients:
- 1 big celeriac, cut into medium sticks
- 1 tbsp. olive oil
- Salt and black pepper to the taste

Instructions:
1. In your Foodi's basket, mix all the ingredients, toss, set the machine on Air Crisp and cook at 380°F for 20 minutes
2. Divide the sticks into bowls and serve as a snack

Celery Dip

(Prep + Cook Time: 25 Minutes | **Servings:** 6)

Ingredients:
- 4 garlic cloves, minced
- 28 oz. canned tomatoes, crushed.
- 4 celery ribs, chopped.
- 1/4 cup veggie stock
- 1 yellow onion, chopped.
- Cooking spray
- A pinch of basil, dried
- Salt and black pepper to the taste

Instructions:
1. Put the reversible rack in the Foodi, add the baking pan inside and grease it with cooking spray
2. Combine all the ingredients inside, set the machine on Baking mode and cook at 380°F for 20 minutes.
3. Divide into bowls and serve as a snack

Chickpeas Salad

(Prep + Cook Time: 30 Minutes | **Servings:** 4)

Ingredients:
- 20 oz. canned tomatoes, crushed.
- 3 garlic cloves, minced
- 1/4 cup veggie stock
- 1 cup baby spinach
- 2 cups canned chickpeas, drained.
- Salt and black pepper to the taste

Instructions:
1. In your Foodi, combine all the ingredients except the spinach, put the pressure lid on and cook on High for 20 minutes.
2. Release the pressure naturally for 10 minutes
3. Divide the spinach into bowls, also divide the chickpeas salsa, toss and serve as an appetizer

Lime Cabbage

(Prep + Cook Time: 25 Minutes | **Servings:** 4)

Ingredients:
- 1 big red cabbage head, shredded.
- 2 tsp. canola oil
- 1/2 cup veggie stock
- Salt and black pepper to the taste
- Juice of 2 limes

Instructions:
1. In your Foodi, mix all the ingredients, put the pressure lid on and cook on High for 15 minutes
2. Release the pressure naturally for 10 minutes, divide the mix between plates and serve as a side dish

Black Olives Spread

(Prep + Cook Time: 10 Minutes | **Servings:** 4)

Ingredients:
- 12 black olives, pitted and minced.
- 2 tbsp. basil pesto
- 4 oz. cream cheese
- Salt and black pepper to the taste

Instructions:
1. In your Foodi, mix all the ingredients, toss, put the pressure lid on and cook on High for 5 minutes
2. Release the pressure fast for 4 minutes, blend the mix a bit using an immersion blender, divide into bowls and serve

Pork Bites

(Prep + Cook Time: 26 Minutes | **Servings:** 2)

Ingredients:
- 5 oz. pork stew meat, cubed.
- 1/2 tsp. garlic, minced
- 1 yellow onion, chopped.
- 1 tbsp. olive oil
- Salt and black pepper to the taste
- 3 tbsp. red wine

Instructions:
1. Set the Foodi on Sauté mode, add the oil, heat it up, add the garlic, onion, salt and pepper and sauté for 3 minutes
2. Add the meat cubes and the wine, toss, put the pressure lid on and cook on High for 15 minutes.
3. Release the pressure fast for 6 minutes, divide the bites into bowls and serve

Peppers Salsa

(Prep + Cook Time: 20 Minutes | **Servings:** 4)

Ingredients:
- 1 yellow bell pepper, cut into strips
- 2 oz. tomato sauce
- 1 green onion, chopped.
- 1 orange bell pepper, cut into strips
- 2 tbsp. oregano, chopped.
- Salt and black pepper to the taste

Instructions:
1. In your Foodi, mix all the ingredients, toss, put the pressure lid on and cook on High for 12 minutes.
2. Release the pressure fast for 5 minutes, divide the salsa into bowls and serve as an appetizer

Simple Green Beans

(Prep + Cook Time: 25 Minutes | **Servings:** 4)

Ingredients:
- 1 tbsp. olive oil
- 3 garlic cloves, minced.
- 1 lb. green beans
- Juice of 1 lime

Instructions:
1. In your Foodi's basket, combine all the ingredients, toss and cook on Air Crisp at 370°F for 15 minutes.
2. Divide between plates and serve as a side dish

Lentils Salsa

(Prep + Cook Time: 25 Minutes | **Servings:** 4)

Ingredients:
- 1 yellow onion, chopped.
- 2 garlic cloves, minced
- 1 cup tomato puree
- 2 cups canned lentils, drained
- 1 tbsp. olive oil
- 4 tbsp. white vinegar
- 1 tsp. Tabasco sauce
- Salt and black pepper to the taste

Instructions:
1. In your Foodi, mix all the ingredients, put the pressure lid on and cook on High for 15 minutes
2. Release the pressure naturally for 10 minutes, divide the mix into bowls and serve as an appetizer

Minty Turkey Bites

(Prep + Cook Time: 30 Minutes | **Servings:** 4)

Ingredients:
- 1 big turkey breast, skinless, boneless and cubed.
- 1 tbsp. mint, chopped.
- 2 tbsp. olive oil
- 1/3 cup red wine

Instructions:
1. In your Foodi, combine all the ingredients, toss, set the machine on Baking mode and cook at 390°F for 20 minutes
2. Divide into bowls and serve as a snack.

Caramel Sauce

(Prep + Cook Time: 20 Minutes | **Servings:** 1 cup)

Ingredients:
- 1/3 cup heavy cream
- 1 cup sugar
- 3 tbsp. butter, cut into 1/2-inch pieces
- 1/2 tsp. sea salt
- 1/3 cup water
- 1/2 tsp. vanilla

Instructions:
1. Press the *Sauté* key of the Foodi. Add the water and the sugar. Stir to combine and let cook for 13 minutes without touching the pot
2. When 13 minutes are up, immediately whisk the butter in the pot, followed by the cream. Whisk until smooth.
3. Add the vanilla and the salt
4. Press the *Cancel* key and with an oven mitt gloved hand, remove the inner pot from the housing to remove from heat
5. Pour the salted caramel into a heat-safe glass and let cool. Store in the fridge for up to 5 days.

Basil Beet Chips

(Prep + Cook Time: 30 Minutes | **Servings:** 6)

Ingredients:
- 1 lb. beets, thinly sliced
- 1 bunch basil, chopped.
- 1/3 cup olive oil
- 4 garlic cloves, minced.

Instructions:
1. In a bowl, mix all the ingredients and toss
2. Put the chips in your Foodi's basket and cook them on Air Crisp at 390°F for 20 minutes.
3. Serve as a snack

Herbed Squash

(Prep + Cook Time: 30 Minutes | **Servings:** 4)

Ingredients:
- 2 pounds squash, peeled and cubed.
- 1 tbsp. mixed herbs, dried
- 2 tsp. parsley, chopped.
- A drizzle of olive oil
- Salt and black pepper to the taste

Instructions:
1. In your Foodi's basket combine all the ingredients, toss and cook on Air Crisp at 400°F for 20 minutes.
2. Divide the squash between plates and serve as a side dish

Chives Chips

(Prep + Cook Time: 30 Minutes | **Servings:** 4)

Ingredients:
- 4 gold potatoes, thinly sliced.
- 1 tbsp. chives, chopped.
- 2 tsp. olive oil
- Salt and black pepper to the taste

Instructions:
1. In a bowl, mix all the ingredients and toss
2. Put the Foodi's basket in the machine, put the chips inside and cook on Air Crisp at 380°F for 20 minutes.
3. Serve as a snack

Cranberry Apple Sauce

(Prep + Cook Time: 20 Minutes | **Servings:** 2 Cups)

Ingredients:
- 10 oz. cranberries, frozen or fresh, preferably organic
- 1/2 cup maple syrup OR honey OR omit
- 1 to 2 apples; medium-sized, peeled, cored, and then cut into chunks
- 1/4 tsp. sea salt
- 1/4 cup lemon juice
- 1 tsp. cinnamon

Instructions:
1. Put all of the ingredients in the Foodi and combine. Cover and lock the lid. Press the *Pressure* key, set the pressure to HIGH, and set the timer for 1 minute
2. When the Foodi timer beeps, let the pressure release naturally for 10 to 15 minutes or until the valve drops. Press the *Cancel* key and unplug the Foodi
3. Unlock and carefully open the lid. Using a wooden spoon, mash the fruit a bit.
4. Select the *Sauté* key and simmer for 1 to 2 minutes to allow some of the water to evaporate and the mix to thicken
5. Press the *Cancel* key. If you omitted the maple syrup/ honey and want to sweeten with stevia, then add to taste. Stir to combine. Transfer into a pint jar and refrigerate.

Basil Shrimp

(Prep + Cook Time: 15 Minutes | **Servings:** 6)

Ingredients:
- 1 lb. shrimp, peeled and deveined.
- 1 tbsp. basil, chopped.
- 2 tsp. olive oil
- Salt and black pepper to the taste

Instructions:
1. In your Foodi's basket, mix all the ingredients, toss, set the machine on Air Crisp and cook the shrimp at 370°F for 8 minutes
2. Divide into bowls and serve as an appetizer

Chinese Beet Slices

(Prep + Cook Time: 30 Minutes | **Servings:** 4)

Ingredients:
- 4 beets, thinly sliced.
- 2 tsp. olive oil
- 1 tsp. sweet paprika
- 2 tbsp. soy sauce

Instructions:
1. In a bowl, mix all the ingredients and toss
2. Put the beet slices in your Foodi's basket and cook on Air Crisp at 390°F for 20 minutes.
3. Serve as a snack

Vegetable Stock

(Prep + Cook Time: 30 Minutes | **Servings:** 8 Cups)

Ingredients:
- 4 medium-sized carrots, peeled and chopped
- 2 bay leaves
- 8 black peppercorns
- 4 celery stalks; chopped
- 2 green onions; sliced
- 6 parsley sprigs
- 4 thyme sprigs
- 8 cups water
- 2 tsp. minced garlic
- 1½ tsp. salt

Instructions:
1. Prepare vegetables. In a Foodi, pour the water and add all the ingredients except salt. Plug in and switch on the Foodi, and secure pot with lid
2. Select SOUP option, and adjust cooking time to 30 minutes and let cook. Foodi will take 10 minutes to build pressure before cooking timer starts
3. When the timer beeps, switch off the Foodi and let pressure release naturally for 10 minutes and then do quick pressure release
4. Then uncover the pot and pass the mixture through a strainer placed over a large bowl to collect stock and vegetables on the strainer. Stir salt into the stock and let cool completely before storing or use it later for cooking.

Carrot Sticks

(Prep + Cook Time: 20 Minutes | **Servings:** 8)

Ingredients:
- 2 eggs, whisked
- 1 cup bread crumbs
- 8 carrots, cut into sticks
- 1 tbsp. Italian seasoning
- Salt and black pepper to the taste
- A drizzle of olive oil

Instructions:
1. In a bowl, mix the bread crumbs with seasoning, salt and pepper and toss.
2. Put the eggs in a separate bowl
3. Dredge the carrots sticks in the egg and then coat in bread crumbs
4. Put the sticks in your Foodi's basket and cook them on Air Crisp mode at 390°F for 15 minutes.
5. Serve as a snack.

Vegetables

Curried Cauliflower

(Prep + Cook Time: 12 Minutes | **Servings:** 4)

Ingredients:
- 1 whole head cauliflower, base trimmed flat and any leaves removed
- 1 cup Chicken Stock or low-sodium broth
- 1/2 cup white wine
- 2 tbsp. unsalted butter or olive oil
- 2 tsp. curry powder
- 2 tsp. kosher salt

Instructions:
1. Turn the Foodi to *Sautéing/Browning* pour in the white wine and Chicken Stock. Add the butter, curry powder, and kosher salt. Simmer for about 1 minute, or until the butter just melts and is incorporated into the sauce. Add the cauliflower
2. Lock the lid in place, and bring the pot to High pressure. Cook at High pressure for 7 minutes. To get 7 minutes cook time, press *Pressure* button and use the *Time Adjustment* button to adjust the cook time to 7 minutes.
3. Use the Quick Pressure Release method
4. Unlock and remove the lid. Using two large forks or slotted spatulas, transfer the cauliflower to a cutting board.
5. Turn the Foodi to *Sautéing/Browning*Simmer the sauce for about 6 minutes, or until reduced by about two-thirds.
6. Meanwhile, break the cauliflower into florets. Discard the core. When the sauce has reduced to the desired consistency, add the cauliflower, toss to coat, and serve
7. If you are a fan of mashed cauliflower, cook the whole cauliflower for 15 minutes on High pressure with a quick release for cauliflower so soft it will practically mash itself. Reduce the sauce by about half, and then mash the cauliflower into it, adding more broth or butter as desired

Potato Salad

(Prep + Cook Time: 15 Minutes | **Servings:** 4)

Ingredients:
- 24 oz. Yukon gold potatoes; peeled and diced
- 1 tbsp. (15 ml) organic yellow mustard
- 1/2 sweet onion; minced
- 1 rib celery; minced
- 1/4 tsp. dried or fresh dill; minced
- 1/2 cup water
- 1/4 cup + 1 tbsp. high-quality store-bought mayonnaise
- 1 tsp. apple cider vinegar
- Pinch ground black pepper
- 1/2 tsp. celery salt
- Optional: paprika to garnish

Instructions:
1. Place the diced potatoes and water into the bowl of your Foodi
2. Lock the lid on the Foodi and then cook On High pressure for 10 minutes. To get 10 minutes' cook time, press *Pressure* button
3. Allow the potatoes to cook. Quick-release the pressure valve once the cycle is complete.
4. Remove the lid once safe to do so. Drain the water from the potatoes (unless you want soupy potato salad) and stir in all the remaining ingredients.
5. Sprinkle a bit of paprika on top to garnish. Serve

Braised Red Cabbage and Apples

(Prep + Cook Time: 18 minutes | **Servings:** 4)

Ingredients:
- 1 medium red cabbage (about 2 lb.); cored and thinly sliced
- 1 medium tart green apple; such as Granny Smith; peeled, cored and chopped.
- 4 thin bacon slices; chopped.
- 1/2 cup chicken broth
- 1 small red onion; chopped.
- 1 tsp. dried thyme
- 1/4 tsp. ground allspice
- 1/4 tsp. ground mace
- 1 tbsp. balsamic vinegar
- 1 tbsp. packed dark brown sugar

Instructions:
1. Fry the bacon in the Foodi turned to the *air crisp* function, until crisp, about 4 minutes
2. Add the onion to the pot; cook, often stirring, until soft, about 4 minutes. Add the apple, thyme, allspice and mace. Cook about 1 minute, stirring all the while, until fragrant
3. Stir in the brown sugar and vinegar; keep stirring until bubbling, about 1 minute
4. Add the cabbage; toss well to mix evenly with the other ingredients. Drizzle the broth over the cabbage mixture.
5. High pressure for 13 minutes. Lock the lid on the Foodi Multi-cooker and then cook for 13 minutes.
6. To get 13 minutes' cook time, press *Pressure* button and use the Time Adjustment button to adjust the cook time to 13 minutes
7. Pressure Release. Use the quick release method to return the pot to normal pressure
8. Unlock and open the pot. Close the crisping lid. Select "BROIL" and set the time to 5 minutes. Select START/STOP to begin. Cook until top is browned. Serve

Sugar Glazed Carrots

(Prep + Cook Time: 10 Minutes | **Servings:** 4)

Ingredients:
- 8 moderately large carrots (about 6 oz. each), peeled and cut into 1-inch segments
- 1 tbsp. unseasoned rice vinegar
- 2 tbsp. unsalted butter
- 1 tbsp. sugar

Instructions:
1. Put the carrots in the Foodi; add enough cool tap water that they're submerged by 2 inches
2. Lock the lid onto the pot Set the Foodi to cook at High pressure for 3 minutes. To get 3minutes cook time, press *Pressure* button and use the *Time Adjustment* button to adjust the cook time to 3 minutes.
3. Use the Quick Pressure Release method to return the pot's pressure to normal
4. Unlock and open the pot. Drain the carrots in a colander set in the sink. Turn the Foodi to its *Sautéing/Browning* function. Add the butter; when it has melted, stir in the sugar and cook until it melts and becomes bubbly, stirring all the while, less than 1 minute
5. Add the carrots and vinegar; toss over the heat for 1 minute to glaze the carrots evenly and thoroughly.

Smashed Sweet Potatoes with Pineapple and Ginger

(Prep + Cook Time: 18 Minutes | **Servings:** 8)

Ingredients:
- 4 lb. medium sweet potatoes (about 6 potatoes), peeled and cut into 1½-inch chunks
- 2 tbsp. frozen unsweetened pineapple juice concentrate, thawed
- 3 tbsp. unsalted butter
- 1/4 tsp. ground cinnamon
- 1/4 tsp. grated nutmeg
- 1/2 tsp. ground ginger
- 1 tsp. salt

Instructions:
1. Place the sweet potatoes and 3 cups water in the Foodi
2. Lock the lid on the Foodi and then cook On High pressure for 12 minutes. To get 12 minutes' cook time, press *Pressure* button, and use the *Time Adjustment* button to adjust the cook time to 12 minutes.
3. Use the Quick Pressure Release method to bring the pot's pressure back to normal
4. Unlock and open the cooker. Drain the sweet potatoes in a colander set in the sink. Turn the electric cooker to its browning function. Melt the butter in the cooker, then add the ginger, cinnamon, and nutmeg; cook until aromatic, stirring constantly, less than 1 minute
5. Stir in the pineapple juice concentrate and salt, and then turn off the electric cooker. Add the potatoes and stir well with a wooden spoon, smashing them a bit, until you have a vaguely smooth puree with chunks of sweet potato.

Brussels Sprouts

(Prep + Cook Time: 5 Minutes | **Servings:** 4)

Ingredients:
- 1 lb. Brussels sprouts
- 1/4 cup pine nuts
- Salt and pepper to taste
- Olive oil
- 1 cup water

Instructions:
1. Pour the water into the Foodi. Set the steamer basket. Put the Brussels sprouts into the steamer basket.
2. Close and lock the lid. Press the *Pressure* button. Set the pressure to HIGH and set the time to 3 minutes.
3. When the timer beeps, turn the valve to Venting to quick release the pressure
4. Transfer the Brussels sprouts into a serving plate, season with olive oil, salt, pepper, and sprinkle with the pine nuts

Notes: To prepare the Brussels sprouts, wash them and remove the outer leaves. If some of them are quite large, cut those in half for uniformity, so that they will cook evenly.

Wrapped Carrot with Bacon

(Prep + Cook Time: 25 Minutes | **Servings:** 8)

Ingredients:
- 1 lb. carrot
- 9 oz. bacon
- 1/4 cup chicken stock
- 1 tbsp. olive oil
- 1/4 tsp. marjoram
- 1/2 tsp. ground black pepper
- 1 tsp. ground white pepper
- 1 tsp. paprika
- 1 tsp. salt

Instructions:
1. Wash the carrot carefully and peel it. Sprinkle the carrot with the ground black pepper.
2. Combine the salt, ground white pepper, paprika, and marjoram together. Stir the mixture
3. Slice the bacon. Then combine the sliced bacon and spice mixture together. Stir it carefully.
4. Then wrap the carrot in the sliced bacon

5. Pour the olive oil in the Foodi and add wrapped carrot. Close the lid and *Sauté* the carrot for 10 minutes
6. Then add the chicken stock, close and lock the lid. Select *Pressure* and cook at HIGH pressure for 8 minutes more.
7. When the time is over; quick release the remaining pressure and open the lid. Chill the carrot little.

Rye Berry and Celery Root Salad

(**Prep + Cook Time:** 45 minutes | **Servings:** 4)

Ingredients:
- 1 medium celeriac (celery root); peeled and shredded through the large holes of a box grater
- 3/4 cup rye berries
- 2 tbsp. honey
- 2 tbsp. apple cider vinegar
- 2 tbsp. unsalted butter
- 1/2 tsp. salt
- 1/2 tsp. ground black pepper

Instructions:
1. Place the rye berries in the Foodi Multi-cooker; pour in enough cold tap water, so the grains are submerged by 2 inches.
2. High pressure for 40 minutes. Lock the lid on the Foodi Multi-cooker and then cook for 40 minutes.
3. To get 40 minutes' cook time, press *Pressure* button and use the Time Adjustment button to adjust the cook time to 40 minutes
4. Pressure Release. Use the quick release method to bring the pot's pressure back to normal
5. Finish the dish. Unlock and open the cooker. Stir in the shredded celeriac. Cover the pot without locking it and set aside for 1 minute. Drain the pot into a large colander set in the sink. Wipe out the cooker
6. Melt the butter in the Foodi Multi-cooker; turned to it sauté function. Add the honey and cook for 1 minute, constantly stirring.
7. Add the drained rye berries and celeriac; cook, constantly stirring, for 1 minute. Stir in the vinegar, salt and pepper to serve

Quinoa and Potato Salad

(**Prep + Cook Time:** 20 minutes | **Servings:** 4)

Ingredients:
- 1 ½ lb. tiny white potatoes; halved
- 1/4 cup white balsamic vinegar
- 1 cup blond (white) quinoa
- 1 medium shallot; minced
- 2 medium celery stalks; thinly sliced
- 1 large dill pickle; diced
- 1 tbsp. Dijon mustard
- 1 tsp. sweet paprika
- 1/2 tsp. ground black pepper
- 1/4 tsp. celery seeds
- 1/4 tsp. salt
- 1/4 cup olive oil

Instructions:
1. Whisk the vinegar, mustard, paprika, pepper, celery seeds and salt in a large serving bowl until smooth; whisk in the olive oil in a thin, steady stream until the dressing is fairly creamy.
2. Place the potatoes and quinoa in the Foodi Multi-cooker; add enough cold tap water so that the ingredients are submerged by 3 inches (some of the quinoa may float)
3. High pressure for 10 minutes. Lock the lid on the Foodi Multi-cooker and then cook for 10 minutes.
4. To get 10 minutes' cook time, press *Pressure* button and use the Time Adjustment button to adjust the cook time to 10 minutes.
5. Pressure Release. Use the quick release method to bring the pot's pressure back to normal
6. Finish the dish. Unlock and open the pot. Close the crisping lid. Select "BROIL" and set the time to 5 minutes. Select START/STOP to begin
7. Cook until top is browned. Drain the contents of the pot into a colander lined with paper towels or into a fine-mesh sieve in the sink. Do not rinse.

8. Transfer the potatoes and quinoa to the large bowl with the dressing. Add the shallot, celery and pickle; toss gently and set aside for a minute or two to warm up the vegetables.

Braised Celery and Tomatoes

(Prep + Cook Time: 18 Minutes | Servings: 4)

Ingredients:
- 1 (1 lb.) celery bunch, cut into 1-inch pieces (about 4 cups)
- 3 bacon slices; diced (about 1/2 cup)
- 1/3 cup dry white wine
- 1 (14.5 oz.) can diced tomatoes, drained
- 1-teaspoon olive oil
- 2 cups thinly sliced onion
- 1/2 tsp. kosher salt; plus, additional for seasoning
- Freshly ground black pepper
- 1/2 cup pale yellow celery leaves; roughly chopped (optional)

Instructions:
1. Turn the Foodi to *Sautéing/Browning* add the olive oil and bacon. Cook for about 3 minutes, stirring, until the bacon has released most of its fat and just begun to brown. Add the onion, and sprinkle with ½ tsp. of kosher salt. Cook for about 2 minutes, stirring, until the onions begin to soften; then add the celery. Stir to coat the celery with the bacon fat. Add the white wine and tomatoes
2. Lock the lid in place, and bring the pot to High pressure. Cook at High pressure for 12 minutes. To get 12 minutes' cook time, press *Pressure* button
3. Use the Quick Pressure Release method
4. Unlock and remove the lid. If there is a lot of liquid in the Foodi, turn the Foodi to *Sautéing/Browning* and simmer until most of the liquid is gone. Season to taste with a few grinds of pepper and additional salt, if necessary. Garnish with the celery leaves (if using), and serve
5. This dish works best with the larger, outer celery stalks. Reserve the small, pale inside stalks for another use. One large bunch of celery should provide the 4 cups called for in this recipe.

Zucchini and Mushrooms

(Prep + Cook Time: 20 Minutes | Servings: 4)

Ingredients:
- 4 medium zucchini, cut into ½-inch slices (about 8 cups)
- 8 to 12 oz. mushrooms; sliced or separated depending on type of mushroom
- 1 can (15 oz.) crushed or diced tomatoes with juice
- 1 large sprig fresh basil; sliced
- 2 cloves garlic, minced
- 1½ cups onions; diced
- 1 tbsp. extra-virgin olive oil
- 1/2 tsp. black pepper; or to taste
- 1/2 tsp. salt, or to taste

Instructions:
1. Press the *Sauté* button of the Foodi. Add the olive oil and heat. Add the garlic, onions, and mushrooms; cook, frequently stirring, until the onions are soft and the mushrooms lose their moisture
2. Add the basil and sprinkle with the salt and pepper. Sauté for 5 minutes until the mushrooms are soft
3. Add the zucchini, stir. Add the tomatoes with the juices over the zucchini; do not stir.
4. Close and lock the lid. Press the *Pressure* button. Set the pressure to LOW and the timer to 1 minute. (Allow cooking for 1 minute then Stop).
5. When the timer beeps, turn the steam valve to quick release the pressure. Carefully remove the cover
6. If the zucchinis are still a little undercooked, just cover the pot and let rest for 1 minutes to allow the zucchinis to soften.
7. Serve over pasta, rice, baked potatoes, or polenta. If desired, you can stir a can of white beans.

Buttered Brussels Sprouts

(Prep + Cook Time: 10 Minutes | Servings: 4)

Ingredients:
- 1 lb. Brussels sprouts
- 1/2 tsp. salt; plus, more if desired
- 1 tbsp. unsalted butter, diced, at room temperature
- Brussels sprouts does not exceed two-thirds of the cooker's capacity.
- 1 tbsp. grated orange zest
- Freshly ground black pepper

Instructions:
1. Add 1 cup of water (or the minimum amount required by your cooker to reach pressure) to the Foodi base. To ensure even cooking, cut any large sprouts in half from top to bottom. Place the sprouts in the steamer basket in an even layer and lower it into the cooker; sprinkle with 1/2 tsp. salt
2. Close and lock the lid of the Foodi. Cook at High pressure for 3 minutes, to get 3 minutes cook time, press *Pressure* button and use the *Time Adjustment* button to adjust the cook time to 3 minutes.
3. When the time is up, open the cooker with the Natural release method
4. Lift the steamer basket out of the cooker and immediately tumble the sprouts into a serving dish to keep them from overcooking. Toss with the butter and orange zest and season with pepper and more salt if you wish.

Polenta with Honey and Pine Nuts

(Prep + Cook Time: 25 Minutes | Servings: 6)

Ingredients:
- 1 cup polenta
- 5 cups water
- 1/2 cup honey
- 1/4 cup pine nuts
- 1/2 cup heavy cream
- Salt to taste

Instructions:
1. Mix pine nuts and honey with water in your Foodi.
2. Turn on the *Sauté* function and bring to a boil while stirring
3. Mix in polenta. Close and seal lid. Select *Pressure* and adjust time to 12 minutes
4. When time is up, press *Cancel* and quick release the pressure. Mix in cream and wait 1 minute before serving with a sprinkle of salt.

Collard Greens in A Tomato Sauce

(Prep + Cook Time: 11 Minutes | Servings: 6)

Ingredients:
- 1½ lb. collard greens, tough stems removed, the leaves chopped (about 8 packed cups)
- 1/2 cup canned tomato puree
- 1/2 cup vegetable or chicken broth
- 1/2 cup moderately sweet white wine; such as a dry Riesling
- 2 tbsp. olive oil
- 1 tbsp. minced garlic
- 1/2 tsp. red pepper flakes
- 1/2 tsp. salt

Instructions:
1. Heat the oil in the Foodi turned to the *Sautéing/Browning* function. Add the garlic and red pepper flakes; cook, stirring all the while, until aromatic, less than 1 minute
2. Add the collards; toss over the heat for 2 minutes. Add the tomato puree, broth, wine, and salt, and stir well.
3. Lock the lid on the Foodi and then cook On High pressure for 6 minutes. To get 6 minutes' cook time, press *Pressure* button and use the *Time Adjustment* button to adjust the cook time to 6 minutes
4. Use the Quick Pressure Release method. Unlock and open the cooker. Stir well before serving.

Pumpkin Puree

(Prep + Cook Time: 30 Minutes | **Servings:** 6)

Ingredients:
- 2 lb. small-sized sugar pumpkin or pie pumpkin, halved and seeds scooped out
- 1/2 cup water

Instructions:
1. Pour the water into the Foodi and set the steamer rack
2. Put the pumpkin halves on the rack. Select *Pressure* and cook at HIGH pressure for 13 or 15 minutes.
3. When the timer beeps, turn the valve to quick release the pressure. Let the pumpkin cool
4. When cool enough, scoop out the flesh into a bowl. Puree using an immersion blender or puree in a blender.

Notes:
You can stir pumpkin into your oatmeal, use it to make a dessert, stir some with an applesauce for instant pumpkin applesauce, mix with softened butter with some sugar and spices like cinnamon, nutmeg, or cloves to make a compound butter for biscuits, blend it to make a creamy soup, and much more.

Vinegary Collard Greens

(Prep + Cook Time: 11 Minutes | **Servings:** 4)

Ingredients:
- 1½ lb. collard greens, tough stems removed and the leaves chopped (about 8 packed cups)
- 1/2 cup chicken broth
- 4 oz. slab bacon; diced
- 1 small yellow onion; chopped
- 2 tsp. minced garlic
- 3 tbsp. balsamic vinegar
- 2 tbsp. canned tomato paste
- 1 tbsp. packed dark brown sugar

Instructions:
1. Put the bacon in the Foodi turned to the *Sautéing/Browning* function; fry until crisp and well browned, stirring occasionally, about 4 minutes
2. Add the onion; cook, stirring often, until translucent, about 2 minutes. Add the garlic, stir well, and add the collard greens. Stir over the heat for 2 minutes, then pour in the broth, vinegar, tomato paste, and brown sugar until the latter two items dissolve into the sauce. Stir well one more time
3. Lock the lid onto the pot. Set the Foodi to cook at High pressure for 6 minutes. To get 6 minutes' cook time, press *Pressure* button, and use the *Time Adjustment* button to adjust the cook time to 6 minutes.
4. Use the Quick Pressure Release method. Unlock and open the pot. Stir well before serving.

Crispy Ratatouille Recipe

(Prep + Cook Time: 14 minutes | **Servings:** 4)

Ingredients:
- 1 (14.5 oz.) can diced tomatoes; undrained
- 1 small red bell pepper; cut into ½-inch chunks (about 1 cup)
- 1 small green bell pepper; cut into ½-inch chunks (about 1 cup)
- 1 rib celery; sliced (about 1 cup)
- Kosher salt; for salting and seasoning
- 1 small eggplant; peeled and sliced 1/2-inch thick
- 1 medium zucchini; sliced 1/2-inch thick
- 2 tbsp. olive oil
- 1 cup chopped onion
- 3 garlic cloves; minced or pressed
- 1/2 tsp. dried oregano
- 1/4 tsp. freshly ground black pepper
- 2 tbsp. minced fresh basil
- 1/4 cup water
- 1/4 cup pitted green or black olives (optional)

Instructions:
1. Place a rack on a baking sheet. With kosher salt, very liberally salt one side of the eggplant and zucchini slices and place them, salted-side down, on the rack. Salt the other side.
2. Let the slices sit for 15 to 20 minutes or until they start to exude water (you'll see it beading up on the surface of the slices and dripping into the sheet pan). Rinse the slices and blot them dry. Cut the zucchini slices into quarters and the eggplant slices into eighths.
3. Turn the Foodi Multi-cooker to *Sauté*, heat the olive oil until it shimmers and flows like water. Add the onion and garlic and sprinkle with a pinch or two of kosher salt. Cook for about 3 minutes, stirring until the onions just begin to brown
4. Add the eggplant, zucchini, green bell pepper, red bell pepper, celery and tomatoes with their juice, water and oregano
5. High pressure for 4 minutes. Lock the lid on the Foodi Multi-cooker and then cook for 4 minutes.
6. To get 4 minutes' cook time, press *Pressure* button and use the Time Adjustment button to adjust the cook time to 4 minutes.
7. Pressure Release. Use the quick release method.
8. Finish the dish. Unlock and remove the lid. Close the crisping lid. Select "BROIL" and set the time to 5 minutes. Select START/STOP to begin. Cook until top is browned
9. Stir in the pepper, basil and olives (if using). Taste, adjust the seasoning as needed and serve.
10. While this vegetable dish is usually served on its own, it's great tossed with cooked pasta or served over polenta

Steamed Artichokes

(Prep + Cook Time: 45 Minutes | **Servings:** 4)

Ingredients:
- 2 medium-sized whole artichokes (about 5 ½ oz. each)
- 1 cup water
- 1 lemon wedge

Instructions:
1. Rinse the artichokes clean and remove any damaged outer leaves
2. With a sharp knife, trim off the stem and top third of each artichoke carefully. Rub the cut top with a lemon wedge to prevent browning.
3. Pour 1 cup of water into the Foodi and set the steamer basket or rack. Pout the artichokes on the steamer/rack
4. Select *Pressure* and cook at HIGH pressure for 20 minutes. When the timer beeps, press *Cancel* to turn off the warming function. Let the pressure release naturally for 10 minutes.
5. Open the lid and with tongs, remove the artichokes from the pot. Serve warm with your dipping sauce of choice

Notes: If cooking larger artichokes, set the timer to 25 minutes and if cooking smaller artichokes, set the timer to 15 minutes.

Carrots Escabeche

(Prep + Cook Time: 10 Minutes | **Servings:** 4)

Ingredients:
- 1 lb. carrots, peeled and cut into ½-inch-thick slices
- 1/3 cup olive oil
- 1/4 cup white wine vinegar
- 1 garlic clove; minced
- 3 tbsp. chopped fresh cilantro
- 2 tbsp. chopped fresh flat-leaf parsley
- 2 tsp. chopped fresh mint
- 1/2 tsp. kosher salt

Instructions:
1. In the Foodi, place the carrots, and pour in enough water to cover them. Lock the lid in place, and bring the pot to High pressure. Cook at High pressure for 3 minutes. To get 3 minutes' cook time, press *Pressure* button and use the *Time Adjustment* button to adjust the cook time to 3 minutes

2. Use the Quick Pressure Release method
3. Drain the carrots, and transfer them to a medium bowl. In a small bowl, whisk together the white wine vinegar, olive oil, and kosher salt. Pour the mixture over the hot carrots, and stir gently. Cool the carrots to room temperature, then add the cilantro, parsley, mint, and garlic. Stir gently to combine. Serve slightly chilled or at room temperature

Butter Spaghetti Squash

(Prep + Cook Time: 18 minutes | **Servings:** 6)

Ingredients:
- 1 (3- to 3½ lb) spaghetti squash; halved lengthwise and seeded
- 1/2 cup finely grated Parmesan cheese (about 1 oz.)
- 2 tbsp. packed fresh sage leaves; minced
- 6 tbsp. unsalted butter
- 1/2 tsp. salt
- 1/2 tsp. ground black pepper

Instructions:
1. Put the squash cut side up in the cooker; add 1 cup water.
2. High pressure for 12 minutes. Lock the lid on the Foodi Multi-cooker and then cook for 12 minutes.
3. To get 12 minutes' cook time, press *Pressure* button and use the Time Adjustment button to adjust the cook time to 12 minutes
4. Pressure Release. Use the quick release method to bring the pot's pressure back to normal
5. Finish the dish. Unlock and open the cooker. Transfer the squash halves to a cutting board; cool for 10 minutes. Discard the liquid in the cooker. Use a fork to scrape the spaghetti-like flesh off the skin and onto the cutting board; discard the skins.
6. Melt the butter in the electric cooker turned to its browning function. Stir in the sage, salt and pepper, then add all of the squash. Stir and toss over the heat until well combined and heated through about 2 minutes. Add the cheese, toss well.
7. Close the crisping lid. Select "BROIL" and set the time to 5 minutes. Select START/STOP to begin. Cook until top is browned. Serve

Cauliflower Mac and Cheese

(Prep + Cook Time: 30 Minutes | **Servings:** 4)

Ingredients:
- 2 cups Cauliflower Rice
- 1/2 cup half-and-half
- 1/2 cup grated sharp Cheddar cheese
- 2 tbsp. cream cheese; at room temperature
- 1 tsp. salt
- 1 tsp. freshly ground black pepper

Instructions:
1. In a heatproof bowl, mix the cauliflower, cream cheese, half-and-half, Cheddar cheese, salt, and pepper together. Cover the bowl with aluminum foil
2. Pour 2 cups of water into the inner cooking pot of the Pressure Cooker, then place a trivet in the pot. Place the bowl on the trivet
3. Lock the lid into place. Select Manual or Pressure Cook and adjust the pressure to High. Cook for 5 minutes. When the cooking is complete, let the pressure release naturally for 10 minutes, then Quick Pressure Release any remaining pressure. Unlock the lid and carefully remove the bowl. Remove the foil
4. Place the cooked cauliflower under the broiler, and broil until the cheese is brown and bubbling, 3 to 5 minutes. Serve immediately.

Breakfast Kale

(Prep + Cook Time: 10 Minutes | Servings: 4)

Ingredients:
- 10 oz. kale
- 2 tsp. vinegar; your favorite flavored
- For the faux parmesan cheese:
- 1 cup raw cashews
- 1/2 cup nutritional yeast
- 1 tbsp. salt-free seasoning I have used Benson's
- 1/2 cup water

Instructions:
1. Fill the Foodi container with washed and chopped kale
2. Pour the water. Close and lock the lid. Select *Pressure* and cook at HIGH pressure for 4 minutes.
3. Meanwhile, put all the faux Parmesan ingredients into a food processor. Process until the mixture is powdery. If you prefer it chunkier, process less
4. When the timer beeps, use a quick release and carefully open the lid. Transfer the kale in a serving plate.
5. Pour about 2 tsp. of your favorite flavored vinegar
6. Top with the faux parmesan. Serve over cooked brown rice or with a small potato.

Mushroom Gravy

(Prep + Cook Time: 45 Minutes | Servings: 4)

Ingredients:
- 8 oz. sliced white mushrooms
- 2 fluid oz. vegetable broth
- 2 fluid oz. almond milk
- 2 tbsp. olive oil
- 4 tbsp. all-purpose flour
- 4 tbsp. vegan butter
- 22 fluid oz. water

Instructions:
1. Select *Sauté* and preheat the Foodi. Add olive oil. Then add mushrooms and cook for 5 to 7 minutes or until nicely golden brown
2. Pour in broth and continue cooking until mushrooms turn into dark color
3. Press *Cancel*, then pour the water and stir until just mixed. Close and lock the lid, select *Pressure* and cook at HIGH pressure for 5 minutes.
4. Foodi will take 10 minutes to build pressure before cooking timer starts
5. When the timer beeps, switch off the Foodi and let pressure release naturally for 10 minutes and then do quick pressure release.
6. Then uncover the pot, drain mushrooms and return to the pot, reserve broth.
7. Place a medium-sized saucepan over medium heat, add butter and let heat until melt completely
8. Then gradually stir in flour and then slowly whisk in reserved broth until combined.
9. Pour in milk, stir in mushrooms and bring the mixture to simmer, whisk occasionally
10. Simmer mixture for 8 minutes until gravy reaches desired thickness and then ladle into serving platters. Serve immediately.

Simple Potato Wedges

(Prep + Cook Time: 45 minutes | **Servings:** 4)

Ingredients:
- 4 Idaho potatoes, cut in 2-inch wedges
- 1 tbsp. fresh oregano leaves, minced
- 4 cloves garlic, peeled, minced
- Juice of 1 lemon
- 2 tbsp. extra virgin olive oil, divided.
- 2 tsp. kosher salt
- 1/2 cup water
- 1 tsp. ground black pepper

Instructions:
1. Pour water into the pot. Place potatoes into the Cook & Crisp Basket and place basket into pot.
2. Assemble pressure lid, making sure the PRESSURE RELEASE valve is in the SEAL position. Select PRESSURE and set to LOW. Set time to 3 minutes. Select START/STOP to begin.
3. While potatoes are cooking, stir together 1 tbsp. olive oil with oregano, garlic, lemon juice, salt, and pepper in a small bowl. Set aside
4. When pressure cooking is complete, quick release the pressure by moving the PRESSURE RELEASE valve to the VENT position. Carefully remove lid when unit has finished releasing pressure.
5. Pour remaining olive oil over the potatoes in the basket, shaking to coat evenly
6. Close the crisping lid. Select AIR CRISP, set temperature to 400°F, and set time to 18 minutes.
7. Select START/STOP to begin. Check potatoes after 12 minutes. Continue cooking for up to 18 minutes for desired crispiness. When cooking is complete, remove potatoes from basket. Toss with oregano dressing and serve

Buffalo Cauliflower Bites

(Prep + Cook Time: 1 hour 20 minutes | **Servings:** 6)

Ingredients:
- 2 heads cauliflower, trimmed, cut in 2-inch florets
- 1 ½ cups water, divided.
- 1 tsp. garlic powder
- 1 tsp. onion powder
- 1 tsp. kosher salt
- 1 ½ cups cornstarch
- 1 tsp. black pepper
- 2 eggs
- 1/2 cup all-purpose flour
- 2 tsp. baking powder
- 1/3 cup buffalo wing sauce

Instructions:
1. Place cauliflower and 1/2 cup water into the pot. Assemble pressure lid, making sure the PRESSURE RELEASE valve is in the SEAL position. Select PRESSURE and set to LOW. Set time to 2 minutes. Select START/STOP to begin.
2. When pressure cooking is complete, quick release the pressure by turning the PRESSURE RELEASE valve to the VENT position. Carefully remove lid when unit has finished releasing pressure. Drain cauliflower and chill in refrigerator until cooled, about 10 minutes
3. Whisk together cornstarch, flour, baking powder, garlic powder, onion powder, salt, and pepper. Whisk in eggs and 1 cup water until batter is smooth
4. Add chilled cauliflower to bowl with batter and gently toss until well coated. Transfer coated cauliflower to baking sheet and chill in freezer for 20 minutes
5. Close crisping lid. Preheat the unit by selecting AIR CRISP, setting the temperature to 360°F, and setting the time to 5 minutes.
6. Meanwhile, arrange half the cauliflower in an even layer in the bottom of the Cook & Crisp Basket. After 5 minutes, place basket into the pot
7. Close crisping lid. Select AIR CRISP, set temperature to 360°F, and set time to 20 minutes. Select START/STOP to begin. When first batch of cauliflower is crisp and golden, transfer to a bowl. Repeat with remaining chilled cauliflower.
8. When cooking is complete, microwave hot sauce for 30 seconds, then toss with cooked cauliflower. Serve immediately

One Pot Pasta Puttanesca

(Prep + Cook Time: 14 minutes | **Servings:** 4)

Ingredients:
- 8 oz. dried whole wheat ziti
- 1 small red onion; chopped.
- 1 tbsp. drained and rinsed capers; minced
- 1 tbsp. minced garlic
- 1 lb. eggplant (about 1 large); stemmed and diced (no need to peel)
- 1 (28 oz.) can diced tomatoes (about 3 ½ cups)
- 2 medium yellow bell peppers; stemmed, cored and chopped.
- 2 tbsp. olive oil
- 1 ¼ cups vegetable broth
- 2 tbsp. canned tomato paste
- 2 tsp. dried rosemary
- 1 tsp. dried thyme
- 1/2 tsp. ground black pepper

Instructions:
1. Heat the oil in the Foodi Multi-cooker turned to the *Sauté* function. Add the onion, capers and garlic; cook, often stirring, just until the onion first begins to soften, about 2 minutes.
2. Add the eggplant and bell peppers; cook, often stirring, for 1 minute. Mix in the tomatoes, broth, tomato paste, rosemary, thyme and pepper, stirring until the tomato paste coats everything. Stir in the ziti until coated
3. High pressure for 8 minutes. Lock the lid on the Foodi Multi-cooker and then cook for 8 minutes.
4. To get 8 minutes' cook time, press *Pressure* button and use the Time Adjustment button to adjust the cook time to 8 minutes.
5. Pressure Release. Use the quick release method to drop the pressure in the pot back to normal. Unlock and open the cooker. Stir well before serving

Artichoke Hearts

(Prep + Cook Time: 50 Minutes | **Servings:** 4)

Ingredients:
- 4 artichokes, washed, stems and petal tips cut off
- 1/4 cup extra virgin olive oil
- 2 tsp. balsamic vinegar
- 2 tbsp. lemon juice
- 1 tsp. dried oregano
- 2 cups water
- 2 garlic cloves; peeled and minced
- Salt and ground black pepper, to taste

Instructions:
1. Put the artichokes in the steamer basket of the Foodi. Add the water to the Foodi.
2. Cover and cook them on Egg mode for 8 minutes. In a bowl, mix lemon juice with vinegar, oil, salt, pepper, garlic, and oregano, and stir very well. Release the pressure from the Foodi, transfer artichokes to a plate, cut them into halves, take out the hearts and arrange them on a platter
3. Drizzle the vinaigrette over artichokes and let them marinate for 30 minutes. Heat up a grill over medium heat, add the artichokes, and cook for 3 minutes on each side. Serve them warm.

Carrot Puree

(Prep + Cook Time: 25 Minutes | **Servings:** 4)

Ingredients:
- 1 ½ lb. carrots, peeled and roughly chopped
- Brown Sugar as needed for more sweetness
- 1 tbsp. soy butter; softened
- 1 tbsp. honey
- 1 cup water
- 1/2 tsp. salt

Instructions:
1. Rinse peeled carrots, pat dry and then chop roughly into small pieces. Pour water and then insert a steamer basket in the Foodi
2. Place chopped carrots into the basket and secure pot with lid.
3. Select *Pressure* and cook at HIGH pressure for 4 minutes.
4. When the timer beeps, switch off the Foodi and do a quick pressure release
5. Then uncover the pot and transfer carrots to a food processor or blender.
6. Pulse until smooth and transfer puree to a bowl. Stir in honey, salt, and butter. For more sweetness stir in brown sugar to taste and serve immediately.

Roasted Rainbow Fingerling Potatoes

(Prep + Cook Time: 25 Minutes | **Servings:** 4)

Ingredients:
- 2 lb. rainbow fingerling potatoes
- 1/2 cup diced onion
- 2 tbsp. ghee
- 1 tbsp. olive oil
- 1/2 tsp. onion powder
- 1/4 tsp. black pepper
- 1/2 tsp. paprika
- Up to 1 tsp. sea salt

Instructions:
1. Begin by sautéing the onion in your Foodi in the ghee and olive oil for 5 minutes.
2. Add in the potatoes and seasonings and secure the lid
3. Lock the lid on the Foodi and then cook On High pressure for 20 minutes. To get 20 minutes' cook time, press *Pressure* button and use the *Time Adjustment* button to adjust the cook time to 20 minutes
4. Quick-release the pressure valve when complete and carefully remove the lid. Serve warm.

Spaghetti Squash and Spinach Walnut Pesto

(Prep + Cook Time: 15 minutes | **Servings:** 4)

Ingredients:
- 4 lb. Spaghetti Squash

For the Pesto
- 1/2 cup spinach, chopped
- 1/3 cup extra virgin olive oil
- 2 Garlic Cloves, minced
- 1 cup Water
- 2 tbsp. Walnuts
- Salt and ground pepper, to taste
- Zest and juice from ½ lemon

Instructions:
1. In a food processor put all the pesto ingredients and blend until everything is well incorporated. Season to taste and set aside.
2. Put the squash on a flat surface and use a knife to slice in half lengthwise. Scoop out all seeds and discard them
3. Next, open the Foodi, pour the water into it and fit the reversible rack at the bottom. Place the squash halves on the rack, close the lid, secure the pressure valve, and select Steam on High pressure for 5 minutes. Press Start/Stop
4. Once the timer has ended, do a quick pressure release, and open the lid

5. Remove the squash halves onto a cutting board and use a fork to separate the pulp strands into spaghetti-like pieces. Return to the pot and close the crisping lid. Cook for 2 minutes on Broil mode
6. Scoop the spaghetti squash into serving plates and drizzle over the spinach pesto

Spring Vegetable Ragù

(Prep + Cook Time: 10 Minutes | **Servings:** 4)

Ingredients:
- 1 (14 oz.) can crushed tomatoes (about 1¾ cups)
- 1 large yellow onion; chopped
- 12 oz. baby zucchini; halved crosswise
- 2 tbsp. packed dark brown sugar
- 12 oz. sugar snap peas; trimmed and halved crosswise
- 1 cup shelled fresh peas, or frozen peas, thawed
- 1/3 cup olive oil
- 1 tbsp. minced garlic
- 1 tbsp. minced fresh ginger
- 1 tsp. ground coriander
- 1 tsp. ground cumin
- 1/4 tsp. ground cloves
- 1/2 tsp. ground cinnamon
- 1/2 tsp. salt

Instructions:
1. Heat the oil in the Foodi turned to the *Sautéing/Browning* function. Add the onion and cook, stirring often, until soft, about 4 minutes
2. Stir in the garlic, ginger, coriander, cumin, cinnamon, salt, and cloves until aromatic, less than a minute. Add the tomatoes, zucchini, and brown sugar; stir until the brown sugar dissolves
3. Lock the lid onto the cooker. Set the Foodi to cook at High pressure for 3 minutes. To get 3 minutes' cook time, press *Pressure* button and use the *Time Adjustment* button to adjust the cook time to 3 minutes.
4. Use the Quick Pressure Release method
5. Unlock and open the pot. Turn the Foodi to its *Sautéing/Browning* function. Bring the sauce to a simmer, then stir in the sugar snaps and peas. Simmer for 2 minutes, stirring occasionally, until the vegetables are crisp yet tender. Serve at once.

Polenta with Fresh Herbs

(Prep + Cook Time: 20 Minutes | **Servings:** 6)

Ingredients:
- 1 cup coarse-ground polenta
- 1/2 cup minced onion
- 4 cups veggie broth
- 1 bay leaf
- 3 tbsp. fresh; chopped basil
- 2 tbsp. fresh, chopped Italian parsley
- 2 tsp. fresh; chopped oregano
- 2 tsp. minced garlic
- 1 tsp. fresh; chopped rosemary
- 1 tsp. salt

Instructions:
1. Select *Sauté* and preheat your Foodi. Dry sauté the onion for about a minute. Add the minced garlic and cook for one more minute
2. Pour the broth, along with the oregano, rosemary, bay leaf, salt, half the basil, and half the parsley. Stir.
3. Sprinkle the polenta in the pot, but don't stir. Close and seal the lid
4. Select *Pressure* and cook at HIGH pressure for 5 minutes.
5. When the timer beeps, press *Cancel* and wait 10 minutes.
6. Pick out the bay leaf. Using a whisk, stir the polenta to smooth it
7. If it's thin, simmer on the *Sauté* setting until it reaches the consistency you like. Season to taste with salt and pepper before serving.

Vegetable Stew Recipe

(Prep + Cook Time: 55 minutes | **Servings:** 6)

Ingredients:
- 6 cups vegetable stock (or beef/chicken stock)
- 1/2 cup red wine or rice wine (red wine is preferred)
- 2 large carrots; cut into bite size pieces
- 3 potatoes cut into chunks
- 4 celery stalks cut into bite size pieces
- 2 cups of sliced white mushrooms
- 1 large onion; diced
- 6 tomatoes; diced
- 3 gloves garlic; minced
- 1 cup pearl barley
- 1 tbsp. dried parsley flakes
- 1 tbsp. dried thyme
- 1 bay leaf

Instructions:
1. In a nonstick pan add a drizzle of olive oil and quickly sauté the white mushrooms with the minced garlic and onions until golden brown (2 - 3 minutes on medium heat) then add in the red wine and cook for another minute. Set aside.
2. In the Foodi Multi-cooker add the rest of the ingredients not including the barley
3. High pressure for 20 minutes. Lock the lid on the Foodi Multi-cooker and then cook for 20 minutes.
4. To get 20 minutes' cook time, press *Pressure* button and adjust the time
5. Pressure Release. Use the quick release method to bring the pot's pressure back to normal
6. Add the mushrooms and barley, give it a good stir and add 2 pinches of salt and pepper
7. High pressure for 10 minutes. Lock the lid on the Foodi Multi-cooker and then cook for 10 minutes.
8. To get 10 minutes' cook time, press *Pressure* button and use the Time Adjustment button to adjust the cook time to 10 minutes.
9. Pressure Release. Use the quick release method to bring the pot's pressure back to normal.
10. Finish the dish. At this point the potatoes and carrots should have softened. Add salt and pepper to taste.
11. Serve with your favorite pasta dish fresh baked biscuits

Stewed Broccoli

(Prep + Cook Time: 10 Minutes | **Servings:** 4 to 6)

Ingredients:
- 2 lb. broccoli (with or without main stems)
- 3 oil-packed anchovies (optional)
- 1/2 cup of red wine (something tart, such as Chianti)
- 1 cup water, more as needed
- 1/2 cup shaved Caciocavallo or Pecorino Romano cheese (shaved using a vegetable peeler)
- 1 tbsp. olive oil
- 2 garlic cloves; coarsely chopped
- 1 tsp. salt

Instructions:
1. If using broccoli stems, cut them from the crowns and chop them. Separate the crowns into florets. Set the broccoli aside
2. Heat the Foodi using the *Sauté* mode, add the oil, and heat briefly. Stir in the garlic and the anchovies if using. Sauté for 2 minutes until the garlic is golden and the anchovies have dissolved. To deglaze the cooker, pour in the wine and continue to cook until it has almost completely evaporated, about 3 minutes. Stir in the broccoli stems if using. Arrange the florets on top and sprinkle with the salt and pour 1 cup water (or the minimum amount required by your cooker to reach pressure)
3. Close and lock the lid of the Foodi. Cook at High pressure for 5 minutes. To get 5 minutes' cook time, press *Pressure* button, and use the *Time Adjustment* button to adjust the cook time to 5 minutes.
4. When the time is up, open the cooker using the Natural release method.
5. Delicately tumble the broccoli into a serving dish, pouring the cooking liquid over the top. Decorate with the cheese just before serving.

Maple Mustard Brussels Sprouts

(Prep + Cook Time: 25 Minutes | **Servings:** 8)

Ingredients:
- 16 Brussels sprouts, medium or large-sized (about 1 to 2-inch diameter), cut into halves or into quarters to make 3 cups total
- 1/2 cup onion; diced
- 1/2 cup vegetable stock OR water
- 1 ½ to 2 tbsp. Dijon mustard
- 1 tsp. olive oil
- 1/2 to 1 tbsp. maple syrup
- 2 tsp. pure sesame OR sunflower oil; optional
- Salt and freshly ground black pepper

Instructions:
1. Set the Foodi to *Sauté*. Pour the oil in the pot. Add onion and sauté for about 1 to 2 minutes or until starting to soften.
2. In a glass jar or in a jar, whisk the stock with the mustard. Set aside
3. Add the Brussels sprouts and then the stock mix in the pot.
4. Stir to coat and then drizzle the maple syrup over the veggies without stirring. Close and lock the lid. Select *Pressure* and cook at LOW pressure for 3 minutes
5. When the timer beeps, turn the steam valve to Venting for quick pressure release. Carefully unlock and open the lid.
6. Transfer the sprouts into a bowl. If desired, season to taste with salt and pepper

Notes: If you are using small sprouts, do not cut them into halves. The cooking time indicated for this recipe cooks the sprouts al dente. If you want then softer, cook them for 1 to 2 minutes more.

Zucchini Fries with Marinara Sauce

(Prep + Cook Time: 1 hour and 20 minutes | **Servings:** 4)

Ingredients:
- 2 large zucchinis, cut in sticks 3-inches long and 1/4-inch thick
- 2 tsp. kosher salt
- 2 cups all-purpose flour
- 3 eggs, beaten
- 3 cups seasoned bread crumbs
- 1/4 cup grated Parmesan cheese
- 1 tbsp. garlic powder
- 2 tsp. onion powder
- Marinara sauce, for serving

Instructions:
1. Place the zucchini sticks onto a plate and sprinkle with salt. Allow for 15 minutes to remove excess liquid. Pat dry.
2. Place flour into a bowl. Place beaten eggs in another bowl. Combine bread crumbs, Parmesan, garlic powder, and onion powder in a third bowl.
3. First, dredge fries in the flour, then shake off any excess and coat in the egg. Then coat in bread crumb mixture and return to a clean plate. Repeat with remaining zucchini. Cover plate with plastic wrap and place in the freezer for 30 to 40 minutes
4. Once coating has hardened, place the Cook & Crisp Basket in the pot. Close crisping lid. Preheat the unit by selecting AIR CRISP, setting the temperature to 360°F, and setting the time to 5 minutes. Press START/STOP to begin
5. After 5 minutes, open lid and add zucchini fries to basket. Close lid. Select AIR CRISP, set temperature to 360°F, and set time to 24 minutes. Press START/STOP to begin
6. After 12 minutes, open lid, then lift basket and shake zucchini fries or toss them with silicone-tipped tongs. Lower basket back into pot and close lid to resume cooking.
7. After 20 minutes, check fries for desired doneness. Cook for up to 5 more minutes for crispier results. When cooking is complete, serve fries immediately with marinara sauce

Greens and Beets with Horseradish Sauce

(Prep + Cook Time: 15 minutes | **Servings:** 4)

Ingredients:
- 2 large or 3 small beets with greens; scrubbed and root ends trimmed
- 2 tsp. unsalted butter
- 1 tbsp. minced fresh chives
- 1 cup water; for steaming
- 1 tbsp. whole milk
- 2 tbsp. sour cream
- 1 tsp. prepared horseradish
- 1/4 tsp. lemon zest
- 1/8 tsp. kosher salt; divided.

Instructions:
1. Trim off the beet greens and set aside. If the beets are very large (3 inches or more in diameter), quarter them; otherwise, halve them
2. Add the water and insert the steamer basket or trivet. Place the beets on the steamer insert.
3. High pressure for 10 minutes. Lock the lid on the Foodi Multi-cooker and then cook for 10 minutes.
4. To get 10 minutes' cook time, press *Pressure* button and use the Time Adjustment button to adjust the cook time to 10 minutes.
5. When the timer goes off, turn the cooker off. (Warm* setting, turn off)
6. Pressure Release. Let the pressure to come down naturally.
7. While the beets are cooking and the pressure is releasing, wash the greens and slice them into 1/2-inch-thick ribbons, removing any tough stems. In a small bowl, whisk together the sour cream, milk, horseradish, lemon zest and $1/16$ tsp. of kosher salt.
8. Finish the dish. When the pressure has released completely, unlock and remove the lid. Remove the beets and cool slightly; then use a paring knife or peeler to peel them. Slice them into large bite-size pieces and set aside
9. Remove the steamer from the Foodi Multi-cooker and pour out the water. Turn the Foodi Multi-cooker to *Sauté*. Add the butter to melt. When the butter stops foaming, add the beet greens and sprinkle with the remaining $1/16$ tsp. of kosher salt. Cook for 3 to 4 minutes, stirring until wilted
10. Return the beets to the Foodi Multi-cooker and heat for 1 or 2 minutes, stirring. Transfer the beets and greens to a platter and drizzle with the sour cream mixture. Sprinkle with the chives and serve.
11. It may be tempting to cool the beets entirely before you peel them, but that would be a mistake. Beets are easiest to peel when they're just cool enough to handle; if they get too cold the skins tend to stick

Smooth Carrots with Pancetta

(Prep + Cook Time: 18 minutes | **Servings:** 4)

Ingredients:
- 1 lb. baby carrots
- 1 medium leek; white and pale green parts only, sliced lengthwise, washed and thinly sliced
- 4 oz. pancetta; diced
- 1/4 cup moderately sweet white wine; such as a dry Riesling
- 1/2 tsp. ground black pepper
- 2 tbsp. unsalted butter; cut into small bits

Instructions:
1. Put the pancetta in the Foodi turned to the *Air crisp* function and use the Time Adjustment button to adjust the cook time to 5 minutes.
2. Add the leek; cook, often stirring, until softened. Pour in the wine and scrape up any browned bits at the bottom of the pot as it comes to a simmer
3. Add the carrots and pepper; stir well. Scrape and pour the contents of the Foodi Multi-cooker into a 1-quart, round, high-sided soufflé or baking dish
4. Dot with the bits of butter. Lay a piece of parchment paper on top of the dish, then a piece of aluminum foil. Seal the foil tightly over the baking dish
5. Set the Foodi Multi-cooker rack inside and pour in 2 cups water. Use aluminum foil to build a sling for the baking dish; lower the baking dish into the cooker

6. High pressure for 7 minutes. Lock the lid on the Foodi Multi-cooker and then cook for 7 minutes.
7. To get 7 minutes' cook time, press *Pressure* button and use the Time Adjustment button to adjust the cook time to 7 minutes
8. Pressure Release. Use the quick release method to return the pot's pressure to normal.
9. Finish the dish. Close the crisping lid. Select "BROIL" and set the time to 5 minutes. Select START/STOP to begin. Cook until top is browned.
10. Unlock and open the pot. Use the foil sling to lift the baking dish out of the cooker. Uncover, stir well and serve

Chickpea Stew with Carrots

(Prep + Cook Time: 18 minutes | **Servings:** 4)

Ingredients:

- 1 (9 oz.) box frozen artichoke heart quarters; thawed and squeezed of excess moisture
- 1 (14 oz.) can diced tomatoes (about 1 ¾ cups)
- 1 lb. baby-carrots; cut into 1-inch pieces
- 6 pitted dates; preferably Medjool, chopped.
- 1 medium red onion; halved and sliced into thin half-moons
- 1 ½ cups dried chickpeas
- 2 cups chicken broth
- 2 tbsp. all purpose flour
- 2 ½ tbsp. olive oil
- 2 tsp. minced garlic
- 1/2 tsp. ground cinnamon
- 1/2 tsp. ground coriander
- 1/2 tsp. ground cumin
- 1/2 tsp. salt
- 1 tbsp. sweet paprika

Instructions:

1. Soak the chickpeas in a big bowl of water for at least 12 hours or up to 16 hours.
2. Drain the chickpeas in a colander set in the sink. Whisk the broth and flour in a medium bowl until the flour dissolves
3. Heat 1 ½ tbsp. oil in the Foodi Multi-cooker turned to the Sauté function. Add the onion and cook, often stirring, until softened, about 4 minutes.
4. Stir in the garlic, paprika, cinnamon, coriander, cumin and salt until aromatic, about 30 seconds. Pour in the tomatoes as well as the broth mixture. Stir well, then add the carrots, dates and drained chickpeas.
5. High pressure for 12 minutes. Lock the lid on the Foodi Multi-cooker and then cook for 12 minutes.
6. To get 12 minutes' cook time, press *Pressure* button and use the Time Adjustment button to adjust the cook time to 12 minutes
7. Pressure Release. Use the quick release method to drop the pot's pressure back to normal
8. Finish the dish. Unlock and open the cooker. Heat the remaining tbsp. oil in a large nonstick skillet set over medium-high heat
9. Add the artichoke heart quarters; fry until brown and crisp, stirring and occasionally turning about 10 minutes. Dish up the chickpea mixture into big bowls and top with the crisp artichoke bits.

Rice & Pasta

Lentil Sauce for Pasta

(Prep + Cook Time: 20 Minutes | **Servings:** 4 with pasta)

Ingredients:
- 1 large yellow onion; chopped
- 2 cups vegetable broth
- 1 cup brown lentils
- 3 medium Roma (plum) tomatoes; chopped
- 2 tbsp. canned tomato paste
- 1 tbsp. minced garlic
- 1/2 tsp. ground allspice
- 2 tbsp. olive oil
- 1/2 tsp. ground coriander
- 1/2 tsp. ground cumin
- 1/2 tsp. salt
- 1/4 tsp. red pepper flakes

Instructions:
1. Heat the oil in the Foodi turned to the *Sautéing/Browning* function. Add the onion and cook, stirring often, until softened, about 4 minutes
2. Stir in the garlic, allspice, coriander, cumin, salt, and red pepper flakes; cook until fragrant, stirring all the while, less than 1 minute. Add the broth, lentils, tomatoes, and tomato paste; stir well until the paste has coated everything
3. Lock the lid onto the pot. Set the Foodi to cook at High pressure for 15 minutes. To get 15 minutes' cook time, press *Pressure* button and use the *Time Adjustment* button to adjust the cook time to 15 minutes
4. Turn off the Foodi or unplug it so it doesn't flip to its keep-warm setting. Let its pressure return to normal naturally, 10 to 15 minutes. Unlock and open the pot. Stir well before serving.

Brown Rice Pilaf with Cashews

(Prep + Cook Time: 38 Minutes | **Servings:** 6)

Ingredients:
- 1 large leek, white and pale green parts only, halved lengthwise, washed, and thinly sliced
- 1/2 cup chopped roasted unsalted cashews
- 1½ cups long-grain brown rice; such as brown basmati
- 3 cups vegetable or chicken broth
- 3 tbsp. unsalted butter
- 1/2 tsp. dried thyme
- 1/2 tsp. salt
- 1/8 tsp. ground turmeric

Instructions:
1. Melt the butter in the Foodi turned to the *Sautéing/Browning* function. Add the leek and cook, stirring often, until softened, about 2 minutes. Stir in the thyme, salt, and turmeric until fragrant, less than half a minute. Add the rice and cook for 1 minute, stirring all the while. Pour in the broth and stir well to get any browned bits off the bottom of the cooker
2. Lock the lid on the Foodi and then cook On High pressure for 33 minutes. To get 33 minutes' cook time, press *Pressure* button and use the *Time Adjustment* button to adjust the cook time to 33 minutes
3. Use the Quick Pressure Release method to return the pot's pressure to normal but do not open the cooker. Set aside for 10 minutes to steam the rice. Unlock and open the pot. Stir in the chopped cashews before serving.

Tasty Ninja Fagiole

(Prep + Cook Time: 13 Minutes | **Servings:** 6)

Ingredients:
- 1 (28 oz.) can whole tomatoes; cut into chunks (and with their juice-about 3½ cups)
- 1 medium green bell pepper; stemmed, cored, and chopped
- 1 (15 oz.) can small red beans, drained and rinsed (about 1¾ cups)
- 1 small yellow onion; chopped
- 1 cup dried whole wheat ziti (about 3 oz.)
- 1 tsp. dried oregano
- 1 tsp. dried thyme
- 1/4 tsp. grated nutmeg
- 1/4 tsp. red pepper flakes
- 1/4 tsp. salt

Instructions:
1. Mix everything in the Foodi.
2. Lock the lid onto the pot. Set the Foodi to cook at High pressure for 8 minutes. To get 8 minutes' cook time, press *Pressure* button and use the *Time Adjustment* button to adjust the cook time to 8 minutes
3. Use the Quick Pressure Release method to drop the pot's pressure back to normal. Unlock and open the lid; stir the soup before serving.

Turkey and Veggie Casserole

(Prep + Cook Time: 13 Minutes | **Servings:** 4 to 6)

Ingredients:
- 1 lb. turkey breast cutlets; diced into 1/2-inch pieces
- 8 oz. dried ziti or penne
- 2 cups frozen peas and carrots (do not thaw)
- 1 small yellow onion; chopped
- 2 cups grated Gruyère cheese (about 8 oz.)
- 1 cup heavy or light cream
- 3/4 cup whole milk
- 1 tbsp. Worcestershire sauce
- 1 tbsp. all-purpose flour
- 1 tsp. dried sage
- 1/2 tsp. ground black pepper
- 2 tbsp. unsalted butter

Instructions:
1. Whisk the cream, milk, Worcestershire sauce, flour, sage, and pepper in a large bowl until the flour dissolves; set aside
2. Place the turkey, pasta, and 6 cups water in the Foodi.
3. Lock the lid onto the pot. Set the Foodi to cook at High pressure for 8 minutes. To get 8 minutes' cook time, press *Pressure* button and use the *Time Adjustment* button to adjust the cook time to 8 minutes.
4. Use the Quick Pressure Release method to drop the pot's pressure to normal
5. Place the peas and carrots in a large colander set in the sink. Unlock and open the pot, then pour its contents over the vegetables in the colander. Set aside for 5 minutes. Wipe out the cooker
6. Melt the butter in the Foodi turned to the *Sautéing/Browning* function. Add the onion and cook, stirring often, until softened, about 3 minutes. Add the milk mixture and whisk until bubbling, about 2 minutes. Stir in the contents of the colander, then the cheese. Cover loosely and set aside off the heat for a few minutes to warm everything through and melt the cheese.

Seafood Risotto

(Prep + Cook Time: 16 Minutes | **Servings:** 4)

Ingredients:
- 3 cups mixed seafood (shrimp, calamari, clams, etc.)
- 3 garlic cloves; chopped
- 3 oil-packed anchovies
- 2 cups Arborio or Carnaroli rice
- 1 bunch flat-leaf parsley; chopped
- Lemon wedges; for serving
- Water, as needed
- 2 tbsp. olive oil; plus, more to finish
- Freshly squeezed juice of 1 lemon
- 2 tsp. salt
- 1/4 tsp. ground white pepper

Instructions:
1. Separate the shellfish from the other seafood and set the shellfish aside. Add the remaining seafood to a 4 cup measuring cup and add water to just over the 4 cup mark
2. Heat the Foodi using the *Sauté* mode, add the oil, and heat briefly. Stir in the garlic and anchovies and sauté until the garlic is golden and the anchovies are broken up. Add the rice, stirring to coat well. While you continue to stir, look carefully at the rice, it will first become wet and look slightly transparent and pearly; then it will slowly begin to look dry and solid white again. At that point pour in the lemon juice. Scrape the bottom of the Foodi gently, and keep stirring until all of the juice has evaporated. Stir in the seafood and water and the salt and pepper. Place the shellfish on top without stirring any further
3. Lock the lid on the Foodi and then cook on High Pressure for 6 minutes. To get 6 minutes' cook time, press *Pressure* button and use the *Time Adjustment* button to adjust the cook time to 6 minutes.
4. Pressure Release When the time is up, open the Foodi with the Natural Release method
5. Stir the risotto. Swirl some oil over the top and sprinkle with parsley. Serve with lemon wedges.

Cannellini in Tomato-Sage Sauce

(Prep + Cook Time: 25 Minutes | **Servings:** 4 to 6)

Ingredients:
- 1 lb. ripe tomatoes, coarsely chopped (or whole cherry tomatoes or one 14.5 oz. can, chopped tomatoes with their juices)
- 1 cup dried cannellini beans; soaked, rinsed, and drained
- 3 garlic cloves; 2 smashed; 1 minced and reserved
- 1 tbsp. olive oil
- 2 fresh sage sprigs (reserve 2 leaves for a garnish)
- Extra-virgin olive oil
- 1 cup water
- 1½ tsp. salt
- 1/2 tsp. freshly ground black pepper

Instructions:
1. Add the 2 smashed garlic cloves to the cooker base with the everyday olive oil and sage sprigs and heat on low heat (turn the Foodi to "keep warm" setting) to slowly infuse the oil with the garlic and sage. Swish the contents around occasionally. When the garlic starts to turn golden, after about 4 minutes, add the water, tomatoes, and cannellini beans
2. Close and lock the lid of the Foodi. Cook at High pressure for 20 minutes. To get 20 minutes' cook time, press *Pressure* button
3. When the time is up, open the Foodi with the Natural Release method; this should take 20 to 30 minutes
4. When the cooker is open, remove and discard the sage stems and stir in the minced garlic, salt, and pepper; taste and adjust the seasoning if you wish. Using a slotted spoon, transfer the beans to a serving dish, swirl in a little extra-virgin olive oil and decorate with the reserved sage leaves.

Fried Rice

(Prep + Cook Time: 15 Minutes | **Servings:** 4)

Ingredients:
- 1 cup basmati rice; uncooked
- 1/4 cup soy sauce
- 1½ cups chicken stock
- 1/2 cups peas; frozen OR your preferred vegetable
- 1 tbsp. butter (or oil)
- 1 medium onion; diced
- 2 cloves garlic; minced
- 1 egg

Instructions:
1. Select *Sauté* mode and preheat the Foodi. Put the oil in the pot. Add the garlic and the onion. Sauté for 1 minute
2. Add the egg, scramble with the garlic mix for about 1 to 2 minutes.
3. Add the rice, stock, and soy sauce in the pot. Press *Cancel*. Close and lock the lid. Press "RICE" and set the time for 10 minutes
4. When the timer beeps, quick release the pressure. Carefully open the lid. Stir in the frozen peas or veggies. Let sit until the peas/ veggies are warmed through.

Wild Rice Salad with Apples

(Prep + Cook Time: 25 Minutes | **Servings:** 4)

Ingredients:
- 1/2 cup walnut pieces; toasted
- 2 or 3 celery stalks; thinly sliced (about 1 cup)
- 1 medium Gala, Fuji, or Braeburn apple, cored and cut into ½-inch pieces
- 4 cups water
- 1¼ tsp. kosher salt; divided
- 1 cup wild rice
- Pinch granulated sugar
- 1/3 cup walnut or olive oil
- 3 tbsp. cider vinegar
- 1/4 tsp. celery seed
- 1/8 tsp. freshly ground black pepper

Instructions:
1. Add the water into the Foodi, and 1 tsp. of kosher salt. Stir in the wild rice
2. Lock the lid on the Foodi and then cook On High pressure for 18 minutes. To get 18 minutes' cook time, press Pressure button and use the *Time Adjustment* button to adjust the cook time to 18 minutes
3. Use the Natural Pressure Release method. Unlock and remove the lid. The rice grains should be mostly split open. If not, simmer the rice for several minutes more, in the Foodi set to *Sautéing/Browning* until at least half the grains have split. Drain and cool slightly
4. To a small jar with a tight-fitting lid, add the walnut oil, cider vinegar, celery seed, the remaining 1/4 tsp. of kosher salt, the pepper, and the sugar, and shake until well combined
5. To a medium bowl, add the cooled rice, walnuts, celery, and apple. Pour half of the dressing over the salad, and toss gently to coat, adding more dressing as desired. Serve.

Rice Stuffed Acorn Squash

(Prep + Cook Time: 20 Minutes | **Servings:** 4)

Ingredients:
- 2 medium-sized; halved acorn squash
- 1 cup diced onion
- 1/2 cup quinoa
- 1/2 cup vegan cheese
- 3¾ cups veggie stock
- 1 cup white rice
- 2 minced garlic cloves
- 1 tbsp. Earth Balance spread (or any vegan butter)
- 1 tsp. chopped rosemary
- 1 tsp. chopped thyme
- 1 tsp. chopped sage

Instructions:
1. Turn your Foodi to *Sauté* and melt the Earth Balance. Add onion and salt, and cook for two minutes.
2. Toss in the garlic and cook for another minute or so. Add rice, quinoa, herbs, and pour in the broth. Stir.
3. Put your de-seeded squash halves with the cut-side up in a steamer basket
4. Put the trivet in the cooker, and place the basket on top. Close and seal the lid
5. Hit *Pressure* and cook for 6 minutes on HIGH pressure.
6. When the timer beeps, carefully Quick Pressure Release the pressure after hitting *Cancel*.
7. Take out the steamer basket and drain any liquid that's hanging around in the squash
8. Add vegan cheese to the pot and stir. Wait 5 minutes or so for the stuffing to thicken. Fill the squash and sprinkle on some extra cheese. Serve!

Curried Chicken and Pasta

(Prep + Cook Time: 13 Minutes | **Servings:** 4)

Ingredients:
- 1 lb. boneless skinless chicken breasts; cut into ½-inch pieces
- 1/4 cup heavy cream
- 4 medium carrots; shredded through the large holes of a box grater
- 8 oz. dried ziti pasta
- 3 cups chicken broth
- 2 tbsp. all-purpose flour
- 2 tbsp. unsalted butter
- 1 large yellow onion; chopped
- 2 tsp. yellow curry powder

Instructions:
1. Whisk the broth and flour in a medium bowl until smooth; set aside.
2. Melt the butter in the Foodi turned to the *Sautéing/Browning* function. Add the onion; cook, stirring often, until softened, about 4 minutes. Stir in the curry powder until aromatic, less than a minute. Then stir in the carrots and cook for 1 minute
3. Pour in the broth mixture. Add the pasta and chicken; stir well
4. Lock the lid onto the pot. Set the Foodi to cook at High pressure for 8 minutes. To get 8 minutes' cook time, press *Pressure* button and use the *Time Adjustment* button to adjust the cook time to 8 minutes.
5. Use the Quick Pressure Release method
6. Unlock and open the cooker. Stir in the cream. Put the lid loosely on the pot and set aside for 2 minutes to heat through. Serve in bowls.

Rice and Kale

(Prep + Cook Time: 20 Minutes | **Servings:** 6)

Ingredients:
- 8 oz. kale, washed, stemmed, and chopped (about 2 cups packed)
- 3 cups vegetable; chicken, or beef broth
- 1⅓ cups long-grain white basmati rice
- 1 tbsp. olive oil
- 1 tbsp. minced garlic
- 1/2 tsp. cumin seeds

Instructions:
1. Heat the oil in the Foodi turned to the *Sautéing/Browning* function. Add the garlic and cumin; stir until aromatic, until the cumin seeds start to pop, about 1 minute
2. Add the kale and stir until wilted, about 1 minute. Stir in the broth and scrape up any browned bits in the bottom of the cooker. Add the rice and stir well.
3. Lock the lid onto the pot.
4. Set the Foodi to cook at High pressure. Set the Foodi timer to cook at High pressure for 15 minutes. To get 15 minutes' cook time, press *Pressure* button
5. Bring the pot's pressure back to normal with the Quick Pressure Release method but do not open the cooker. Set aside for 10 minutes to steam the rice. Unlock and open the cooker. Stir before serving.

Pasta Puttanesca

(Prep + Cook Time: 13 Minutes | **Servings:** 4)

Ingredients:
- 1 lb. eggplant (about 1 large), stemmed and diced (no need to peel)
- 2 medium yellow bell peppers; stemmed, cored, and chopped
- 1 (28 oz.) can diced tomatoes (about 3½ cups)
- 8 oz. dried whole wheat ziti
- 2 tbsp. olive oil
- 1 small red onion; chopped
- 1 tbsp. drained and rinsed capers, minced
- 1 tbsp. minced garlic
- 1¼ cups vegetable broth
- 2 tbsp. canned tomato paste
- 2 tsp. dried rosemary
- 1 tsp. dried thyme
- 1/2 tsp. ground black pepper

Instructions:
1. Heat the oil in the Foodi turned to the *Sautéing/Browning* function. Add the onion, capers, and garlic; cook, stirring often, just until the onion first begins to soften, about 2 minutes
2. Add the eggplant and bell peppers; cook, stirring often, for 1 minute. Mix in the tomatoes, broth, tomato paste, rosemary, thyme, and pepper, stirring until the tomato paste coats everything. Stir in the ziti until coated
3. Lock the lid onto the pot. Set the Foodi to cook at High pressure for 8 minutes. To get 8 minutes' cook time, press *Pressure* button and use the *Time Adjustment* button to adjust the cook time to 8 minutes.
4. Use the Quick Pressure Release method to drop the pressure in the pot back to normal. Unlock and open the cooker. Stir well before serving.

Italian Pasta Casserole

(Prep + Cook Time: 13 Minutes | **Servings:** 4)

Ingredients:
- 1 lb. lean ground beef (preferably 93% lean)
- 1 medium yellow bell pepper; stemmed, cored, and chopped
- 1 medium yellow onion; chopped
- 1 medium green bell pepper; stemmed, cored, and chopped
- 3/4 cup dry, fruit-forward red wine; such as Zinfandel
- 1 (28 oz.) can crushed tomatoes (about 3½ cups)
- 2 tbsp. olive oil
- 8 oz. dried ziti
- 2 tsp. dried basil
- 1 tsp. dried oregano or marjoram
- 1 tsp. dried thyme
- 1/2 tsp. fennel seeds
- 1/2 tsp. salt
- 1/4 tsp. red pepper flakes

Instructions:
1. Heat the oil in the Foodi turned to the *Sautéing/Browning* function. Add the ground beef; cook, stirring often, until browned, about 5 minutes. Use a slotted spoon to transfer the beef to a bowl
2. Add the onion and chopped peppers to the pot; cook, stirring often, until the onion softens, about 5 minutes. Stir in the basil, oregano or marjoram, thyme, fennel seeds, salt, and red pepper flakes. Pour in the wine and scrape up any browned bits in the pot as the mixture comes to a simmer. Return the ground beef to the pot along with the crushed tomatoes and pasta. Stir well
3. Lock the lid onto the pot. Switch the Foodi to cook at High pressure for 8 minutes. To get 8 minutes' cook time, press *Pressure* button and use the *Time Adjustment* button to adjust the cook time to 8 minutes
4. Turn off or unplug the Foodi; set aside for 5 minutes
5. Use the Quick Pressure Release method. Unlock and open the lid. Stir well before serving.

Armenian Rice Pilaf

(Prep + Cook Time: 10 Minutes | **Servings:** 4)

Ingredients:
- 2 cups long-grain white or basmati rice
- 1/2 cup vermicelli or angel hair pasta; broken into 1-inch pieces
- 4 cups salt-free Chicken Stock; preferably double-strength
- 2 tbsp. unsalted butter
- 2 tsp. salt
- 1 tbsp. olive oil

Instructions:
1. Heat the Foodi using the *Sauté* Function, add the butter and oil, and cook until the butter has melted. Add the vermicelli and stir well to coat. Sauté until the pieces just begin to turn golden. Add the rice; stir well to coat and toast for about 1 minute. Add the chicken stock and salt
2. Lock the lid on the Foodi and then cook On High pressure for 3 minutes. To get 3 minutes' cook time, press *Pressure* button and use the *Time Adjustment* button to adjust the cook time to 3 minutes
3. When the time is up, open the Foodi with the 10-Minute Natural Release method. Mix the pilaf well, pulling up the rice from the bottom of the Foodi to the top before serving.

Rice & Chickpea Stew

(Prep + Cook Time: 35 Minutes | Servings: 6)

Ingredients:
- 1 lb. sweet potato; peeled and diced
- 6 oz. brown basmati rice; rinsed
- 3 medium-sized onions; peeled and sliced
- 30 oz. cooked chickpeas
- 4 cups vegetable broth
- 4 oz. chopped cilantro
- 2 tsp. ground cumin
- 2 tsp. ground coriander
- 8 fluid oz. orange juice
- 1 tbsp. olive oil
- 1/4 tsp. salt
- 1/4 tsp. ground black pepper

Instructions:
1. Plug in and switch on a Foodi, select *Sauté* option, add oil and onion and let cook for 8 to 10 minutes or until browned
2. Stir in coriander and cumin and continue cooking for 15 seconds or until fragrant.
3. Add remaining ingredients into the pot except for black pepper and cilantro and stir until just mixed.
4. Press *Cancel* and secure pot with lid. Then position pressure indicator, select *Pressure* option and adjust cooking time on timer pad to 5 minutes and let cook on HIGH pressure
5. Foodi will take 10 minutes to build pressure before cooking timer starts
6. When the timer beeps, switch off the Foodi and let pressure release naturally for 10 minutes and then do quick pressure release
7. Then uncover the pot and stir in pepper until mixed. Garnish with cilantro and serve.

Portuguese Tomato Rice with Shrimp

(Prep + Cook Time: 35 Minutes | Servings: 4)

Ingredients:
- 2 ¾ cups passata or thin tomato puree (if the passata is very thick use 2¼ cups passata and 1¼ cups of stock)
- 1 large onion finely chopped
- 1 handful parsley freshly chopped
- 24 raw shrimp shelled and deveined; optional
- 2 tbsp. tomato paste
- 4 cloves garlic finely chopped
- 3/4 cup chicken stock
- 2 tbsp. olive oil
- 2 bay leaves
- 1½ cups Arborio rice
- 2 tsp. paprika
- Kosher salt to taste
- Black pepper to taste
- 1 cup tomato diced; heaping cup
- 3 - 4 tbsp. butter

Instructions:
1. Hit the *Sauté* button on your Foodi and when says it's 'Hot', add in the oil and the onions and sauté for 3 or 4 minutes, until the onions are nice and soft.
2. Add in the tomato paste and cook for another couple of minutes, stirring constantly so the tomato paste doesn't burn.
3. Now add the garlic and bay leaves, stir another minute before adding in the rice
4. Pour in the stock, the tomatoes, paprika and good pinch of kosher salt (start with 1 tsp. and taste) and a few grinds of black pepper. Lastly, stir in the chopped tomatoes
5. Close up the lid, seal the vent and press the *Pressure* button to program your Foodi to cook for 6 minutes at HIGH pressure
6. When the time is up, quick release the pressure, open the lid and give the rice a good stir. It will be quite soupy
7. If you are adding shrimp, add them now, stir them into the rice and add the lid back on and let the rice sit for 3 or 4 minutes to cook them. If you are NOT adding shrimp, you can leave the lid off but continue to stir the rice occasionally for another minute or so to thicken the rice up a bit. Just before serving, stir in the butter and parsley.

Lentil and Wild Rice Pilaf

(Prep + Cook Time: 20 + 30 Minutes | **Servings:** 6)

Ingredients:
For the lentils and rice (soak for 30 minutes before cooking):
- 1/2 cup black or green lentils
- 1/4 cup black/wild rice
- 1/4 cup brown rice

For the vegetables:
- 1/2 onion, medium-sized, finely chopped
- 1 cup mushrooms; sliced
- 3 cloves garlic; pressed/minced
- 1 stalk celery, finely chopped

For the spices:
- 2 cups vegetable broth
- 1 tsp. dried coriander
- 1 bay leaf
- 1 tsp. fennel seeds
- 1 tbsp. Italian seasoning blend (no-salt added)
- 1/2 tsp. ground black pepper
- 1/4 tsp. red pepper flakes

Instructions:
1. Combine the rice and the lentils in a medium-sized bowl. Let soak for 30 minutes. Drain and then rinse thoroughly
2. Set the Foodi to *Sauté*. Put the veggies in the inner pot and sauté for 3 to 5 minutes.
3. If needed, add a bit of water to prevent the veggies from burning.
4. Add the rice and lentils, vegetable broth, and spices into the pot. Close and lock the lid
5. Press *Pressure*, set the pressure to HIGH, and set the timer to 9 minutes
6. When the timer beeps, let the pressure release naturally. Open the lid. Stir the pilaf
7. If liquid remains, let sit for 5 minutes uncovered to allow the pilaf to absorb more liquid. Serve this dish with steamed or fresh veggies.

Notes: If you don't like fennel seeds, then use 1 tbsp. of your preferred dried herbs, such as thyme, rosemary, parsley, basil, or oregano. If you don't have black or wild rice on hand, you can use all brown rice.

Ninja Brown Rice

(Prep + Cook Time: 27 Minutes | **Servings:** 4)

Ingredients:
- 1½ cups brown rice
- 2½ cups water
- 1 tsp. olive oil
- 1/2 tsp. salt

Instructions:
1. Place the rice, water, salt, and oil in the Foodi base
2. Lock the lid on the Foodi and then cook on High Pressure for 20 minutes. To get 20 minutes' cook time, press Pressure button and use the *Time Adjustment* button to adjust the cook time to 20 minutes
3. When the time is up, open the Foodi with the 10-Minute Natural Release method. Fluff the rice with a fork and serve.

Rice and Artichokes

(Prep + Cook Time: 30 Minutes | Servings: 4)

Ingredients:
- 6 oz. graham crackers, crumbled
- 8 oz. veggie stock
- 8 oz. water
- 6 oz. arborico rice
- 16 oz. vegan cream cheese; soft
- 14 oz. artichoke hearts; chopped
- 1½ tbsp. vegan cheese; grated
- 2 garlic cloves, minced
- 2 tbsp. white wine
- Salt and black pepper to taste
- 1 tbsp. vegetable oil
- 1 ½ tbsp. thyme, finely chopped

Instructions:
1. Heat up a pan with the oil over medium high heat, add rice and garlic, stir and cook for 3 minutes
2. Transfer everything to your Foodi, add stock, wine, water, cover and Select *Pressure* and cook at HIGH pressure for 10 minutes
3. Release pressure naturally for 5 minutes. Add crackers, add artichokes, vegan cheese, vegan cream cheese, salt, pepper and thyme, stir well, divide into bowls and serve right away.

Quinoa Risotto with Bacon

(Prep + Cook Time: 16 Minutes | Servings: 4)

Ingredients:
- 3 oz. slab bacon; diced
- 1/4 cup finely grated Parmesan cheese (about 1/2 oz.)
- 6 medium scallions; thinly sliced
- 12 cherry tomatoes; halved
- 3½ cups chicken broth
- 1½ cups white or red quinoa; rinsed if necessary
- 1/4 cup dry vermouth
- 3 fresh thyme sprigs
- 1/2 tsp. ground black pepper

Instructions:
1. Place the bacon in the Foodi turned to the *Sautéing/Browning* function. Fry until crisp, stirring occasionally, about 4 minutes
2. Add the scallions; stir over the heat until softened, about 1 minute. Put in the tomatoes; cook just until they begin to break down, about 2 minutes, stirring occasionally. Pour in the vermouth; as it comes to a simmer, scrape up any browned bits in the bottom of the cooker
3. Stir in the broth, quinoa, and thyme sprigs.
4. Lock the lid on the Foodi and then cook On High pressure for 9 minutes. To get 9 minutes' cook time, press *Pressure* button and use the *Time Adjustment* button to adjust the cook time to 9 minutes.
5. Return the pot's pressure to normal with the Quick Pressure Release method
6. Unlock and open the cooker. Turn the Foodi to its *Sautéing/Browning* function. Discard the thyme sprigs. Bring the mixture in the pot to a simmer; cook, stirring often, until thickened, 2 to 3 minutes. Stir in the cheese and pepper to serve.

Chicken in Peanut Sauce

(Prep + Cook Time: 13 Minutes | Servings: 4)

Ingredients:
- 1 lb. boneless skinless chicken breasts, cut into 1/2-inch cubes
- 1 (14 oz.) can diced tomatoes (about 1¾ cups)
- 2 tbsp. peanut oil
- 1 medium yellow onion; chopped
- 1 tbsp. minced fresh ginger
- 2 tsp. minced garlic
- 6 tbsp. creamy natural-style peanut butter
- 1 tbsp. packed dark brown sugar
- 1/4 tsp. cayenne
- 2¼ cups chicken broth
- 8 oz. dried whole wheat ziti
- 1/2 tsp. ground allspice
- 1/2 tsp. ground cinnamon
- 1/2 tsp. ground cloves
- 1/2 tsp. salt

Instructions:
1. Heat the oil in the Foodi turned to the *Sautéing/Browning* function. Add the onion, ginger, and garlic; cook until the onion softens, about 3 minutes, stirring often. Add the chicken and cook until it loses its raw color, about 3 minutes, stirring more frequently
2. Stir in the tomatoes, peanut butter, brown sugar, allspice, cinnamon, cloves, salt, and cayenne until the peanut butter dissolves. Add the broth and pasta; stir well
3. Lock the lid onto the pot. Set the Foodi to cook at High pressure for 8 minutes. To get 8 minutes' cook time, press *Pressure* button and use the *Time Adjustment* button to adjust the cook time to 8 minutes
4. Use the Quick Pressure Release method to bring the pot's pressure to normal. Unlock and open the pot. Stir well before serving in bowls.

Wild Rice with Sweet Potatoes

(Prep + Cook Time: 50 Minutes | Servings: 6)

Ingredients:
- 1 medium yellow onion, chopped
- 2 medium celery stalks; chopped
- 1½ cups black wild rice (about 8 oz.)
- 3 cups vegetable or chicken broth
- 1 large sweet potato (about 1 lb.); peeled and diced
- 1/4 cup dried cranberries
- 2 tbsp. olive oil
- 1 tbsp. packed fresh sage leaves; minced
- 2 tsp. fresh thyme leaves
- 1/2 tsp. salt
- 1/2 tsp. ground black pepper

Instructions:
1. Heat the olive oil in the Foodi turned to the *Sautéing/Browning* function. Add the onion and celery; cook, stirring often, until the onion softens, about 4 minutes. Mix in the sage and thyme; cook until fragrant, about 30 seconds. Stir in the rice and toss well to coat. Pour in the broth; stir well to get up any browned bits in the bottom of pot.
2. Lock the lid on the Foodi and then cook On High pressure for 30 minutes. To get 30 minutes' cook time, press *Pressure* button
3. Pressure Release Use the Quick Pressure Release method to return the pot's pressure to normal.
4. Unlock and open the cooker. Stir in the sweet potato, cranberries, salt, and pepper.
5. Lock the lid back on the Foodi and then cook On High pressure for 15 minutes. To get 15 minutes' cook time, press *Pressure* button
6. Pressure Release Use the Quick Pressure Release method to return the pot's pressure to normal. Unlock and open the cooker. Stir well before serving.

Beetroot Rice

(Prep + Cook Time: 35 Minutes | **Servings:** 2 to 4)

Ingredients:
- 1 cup Basmati rice
- 1 beet cut into small pieces
- 1/2 cup green peas
- 1 tbsp. lemon juice
- 1¼ cup water
- 1 tbsp. ghee or oil
- 1/2 tsp. cumin seeds or Jeera
- 1/2 tbsp. ginger paste
- 1/2 tbsp. garlic paste
- 1/2 onion thinly sliced

Whole Spices (optional):
- 1 inch stick cinnamon or Dal chini
- 3 cloves or Laung
- 1 bay leaf or Tej Patta
- 1-star anise
- 6 black peppercorns

Spices:
- 1/2 tsp. garam masala
- 1 tsp. coriander or Dhania powder (optional)
- 1/2 tsp. cayenne or red chili powder
- 1/4 tsp. turmeric or Haldi powder
- 2 tsp. salt

Instructions:
1. Start the Foodi In *Sauté* mode and heat it. Add ghee, cumin seeds and whole spices and sauté them for 30 seconds until the cumin seeds change color
2. Add the sliced onions, ginger, garlic and sauté for 3 minutes.
3. Add the beets, green peas and spices. Mix well
4. Add the rice and water to the pot. Stir the ingredients in the pot
5. Change the Foodi setting to *Pressure*, close the lid and cook for 4 minutes at HIGH pressure.
6. When the Foodi beeps, do a 10-minute natural release, then release the remaining pressure.
7. Add the lemon juice and fluff the rice. Beet Pulao is ready. Enjoy with homemade yogurt or raita.

Note for you:

8. Adding whole spices is optional. You can enjoy this beet pulao even if you don't have all the whole spices in your pantry.
9. To reduce spice, skip the cayenne
10. I added green peas along with the beets, as that is what I had at hand. Other possible options to add are potatoes, bell peppers, carrots and edamame.

Spanish Rice

(Prep + Cook Time: 30 Minutes | **Servings:** 4)

Ingredients:
- 2 cups long grain rice
- 1½ cups chicken stock or water
- 2 tbsp. butter
- 1/2 tsp. garlic powder
- 1/2 tsp. onion powder
- 8 oz. tomato sauce
- 1 tsp. cumin
- 1 tsp. chili powder
- 1/2 tsp. salt

Instructions:
1. Set the Foodi to *Sauté* setting.
2. Sauté butter and dry rice together for 4 minutes
3. Stir in chicken stock, tomato sauce, cumin, chili powder, garlic powder and onion powder into the rice.
4. Close and lock the lid. Select *Pressure* and cook at HIGH pressure for 10 minutes
5. Once the time is up, let the pressure release naturally. Fluff the rice with a fork and serve.

Barley Risotto with Fresh Spinach

(Prep + Cook Time: 26 Minutes | **Servings:** 6)

Ingredients:
- 1 cup pearled barley
- 4 cups chicken stock or broth
- 4 cups baby spinach
- 1/4 cup grated Parmesan cheese
- 1 tbsp. olive oil
- 1 tbsp. light margarine
- 1 yellow onion; diced
- Juice of 1 lemon
- 1 tbsp. minced garlic
- Salt and pepper

Instructions:
1. With the cooker's lid off, heat oil and margarine on *Sautéing/Browning* until oil is sizzling and margarine is melted
2. Place diced onion in the cooker, and sauté until translucent, 5 minutes. Stir in barley, and sauté 1 additional minute
3. Add the chicken broth, lemon juice, and minced garlic.
4. Lock the lid on the Foodi and then cook On High pressure for 25 minutes. To get 25 minutes' cook time, press *Pressure* button and use the *Time Adjustment* button to adjust the cook time to 25 minutes
5. Let the pressure release naturally 5 minutes before performing a quick release for any remaining pressure.
6. With the cooker's lid off, set to *Sautéing/Browning* to sauté, and stir in spinach and Parmesan cheese, simmering until spinach cooks down. Season with salt and pepper to taste before serving.

Wild and Brown Rice Pilaf

(Prep + Cook Time: 32 Minutes | **Servings:** 4)

Ingredients:
- 1/3 cup wild rice
- 1/2 cup brown rice
- 3/4 cup low-sodium vegetable broth
- 1/4 cup dry white wine
- 1 bay leaf
- 1 fresh thyme sprig; or 1/4 tsp. dried thyme
- 1 tbsp. olive oil
- 3/4 cup diced onion
- 1 garlic clove; minced
- 2 tbsp. chopped fresh parsley
- 2/3 cup water
- 1/2 tsp. kosher salt, divided, plus additional for seasoning

Instructions:
1. Set the Foodi to *Sautéing/Browning* heat the olive oil until it shimmers and flows like water. Add the onion and garlic, and cook for about 3 minutes, stirring, until the garlic is fragrant and the onions soften and separate. Add the wild rice, water, and 1/4 tsp. of kosher salt, and stir
2. Lock the lid on the Foodi and then cook On High pressure for 15 minutes. To get 15 minutes' cook time, press *Pressure* button.
3. Use the Quick Pressure Release method
4. Unlock and remove the lid. Stir in the brown rice, vegetable broth, remaining 1/4 tsp. of kosher salt, white wine, bay leaf, and thyme.
5. Lock the lid on the Foodi and then cook On High pressure for 12 minutes. To get 12 minutes' cook time, press *Pressure* button
6. When the timer goes off, turn the cooker off. ("*Keep Warm*" setting, turn off).
7. After cooking, use the natural method to release pressure for 12 minutes, then the quick method to release the remaining pressure.
8. Unlock and remove the lid. Remove the bay leaf and thyme sprig, and stir in the parsley. Taste and adjust the seasoning, as needed. Replace but do not lock the lid. Let the rice steam for about 4 minutes, fluff gently with a fork, and serve.

Pineapple Fried Rice

(Prep + Cook Time: 35 Minutes | **Servings:** 2)

Ingredients:
- 3 stalks spring onion, chopped, white and green parts separated
- 1/2 red bell pepper
- 1/2 cup mix of carrots & peas (I used frozen carrot & peas and put them in warm water for 5 minutes before using in the recipe)
- 1¼ cups pineapple chunks; I used canned pineapple chunks
- 1½ cups jasmine rice
- 1½ cups water
- 2 tbsp. sesame oil
- 3 - 4 garlic cloves; minced
- 1/2 tbsp. grated ginger
- 1 small onion; chopped
- 2½ tbsp. soy sauce
- 1/4 tsp. white pepper powder, or to taste
- Salt to taste

Instructions:
1. Rinse rice with cold water till the water is no longer cloudy and turns clear. This might take 60 to 90 seconds and is an extremely important step in order to get the perfect texture of rice
2. Drain the rice completely and then transfer it to the pot. Add water and stir
3. Close the lid of the Foodi, set valve to sealing.
4. Press *Pressure* and cook at HIGH pressure for 3 minutes
5. Once the time is up, let the pressure release naturally for 10 minutes and then release the remaining pressure.
6. Open the lid and fluff the rice using a fork. Transfer rice to a bowl and set aside.
7. Now press the *Sauté* button. Add oil to the pot (there's no need to clean it).
8. Once oil is hot, add garlic and ginger and sauté for few seconds.
9. Add in chopped onion and spring onion whites. Sauté for a minute
10. Then add carrot, green peas and pepper. Sauté for another minute
11. Stir in the pineapple chunks and cook for 1 more minute.
12. Push all the veggies to the side and add the soy sauce
13. Put the cooked rice back in the pot again. You may press *Cancel* button at this point.
14. Stir till everything is well combined and all the rice is coated with the sauce.
15. Add white pepper powder, salt and mix to combine. Garnish with spring onion greens and enjoy the pineapple fried rice!

Long Grain White Rice

(Prep + Cook Time: 27 Minutes | **Servings:** 4)

Ingredients:
- 1½ cups long-grain white rice
- 1 tsp. vegetable oil or unsalted butter
- 3 cups water
- 1/2 tsp. salt

Instructions:
1. Place the rice, water, salt, and oil in the Foodi base.
2. Lock the lid on the Foodi and then cook On High pressure for 4 minutes. To get 4 minutes' cook time, press *Pressure* button and use the *Time Adjustment* button to adjust the cook time to 4 minutes
3. When the time is up, open the Foodi with the 10-Minute Natural Release method. Fluff the rice with a fork and serve.

Tiger Prawn Risotto

(Prep + Cook Time: 40 Minutes | **Servings:** 2 to 4)

Ingredients:
- 1/2 lb. frozen tiger prawns, thawed and peeled
- 1 oz. Parmesan cheese; finely grated
- 2 stalk green onions; thinly sliced
- 1 shallot; minced
- 3 cloves garlic; minced
- 2 cups Arborio rice
- 3/4 cup cooking sake
- 2 tsp. soy sauce
- 3 tbsp. olive oil
- 4 tbsp. butter
- 4 cups fish stock or Japanese Dashi
- 1 tsp. salt
- 1 tsp. white pepper

Instructions:
1. In mixing bowl season the prawns with salt and white pepper. Set the Foodi on brown and add the olive oil and butter and sauté prawns for 5 to 10 minutes with the shallot and garlic, the prawns should be about 80% cooked. Remove and set aside
2. Add the Arborio rice, cooking sake, soy sauce and fish stock into Foodi with a swirl of olive oil. Stir and combine, make sure the rice is coated with the liquids or Japanese Dashi.
3. Lock the lid on the Foodi and then cook On High pressure for 25 minutes. To get 25 minutes' cook time, press *Pressure* button and use the *Time Adjustment* button to adjust the cook time to 25 minutes.
4. Pressure Release Use the Quick Pressure Release method to return the pot's pressure to normal
5. Place the prawns on top of the risotto and sprinkle the Parmesan cheese over the prawns and risotto.
6. Cover and lock the lid again and cook on High Pressure for another 5 minutes. To get 5 minutes' cook time, press *Pressure* button and use the *Time Adjustment* button to adjust the cook time to 5 minutes.
7. Pressure Release Use the Quick Pressure Release method to return the pot's pressure to normal. Garnish with the sliced green onions.

Brown Rice Stuffed Cabbage Rolls with Pine Nuts and Currants

(Prep + Cook Time: 35 Minutes | **Servings:** 4)

Ingredients:
- 1 large head green cabbage cored
- 1 can crushed tomatoes undrained; 14.5 oz.
- 3 cups brown rice cooked
- 3 oz. feta cheese crumbled; about 3/4 cup
- 1/2 cup currants dried
- 2 tbsp. pine nuts toasted
- Parsley additional; chopped and fresh, optional
- 1/2 cup apple juice
- 1 tbsp. cider vinegar
- 1 tbsp. olive oil
- 1½ cups onion finely chopped
- 2 tbsp. parsley fresh chopped
- 1/4 tsp. salt
- 1/2 tsp. black pepper freshly ground

Instructions:
1. Steam cabbage head 8 minutes; cool slightly. Remove 16 leaves from cabbage head; discard remaining cabbage. Cut off raised portion of the center vein of each cabbage leaf (do not cut out vein); set trimmed cabbage leaves aside
2. Heat oil in a large nonstick skillet over medium heat; swirl to coat. Add onion; cover and cook 6 minutes or until tender.
3. Remove from heat; stir in brown rice, add feta cheese, currants dried, pine nuts and parsley. Stir in 1/4 tsp. of the salt and 1/8 tsp. of the pepper
4. Place cabbage leaves on a flat surface; place about 1/3 cup rice mixture into center of each cabbage leaf. Fold in edges of leaves over rice mixture; roll up. Arrange cabbage rolls in bottom of the inner pot of a Foodi.

5. Combine the remaining 1/4 tsp. salt, remaining 1/8 tsp. pepper, apple juice, vinegar, and tomatoes; pour evenly over cabbage rolls
6. Close and lock the lid of the Foodi. Turn the steam release handle to Venting position. Press SLOW COOK, and select 2 hours' cook time. Serve sprinkled with parsley, if desired.

Mexican Rice

(Prep + Cook Time: 25 Minutes | **Servings:** 4)

Ingredients:
- 2⅓ cups chicken stock
- 2 cups long grain white rice
- 1 tbsp. olive oil
- 1/4 cup onion; diced
- 1 cup salsa
- 1 tsp. salt

Instructions:
1. Set the Foodi to *Sauté* setting. Sauté olive oil and onion until translucent about 1 to 2 minutes
2. Add in rice and sauté for 2 to 3 minutes.
3. Stir in chicken stock, salsa, and salt into the rice
4. Close and lock the lid. Select *Pressure* and cook at HIGH pressure for 10 minutes
5. Once the time is up, let the pressure release naturally. Fluff the rice with a fork and serve.

Brown Rice with Lentils

(Prep + Cook Time: 40 Minutes | **Servings:** 8)

Ingredients:
- 3 large onions, halved through the root (flatter) end, then sliced into thin half-moons
- 2 cups long-grain brown rice; preferably basmati
- 1 tsp. sugar
- 4½ cups vegetable or chicken broth
- 1/2 cup green lentils (French lentils or lentils de Puy)
- 1 tsp. coriander seeds
- 5 tbsp. olive oil
- 1 tsp. cumin seeds
- 1/2 tsp. ground turmeric
- 1/2 tsp. ground allspice
- 1/2 tsp. ground cinnamon
- 1 tsp. ground black pepper
- 1/2 tsp. salt

Instructions:
1. Heat 1½ tbsp. oil in the Foodi turned to the *Sautéing/Browning* function. Add half the onions and cook until well browned and crisp at the edges, at least 10 minutes, stirring occasionally. Transfer the cooked onions to a large bowl; repeat with 1½ tbsp. more oil and the rest of the onions
2. Add the remaining 2 tbsp. oil to the cooker; stir in the coriander, cumin, turmeric, allspice, and cinnamon until aromatic, about 1 minute. Add the rice, sugar, pepper, and salt; stir for 1 minute. Stir in the broth, scraping up any brown bits in the cooker. Stir in the lentils
3. Lock the lid on the Foodi and then cook On High pressure for 35 minutes. To get 35 minutes' cook time, press *Pressure* button and use the *Time Adjustment* button to adjust the cook time to 35 minutes.
4. Turn off the Foodi or unplug it so it doesn't flip to the keep-warm setting. Let its pressure return normal naturally, 14 to 20 minutes
5. Unlock and open the cooker. Spoon the caramelized onions on top of the rice; set the lid back on the cooker without locking it in place, and set aside for 10 minutes to warm the onions. Serve by scooping up big spoonfuls with onions and rice in each.

Lamb Pasta Casserole

(Prep + Cook Time: 13 Minutes | **Servings:** 4)

Ingredients:
- 1½ lb. lean ground lamb
- 1 small eggplant (about 3/4 lb.); stemmed and diced
- 3/4 cup dry red wine; such as Syrah
- 2¼ cups chicken broth
- 1/2 cup canned tomato paste
- 1 medium red onion; chopped
- 1 tbsp. minced garlic
- 1 tsp. ground cinnamon
- 8 oz. dried spiral-shaped pasta, such as rotini
- 2 tbsp. olive oil
- 1/2 tbsp. dried oregano
- 1/2 tsp. dried dill
- 1/2 tsp. salt
- 1/2 tsp. ground black pepper

Instructions:
1. Heat the oil in the Foodi turned to the *Sautéing/Browning* function. Add the onion and cook, stirring often, until softened, about 4 minutes. Add the garlic and cook until aromatic, less than 1 minute
2. Crumble in the ground lamb; cook, stirring occasionally, until it has lost its raw color, about 5 minutes. Add the eggplant and cook for 1 minute, stirring often, to soften a bit. Pour in the red wine and scrape up any browned bits in the pot as it comes to a simmer.
3. Stir in the broth, tomato paste, cinnamon, oregano, dill, salt, and pepper until everything is coated in the tomato sauce. Stir in the pasta until coated
4. Lock the lid onto the pot. Set the Foodi to cook at High pressure for 8 minutes. To get 8 minutes' cook time, press *Pressure* button and use the *Time Adjustment* button to adjust the cook time to 8 minutes
5. Use the Quick Pressure Release method. Unlock and open the pot. Stir well before serving.

Foodi Brown Rice

(Prep + Cook Time: 30 Minutes | **Servings:** 6)

Ingredients:
- 2 cups brown rice
- 2 ½ cups any kind vegetable broth or water
- 1/2 tsp. of sea salt

Instructions:
1. Put the rice into the Foodi
2. Pour in the broth or water and salt. Close and lock the lid. Press the *Pressure* and set the pressure to HIGH and the timer to 22 minutes
3. When the timer beeps, naturally release the pressure for 10 minutes. Carefully open the lid. Serve.

Brown Rice Medley

(Prep + Cook Time: 35 Minutes | **Servings:** 4)

Ingredients:
- 3 to 4 tbsp. red; wild or black rice
- 1½ cups water
- 3/4 cup (or more) short grain brown rice
- 3/8 to 1/2 tsp. sea salt; optional

Instructions:
1. Put as much as 3 - 4 tbsp. of red, wild, or black rice or use all three kinds in 1 cup measuring cup.
2. Add brown rice to make 1 cup total of rice. Put the rice in a strainer and wash. Put the rice in the Foodi.
3. Add 1½ cups water in the pot. If desired, add salt
4. Stir and then check the sides of the pot to make sure the rice is pushed down into the water. Close and lock the lid. Press *Pressure* and set the time to 23 minutes

5. When the timer beeps, let the pressure release naturally for 5 minutes, then turn the steam valve and release the pressure slowly. If you have time, let the pressure release naturally for 15 minutes. Stir and serve.

Risotto with Butternut Squash and Porcini

(Prep + Cook Time: 15 Minutes | **Servings:** 6)

Ingredients:
- 1/2 oz. dried porcini mushrooms; crumbled
- 1 medium leek; white and pale green parts only, halved lengthwise, washed, and thinly sliced
- 1/2 cup finely grated Parmesan cheese (about 1 oz.)
- 1½ cups white Arborio rice
- 1/4 cup dry vermouth
- 4 cups (1 quart) vegetable broth
- 2 cups seeded; peeled, and finely chopped butternut squash
- 2 tbsp. unsalted butter
- 1 tsp. dried thyme
- 1/4 tsp. saffron threads

Instructions:
1. Melt the butter in the Foodi turned to the *Sautéing/Browning* function. Add the leek and cook, stirring often, until softened, about 2 minutes.
2. Add the rice; stir until coated in the butter. Pour in the vermouth; stir over the heat until fully absorbed into the grains, 1 to 2 minutes. Add the broth, squash, dried porcini, thyme, and saffron
3. Lock the lid on the Foodi and then cook On High pressure for 10 minutes. To get 10 minutes' cook time, press *Pressure* button and use the *Time Adjustment* button to adjust the cook time to10 minutes.
4. Use the Quick Pressure Release method
5. Unlock and open the cooker. Turn the Foodi to its *Sautéing/Browning* function. Bring to a simmer, stirring until thickened, about 2 minutes
6. Stir in the cheese. Put the lid onto the cooker without locking it in place. Set aside for 5 minutes to melt the cheese and blend the flavors. Stir again before serving. Serve.

Risotto with Peas and Shrimp

(Prep + Cook Time: 11 Minutes | **Servings:** 4)

Ingredients:
- 1/2 lb. raw medium shrimp, shelled and deveined
- 1/2 cup frozen peas; thawed
- 1/4 cup grated Parmigiano-Reggiano or similar cheese
- 1/2 cup chopped onion
- 2¾ cups Chicken Stock or low-sodium broth; divided
- 1 cup Arborio rice
- 1/3 cup white wine
- 1 tbsp. unsalted butter

Instructions:
1. Turn the Foodi to *Sautéing/Browning* heat the butter until it stops foaming. Add the onion, and cook for about 2 minutes, stirring, until soft. Add the rice, and stir to coat with the butter. Cook for 1 minute, stirring. Stir in the white wine, and cook for 1 to 2 minutes, or until it's almost evaporated. Add 2½ cups of Chicken Stock, and stir to make sure no rice is sticking to the bottom of the cooker
2. Lock the lid on the Foodi and then cook On High pressure for 6 minutes. To get 6 minutes' cook time, press *Pressure* button and use the *Time Adjustment* button to adjust the cook time to 6 minutes.
3. Pressure Release Use the Quick Pressure Release method
4. Unlock and remove the lid. Turn the Foodi to *Sautéing/Browning* Continue to cook the rice, stirring, for 1 to 2 minutes more, or until the rice is firm just in the very center of the grain and the liquid has thickened slightly. Add the shrimp and peas, and continue to cook for about 4 minutes more, or until the shrimp are cooked. Stir in the Parmigiano-Reggiano. If the risotto is too thick, stir in a little of the remaining 1/4 cup of Chicken Stock to loosen it up. Serve immediately

5. Risotto is one of those dishes that lend themselves to almost endless variation. Leftover ham is a great addition, as is smoked salmon or trout, or go vegetarian with "Sautéed" Mushrooms, roasted peppers, or even beets.

Asian Veggie Pullow

(Prep + Cook Time: 15 Minutes | **Servings:** 4)

Ingredients:
- 1 large onion, finely chopped
- 3 cardamom pods; lightly crushed
- 3 or 4 whole cloves; lightly crushed
- 1 cup frozen petite green peas
- 1 cup coarsely chopped cauliflower florets (1-inch pieces)
- 1/2 cup cashews
- 2 cups basmati rice
- 1 tbsp. smashed garlic
- 4 tbsp. ghee or vegetable oil
- 1 tbsp. peeled and grated fresh ginger
- 1/2 tsp. crushed red pepper flakes
- 1 tsp. ground coriander
- 1/2 tsp. ground turmeric
- 1/2 tsp. ground cinnamon
- 2 carrots; peeled and diced
- 3 cups water
- 2 tsp. salt

Instructions:
1. Toast the cashews in a dry skillet over low heat until golden. Place the rice in a fine-mesh strainer and rinse it. Rest the strainer with the rice in a bowl and cover with water to soak
2. Meanwhile, heat the Foodi using the Sauté Mode, add the ghee, and heat briefly. Stir in the onion and fry until golden, about 7 minutes. Stir in the cardamom and cloves and sauté for about 1 minute. Lift the strainer so the rice can drain. Add the garlic, ginger, red pepper flakes, coriander, turmeric, and cinnamon to the onion mixture and sauté for another 30 seconds. Then add the peas, cauliflower, carrots, and rice; mix well. Sauté for about 3 more minutes. Stir in the water and salt
3. Close and lock the lid of the Foodi. Cook at High pressure for 3 minutes. To get 3 minutes' cook time, press *Pressure* button and use the *Time Adjustment* button to adjust the cook time to 3 minutes.
4. When the time is up, open the Foodi with the 10-Minute Natural Release method. Fluff the pullow with a fork; taste and add more salt if you wish. Sprinkle the cashews over the top.

Rice and Mushrooms

(Prep + Cook Time: 20 Minutes | **Servings:** 6)

Ingredients:
- 8 oz. baby bella or cremini mushrooms, thinly sliced
- 1½ cups long-grain white rice; preferably jasmine
- 8 medium scallions; thinly sliced
- 3 cups chicken broth
- 2 tbsp. mirin
- 2 tbsp. soy sauce
- 2 tbsp. peanut oil
- 1 tbsp. minced fresh ginger

Instructions:
1. Heat the oil in the Foodi turned to the *Sautéing/Browning* function. Add the scallions and mushrooms; cook, stirring often, until both soften and the mushrooms give off their liquid, about 5 minutes.
2. Add the rice and ginger; stir for 1 minute. Pour in the broth, soy sauce, and mirin; scrape up any browned bits in the bottom of the cooker.
3. Lock the lid onto the pot, Cook at High pressure for 15 minutes. To get 15 minutes cook time, press *Pressure* button
4. Use the Quick Pressure Release method to return the pot's pressure to normal but do not open the cooker. Set aside for 10 minutes to steam the rice. Unlock and open the cooker. Stir before serving.

Rice and Lentils

(Prep + Cook Time: 55 Minutes | **Servings:** 4)

Ingredients:
For the sauté:
- 1 tbsp. oil, OR dry sauté (or add a little water/vegetable broth)
- 2 cloves garlic; minced
- 1/2 cup onion; chopped

For the porridge:
- 2-inch sprig fresh rosemary
- 3½ cups water
- 1½ cups brown rice
- 1 cup rutabaga; peeled and diced, OR potato OR turnip
- 1 cup brown lentils
- 1 tbsp. dried marjoram (or thyme)
- Salt and pepper to taste

Instructions:
1. Press the *Sauté* key of the Foodi and select the Normal option. Put the oil/ broth in the pot and, if using oil, heat. When the oil is hot, add the onion and sauté for 5 minutes or until transparent.
2. Add the garlic and sauté for 1 minute
3. Add the lentils, brown rice, rutabaga, marjoram, rosemary, and pour in the water into the pot and stir to combine. Press the *Cancel* key to stop the *Sauté* function
4. Press the *Pressure* key, set the pressure to HIGH, and set the timer for 23 minutes
5. When the Foodi timer beeps, press the *Cancel* key. Let the pressure release naturally for 10 to 15 minutes or until the valve drops. Release remaining pressure. Unlock and carefully open the lid.
6. Taste and, if needed, season with pepper and salt to taste. If needed, add more ground rosemary and more marjoram.

Fresh Tomato and Basil Sauce

(Prep + Cook Time: 10 Minutes | **Servings:** 4)

Ingredients:
- 1½ lb. ripe tomatoes (4 to 5 tomatoes)
- 1 bunch fresh basil
- 2 tbsp. olive oil
- 1 tbsp. extra-virgin olive oil
- 3 garlic cloves; coarsely chopped
- 1/4 cup water
- 1/2 tsp. salt

Instructions:
1. Halve as many of the tomatoes as will cover the base of your Foodi (3 to 4). Chop the rest in large pieces and transfer them to a bowl, scraping in their liquid, too. Sprinkle the salt over the chopped tomatoes. Reserve 1 sprig of the basil and snip the leaves off the remaining basil, chop them, and set them aside
2. Heat the Foodi using the *Sauté* function, add the 2 tbsp. of everyday olive oil, and heat briefly. Arrange the tomato halves, cut side down, in the cooker base and let them fry, without stirring, until caramelized, about 4 minutes. Flip the tomatoes over, sprinkle with the garlic, and pour the chopped tomatoes and their juices into the cooker. Add the water if using. Lay the reserved basil sprig on top
3. Close and lock the lid of the Foodi. Cook at High pressure for 5 minutes. To get 5 minutes' cook time, press *Pressure* button and use the *Time Adjustment* button to adjust the cook time to 5 minutes.
4. When the time is up, open the Foodi with the Natural release method.
5. Fish out and discard the basil stem. Using a fork, break up the tomato halves and their skins. Return the uncovered cooker base to medium-high heat and cook until the contents have reduced to a sauce consistency, about 5 minutes more
6. Pour the sauce over pasta, sprinkle with the chopped basil, and swirl on the extra-virgin olive oil. Serve immediately.

Beans & Grains

Stewed Tomatoes and Green Beans

(Prep + Cook Time: 15 Minutes | **Servings:** 10)

Ingredients:
- 1 lb. trimmed green beans
- 2 cups fresh; chopped tomatoes
- 1 crushed garlic clove
- 1 tsp. olive oil
- 1/2 cup water
- Salt to taste

Instructions:
1. Set *Sauté* setting and preheat your Foodi. When warm, add 1 tsp. of olive oil and garlic.
2. When the garlic has become fragrant and golden, add tomatoes and stir. If the tomatoes are dry, add 1/2 cup water
3. Fill the steamer basket with the green beans and sprinkle on salt. Lower into cooker
4. Close and seal the lid. Select *Pressure* and cook at HIGH pressure for 5 minutes
5. When the timer beeps, turn off cooker and Quick Pressure Release the pressure.
6. Carefully remove the steamer basket and pour beans into the tomato sauce
7. If the beans aren't quite tender enough, simmer in sauce for a few minutes. Serve.

White Bean Dip with Tomatoes

(Prep + Cook Time: 15 Minutes | **Servings:** 8)

Ingredients:
- 1 can cannellini beans; soaked overnight
- 1 small white onion; peeled and diced
- 6 sun-dried tomatoes
- 3 tbsp. chopped parsley
- 1½ tsp. minced garlic; divided
- 1¼ cups water
- 1 tsp. paprika
- 3 tbsp. olive oil
- 2 tbsp. lemon juice
- 1 tbsp. capers
- 1 tsp. salt
- 1/8 tsp. ground black pepper

Instructions:
1. Drain beans and place in the Foodi. Pour in water and add 1 tsp. garlic, salt, and black pepper.
2. Plug in and switch on the Foodi and secure with lid. Then position pressure indicator, select *Pressure* and cook at HIGH pressure for 14 minutes
3. When the timer beeps, switch off the Foodi and let pressure release naturally for 10 minutes and then do quick pressure release.
4. In the meantime, place a small non-stick frying pan over medium heat, add oil and let heat.
5. Then add onion and remaining garlic and cook for 3 to 5 minutes or until onions are nicely golden brown.
6. When the onions are done, set pan aside until required. Then uncover the pot and drain beans, reserve 1/2 cup of cooking liquid
7. Let beans cool slightly and then transfer to a food processor and add onion-garlic mixture, paprika, and lemon juice.
8. Pulse until smooth; slowly blend in reserved cooking liquid until dip reaches to desired thickness. Tip mixture into a serving bowl
9. Dice tomatoes and stir together with capers and parsley
10. Add this mixture into bean dip and stir until mixed well. Adjust the seasoning and serve immediately.

Pinto beans with bacon

(Prep + Cook Time: 24 Minutes | Servings: 4)

Ingredients:
- 1 (4½ oz.) can chopped mild green chiles (about 1/2 cup)
- 1 medium yellow or white onion; chopped
- 3 thin bacon slices; chopped
- 1/2 cup chopped pecans
- 1 cup dried pinto beans
- 1 tbsp. unsalted butter
- 1/2 tsp. dried oregano
- 1/2 tsp. ground cumin
- 1/4 tsp. ground coriander

Instructions:
1. Soak the beans in a large bowl of water on the counter overnight, for at least 12 hours or up to 16 hours.
2. Drain the beans in a colander set in the sink; pour them into the Foodi. Add enough cool tap water that they're submerged by 2 inches
3. Lock the lid on the Foodi and then cook On High pressure for 18 minutes. To get 18 minutes' cook time, press *Pressure* button and use the time adjustment button to adjust the cook time to 18 minutes.
4. Pressure release use the Quick Pressure Release method
5. Unlock and open the cooker. Scoop out 1 cup of the cooking liquid and reserve it. Drain the beans in a colander set in the sink. Wipe out the cooker.
6. Melt the butter in the Foodi turned to its *Sautéing/Browning* function. Add the bacon and pecans; fry until both are lightly browned, stirring occasionally, about 3 minutes. Add the onion and cook, stirring often, until softened, about 3 minutes
7. Stir in the oregano, cumin, and coriander until aromatic, about 20 seconds. Then pour in the drained beans, green chiles, and 1/4 cup of the reserved cooking liquid. Cook, stirring often, until the beans are just heated through, adding more of the reserved cooking liquid in 1/4 cup increments when the mixture gets too dry.

Refried Bean Nachos

(Prep + Cook Time: 35 Minutes | Servings: 6)

Ingredients:
- 2 cups pinto beans dried, (rinsed well, but not soaked)
- 1/2 cup salsa Cilantro; to taste (optional)
- 3 cups vegetable broth OR water OR combination of the two
- 1 onion; large-sized, cut into fourths (or diced if you like to leave your beans chunky)
- 4 cloves garlic; peeled and roughly chopped
- 1 jalapeno pepper, seeded (more or less to taste, optional)
- 1 tsp. salt
- 1 tsp. paprika
- 1 tsp. chili powder
- 1 tsp. cumin
- 1/2 tsp. black pepper

Instructions:
1. Put all of the ingredients in the Foodi and stir well to incorporate. Close and lock the lid. Press *Pressure* and cook at HIGH pressure for 28 minutes
2. When the timer beeps, let the pressure release naturally for 10 minutes. Turn the valve to release any remaining pressure. Carefully open the lid and stir the dish
3. With a potato masher or in a blender, mash or blend the beans to desired consistency; be careful because the beans are hot.
4. If you prefer your beans thick, drain some of the water before mashing or blending. Serve warm

Notes: This dish is freezer-friendly. Store in portion-sized containers and freeze.

Cuban black beans with ham

(Prep + Cook Time: 18 Minutes | **Servings:** 8)

Ingredients:
- 1/2 lb. smoked ham; any rind removed, the meat chopped
- 2 medium yellow onions; chopped
- 1 large green bell pepper, stemmed, cored, and chopped
- 2 cups dried black beans
- 2 tbsp. olive oil
- 1 tbsp. finely grated orange zest
- 2 tsp. minced garlic
- 1/2 tbsp. dried oregano
- 1/2 tsp. red pepper flakes
- 2 bay leaves
- 1 (4-inch) cinnamon stick
- 3 tbsp. sherry vinegar
- 1 tbsp. packed dark brown sugar
- 4 cups (1 quart) chicken broth
- 1/4 cup packed fresh cilantro leaves; chopped

Instructions:
1. Soak the beans in a big bowl of water on the counter overnight, for at least 12 hours or up to 16 hours. Drain in a colander set in the sink.
2. Heat the oil in the Foodi turned to the browning function. Add the ham and fry until well browned, about 5 minutes, stirring occasionally. Add the onions and pepper; cook, stirring often, until the onion turns translucent, about 4 minutes
3. Stir in the orange zest, garlic, oregano, red pepper flakes, bay leaves, and cinnamon stick until aromatic, less than 1 minute. Add the vinegar and brown sugar; stir until the brown sugar melts. Pour in the broth and scrape up any browned bits in the bottom of the cooker. Stir in the beans and cilantro
4. Lock the lid on the Foodi and then cook On High pressure for 18 minutes. To get 18 minutes' cook time, press *Pressure* button and use the time adjustment button to adjust the cook time to18 minutes
5. Pressure release use the Quick Pressure Release method to return the pot's pressure to normal
6. unlock and open the cooker. Discard the bay leaves and cinnamon stick. Turn the electric cooker to its browning function. Bring to a simmer; cook, uncovered and stirring often, until the remaining liquid in the pot is reduced by half, between 5 and 10 minutes.

Perfect Refried Beans

(Prep + Cook Time: 55 Minutes | **Servings:** 8)

Ingredients:
- 2 lb. pinto beans, dried, sorted
- 4 to 5 garlic cloves; roughly chopped
- 1 ½ cups onion; chopped
- 2 tsp. dried oregano
- 3 tbsp. vegetable OR shortening lard
- 4 cups vegetable broth
- 1 jalapeno; seeds removed and chopped
- 4 cups water
- 1½ tsp. ground cumin
- 1 to 2 tsp. sea salt
- 1/2 tsp. ground black pepper

Instructions:
1. Put the sorted pinto beans into a large-sized mixing bowl. Fill the bowl with just enough water to cover the beans by several inches. Set aside to soak for 15 minutes
2. Meanwhile, put the garlic cloves, onion, dried oregano, jalapeno, cumin, lard, vegetable broth, black pepper, and water in the Foodi. Stir to mix
3. Put the soaked beans in a colander to strain. Discard the soaking liquid. Rinse the beans with fresh water.
4. Add the beans into the pot. Stir to mix. It's ok if the lard is still a lump. It will melt as the pot heats up. Cover and lock the lid.
5. Press the *Pressure* button and adjust the time to 45 minutes
6. When the timer beeps, let the pressure down naturally, about 40 minutes
7. When the pressure is released, carefully open the lid and season the beans with sea salt to taste.

8. With an immersion blender, blend the beans to desired consistency. It will appear soupy, but as the beans cool, it will thicken.

Spice Black Bean and Brown Rice Salad

(Prep + Cook Time: 35 Minutes | **Servings:** 8)

Ingredients:
- 1 can (14 oz.) black beans; drained and rinsed
- 12 grape tomatoes; quartered
- 1 cup brown rice
- 1 avocado; diced
- 1½ cups water
- 1/4 cup cilantro; minced
- 1/4 tsp. salt

For the spicy dressing:
- 2 garlic cloves; pressed or minced
- 2 tsp. Tabasco or Cholula
- 3 tbsp. lime juice; fresh squeezed
- 3 tbsp. extra-virgin olive oil
- 1/8 tsp. salt
- 1 tsp. agave nectar

Instructions:
1. Combine the rice with the water and salt in the Foodi. Close and lock the lid. Select *Pressure* and cook at HIGH pressure for 24 minutes
2. When the timer beeps, release the pressure naturally for 10 minutes. Turn the steam valve to release any remaining pressure. Carefully open the lid.
3. Using a fork, fluff the rice and let cool to room temperature.
4. When cool, refrigerate until ready to use. In a large-sized bowl, stir the brown rice with the black beans, avocado, tomato, and cilantro
5. In a small-sized bowl, except for the olive oil, whisk the dressing ingredients together. While continuously whisking, slowly pour in the olive oil
6. Pour the dressing over the brown rice mix and stir to combine.

Spicy Black Eyed Peas

(Prep + Cook Time: 28 Minutes | **Servings:** 6)

Ingredients:
- 4 oz. slab bacon; chopped
- 1 (14 oz.) can diced tomatoes (about 1¾ cups)
- 1 (4½ oz.) can chopped hot green chiles (about ½ cup)
- 1 medium yellow onion; chopped
- 2 cups dried black-eyed peas
- 1 tbsp. dried oregano

Instructions:
1. Fry the bacon in the Foodi turned to its *Sautéing/Browning* function until it begins to brown and give off its fat, about 2 minutes
2. Add the onion and cook, stirring often, until it turns translucent, about 4 minutes. Pour in 3 cups water; add the black-eyed peas, tomatoes, chiles, and oregano, and stir well
3. Lock the lid on the Foodi and then cook On High pressure for 22 minutes. To get 22 minutes' cook time, press *Pressure* button and use the time adjustment button to adjust the cook time to 22 minutes.
4. Use the Quick Pressure Release method.
5. Unlock and open the cooker. Stir well before serving. Serve and enjoy.

Basic Boiled Beans

(Prep + Cook Time: 18 Minutes | **Servings:** 5)

Ingredients:
- 1 to 3 aromatics, choose one from each: garlic, onion, shallots carrot, bell pepper celery, fennel, green bell pepper, parsley stems
- 2 cups dried beans; soaked, rinsed, and drained
- 1 herb; choose one: bay leaf, fresh thyme sprig, fresh sage sprig
- 1 tbsp. fat, choose one: vegetable oil, butter, margarine, rendered fat, 1 thick slice of bacon
- 4 cups water

Instructions:
1. Place the beans in the Foodi base and add the water. Then add your chosen herb, aromatics, and fat.
2. Close and lock the lid of the Foodi. Cook at High pressure for the time appropriate for the type of bean, using the *Pressure* button and de ADJUSTMENT TIME button
3. When the time is up, open the Foodi with the Natural Release method; this should take 20 to 30 minutes
4. Drain the beans in a colander set over a bowl. Remove the herb and aromatics and reserve the cooking liquid to use in place of stock at a later time. Use the beans in any recipe calling for cooked beans.

White Bean, Sausage, And Escarole Stew

(Prep + Cook Time: 20 Minutes | **Servings:** 6)

Ingredients:
- 1 lb. mild Italian sausage, cut into 1-inch pieces
- 2 tbsp. white wine vinegar
- 1/2 cup finely grated parmesan cheese (about 1 oz.)
- 4 cups (1 quart) chicken broth
- 2 cups dried great northern beans
- 2 tbsp. olive oil
- 2 small escarole heads; cored and chopped

Instructions:
1. Soak the beans in a big bowl of water on the counter overnight, for at least 12 hours or up to 16 hours. Drain them in a colander set in the sink
2. Heat the oil in the Foodi turned to the browning function. Add the sausage and brown on all sides, turning occasionally with kitchen tongs, about 6 minutes. Pour in the broth and the drained beans
3. Lock the lid on the Foodi and then cook On High pressure for 15 minutes. To get 15 minutes' cook time, press *Pressure* button.
4. Use the Quick Pressure Release function to bring the pot's pressure back to normal.
5. Unlock and open the pot. Stir in the escarole and vinegar
6. Lock the lid on the Foodi and then cook On High pressure for 3 minutes. To get 3 minutes' cook time, press *Pressure* button and use the time adjustment button to adjust the cook time to 3 minutes.
7. Use the Quick Pressure Release method to bring the pressure back to normal. Then open the pot. Stir well and serve with the cheese sprinkled over each bowlful.

Green Bean Casserole

(Prep + Cook Time: 30 Minutes | Servings: 4)

Ingredients:
- 16 oz. green beans (I used Frozen)
- 1 onion; small-sized
- 1/2 cup French's onions, for garnishing
- 1 cup heavy cream
- 1 cup chicken broth
- 12 oz. mushroom; sliced
- 2 tbsp. butter

Instructions:
1. Press *Sauté* key of the Foodi. Put the butter in the pot and melt. Add the onion and mushrooms; sauté for about 2 to 3 minutes or until the onions are soft
2. Add the green beans, heavy cream, and chicken broth. Press the *Cancel* key to stop the *Sauté* function. Cover and lock the lid.
3. Press the *Pressure* key, set the pressure to HIGH, and set the timer for 15 minutes.
4. When the Foodi timer beeps, press the *Cancel* key and unplug the Foodi. Turn the steam valve to quick release the pressure. Unlock and carefully open the lid
5. While the dish is still hot, add 2 tbsp. cornstarch to thicken. Serve topped with French's onions.

Cracked Wheat Surprise

(Prep + Cook Time: 18 Minutes | Servings: 2)

Ingredients:
- 2 cups light brown sugar
- 2 cups cracked wheat
- 1 tsp. fennel seeds
- 2½ cups butter
- 3 cloves
- 1 cup milk
- Almonds; chopped
- Salt to taste
- 3 cups water

Instructions:
1. Set the Foodi on *Sauté* mode, add the butter and heat it up. Add the cracked wheat, stir, and cook for 5 minutes. Add the cloves and fennel seeds, stir, and cook for 2 minutes. Add the sugar, a pinch of salt, milk, and water, stir.
2. Cover, and cook on the *Pressure* setting for 10 minutes. Release the pressure, uncover the Foodi, divide into bowls, and serve with chopped almonds on top

Barley with Vegetables

(Prep + Cook Time: 35 Minutes | Servings: 4)

Ingredients:
- 1 cup Parmesan cheese, grated
- 1/3 cup mushrooms; chopped
- 4 cups vegetable stock
- 3 tbsp. fresh parsley; chopped
- 1½ cups pearl barley; rinsed
- 1 white onion, peeled and chopped
- 1 garlic clove; peeled and minced
- 1 celery stalk; chopped
- 1 tbsp. extra virgin olive oil
- 1 tbsp. butter
- 2¼ cups water
- Salt and ground black pepper, to taste

Instructions:
1. Set the Foodi on *Sauté* mode, add the oil and butter and heat them up. Add the onion and garlic, stir, and cook for 4 minutes. Add the celery and barley and toss to coat. Add the mushrooms, water, stock, salt, and pepper, stir.
2. Cover the Foodi and cook on the *Pressure* setting for 18 minutes. Release the pressure, uncover the Foodi, add the cheese and parsley and more salt and pepper, if needed, stir for 2 minutes, divide into bowls, and serve

Italian Cannellini Beans and Mint Salad

(Prep + Cook Time: 15 Minutes | Servings: 4)

Ingredients:
- 1 cup cannellini beans; soaked overnight
- 1 bay leaf
- 1 sprig mint fresh
- 1 dash vinegar
- 4 cups water
- 1 clove garlic smashed
- Olive oil
- Salt to taste
- Pepper to taste

Instructions:
1. Add soaked beans, water, garlic clove and bay leaf to the Foodi
2. Close and lock the lid. Press *Pressure* and cook at HIGH pressure for 8 minutes.
3. When time is up, open the Foodi using natural release
4. Strain the beans and mix with mint, vinegar, olive oil, salt and pepper.

Hummus

(Prep + Cook Time: 18 Minutes | Servings: 8)

Ingredients:
- 2 cups dried chickpeas
- 1/4 cup olive oil
- 1/4 cup tahini
- 1 tsp. baking soda
- 6 tbsp. fresh lemon juice
- 2 or 3 medium garlic cloves
- 1/2 tsp. ground cumin
- 1/2 tsp. dried oregano
- 1/2 tsp. dried sage
- 1/2 tsp. salt
- 1/2 tsp. ground black pepper

Instructions:
1. Soak the chickpeas in a big bowl of water on the counter for at least 12 hours or up to 16 hours
2. Drain the chickpeas in a colander set in the sink, then pour them into the Foodi. Add enough cool tap water so they're submerged by 2 inches. Stir in the baking soda
3. Lock the lid on the Foodi and then cook On High pressure for 12 minutes. To get 12 minutes' cook time, press Pressure button and use the time adjustment button to adjust the cook time to 12 minutes
4. Pressure release use the Quick Pressure Release method to bring the pot's pressure back to normal
5. Unlock and open the cooker. Drain the chickpeas into a colander set in the sink; rinse with cool water to bring them back to room temperature. Pour the chickpeas into a large bowl and cover with cool tap water; agitate the water to loosen their skins. Rub off and discard the skins. (you should have about 4 cups of peeled chickpeas.)
6. Pour the peeled chickpeas into a food processor fitted with the chopping blade. Add the olive oil, tahini, lemon juice, garlic, cumin, oregano, sage, salt, and pepper. Cover and process until a thick, velvety spread, scraping down the inside of the canister at least once and adding a tbsp. or more of water if the paste is too thick.
7. Scrape into a serving bowl, cover, and refrigerate for at least 2 hours or up to 3 days.

Black bean and corn salad

(Prep + Cook Time: 24 Minutes | **Servings:** 8)

Ingredients:
- 2 cups dried black beans
- 1 medium fresh jalapeño chili; stemmed and split lengthwise
- 2 cups fresh corn kernels (about 2 large ears), or frozen kernels, thawed
- 1 large globe or beefsteak tomato; chopped
- Up to 6 medium scallions; thinly sliced
- 1 medium yellow bell pepper, stemmed, cored, and diced
- 2 tbsp. olive oil
- 2 tsp. cumin seeds
- 2 tsp. minced garlic
- 1/4 cup fresh lime juice
- 3 tbsp. olive oil
- 1 tbsp. sherry vinegar
- 1 tbsp. honey
- 1 tsp. salt

Instructions:
1. Soak the beans in a large bowl of water on the counter overnight, for at least 12 hours or up to 16 hours. Drain them in a colander set in the sink
2. Heat the oil in the Foodi turned to the *Sautéing/Browning* function. Add the cumin seeds and garlic; cook for 1 minute, stirring constantly, just until the garlic begins to brown. Pour in the drained beans; add the jalapeño. Add enough cool tap water so that the ingredients are submerged by 2 inches (the seeds will float).
3. Lock the lid on the Foodi and then cook On High pressure for 18 minutes. To get 18 minutes' cook time, press *Pressure* button and use the time adjustment button to adjust the cook time to 18 minutes.
4. Pressure release use the Quick Pressure Release method
5. Unlock and open the cooker. Drain the contents of the cooker into a colander set in the sink. Discard the jalapeño
6. Transfer the bean mixture to a large bowl; stir in the corn, tomato, scallions, and bell pepper. Whisk the lime juice, olive oil, vinegar, honey, and salt in a small bowl until smooth; pour over the salad and toss well.

Barley and Mushroom Risotto

(Prep + Cook Time: 40 Minutes | **Servings:** 4)

Ingredients:
- 1 cup pearl barley
- 2 cups yellow onions; peeled and chopped
- 1.5 oz. dried mushrooms
- 1/4 cup Parmesan cheese; grated
- 1 tbsp. olive oil
- 1 tsp. fennel seeds
- 2 tbsp. black barley
- 3 cups chicken stock
- 1/3 cup dry sherry
- 1½ cups water
- Salt and ground black pepper; to taste

Instructions:
1. Set the Foodi on *Sauté* mode, add the oil, and heat it up. Add the fennel and onions, stir, and cook for 4 minutes. Add the barley, sherry, mushrooms, stock, water, salt, and pepper and stir well
2. Cover the Foodi, cook on the "Rice" setting for 18 minutes, release the pressure, uncover the Foodi, and set it on *Sauté* mode. Add more salt and pepper, if needed, stir and cook for 5 minutes. Divide into bowls, add the cheese on top, and serve

Quick Soaking Dry Beans

(Prep + Cook Time: 15 Minutes | **Servings:** 3)

Ingredients:
- 1 cup beans
- 4 cups water
- 1 tsp. salt, optional

Instructions:
1. Place water, beans and salt into the Foodi.
2. Set Foodi to *Pressure* and cook for 2 to 8 minutes at HIGH pressure.
3. Once time is up, slow release the pressure from the Foodi
4. Strain, rinse and drain the beans. You are now able to use these beans in any recipe at normal

Notes: You can double, triple, or half this recipe as long as you keep the ratio of beans to water at 1:4.

Wheat Berry Salad

(Prep + Cook Time: 45 Minutes | **Servings:** 6)

Ingredients:
- 1½ cups wheat berries
- 1 tbsp. extra virgin olive oil
- 4 cups water
- Salt and ground black pepper; to taste

For the salad:
- 2 oz. feta cheese; crumbled
- 1/2 cup Kalamata olives, pitted and chopped
- 1/2 cup fresh basil leaves; chopped
- 1 cup cherry tomatoes; cut into halves
- 2 green onions; chopped
- 1/2 cup fresh parsley, chopped
- 1 tbsp. balsamic vinegar
- 1 tbsp. extra virgin olive oil

Instructions:
1. Set the Foodi on *Sauté*, add the tbsp. oil and heat it up. Add the wheat berries, stir, and cook for 5 minutes. Add the water, salt, and pepper.
2. Cover the Foodi, and cook on *Pressure* mode for 30 minutes. Release the pressure for 10 minutes, uncover the Foodi, drain the wheat berries, and put them in a salad bowl. Add the salt and pepper, 1 tbsp. oil, balsamic vinegar, tomatoes, green onions, olives, cheese, basil, and parsley, toss to coat, and serve.

Rich and creamy lentils

(Prep + Cook Time: 20 Minutes | **Servings:** 6)

Ingredients:
- 1 large yellow onion, chopped
- 2 cups brown lentils
- 1½ cups chicken broth
- 3/4 cup canned crushed tomatoes
- 2 tbsp. olive oil
- 2 bay leaves
- 1 cup plain whole-milk yogurt
- 1 tbsp. minced garlic
- 1 tbsp. minced fresh ginger
- 1 tbsp. garam masala

Instructions:
1. Heat the oil in the Foodi turned to the browning function. Add the onion and cook, stirring often, until softened, about 4 minutes. Add the garlic and ginger; cook, stirring constantly, until aromatic, about 1 minute.
2. Stir in the garam masala until aromatic, less than a minute; then add the lentils, broth, tomatoes, and bay leaves. Stir well
3. Lock the lid on the Foodi and then cook On High pressure for 15 minutes. To get 15 minutes' cook time, press *Pressure* button
4. Pressure release use the Quick Pressure Release method to bring the pot's pressure back to normal.

5. Unlock and open the cooker. Turn the electric cooker to its browning function. Bring to a simmer, stirring often. Cook, stirring almost constantly, until the liquid has evaporated, 5 to 10 minutes. Discard the bay leaves. Stir in the yogurt before serving.

Cracked Wheat and Vegetables

(Prep + Cook Time: 25 Minutes | **Servings:** 4)

Ingredients:
- 2 garlic cloves, peeled and minced
- 1 yellow onion; peeled and chopped
- 2 tomatoes; cored and chopped
- 2 small potatoes; cubed
- 5 cauliflower florets; chopped
- 2 curry leaves
- 3 tsp. vegetable oil
- 1/4 tsp. garam masala
- Cilantro leaves; chopped, for serving
- 1/2 cup cracked whole wheat
- 1½ cups water
- 1/4 tsp. mustard seeds
- 1/4 tsp. cumin seeds
- 1 tsp. ginger; grated
- 1 tbsp. yellow split peas, rinsed
- Salt and ground black pepper, to taste

Instructions:
1. Set the Foodi on *Sauté* mode, add the oil and heat it up. Add the cumin and mustard seeds, stir, and cook for 1 minute. Add the onion, garlic, split peas, garam masala, ginger, and curry leaves, stir, and cook for 2 minutes. Add the cauliflower, potatoes, and tomatoes, stir, and cook for 4 minutes. Add the wheat, salt, pepper, and water, stir
2. Cover, and cook on *Pressure* mode for 5 minutes. Release the pressure, uncover the Foodi, transfer the wheat and vegetables to plates, sprinkle cilantro on top, and serve

Franks and Beans

(Prep + Cook Time: 14 Minutes | **Servings:** 4)

Ingredients:
- 2 (15 oz.) cans pinto beans, drained and rinsed (about 3½ cups)
- 3 oz. slab bacon; chopped
- 1 lb. hot dogs; cut into 2-inch pieces
- 1 medium yellow onion; chopped
- 2 tsp. minced garlic
- 1/2 cup ketchup
- 1/4 cup maple syrup; preferably Grade B or 2
- 2 tbsp. Dijon mustard
- 2 tbsp. packed dark brown sugar
- 1/2 tsp. ground black pepper
- 1/4 tsp. ground cloves

Instructions:
1. Fry the bacon until brown and crisp, stirring occasionally, in the Foodi turned to the *Sautéing/Browning* function, about 3 minutes
2. Add the onion and cook until softened, about 4 minutes, stirring occasionally. Add the garlic and cook until aromatic, less than 1 minute. Stir in the beans, ketchup, maple syrup, mustard, brown sugar, pepper, and cloves until the brown sugar dissolves; then stir in the hot dogs
3. Lock the lid onto the pot. Set the Foodi to cook at High pressure for 7 minutes. To get 7 minutes' cook time, press *Pressure* button and use the *Time Adjustment* button to adjust the cook time to 7 minutes
4. Use the Quick Pressure Release method. Unlock and open the pot. Stir well before serving.

Black Bean and Sweet Potato Hash

(Prep + Cook Time: 15 Minutes | **Servings:** 4)

Ingredients:
- 2 cups peeled; chopped sweet potatoes
- 1 cup cooked and drained black beans
- 1/4 cup chopped scallions
- 1 cup chopped onion
- 2 tsp. hot chili powder
- 1 minced garlic clove
- 1/3 cup veggie broth

Instructions:
1. Prep your veggies. Turn your Foodi to *Sauté* and cook the chopped onion for 2 to 3 minutes, stirring so it doesn't burn.
2. Add the garlic and stir until fragrant. Add the sweet potatoes and chili powder, and stir
3. Pour in the broth and give one last stir before locking the lid. Select *Pressure* and cook at HIGH pressure for 3 minutes.
4. When time is up, Quick Pressure Release the pressure carefully
5. Add the black beans and scallions, and stir to heat everything up. Season with salt and more chili powder if desired.

Refried Beans

(Prep + Cook Time: 26 Minutes | **Servings:** 8)

Ingredients:
- 1½ lb. (3 cups) dried pinto beans
- 1 (3 oz.) salt pork chunk
- Up to 2 cups finely shredded smoked cheddar cheese (about 8 oz.)
- 1 tbsp. minced garlic
- 1/4 cup vegetable or canola oil

Instructions:
1. Soak the beans in a big bowl of water on the counter overnight, for at least 12 hours or up to 16 hours.
2. Drain the beans in a colander set in the sink; pour them into the Foodi. Add the salt pork and garlic; pour in enough cool tap water so that the ingredients are covered by 2 inches of water (the garlic will float).
3. Lock the lid on the Foodi and then cook On High pressure for 21 minutes. To get 21 minutes' cook time, press *Pressure* button and use the *Time Adjustment* button to adjust the cook time to 21 minutes
4. Pressure Release Use the Quick Pressure Release method to drop the pot's pressure back to normal
5. Unlock and open the cooker. Discard the salt pork. Scoop out 1 cup of the soaking water and set aside. Drain the remaining contents of the cooker into a colander set in the sink
6. Transfer the beans and garlic to a large bowl. Use a potato masher to create a thick paste, adding the soaking water in small bits until you've added just enough to get a smooth but not wet paste
7. Heat the oil in a large pot over medium heat. Add the bean paste and cook, stirring often, until hot and bubbling, about 5 minutes. Spread the mixture on a large serving platter or individual plates and top with the shredded cheese.

Dessert Recipes

Chocolate Cheesecake

(Prep + Cook Time: 1 hour 50 Minutes | **Servings:** 12)

Ingredients:
For the crust:
- 1½ cups chocolate cookie crumbs
- 4 tbsp. melted butter

For the filling:
- 24 oz. cream cheese; softened
- 4 oz. white chocolate
- 4 oz. milk chocolate
- 4 oz. bittersweet chocolate
- 1/2 cup Greek yogurt
- 2 tbsp. cornstarch
- 1 cup sugar
- 3 eggs
- 1 tbsp. vanilla extract
- Vegetable oil cooking spray
- 1 cup water

Instructions:
1. In a bowl, mix the cookie crumbs with the butter and stir well. Spray a springform pan with some cooking oil, line with parchment paper, press the crumbs and butter mixture on the bottom and keep in the freezer. In a bowl, mix the cream cheese with cornstarch and sugar and stir using a mixer
2. Add the eggs, yogurt, and vanilla, stir to combine everything and divide into 3 bowls. Put the milk chocolate in a heatproof bowl and heat up in the microwave for 30 seconds
3. Add this to one of the bowls with the batter you made earlier and stir well. Put dark and white chocolate in separate heatproof bowls and heat them up in the microwave for 30 seconds each.
4. Add these to the other 2 bowls with cheesecake batter, stir, and place them all in the refrigerator for 30 minutes. Take the bowls out of the refrigerator and layer your cheesecake
5. Pour the dark chocolate batter in the center of the crust. Add white chocolate batter on top and spread evenly and end with milk chocolate batter. Put the pan in the steamer basket of the Foodi, add 1 cup water to the Foodi
6. Cover, and cook on the "Beans/Risotto" setting for 45 minutes. Release the pressure for 10 minutes, take the cheesecake out of the Foodi , set aside to cool down, and serve.

Vanilla Pudding with Berries

(Prep + Cook Time: 35 minutes 6h for refrigeration | **Servings:** 4)

Ingredients:
- 1 cup Heavy Cream
- 4 Egg Yolks
- 1/2 cup Sugar
- 4 Raspberries
- 4 Blueberries
- 1/2 cup Milk
- 1 tsp. Vanilla
- 4 tbsp. Water + 1 ½ cups Water

Instructions:
1. Turn on your Foodi and select Sear/Sauté mode on Medium(MD)
2. Add 4 tbsp. for water and the sugar. Stir it constantly until it dissolves. Press Stop. Add milk, heavy cream, and vanilla. Stir it with a whisk until evenly combined
3. Crack the eggs into a bowl and add a tablespoon of the cream mixture. Whisk it and then very slowly add the remaining cream mixture while whisking
4. Fit the reversible rack at the bottom of the pot, and pour one and a half cup of water in it. Pour the mixture into four ramekins and place them on the rack
5. Close the lid of the pot, secure the pressure valve, and select Pressure mode on High Pressure for 4 minutes. Press Start/Stop

6. Once the timer has gone off, do a quick pressure release, and open the lid. With a napkin in hand, carefully remove the ramekins onto a flat surface. Let them cool for about 15 minutes and then refrigerate them for 6 hours
7. After 6 hours, remove them from the refrigerator and garnish them with the raspberries and blueberries. Enjoy immediately or refrigerate further until dessert time is ready

Delicious Chocolate Fondue

(Prep + Cook Time: 10 Minutes | **Servings:** 4)

Ingredients:
- 3.5 oz. of cream
- 3.5 oz. of dark chocolate (minimum 70% cocoa)

Instructions:
1. Pour two cups of water into the Foodi and lower the trivet.
2. Put chocolate chunks in a ceramic, heat-proof container that fits into the pressure cooker, and pour over the cream
3. Put into the Foodi. Close and lock the lid. Select *Pressure* and cook at HIGH pressure for 2 minutes.
4. When time is up, press *Cancel* and carefully quick release the pressure
5. Open the lid and remove the container.
6. Whisk quickly until the chocolate becomes smooth. Serve right away!

Notes:
If you want to make your fondue unique, add 1 tsp. of Amaretto liquor before closing up the pressure. Other flavor options include chili powder, peppermint extract, orange extract, or Bailey's.

White chocolate lemon pudding

(Prep + Cook Time: 20 Minutes | **Servings:** 6)

Ingredients:
- 6 oz. white chocolate; chopped
- 1 cup half-and-half
- 4 large egg yolks, at room temperature and whisked in a small bowl
- 1 cup heavy cream
- 1 tbsp. sugar
- 1 tbsp. finely grated lemon zest (about 1 medium lemon)
- 1/4 tsp. lemon extract

Instructions:
1. Put the chopped white chocolate in a large bowl. Mix the cream and half-and-half in a small saucepan and warm over low heat until bubbles fizz around the edges of the pan
2. Pour the warm mixture over the white chocolate and whisk until melted. Whisk in the egg yolks, sugar, zest, and extract. Pour the mixture into six 1/2 cup heat-safe ramekins; cover each tightly with aluminum foil.
3. Set the Foodi rack in the Foodi; pour in 2 cups water. Set the ramekins on the rack, stacking them as necessary without any one ramekin sitting directly on top of another.
4. Lock the lid on the Foodi and then cook On High pressure for 15 minutes
5. Turn off the Foodi or unplug it so it doesn't jump to its *Keep Warm* setting. Let its pressure return to normal naturally, 10 to 14 minutes
6. Unlock and open the cooker. Transfer the (hot!) Ramekins to a cooling rack; uncover each and cool for a few minutes before serving-or store in the refrigerator for up to 3 days, covering the ramekins again after they have chilled.

Rich Chocolate Pudding

(Prep + Cook Time: 35 Minutes | **Servings:** 6)

Ingredients:
- 4 oz. bittersweet chocolate chopped
- 1/3 cup brown sugar packed
- 1½ cups whipping cream
- 4 egg yolks
- 1 tbsp. unsweetened cocoa powder
- 1 tsp. Vanilla
- 1½ cups water
- 1/4 tsp. salt

Instructions:
1. Heat cream to a simmer in medium saucepan over medium heat. Remove from heat. Add chocolate; stir until chocolate is melted and mixture is smooth
2. Whisk egg yolks, brown sugar, cocoa, vanilla and salt in large bowl until well blended. Gradually add hot chocolate mixture, whisking constantly until blended
3. Strain into 6 to 7-inch (1½ -quart) soufflé dish or round baking dish that fits inside Foodi. Cover dish tightly with foil.
4. Pour water into Foodi. Place soufflé dish on rack; lower into pot using handles of rack.
5. Close and lock the lid. Select *Pressure* and cook at LOW pressure for 22 minutes.
6. When cooking is complete, use natural release for 5 minutes, then release remaining pressure
7. Use handles of rack to remove dish from pot. Remove foil; cool to room temperature. Cover and refrigerate at least 3 hours or up to 2 days

Poached peach cups with ricotta and honey

(Prep + Cook Time: 10 Minutes | **Servings:** 4)

Ingredients:
- 4 peaches, cut in half and pitted
- 1 cup part-skim ricotta cheese
- 1/4 cup apple juice
- 1/8 tsp. ground cinnamon
- 1/4 cup water
- 3 tbsp. light brown sugar
- 2 tbsp. honey
- 1/4 tsp. vanilla extract

Instructions:
1. Add peaches, apple juice, water, brown sugar, and cinnamon to the cooker
2. Lock the lid on the Foodi and then cook On High pressure for 5 minutes. To get 5 minutes' cook time, press *Pressure* button, and use the time adjustment button to adjust the cook time to 5 minutes
3. Perform a quick release to release the cooker's pressure
4. Remove peaches from cooking liquid, and set aside. Combine ricotta cheese, honey, and vanilla extract, and serve spooned into the center of each peach half.

Molten gingerbread cake

(Prep + Cook Time: 20 Minutes | **Servings:** 2)

Ingredients:
- ⅔ cup all-purpose flour
- 1/4 cup molasses
- 1/4 cup vegetable oil
- 1/4 cup packed brown sugar
- 1 large egg
- 3 tbsp. very hot water
- 3/4 tsp. ground ginger
- 1/2 tsp. ground cinnamon
- 1/4 tsp. kosher salt
- 1/4 tsp. baking powder
- 1/4 tsp. baking soda
- 1 cup water, for steaming (double-check the Foodi manual to confirm amount, and follow the manual if there is a discrepancy)

Instructions:
1. In a small bowl, using a hand mixer, mix together the hot water, vegetable oil, brown sugar, molasses, and egg. In another small bowl, sift together the flour, ground ginger, cinnamon, kosher salt, baking

powder, and baking soda. Add the dry ingredients to the liquid mixture. Mix on medium speed until the ingredients are thoroughly combined, with no lumps. Pour the batter into a nonstick mini (3-by-5-inch) loaf pan. Cover the pan with aluminum foil, making a dome over the pan
2. Add the water and insert the steamer basket or trivet. Carefully place the loaf pan on the steamer insert.
3. Lock the lid on the Foodi and then cook On High pressure for 15 minutes. To get 15 minutes' cook time, press *Pressure* button and use the time adjustment button to adjust the cook time to 15 minutes.
4. When the timer goes off, turn the cooker off. ("*Keep Warm*" setting, turn off)
5. After cooking, use the natural method to release pressure for 5 minutes, then the quick method to release the remaining pressure
6. Unlock and remove the lid. Using tongs, carefully remove the pan from the Foodi. Let the cake rest for 2 to 3 minutes; remove the foil, slice, and serve
7. to sift the dry ingredients, place a medium-coarse sieve over a small bowl or on a sheet of wax paper or parchment paper. Measure the dry ingredients into the sieve. Tap the side of the sieve to move the contents through the sieve to the bowl or parchment paper; then transfer the sifted ingredients to the wet ingredients.

Chocolate Fondue with Coconut Cream

(Prep + Cook Time: 5 Minutes | **Servings:** 4)

Ingredients:
- 3.5 oz. coconut cream
- 3.5 oz. 70% dark bittersweet chocolate
- 2 cups water
- 1 tsp. sugar

Instructions:
1. Pour 2 cups of water into your Foodi and insert trivet
2. In a heatproof bowl, add chocolate chunks.
3. Add coconut cream and sugar.
4. Put the bowl on top of the trivet. Close and seal the lid
5. Select *Pressure* and cook at HIGH pressure for 2 minutes. (Press Stop when complete 2 Minute).
6. When time is up, press *Cancel* and use a quick release. Carefully remove bowl and whisk with a fork until it becomes smooth. Serve!

Vanilla Pots de Crème

(Prep + Cook Time: 10 Minutes | **Servings:** 4)

Ingredients:
- 6 large egg yolks
- 1 cup heavy cream
- 1 cup whole milk
- ⅔ cup sugar
- 1 tsp. vanilla extract
- Seasonal fruit; for serving

Instructions:
1. Add 2 cups of water to the Foodi base; insert the steamer basket and set aside. In a large bowl, whisk together the egg yolks and sugar until the sugar has dissolved. Add the milk, cream, and vanilla, whisking just enough to combine; do not whip. Pour the mixture through a fine-mesh strainer into six 4 oz. ramekins; cover each tightly with aluminum foil. Arrange in the steamer basket, making sure they are level
2. Close and lock the lid of the Foodi. Cook at High pressure for 5 minutes. To get 5 minutes' cook time, press *Pressure* button, and use the *Time Adjustment* button to adjust the cook time to 5 minutes
3. When the time is up, open the Foodi using the 10-Minute Natural Release method
4. Check the custard for doneness. Lift all the ramekins out of the cooker; remove the foil. Serve the pots de crème warm, topped with seasonal fruit. Or if you prefer to serve them chilled, let them cool for 30 to 45 minutes, then cover tightly with plastic wrap and refrigerate until chilled.
5. Add the fruit when serving.

Pumpkin Pie Pudding

(**Prep + Cook Time:** 28 Minutes | **Servings:** 6)

Ingredients:
- 1/2 cup packed dark brown sugar
- 1½ cups canned pumpkin
- 2 large eggs; at room temperature
- 2 tbsp. all-purpose flour
- 1 tsp. ground cinnamon
- 1/2 cup heavy cream
- 2 tbsp. unsulphured molasses
- 1 tsp. vanilla extract
- 1/4 tsp. salt

Instructions:
1. Lightly butter the inside of a 1-quart round, high-sided soufflé or baking dish; set aside
2. Whisk the pumpkin, brown sugar, cream, eggs, molasses, and vanilla in a large bowl until the brown sugar has dissolved. Whisk in the flour, cinnamon, and salt until smooth
3. Pour the mixture into the prepared baking dish. Butter one side of a 10-inch piece of aluminum foil and set it buttered side down over the baking dish; seal well
4. Set the Foodi rack; pour in 2 cups water. Crimp the ends of the sling to fit inside the cooker.
5. Lock the lid, cook on High pressure for 22 minutes.
6. Turn off the Foodi or unplug it so it doesn't flip to its keep-warm setting.
7. Let its pressure return to normal naturally, 10 to 14 minutes
8. Unlock and open the cooker. Use the foil sling to transfer the baking dish to a wire cooling rack; uncover and set aside for a few minutes, until the pudding is firm and set.
9. Serve by dishing it up warm by the spoonful.

Blackberry swirl cheesecake

(**Prep + Cook Time:** 30 Minutes | **Servings:** 4 to 6)

Ingredients:
- Freshly grated zest from 1 lemon
- Freshly grated zest from half an orange
- 1 cup fresh blackberries
- 1/2 cup powdered sugar
- 4 tbsp. unsalted butter
- 1 cup crushed graham crackers
- 14 oz. cream cheese (one 8 oz. and two 3 oz. packages)
- 1/2 cup granulated sugar
- 2 large eggs

Instructions:
1. Add 2 cups of water to the Foodi base; insert the steamer basket and set aside. Cut a piece of wax paper to fit the bottom of a wide, flat-bottomed 4 cup baking dish; also cut a strip sized to fit the sides of the dish. Line the dish with the paper.
2. Puree the blackberries and powdered sugar in a blender and set aside
3. Melt the butter in a medium saucepan on medium heat. Remove the pan from the heat and mix in the crushed crackers. Scoop the mixture into the prepared baking dish and, using the back of your hand, push it into a flat, thin, even layer that covers the bottom of the dish, and, if there is enough, partway up the sides. Put the dish in the refrigerator to chill, uncovered, while you prepare the filling
4. In a medium bowl, using an electric mixer on medium speed, mix together the cream cheese, granulated sugar, and lemon and orange zests. Add the eggs and mix into a smooth batter, about 5 minutes
5. Remove the dish with the crust from the refrigerator. Slowly pour the batter over the crust, spreading level. To add the blackberry swirl, pour the puree into a squirt bottle (or food storage bag with one corner clipped off) and with it draw a spiral from the center out on top of the batter. Then use a toothpick or skewer to drag radiating lines from the center to the edge of the dish. Using a foil sling, lower the dish into the Foodi; do not cover the dish.
6. Lock the lid on the Foodi and then cook On High pressure for 20 minutes. To get 20 minutes' cook time, press *Pressure* button and use the time adjustment button to adjust the cook time to 20 minutes
7. When the time is up, open the Foodi using the 10-minute natural release method.

8. Lift the dish out of the Foodi and check the cake for doneness, transfer the dish to a wire rack
9. Let the cake cool, uncovered, for about 30 minutes. Then cover the dish with plastic wrap and refrigerate until ready to serve, for at least 4 hours
10. Work quickly and delicately to unmold the chilled cake: invert a plate over the dish and flip the dish and plate over together. Lift the dish off the cake and then peel off the wax paper circle on the base and the strip on the sides. Then invert a serving plate on the cake and gently flip all three components over together; lift off the top plate. Serve the cake cold, cut into wedges.

Pumpkin Chocolate Cake

(Prep + Cook Time: 55 Minutes | **Servings:** 12)

Ingredients:
- 3/4 cup white flour
- 3/4 cup whole wheat flour
- 1/2 cup Greek yogurt
- 8 oz. canned pumpkin puree
- Vegetable oil cooking spray
- 1-quart water
- 1 egg
- 1 tsp. baking soda
- 2 tbsp. canola oil
- 3/4 tsp. pumpkin pie spice
- 3/4 cup sugar
- 1 banana; mashed
- 1/2 tsp. baking powder
- 1/2 tsp. vanilla extract
- ⅔ cup chocolate chips
- Salt

Instructions:
1. In a bowl, mix the flours, salt, baking soda, baking powder, and pumpkin spice, and stir. In another bowl, mix the sugar with the oil, banana, yogurt, pumpkin puree, vanilla, and egg, and stir using a mixer. Combine the 2 mixtures, add the chocolate chips and mix well. Pour into a greased Bundt pan, cover the pan with paper towels and aluminum foil, and place in the steamer basket of the Foodi
2. Add the quart water to the Foodi, cover, and cook on the "Beans/Risotto" setting for 35 minutes. Release the pressure for 10 minutes, uncover the Foodi, leave the cake to cool down before cutting and serving it.

Mango Cake

(Prep + Cook Time: 50 Minutes | **Servings:** 8)

Ingredients:
- 1¼ cups flour
- 1/2 cup sugar
- 1/4 cup coconut oil
- 3/4 cup milk
- 1 cup water
- 1 tbsp. lemon juice
- 1 tsp. mango syrup
- 1 tsp. baking powder
- 1/4 tsp. baking soda
- 1/8 tsp. salt

Instructions:
1. Grease a baking pan that will fit in your Foodi. Mix the sugar, oil, and milk in a bowl until the sugar has melted.
2. Pour in mango syrup and mix again
3. Pour all the dry ingredients through a sieve into the wet
4. Add lemon juice and mix well.
5. Pour into the baking pan.
6. Pour 1 cup of water into the Foodi and place a trivet in the pot
7. Lower the baking pan into the cooker and close the lid
8. Select *Pressure*, and cook at HIGH pressure for 35 minutes.
9. When time is up, press *Cancel* and let the pressure release naturally.
10. Check the cake for doneness before cooling for 10 minutes. Serve!

Pineapple upside-down cake

(Prep + Cook Time: 30 Minutes | Servings: 6)

Ingredients:
- 4 canned pineapple rings packed in syrup
- 2 large eggs; at room temperature
- 1/2 cup regular or low-fat sour cream
- 1/2 cup granulated sugar
- 1/4 cup packed dark brown sugar
- 1 cup all-purpose flour
- 1/4 tsp. ground cinnamon
- 3 tbsp. unsalted butter; melted and cooled
- 2 tsp. vanilla extract
- 3/4 tsp. baking powder
- 1/4 tsp. salt

Instructions:
1. Generously butter the inside of a 2-quart round, high-sided soufflé or baking dish. Place a rack inside the Foodi; pour in 2 cups water. Whisk the flour, baking powder, salt, and cinnamon in a small bowl; set aside.
2. Sprinkle the brown sugar evenly over the bottom of the prepared dish. Lay the pineapple rings in the baking dish. Whisk the eggs, sour cream, sugar, butter, and vanilla in a large bowl until smooth. Whisk in the flour mixture until moistened and uniform; pour into the baking dish. Do not cover
3. Make an aluminum foil sling, set the baking dish on it, and lower it onto the rack in the cooker. Crimp the ends of the sling to fit into the pot.
4. Lock the lid on the Foodi and then cook On High pressure for 25 minutes. To get 25 minutes' cook time, press *Pressure* button and use the time adjustment button to adjust the cook time to 25 minutes.
5. Turn off the Foodi or unplug it so it doesn't flip to its *Keep Warm* setting. Let its pressure return to normal naturally, 8 to 12 minutes
6. Unlock and open the cooker. Use the foil sling to transfer the hot baking dish to a wire rack. Cool for 10 minutes, then set a serving platter over the baking dish, invert it all, and remove the baking dish, thereby unmolding the cake. Serve warm or at room temperature.

Awesome Honey Flans

(Prep + Cook Time: 10 Minutes | Servings: 4)

Ingredients:
- 2 large eggs
- 1 cup whole milk
- 1/3 cup dark honey
- 8 amaretti cookies or gingersnaps, finely crushed, for sprinkling

Instructions:
1. Add 2 cups of water to the Foodi base; insert the steamer basket and set aside
2. Break one of the eggs into a 4 cup measuring cup; separate the other egg, adding the yolk to the measuring cup and reserve the white for another use
3. Add the honey to the eggs and whisk together until well combined, then whisk in the milk. Pour the mixture through a fine-mesh strainer into six 4 oz. ramekins; cover each tightly with aluminum foil.
4. Arrange the ramekins in the steamer basket, making sure they are level
5. Close and lock the lid of the Foodi. Cook at High pressure for 5 minutes. To get 5 minutes' cook time, press *Pressure* button, and use the *Time Adjustment* button to adjust the cook time to 5 minutes.
6. When the time is up, open the Foodi using the 10-Minute Natural Release method
7. Check the flan for doneness. Lift the ramekins out of the cooker
8. Remove the foil and sprinkle crushed cookies over each flan and serve warm. Or if you prefer to serve them chilled, hold off on the crushed cookies. Instead, let the flans cool for about 30 minutes, then cover with plastic wrap and refrigerate.
9. Add the crushed cookies just before serving

Strawberry Shortcake Mug Cake

(Prep + Cook Time: 18 Minutes | **Servings:** 2)

Ingredients:
- 1/2 cup almond flour
- 1/2 tsp. 100% vanilla extract
- 3 tbsp. chopped strawberries (plus more for garnish)
- 1 cup water
- 3 tbsp. coconut whipped cream to garnish
- 1 egg
- 1 tbsp. ghee
- 1 tbsp. maple syrup

Instructions:
1. Combine all of the ingredients, except for the water and whipped cream, into a heat-resistant ceramic coffee mug
2. Pour the cup of water into the stainless steel Foodi bowl and place the wire rack into the basin. Set your mug on top of the rack and secure the lid
3. Lock the lid, cook on High pressure for 12 minutes.
4. Now allow the cake to cook, quick-releasing the pressure valve when the cycle is complete
5. Remove the lid when safe to do so and carefully remove the hot mug. Top with coconut whipped cream and additional fresh strawberries if desired.

Vanilla Ginger Custard

(Prep + Cook Time: 16 Minutes | **Servings:** 2)

Ingredients:
- 1/3 cup heavy (whipping) cream
- 1/3 cup whole milk
- 1/3 cup granulated sugar
- 2 large egg yolks
- 1/2 tsp. vanilla extract
- 1/4 tsp. ground ginger
- 1 cup water; for steaming (double-check the Foodi manual to confirm amount, and follow the manual if there is a discrepancy)
- 2 tsp. chopped crystalized ginger (optional)

Instructions:
1. In a small saucepan set over medium heat, combine the milk, heavy cream, vanilla, and ground ginger, and bring the mixture just to a simmer. Take it off the heat and cool slightly
2. In a small bowl, whisk together the egg yolks and sugar until the sugar is dissolved and the mixture is pale yellow. Working slowly, whisk a few tbsp. of the milk mixture into the egg mixture, then repeat with a little more. Once the egg mixture is warmed, whisk in the remainder of the milk mixture
3. Pour the custard into 2 heatproof custard cups or small ramekins. Cover with aluminum foil, and crimp to seal around the edges
4. Add the water and insert the steamer basket or trivet.
5. Place the custard cups on the steamer insert.
6. Lock the lid in place, and bring the pot to High pressure. Cook at High pressure for 6 minutes. To get 6 minutes' cook time, press *Pressure* button and use the *Time Adjustment* button to adjust the cook time to 6 minutes
7. Use the natural method to release pressure
8. Unlock and remove the lid. Using tongs, carefully remove the custards from the cooker and remove the foil. The custards should be set but still a bit soft in the middle; they'll firm as they cool. Cool for 20 to 30 minutes, then refrigerate for several hours to chill completely. When ready to serve, top with the crystalized ginger.

Chocolate pudding

(Prep + Cook Time: 20 Minutes | **Servings:** 6)

Ingredients:
- 6 oz. semisweet or bittersweet chocolate, chopped
- 4 large egg yolks, at room temperature and whisked in a small bowl
- 1/2 oz. unsweetened chocolate; chopped
- 1 tbsp. vanilla extract
- 6 tbsp. sugar
- 1½ cups light cream
- 1/4 tsp. salt

Instructions:
1. Place all the chopped chocolate and the sugar in a large bowl. Heat the cream in a saucepan over low heat until small bubbles fizz around the inside edge of the pan
2. Pour the warmed cream over the chocolate; whisk until the chocolate has completely melted. Cool a minute or two, then whisk in the yolks, vanilla, and salt. Pour the mixture into six 1/2 cup heat-safe ramekins, filling each about three-quarters full. Cover each with foil
3. Set the rack in the Foodi; pour in 2 cups water. Set the ramekins on the rack, stacking them as necessary without any one ramekin sitting directly on top of another
4. Lock the lid on the Foodi and then cook On High pressure for 15 minutes. To get 15 minutes' cook time, press *Pressure* button.
5. Pressure release turn off the Foodi or unplug it so it doesn't flip to its keep-warm setting. Let its pressure return to normal naturally, 10 to 14 minutes
6. Unlock and open the cooker. Transfer the hot ramekins to a cooling rack, uncover, and cool for 10 minutes before serving-or chill in the refrigerator for up to 3 days, covering again once the puddings have chilled.

Cookies and Cream Cheesecake

(Prep + Cook Time: 1 hour 10 Minutes | **Servings:** 8)

Ingredients:
- 16 oz. cream cheese
- 1 bag of bite-sized Cacao Chocolate sandwich cookies
- 2 eggs
- 1/4 cup sour cream
- 1/2 cup sugar
- 1 tsp. vanilla
- 1 cup water
- 2 tbsp. butter; melted
- **Equipment:** 7-inch springform pan

Instructions:
1. Use a rolling pin or any other heavy tool to convert 1/2 your cookies into sweet crumbs
2. Mix crumbled cookies with the melted butter and press the mixture into the springform pan.
3. Put the eggs, cream cheese, sugar, and sour cream into a mixer. Mix until well combined.
4. Crumble the remaining cookies and then add into the mixture
5. Transfer the batter into the pan and spread into an even layer
6. Cover the spring-form pan with unbleached parchment paper, top it with foil, and secure around the edges.
7. Put a trivet in the Foodi and pour 1 cup of water. Take a long piece of foil and fold it lengthwise to create a strip long enough to allow you to place the cheesecake onto the trivet and retrieve it later when the cooking time is done.
8. Using the foil sling, place the pan onto the trivet. Cover and lock the lid.
9. Press the *Pressure* key, set the pressure to HIGH, and set the timer for 40 minutes
10. When the Foodi timer beeps, press the *Cancel* key and unplug the Foodi. Let the pressure release naturally for 10 to 15 minutes or until the valve drops. Unlock and carefully open the lid.
11. Using the foil sling, carefully remove the cheesecake from the pot
12. Put on the counter and let cool completely. Slice and serve.

Lemon Ricotta Cheesecake with Strawberries

(Prep + Cook Time: 35 minutes | **Servings:** 6)

Ingredients:
- 10 oz. Cream Cheese
- 1/4 cup Sugar
- 1/2 cup Ricotta Cheese
- 1 ½ cups Water
- 10 Strawberries, halved to decorate
- 2 Eggs, cracked into a bowl
- 1 tsp. Lemon Extract
- 3 tbsp. Sour Cream
- One Lemon, zested and juiced

Instructions:
1. In the electric mixer, add the cream cheese, quarter cup of sugar, ricotta cheese, lemon zest, lemon juice, and lemon extract. Turn on the mixer and mix the ingredients until a smooth consistency is formed. Adjust the sweet taste to liking with more sugar
2. Reduce the speed of the mixer and add the eggs. Fold it in at low speed until it is fully incorporated. Make sure not to fold the eggs in high speed to prevent a cracked crust
3. Grease the spring form pan with cooking spray and use a spatula to spoon the mixture into the pan. Level the top with the spatula and cover it with foil
4. Open the Foodi, fit in the reversible rack, and pour in the water. Place the cake pan on the rack. Close the lid, secure the pressure valve, and select Pressure mode on High pressure for 15 minutes. Press Start/Stop.
5. Meanwhile, mix the sour cream and one tbsp. of sugar. Set aside
6. Once the timer has gone off, do a natural pressure release for 10 minutes, then a quick pressure release to let out any extra steam, and open the lid
7. Remove the rack with pan, place the spring form pan on a flat surface, and open it. Use a spatula to spread the sour cream mixture on the warm cake. Refrigerate the cake for 8 hours
8. Top with strawberries; slice it into 6 pieces and serve while firm

Chocolate Zucchini Muffins

(Prep + Cook Time: 35 Minutes | **Servings:** 24)

Ingredients:
- 1/2 cup coconut oil
- 1/3 cup chocolate chips
- 3 tbsp. cocoa powder
- 1 tbsp. melted butter
- 2 tsp. pure vanilla extract
- 3/4 to 1 cup cane juice
- 1 cup water
- 1 cup flour
- 1 cup grated zucchini
- 2 eggs
- 3/4 tsp. cinnamon
- 1/2 tsp. baking soda
- 1/4 tsp. salt

Instructions:
1. Mix cane juice, eggs, coconut oil, and vanilla. In a separate bowl, mix melted butter with cocoa powder.
2. Add to the egg mixture and mix. Add dry ingredients (flour, baking soda, cinnamon, and salt). Add the chocolate chips and zucchini
3. Pour 1 cup of water into your Foodi and lower the trivet
4. Select *Sauté* to preheat the pressure cooker
5. Fill silicone muffin cups 2/3 of the way full with muffin batter. Put cups in the pressure cooker.
6. For the second layer, separate with a piece of parchment paper, foil, and another trivet.
7. Finish layering muffins, and cover again with parchment paper, foil, and then a plate. Close and seal the lid.
8. Select *Pressure* and cook at HIGH pressure for 8 minutes
9. Once cooking is complete, press *Cancel* and wait 15 minutes. Then quick release any leftover pressure.
10. If a toothpick comes out clean from the muffins, they're ready!

Chocolate Brownie

(Prep + Cook Time: 20 Minutes | **Servings:** 2)

Ingredients:
- 1/4 cup all-purpose flour
- 1/3 cup granulated sugar
- 2 tbsp. unsalted butter
- 1 tbsp. dark chocolate chips
- 1 egg
- 1 tbsp. confectioners' sugar or powdered sugar
- 1/8 tsp. vanilla extract
- 2 tbsp. cocoa powder
- 1 cup water, for steaming (double-check the Foodi manual to confirm amount, and follow the manual if there is a discrepancy)

Instructions:
1. In a small microwave-safe bowl, microwave the butter and chocolate chips for 30 seconds on high to melt. Into a small mixing bowl, scrape the chocolate mixture, and add the sugar. Beat for about 2 minutes. Add the egg and vanilla, and beat for about 1 minute more, until smooth. Sift the flour and cocoa powder over the wet ingredients, and beat until just combined
2. Spoon the batter into a nonstick mini springform pan (4½ inches) or a mini loaf pan (3-by-5-inch), and smooth the top
3. Add the water into the Foodi, and insert the steamer basket or trivet. Place the loaf pan on the steamer insert. Place a square of aluminum foil over the pan, but don't crimp it down; it's just to keep steam from condensing on the surface of the cake.
4. Lock the lid in place, and bring the pot to High pressure
5. Cook at High pressure for 15 minutes. To get 15 minutes' cook time, press *Pressure* button.
6. Use the Quick Pressure Release method
7. Unlock and remove the lid. Using tongs, remove the sheet of foil. Transfer the pan to a cutting board or rack to cool. Dust the cake with the confectioners' sugar, slice, and serve.

Apple Bread

(Prep + Cook Time: 1 hour 20 Minutes | **Servings:** 6)

Ingredients:
- 3 cups apples; cored and cubed
- 2 cups white flour
- 1/2 cup butter
- 1 cup water
- 1 cup sugar
- 1 tbsp. vanilla extract
- 2 eggs
- 1 tbsp. apple pie spice
- 1 tbsp. baking powder

Instructions:
1. In a bowl, mix the egg with the butter, apple pie spice, and sugar and stir using a mixer. Add the apples and stir again well. In another bowl, mix the baking powder with flour and stir. Combine the 2 mixtures, stir, and pour into a springform pan. Place in the steamer basket of the Foodi, add the water to the Foodi,
2. Cover, and cook on the "Beans/Risotto" setting for 1 hour and 10 minutes. Release the pressure, fast, leave the bread to cool down, cut, and serve

Blueberry clafouti

(Prep + Cook Time: 16 Minutes | **Servings:** 2)

Ingredients:
- 1/2 cup fresh blueberries; divided
- 1/3 cup whole milk
- 1/4 cup all-purpose flour
- 1 large egg
- 1 tsp. unsalted butter; at room temperature, divided
- 3 tbsp. heavy (whipping) cream
- 3 tbsp. sugar
- 1/4 tsp. vanilla extract
- 1/4 tsp. lemon zest
- 1/8 tsp. ground cinnamon
- 2 tsp. confectioners' sugar or powdered sugar
- 1 cup water; for steaming (double-check the Foodi manual to confirm amount, and follow the manual if there is a discrepancy)
- Pinch fine salt

Instructions:
1. Using ½ tsp. of butter each, coat the insides of each of 2 custard cups or small ramekins. Put 1/4 cup of blueberries in each cup
2. In a medium bowl, combine the milk, heavy cream, sugar, flour, egg, vanilla, lemon zest, cinnamon, and fine salt. Using a hand mixer, beat the ingredients for about 2 minutes on medium speed, or until the batter is smooth. Evenly divide the batter between the 2 cups, filling them about three-fourths full with batter
3. Add the water and insert the steamer basket or trivet. Place the custard cups on the steamer insert. Place a square of aluminum foil over the pan, but don't crimp it down; it's just to keep steam from condensing on the surface of the clafouti
4. Lock the lid on the Foodi and then cook On High pressure for 11 minutes. To get 11 minutes' cook time, press *Pressure* button, and use the time adjustment button to adjust the cook time to 11 minutes.
5. Pressure release use the Quick Pressure Release method
6. Unlock and remove the lid. Using tongs, remove the foil. Transfer the cups to a small baking sheet. Preheat the broiler, and position a rack close to the broiler element. Place the baking sheet under the broiler for 3 to 4 minutes, or until the tops brown slightly. Cool for at least 10 minutes. Sift the confectioners' sugar over the clafouti, and serve warm.

Chocolate Custard

(Prep + Cook Time: 55 Minutes | **Servings:** 6)

Ingredients:
- 13 oz. chopped dark chocolate
- 6 whisked egg yolks Just over
- 1 tsp. vanilla extract
- 1 cup whole milk
- 1/2 cup sugar
- 1 cup cream (1.2 cups)

Instructions:
1. In a saucepan, simmer milk, cream, vanilla, and sugar until sugar has dissolved
2. Take the pan off the heat and add chocolate. When melted, slowly add whisked egg yolks, being careful that they don't cook.
3. Pour into a 7.2 - 8 -inch baking dish. Pour 4 cups of water into your Foodi and insert trivet. Put the custard pan on the trivet and seal the lid
4. Select *Pressure* and cook at HIGH pressure for 30 minutes. When time is up, press *Cancel* and let the pressure release naturally for 10 minutes before quick-releasing.
5. The custard will have a wobbly center, like a jelly. Serve hot or cold.

Apple Ricotta Cake

(**Prep + Cook Time:** 45 Minutes | **Servings:** 6)

Ingredients:
- 1 cup ricotta cheese
- 1 cup flour
- 1 egg
- 1 sliced apple
- 1 diced apple
- 1/4 cup raw sugar
- 1/3 cup sugar
- 2 cups water
- 1 tbsp. lemon juice
- 3 tbsp. olive oil
- 1 tsp. vanilla extract
- 1/8 tsp. cinnamon
- 2 tsp. baking powder
- 1 tsp. baking soda

Instructions:
1. Pour water into your Foodi and lower in steamer basket or trivet. Mix your diced and sliced apple in lemon juice
2. Put a piece of wax paper on the bottom of a 4 cup baking dish (shallow and wide), and oil it, and then dust it with flour.
3. Sprinkle in raw sugar before laying down the apple slices. In a bowl, whisk ricotta, sugar, olive oil, vanilla, and egg.
4. Sift in the cinnamon, flour, baking soda, and baking powder. Stir in the diced apples and then pour into your baking dish. Seal the lid
5. Select *Pressure* and cook for 20 minutes at HIGH pressure
6. When time is up, press *Cancel* and wait 10 minutes before quick-releasing any leftover pressure.
7. To test for doneness, poke a toothpick in the middle. If batter sticks to it, put back in the cooker and bake another 2 minutes under pressure.
8. To serve, chill or eat warm.

Apricot jam

(Prep + Cook Time: 18 Minutes | **Servings:** 4 cups)

Ingredients:
- 2 lb. apricots
- 1 to 1 ½ lb. white sugar
- 2 large navel oranges
- 1 to 2 tsp. fresh orange zest
- 1/4 to 1/2 tsp. almond extract
- 1 tbsp. butter or margarine (optional)

Instructions:
1. Clean the fruit, removing stems, leaves and any bad spots. Cut each apricot in half, discard the pit, and add the fruit halves to the bowl of a blender or food processor. If you want pieces of fruit in your jam to make it more like preserves, peel some of the fruit and add it back in after the rest has been pureed. Remove the colorful surface layer of zest from the orange. You want only the thin outer layer; the white part underneath is bitter
2. Place the zest in a bag or container and refrigerate. Cut a thin slice off the top of the zested oranges. Cut an additional slice if needed to see how thick the orange peel is. Using your knife, cut down the sides of the oranges, in curves along the lines of the oranges, to remove the peel. Cut any remaining pith away from the outside of the orange segments
3. Separate the segments and remove the connective tissue inside. If any orange remains on the peel, hold it over the jam mixture and use your finger to press the juice out. Discard the peel. Either chop the orange segments up very finely with your knife or your food processor. Add the sugar and the finely chopped orange segments to the jam mixture.
4. Let the jam macerate at least an hour, but preferably overnight or 24 hours. If you only have an hour, let it sit on the counter, for longer than that, it should be refrigerated. After maceration, place the apricot jam in the Foodi bowl. With the lid off and set on *Sautéing/Browning*, bring the jam mixture to a hard rolling boil, and cook for 6 minutes. Ignore any foaming at the surface, this will disappear after pressure cooking. As soon as the 6 minutes are up, turn the machine off
5. Lock the lid on the Foodi and then cook On High pressure for 8 minutes. To get 8 minutes' cook time, press *Pressure* button, and use the *Time Adjustment* button to adjust the cook time to 8 minutes.
6. Let its pressure return to normal naturally, 8 to 12 minutes
7. After your pressure cooker has released pressure, carefully remove the lid, and allow any hot liquid to fall back into the pot. Stir in the orange zest and almond extract to taste. Once the jam has cooled, refrigerate.

Chocolate Lava Cake

(Prep + Cook Time: 16 Minutes | **Servings:** 3)

Ingredients:
- 4 tbsp. flour
- 2 tbsp. olive oil
- 4 tbsp. milk
- 1/2 tsp. baking powder
- 1 tbsp. cocoa powder
- 1 egg
- 4 tbsp. sugar
- 1/2 tsp. orange zest
- 1 cup water
- Salt

Instructions:
1. In a bowl, mix the egg with the sugar, oil, milk, flour, salt, cocoa powder, baking powder, and orange zest and stir well. Pour into greased ramekins and place them into the steamer basket of the Foodi
2. Add the water to the Foodi, cover, and cook on the "Beans/Risotto" setting for 6 minutes. Release the pressure, uncover the Foodi, take the lava cakes out, and serve them after they cool down